Soviet Criminal Law and Procedure

Russian Research Center Studies, 50

Soviet Criminal Law and Procedure

THE RSFSR CODES

Introduction and Analysis

Harold J. Berman

Translation

Harold J. Berman and James W. Spindler

SECOND EDITION / HARVARD UNIVERSITY PRESS

CAMBRIDGE, MASSACHUSETTS 1972

Library of Congress Catalog Card Number 72-81269

Preface to the Second Edition

A second edition of this book has been made necessary by the large number of important changes in the Criminal Code and the Code of Criminal Procedure introduced since July 3, 1965, the effective date of the first edition. These changes are discussed in Chapter 5. All together, between January 1, 1961, when the two codes went into effect, and March 1, 1972, the effective date of the present edition, 67 of the 268 original articles of the Criminal Code were amended (some of them more than once), 30 new articles were added, and one was repealed, while 61 of the 413 original articles of the Code of Criminal Procedure were amended (some of them also more than once) and 15 new articles were added. Approximately half of the changes were made since July 3, 1965.

I have taken advantage of the opportunity thus presented to make some changes in the Introduction as well. In this I have been greatly helped by William E. Butler, who was a Research Associate in Law at Harvard Law School from 1968 to 1970 prior to becoming Reader in Soviet Law at University College, London University. Mr. Butler collaborated in writing the new Chapter 5, "Changes in the 1960 RSFSR Code, 1961–1971," and also wrote a new section of Chapter 1, on the codes of other union republics.

In translating the codes Mr. Spindler and I have followed the Soviet style in inserting the dates and sources of amendments at the end of each amended code provision. Also we have made corrections in some of the original translations of code provisions, being aided by the criticisms of several reviewers of the first edition. The translation of the Law on Court Organization has been revised, partly on the basis of the translation of John B. Quigley appearing in Berman and Quigley, *Basic Laws on the Structure of the Soviet State* (Cambridge, Mass., 1969). Thanks are also due to Mr. Quigley, who is now Assistant Professor of Law at Ohio State University, for translations of various amendments to the codes made in the period 1967–1969, when he was a Research Associate in Law at Harvard Law School, and also for criticisms and suggestions concerning both the text and the translations.

Finally, grateful acknowledgment is made of the valuable assistance of Joan Steinman in the final checking and revision of the manuscript.

One reviewer of the first edition deplored the failure to discuss Soviet court decisions applying Code provisions. Actually, reference is made to some decisions, but to discuss cases at any length would result in a full-scale treatise on the whole of Soviet criminal law and procedure, instead of an introduction to the Soviet codes. The reader who wishes to study judicial decisions applying the codes is referred to a collection of 56 Soviet cases on criminal law and procedure published in the journal *Soviet Statutes and Decisions,* I, no. 4 (Summer 1965). That collection has served as a good companion volume to the first edition of the present work; it is not yet out of date, although it should be supplemented by cases involving recent amendments to the codes.

In the latter connection, attention is called to new sections of the Introduction concerning legal control of dissent ((*infra,* pp. 81–83, 87–89). Here it has been essential to discuss some cases in order to understand the reasons for certain changes in the codes since 1966. Also these cases, which have attracted considerable attention throughout the world, illustrate that the Criminal Code and Code of Criminal Procedure are not only a principal means by which the Soviet state has controlled dissent in the post-Stalin period but are also a principal means by which Soviet citizens have claimed and exercised their civil rights and civil liberties.

Harold J. Berman

Cambridge, Massachusetts
April 3, 1972

The final stages of production of the book provide a welcome opportunity to express appreciation for the excellent work of Malcolm E. Hindin in preparing the Index. Readers will recognize that the Index is of special importance in a work of this kind, since it not only gives a detailed table of contents of the codes but also makes it possible to discern their internal patterns and themes by tracing key terms through all the various code provisions in which they appear. Mr. Hindin has carried forward the Index of the first edition and has made many improvements in it.

Preface to the First Edition

The 1960 RSFSR codes of criminal law and procedure, as amended to July 1965, which are translated here, should be, by themselves, of supreme interest to students of criminal law, to students of Soviet social institutions, and to students of the history of the Russian people. Nevertheless, it has seemed necessary to provide an introduction to them, in order to explain certain features that cannot be understood even from a careful study of the texts. The reader must know something about the place of the codes in the system of Soviet law as a whole, and he must know something of the history of the codes. A discussion of the history of the codes has required, in turn, an indication of some of the major changes that they introduced, for they represent an important step in the movement for Soviet law reform which began in the late 1930's but which could only come to fruition in the decade after Stalin's death. Analysis of the reforms reflected in the codes has led inevitably to an explanation of some of the principal concepts of Soviet criminal law and procedure – and especially those concepts that are likely to be unfamiliar to Americans.

Moreover, since the codes presuppose, and make frequent reference to, a system of courts, it has seemed advisable to include a translation of the 1960 RSFSR Law on Court Organization, and this, too, cannot be understood without some discussion of its background and significance. Other important legislation could also have been included, especially the 1955 Statute on Procuratorial Supervision in the USSR, the 1957 Statute on the Supreme Court of the USSR, the 1958 Statute on Military Tribunals, and the 1961 RSFSR Statute on the Bar (*Advokatura*), as well as the USSR and RSFSR Constitutions. These have been omitted in order to keep the volume within reasonable limits; also, they are already available in English translation.[1] Some comments on the military tribunals, the Procuracy, and the bar are nevertheless indispensable to an understanding of the codes of criminal law and procedure.

Those readers who are familiar with European codes of criminal law and procedure will have far less difficulty in understanding and evaluating the Soviet codes than those who are familiar only with traditional American and English law, in which enacted criminal codes, insofar as they exist, usually have the

1. All six of them are translated in Harold J. Berman and John B. Quigley, Jr., *Basic Laws on the Structure of the Soviet State* (Cambridge, Mass., 1969).

character of collections of laws rather than the character of a comprehensive system of general principles as well as of particular crimes, punishments, and procedures.[2] In addition, many of the basic concepts of Soviet criminal law and procedure are in the "Continental" tradition. Therefore, it has seemed necessary to say something concerning the similarities and differences between Soviet criminal law and procedure and that of the Western European countries, for the guidance primarily of those readers who are familiar only with the American system.

Indeed, comparison is implicit in the very act of translation, for all translation from one legal system into another is but the finding of linguistic analogies, often imperfect. To confess this truth is to accept the obligation of explaining it, and, more particularly, of attempting to characterize the linguistic qualities and style of the original Russian text. In addition to a discussion of the language of the codes, a glossary of legal terms is appended for those who read Russian.

Thus what started as a short introduction has turned into a rather long essay on the codes and on Soviet criminal law and procedure generally. Some may wish to read the essay as an introduction to the codes; others may wish to read the codes as appendices to the essay. Either course, it is hoped, will stimulate the reader to extend his explorations into Soviet criminal law and procedure beyond the covers of this book, for it cannot pretend to be more than a foundation for further research and further thought. Indeed, even if the introductory essay succeeds in providing an adequate background for an understanding of the codes, and the codes themselves are mastered, there remain many crucial questions concerning their application in practice. But to answer those questions it would be necessary to analyze Soviet court decisions in criminal cases as well as the enforcement of Soviet criminal law by the Procuracy and the police – which would be another book in itself.

Finally, the reader must be warned that the introductory essay does not attempt to relate, in any systematic way, the development of Soviet criminal law to Soviet political, economic, and social history. The author has attempted to offer such a systematic interpretation elsewhere;[3] the present study is devoted rather to a closer analysis of the raw materials out of which larger interpretations must be constructed.

The author owes a debt of gratitude to James W. Spindler, who collaborated in making the translations included in this volume and who prepared the index to them, first while he was a student at Harvard Law School and thereafter for several months prior to his active service in the United States Marine Corps. In addition, the preparation of the introductory essay was greatly benefited by the

2. Recent American codifications such as the Wisconsin and Illinois criminal codes of 1955 and 1961, respectively, and the 1964 draft of the New York penal code [adopted in 1967], are more comprehensive and systematic than their predecessors, and show the influence of the Model Penal Code of The American Law Institute, which in turn is patterned after European criminal codes.

3. *Justice in the USSR: An Interpretation of Soviet Law*, rev. ed. (Cambridge, Mass.: Harvard University Press, 1963).

comments and suggestions of Peter Maggs, Assistant Professor of Law at the University of Illinois, and of Dr. F. J. Feldbrugge, of the University of Leyden. Needless to say, Professor Maggs and Dr. Feldbrugge are not responsible for any errors that may have been committed, whether of fact or of opinion. Finally, I should like to thank William E. Butler for his valuable assistance in the preparation of footnotes and in indexing the Introduction, as well as Mrs. David Bryden, who helped in the translation of the Code of Criminal Procedure.

The translations of the Criminal Code and the Code of Criminal Procedure appeared originally in the journal *Soviet Statutes and Decisions*, I, no. 1 (Fall 1964), and I, nos. 2-3 (Winter-Spring 1965). Some revisions and corrections have been made for the present publication.

Harold J. Berman

Cambridge, Massachusetts
September 15, 1965

Contents

Introduction

1 The Place of the RSFSR Criminal Code and Code of Criminal Procedure in the Soviet Legal System

On October 27, 1960, the Supreme Soviet of the Russian Soviet Federated Socialist Republic (RSFSR), which is the largest of the 15 union republics of the Union of Soviet Socialist Republics (USSR), adopted a Criminal Code, Code of Criminal Procedure, and Law on Court Organization, to take effect on January 1, 1961.[1]

As of the date it went into effect, the Criminal Code contained – with two qualifications – the entire substantive criminal law applicable in the RSFSR, including in the General Part the Fundamental Principles of Criminal Legislation, which were enacted in December 1958 for the USSR as a whole,[2] and in the Special Part the USSR laws on crimes against the state[3] and on military crimes (which were also enacted in December 1958),[4] as well as other chapters on

1. Law of the RSFSR on the Issuance of the Criminal Code of the RSFSR, October 27, 1960, *Vedomosti RSFSR* (1960), no. 40, item 591; Law of the RSFSR on the Issuance of the Code of Criminal Procedure of the RSFSR, October 27, 1960, *Vedomosti RSFSR* (1960), no. 40, item 592; Law of the RSFSR on the Issuance of the Law on Court Organization of the RSFSR, October 27, 1960, *Vedomosti RSFSR* (1960), no. 40, item 593.

The 1960 RSFSR Criminal Code and Code of Criminal Procedure were translated into English by the Joint Publications Research Service of the U. S. Department of Commerce (Washington, D.C., 1961, mimeographed). They have also been translated, together with the RSFSR Law on Court Organization, into French, German, and other languages. See M. Ancel, ed., *La Réforme Pénale Soviétique: Code Pénale, Code de Procédure Pénale et Loi d'Organisation Judiciaire de la R.S.F.S.R. du 27 Octobre 1960* (Paris, 1962); W. Zülch, T. Pusylewitsch, and H. J. Arnold, transl., *Strafgesetzbuch, Strafprozessordnung, Gerichtsverfassungsgesetz der RSFSR* (Berlin, 1961); H. Fritsche, ed., *Gerichtsverfassung, Strafgesetzbuch und Strafprozessordnung der RSFSR* (Berlin, 1962); T. Pusylewitsch, ed. and transl., *Strafgesetzbuch der RSFSR vom 27 Oktober 1960 in der Fassung vom 6 Mai 1963* (Berlin, 1964).

2. *Osnovy ugolovnogo zakonodatel'stva Soiuza SSR i soiuznykh respublik* (Fundamental Principles of Criminal Legislation of the USSR and the Union Republics), December 25, 1958, *Vedomosti SSSR* (1959), no. 1, item 6. See Table of Corresponding Provisions of the Fundamental Principles of Criminal Legislation of the USSR and the Criminal Code of the RSFSR, Appendix I. The Criminal Code changes the wording of the Fundamental Principles in some instances in order to adapt the provisions from all-union to RSFSR territorial jurisdiction and RSFSR governing bodies. English translations of the Fundamental Principles are listed *infra*, note 11.

3. The phrase "crimes against the state" is used to translate the Russian *gosudarstvennye prestupleniia*, literally "state crimes," or "public crimes."

4. Law on Criminal Responsibility for Crimes Against the State, December 25, 1958, *Vedomosti SSSR* (1959), no. 1, item 8. Law on Criminal Responsibility for Military Crimes, December 25, 1958, *Vedomosti SSSR* (1959), no. 1, item 10. Translations of these laws may

crimes against socialist property, crimes against the person, crimes against political and labor rights of citizens, crimes against personal property, economic crimes, official crimes, crimes against justice, crimes against the system of administration, crimes against public security and against public order and public health, and crimes constituting survivals of local customs.[5]

The first qualification that must be placed on the comprehensive character of the Criminal Code is that a considerable number of its provisions – some 35 articles in all – make it a crime to violate rules which are not themselves contained in the Code but instead have been promulgated, or may be promulgated in the future, by administrative bodies. Thus it is a crime to violate rules concerning currency transactions, rules for protection of labor, rules concerning movement on the territory of the RSFSR by foreigners, transportation regulations of various kinds, safety regulations of various kinds, rules concerning prohibited trades, etc.

By provisions such as these, the Code in effect delegates to administrative bodies some of the legislature's power to make criminal laws. To a certain extent, such a delegation is inevitable in all legal systems, despite the maxim *nullum crimen, nulla poena sine lege* – no crime, no punishment unless a statute so provides (see *infra*, pp. 22, 34, 37). One danger in this is that administrative bodies – infringement of whose decrees has been declared by the legislature, in advance, to be criminally punishable – may issue decrees proscribing acts that ought not to be crimes. Another danger is that people will not know the administrative decrees. These dangers are magnified in a highly centralized political-economic-social structure such as the Soviet, where the scope of administrative regulation is relatively great. They are still further increased by the fact that a very large proportion of Soviet administrative decrees (as well as some statutes) are not published but are instead circulated only to a limited number of people, "for internal use" (*dlia sluzhebnogo pol'zovaniia*).[6] However, the Criminal Code protects a person against a criminal conviction for violating an unpublished decree (or statute) of which he was unaware.[7]

The second qualification which must be placed on the comprehensive character of the Criminal Code derives from the fact that USSR and RSFSR criminal laws enacted prior to its adoption are not expressly declared to be inapplicable. Some Soviet jurists have argued that the definition of a crime (in Article 7) as an

---

be found in *CDSP*, March 11, 1959, p. 5 and in Documentation Office for East European Law, University of Leyden, *The Federal Criminal Law of the Soviet Union*, Law in Eastern Europe no. 3 (Leyden 1959), pp. 73, 87.

5. See the table of contents for pages of the RSFSR Criminal Code.

6. See D. A. Loeber, "Legal Rules 'For Internal Use Only'," *International and Comparative Law Quarterly* 19:70–98 (1970).

7. Cf. V. A. Tumanov, "Vstuplenie v silu norm sovetskogo prava" (The Taking Effect of Norms of Soviet Law), 7 *Uchenye zapiski* (VIIuN) (1958), pp. 85 ff., at pp. 122–123. Nevertheless, ignorance of an increase in criminal penalties introduced by an unpublished statute, as contrasted with ignorance of the rule of law contained in it, does not excuse. Despite Professor Loeber's criticism of this and other loopholes in the Soviet law relating to publication of laws, it is worth stressing that criminal statutes – as contrasted with noncriminal statutes and with administrative decrees imposing sanctions for misconduct – can only take effect upon publication. See *infra*, note 13.

act provided for by the Special Part of the Code implies that no act not so provided for may be punished. Other Soviet jurists take the view that so long as the act is made punishable by a criminal statute, whether in the Code or outside it, it is to be deemed a crime, and in practice the Presidium of the USSR Supreme Soviet and the Presidium of the RSFSR Supreme Soviet have published lists of those laws that have lost their force in the light of the adoption of the Code.[8] Presumably, any prior criminal laws not included in such lists continue to be applicable provided, of course, that they are not inconsistent with the Code.

In addition, a considerable number of criminal laws have been enacted by the RSFSR and USSR Supreme Soviets after the adoption of the Criminal Code; these are ordinarily incorporated in the Code by way of amendment thereof, but the author has found one RSFSR criminal law enacted in 1961 which, prior to its repeal in 1970, was never incorporated in the Criminal Code.[9] No cases have been found, however, in which criminal laws enacted prior to adoption of the Code were applied thereafter, except where the criminal act itself occurred before January 1, 1961.[10]

It may be said with greater confidence that the Code of Criminal Procedure contained, as of the date it went into effect, the entire body of criminal procedure law applicable in the RSFSR, including the Fundamental Principles of Criminal Procedure, which were enacted in December 1958 for the USSR as a whole,[11] as well as more detailed provisions concerning criminal proceedings prior

8. Article 3 of the Law on the Issuance of the Criminal Code of the RSFSR, cited *supra,* note 1, expressly commissions the Presidium of the Supreme Soviet of the RSFSR "to issue a list of legislative acts of the RSFSR which have lost their force in connection with the taking effect of the Criminal Code of the RSFSR." The Presidium of the Supreme Soviet of the USSR has also issued lists of USSR laws which lost their force in connection with the adoption of the 1958 USSR Fundamental Principles of Criminal Legislation and in connection with the promulgation of the RSFSR Criminal Code. Similar lists have been published of RSFSR and USSR laws which lost their force in connection with the adoption of the new legislation on criminal procedure and on court organization.

9. Article 5 of the Law on Strengthening the Struggle Against Persons Who Avoid Socially Useful Work and Lead an Antisocial Parasitic Way of Life, May 4, 1961, *Vedomosti RSFSR* (1961), no. 26, item 371, made Article 186 of the Criminal Code applicable to escape from administrative resettlement; however, Article 186 was never amended to cover this. In 1970 the antiparasite law was included in the Criminal Code and administrative resettlement was eliminated. See *infra,* pp. 77–81.

10. Article 2 of the Law on the Issuance of the Criminal Code of the RSFSR, *supra,* note 1, specifically exempts from the operation of the time limits of Article 24 of the Code cases of persons convicted prior to the adoption of the USSR Fundamental Principles of Criminal Legislation of December 25, 1958, for especially dangerous crimes against the state, and for banditry, intentional homicide under aggravating circumstances, theft of state or social property in large amounts, and assault with intent to rob (*razboi*). Otherwise the retroactive application of the Code is governed by its Article 6, which states that a law establishing the punishability of an act or increasing the punishment for it shall not have retroactive force. See also 1958 USSR Fundamental Principles of Criminal Legislation, Article 6. There being no constitutional provision against retroactivity, the rule contained in Article 6 may be changed by the legislature. In 1961, the death sentence was authorized to be imposed retroactively in a particular case by Edict of the Presidium of the Supreme Soviet of the USSR. See H. J. Berman, *Justice in the USSR: An Interpretation of Soviet Law,* rev. ed. (Cambridge, Mass., 1963), p. 86.

11. *Osnovy ugolovnogo sudoproizvodstva soiuza SSR i soiuznykh respublik* (Fundamental Principles of Criminal Procedure of the USSR and the Union Republics), December 25, 1958, *Vedomosti SSSR* (1959), no. 1, item 15. See Appendix II and *supra,* note 2. The Funda-

to trial, trials, appeals, and protests of decisions before they have taken legal effect, execution of judgments, review of decisions after they have taken legal effect, proceedings in cases of minors, and proceedings for the application of compulsory measures of a medical character.[12] The Code of Criminal Procedure apparently excludes the application of prior procedural law. This is implicit in Article 1, which states that the method of conducting proceedings in criminal cases shall be determined by the Code, by the USSR Fundamental Principles of Criminal Procedure, and by USSR laws enacted in accordance with the Fundamental Principles. Since the USSR Fundamental Principles of Criminal Procedure and all USSR laws enacted in accordance therewith were incorporated in the Code as of the time of its enactment, we do not need to look to other legislation to determine the law of criminal procedure applicable in the RSFSR on January 1, 1961. Moreover, as of March 1, 1972, which is the date of the final preparation of this volume, all USSR and RSFSR laws on criminal procedure enacted after January 1, 1961, seem to have been incorporated into the RSFSR Code by way of amendment[13] – with the exception of a USSR edict of August 1970 (amended in February 1972) expanding the right to counsel in the preliminary investigation and requiring an administrative session of the court for issuance of the indictment in cases of minors and of persons accused of capital offenses.[14]

NONCRIMINAL SANCTIONING UNDER SOVIET LAW

Other limitations upon the comprehensive character of both the Criminal Code

---

mental Principles of Criminal Legislation and of Criminal Procedure are translated in Foreign Languages Publishing House, *Fundamentals of Soviet Criminal Legislation, the Judicial System and Criminal Court Procedure – Official Text and Commentaries* (Moscow, 1960); Documentation Office for East European Law, University of Leyden, *supra*, note 4, pp. 37, 61; *CDSP*, March 4, 1959, p. 3.

12. See the table of contents for the pages of the RSFSR Code of Criminal Procedure.

13. It is not possible to write of this matter with complete assurance, because of the possibility that certain laws and decrees were published that did not come to the author's attention, and because of the possibility that certain laws and decrees were enacted but not published. As far as the published laws and decrees are concerned, these may be found in the official gazettes of the supreme soviets (*Vedomosti SSSR* and *Vedomosti RSFSR*). In addition, however, the Council of Ministers of the USSR and the Council of Ministers of the RSFSR issue decrees which, technically, are not "laws" (*zakony*) but which are technically classified as "legislation" (*zakonodatel'stvo*) if they have general or normative significance. Although individual decrees of the councils of ministers are often published in collections available abroad, foreigners may not subscribe to the journals in which such decrees are systematically published. These journals (*Sobranie postanovlenii soveta ministrov SSSR* and *Sobranie postanovlenii soveta ministrov RSFSR*) are available in libraries in the Soviet Union, and are not considered classified information, but are not generally obtainable in the United States. Without a careful study of all the laws published in the gazettes of the supreme soviets of the USSR and RSFSR, and of all the decrees published in the gazettes of the councils of ministers of the USSR and of the RSFSR, it is impossible to be certain that legislation has not been published affecting criminal law and criminal procedure which has not been incorporated into the codes by way of amendment.

In addition, the question arises whether there may be unpublished laws and unpublished decrees affecting criminal law and criminal procedure. Soviet law since 1958–1959 has required the publication of all laws and decrees which are of "general significance" or are of a "normative character." However, it is the Supreme Soviet of the USSR or of the RSFSR, and the Council of Ministers of the USSR or of the RSFSR, which determine whether a particular law or decree has general significance or is of a normative character. See H. J. Berman, *supra*, note 10, pp. 76–77, 86; D. A. Loeber *supra*, note 6; *supra*, note 7.

14. See *infra*, p. 85.

and the Code of Criminal Procedure arise from the relatively narrow definition of the terms "criminal" (*ugolovnyi*) and "law" (*zakon*) in Soviet legal theory and practice. Various types of cases that would fall within criminal law and criminal procedure in the United States, at least, are considered to be "administrative" in the Soviet Union.

Thus Soviet law imposes sanctions (other than civil sanctions) that are not classified as criminal punishment (*ugolovnoe nakazanie*) for offenses (*narusheniia, prostupki*) that are not called crimes (*prestupleniia*). The imposition of such nonpenal sanctions may be authorized by legislation – whether by a "law" (*zakon*) enacted by the Supreme Soviet of the USSR or by a supreme soviet of a republic, or an "edict" (*ukaz*) enacted by the Presidium of the Supreme Soviet of the USSR or by the presidium of the supreme soviet of a republic;[15] but it may also be authorized not by a legislative act ("law" or "edict") but by an executive "decree" (*postanovlenie*) or "regulation" (*rasporiazhenie*) issued by the Council of Ministers of the USSR, by a republican council of ministers, by an individual all-union or republican ministry or by some other administrative body. A person who commits a noncriminal offense is subject to nonpenal sanctions without the full protection of the rules of the Criminal Code and the Code of Criminal Procedure. Sometimes such sanctions may be imposed by a court, which, however, in such cases is considered to be acting administratively.

More specifically, there are four main categories of offenses that do not fall within the Criminal Code and for whose commission the offender is subject to sanctioning procedures outside the Code of Criminal Procedure. These are (1) administrative offenses, (2) disciplinary offenses, (3) minor antisocial acts that subject the offender to responsibility before "social organizations" (*obshchestvennye organizatsii*), especially comrades' courts, and (4) violations of the laws on "petty speculation," and "malicious disobedience" of the police or the "people's guard." Soviet writers do not treat the fourth category separately, but consider such violations as belonging to the first category.

(1) Administrative Offenses. A variety of violations of administrative decrees and regulations render the violator liable to administrative fines, so-called correctional tasks (which in practice usually amount to fines in the form of deductions from wages), in some cases confiscation of property, and more rarely, preventive detention and arrest. Thus minor traffic violations may render the offender liable to a small fine imposed by a policeman on the spot, with a right of appeal to an administrative commission attached to the executive committee of the local

15. The Presidium of the Supreme Soviet of the USSR consists of 37 members chosen from the Supreme Soviet to conduct its affairs between sessions. It has the power to issue "edicts" that enter into force immediately but are subject to subsequent confirmation by the Supreme Soviet. (The Supreme Soviet usually meets twice a year for less than a week at a time.) The edicts of the Presidium of the Supreme Soviet are of two kinds, one legislative and the other "individual." "Individual" edicts are similar to private bills of American legislatures, for example, the awarding of medals and other honors to individual citizens. The edicts of a legislative character are no different from laws, except that they are subject to subsequent confirmation. The Presidium also has the power to give interpretations of laws of the USSR. See Constitution of the USSR, Article 49. The Presidium of the Supreme Soviet of the RSFSR has the same powers within the jurisdiction of the RSFSR. See Constitution of the RSFSR, Article 33.

government (soviet). A person who appears on the street in an intoxicated condition is subject to a fine of 3 to 5 rubles imposed by an administrative commission. Violations of internal and external passport regulations, of rules concerning travel on railroads, of rules concerning fire protection, of tax regulations, and of a great many other types of administrative regulations, are penalized by more substantial fines, usually not exceeding 50 rubles for officials and 10 rubles for others, although for certain offenses fines of 100 rubles for officials and 50 rubles for others may be imposed, and in practice such fines occasionally exceed 200 rubles. One who drives while intoxicated may have his driver's license suspended for one to three years in an administrative procedure. Contraband goods are subject to confiscation by customs, postal, and other authorities. Such fines and penalties are imposed by the administrative bodies charged with enforcement of the regulations, with rights of appeal to higher administrative bodies or, in the case of a fine, to a district or city people's court.[16]

The distinction between criminal and administrative offenses was flagrantly abused by a 1961 RSFSR law which imposed the "administrative penalty" of "resettlement" in specially designated localities, for two to five years, on persons who "avoid socially useful work" and commit "antisocial acts which enable them to lead a parasitic way of life." The history of this law, which was substantially amended in 1965 and again in 1970, is told in a later chapter. For present purposes it suffices to say that in 1970 the "administrative" character of the procedure and of the penalties was eliminated, the offense was narrowed to that of refusing to obey an order to take specific employment, and such refusal was made an offense under the Criminal Code, with a maximum punishment of deprivation of freedom for one year. The fact that in the Russian Republic for nine years (and in some other republics, under similar laws, for thirteen years) heavy punishment could be imposed "administratively" raised in some minds, both inside and outside the Soviet Union, the specter of a possible return to the duality of law and terror that existed under Stalin. With the changes introduced in the antiparasite law in 1970, the concept of "administrative offenses" has been restricted to relatively minor infractions subject to relatively minor penalties.

(2) Disciplinary Offenses. Under Soviet administrative law, administrative officials (for example, directors of state enterprises or other institutions) may

16. See Articles 39–40, RSFSR Statute on Administrative Commissions, March 30, 1962, *Vedomosti RSFSR* (1962), no. 13, item 166; translated in Harold J. Berman and John B. Quigley, Jr., *Basic Laws on the Structure of the Soviet State* (Cambridge, Mass., 1969), pp. 275–285, and together with other materials on administrative materials, in *Soviet Statutes and Decisions* 6:1–97 (1968). On Soviet administrative law and administrative offenses generally, see V. A. Vlasov and S. S. Studenikin, *Sovetskoe administrativnoe pravo* (Moscow, 1959); G. I. Petrov, *Sovetskoe administrativnoe pravo – chast' obshchaia* (Leningrad, 1960); Iu. M. Kozlov, ed., *Sovetskoe administrativnoe pravo (obshchaia chast')* (Moscow, 1962); Iu. M. Kozlov, ed., *Sovetskoe administrativnoe pravo (osobennaia chast')* (Moscow, 1964); Iu. M. Kozlov, ed., *Voprosy sovetskogo administrativnogo prava na sovremennom etape* (Moscow, 1963); I. F. Bartykov et al., *Administrativnye pravonarusheniia rassmatrivaemye v sudebnom poriadke* (Moscow, 1964); V. D. Sorokin, *Administrativnye komissii pri ispolkomakh raionnykh, gorodskikh sovetov deputatov trudiashchikhsia* (Moscow, 1964); V. A. Vlasov, *Novoe zakonodatel'stvo ob administrativnykh shtrafakh* (Moscow, 1963). See also F. J. Feldbrugge, *Soviet Criminal Law: General Part* (Leyden, 1964), pp. 20–24.

impose upon their subordinates disciplinary penalties for violations of work rules, just as under Soviet military law commanders may impose disciplinary penalties upon their subordinate officers or enlisted men. Also Soviet labor law authorizes the imposition of disciplinary penalties upon workers – for absenteeism, for example, or drunkenness on the job, or damage to property. Disciplinary penalties include censure, reprimand, temporary deprivation of rank or function, and dismissal. Heavy fines, including forfeiture of several months' salary, have sometimes been imposed on officials as a disciplinary penalty. Disciplinary offenses are often treated by Soviet writers as a form of administrative offense. However, it is helpful – at least for the student of comparative law – to distinguish between administrative offenses that may be committed by the public generally and which consist in violations of particular administrative regulations, and administrative offenses that may be committed only by persons in specific relationships of subordination and which may consist in violations of general standards of good conduct.[17] In any event, since neither type of administrative offense is considered a "crime" and neither is subject to criminal penalties, the sanctions applicable to both are imposed without the full protection of the Criminal Code and the Code of Criminal Procedure.

(3) Minor Antisocial Acts Considered by Comrades' Courts. Under the 1961 RSFSR Statute on Comrades' Courts, as amended,[18] persons who commit any of a variety of petty offenses which, because of their insignificance or because of the character of the act committed, fall short of being crimes may be brought before comrades' courts. These are informal nonprofessional tribunals staffed by neighbors or fellow workers in housing units, enterprises or institutions, collective farms, etc., with power to issue warnings, reprimands, recommendations of eviction from an apartment or demotion in a job, fines up to 50 rubles, and transfer to menial work for fifteen days. Comrades' courts are quasi-judicial agencies; they are not subject to the Law on Court Organization, and their sanctions are termed "measures of social pressure" in order to distinguish them both from criminal punishment and from administrative measures. Similarly, the Statute on Comrades' Courts is careful to speak of "members of the comrades' court," rather than of "judges," and of "the person brought before the comrades'

17. The principal legal basis for imposing disciplinary penalties in the Soviet system is the all-union law of October 13, 1929, on the principles of disciplinary legislation of the USSR and the union republics. *Sobranie zakonov i rasporiazhenii raboche-krestianskogo pravitel'stva SSSR* (Collected Laws and Regulations of the Worker-Peasant Government of the USSR), no. 71, item 670. See discussion in Ts. A. Iampol'skaia, "Sluzhebnaia distsiplina i distsiplinarnyi prostupok," *Sovetskoe gosudarstvo i pravo* (1947), no. 12, p. 48; A. I. Turetskii, "Prestuplenie i distsiplinarnyi prostupok," *Sotsialisticheskaia zakonnost'* (1956), no. 10, p. 15; F. J. Feldbrugge, *supra*, note 16, pp. 22–23.

Disciplinary punishment in the armed forces is governed by a special Disciplinary Code and Code of Internal Service of the Armed Forces of the USSR, *Vedomosti SSSR* (1960), no. 34, item 325. Earlier Disciplinary Codes are discussed in H. J. Berman and M. Kerner, *Soviet Military Law and Administration* (Cambridge, Mass., 1955), ch. 2.

18. *Vedomosti RSFSR* (1961), no. 26, item 371; (1963), no. 43, item 750; (1965), no. 4, item 83. The law as amended in 1963 is translated (and discussed with an article-by-article commentary) in H. J. Berman and J. W. Spindler, "Soviet Comrades' Courts," *Washington Law Review* 38:843–910 (1963); and as amended through 1965 in Berman and Quigley, *supra*, note 16, pp. 264–274.

court," rather than the "accused." If it appears that a person brought before the comrades' court should be held criminally responsible, his case is to be transferred to the appropriate agencies for trial under the Criminal Code and the Code of Criminal Procedure and not under the Statute on Comrades' Courts; nevertheless, the criminal courts may transfer for consideration by comrades' courts cases in which the accused committed relatively minor crimes for the first time (RSFSR Criminal Code, Article 51).

(4) Laws Imposing Administrative Confinement. Under a 1957 law on petty speculation,[19] a 1962 law on malicious disobedience of the lawful order or request of a member of the police or of the people's guard,[20] and a 1966 law on hooliganism,[21] an offender may be fined or sentenced to the administrative penalty of "arrest" for a maximum of fifteen days by order of a single judge, in a summary procedure and without right of appeal. However, these examples of administrative confinement by order of a court are only minor departures from the principles of the Criminal Code and Code of Criminal Procedure, since they all involve specifically defined unlawful acts, and the use of the device "arrest"[22] permits relatively light sentences to be meted out speedily to petty offenders. It is expressly provided that the application of administrative sanctions for violations of these laws does not entail a criminal record or an interruption of job seniority.[23]

A far more serious example of the imposition of administrative penalties by courts in administrative session was the antiparasite law of 1961.[24] This law was substantially modified to exclude administrative confinement in February 1970.[25] Despite this important change it remains true that a restricted meaning

19. Edict of the Presidium of the Supreme Soviet of the RSFSR, September 12, 1957, on Responsibility for Petty Speculation, *Vedomosti RSFSR* (1957), no. 1, item 5.

20. Edict of the Presidium of the Supreme Soviet of the USSR, February 15, 1962, on Strengthening Responsibility for Infringing the Life, Health, and Dignity of Workers of the Police and of the People's Guard, Article 1, *Vedomosti SSSR* (1962), no. 8, item 83; Edict on the Application of Measures of Pressure for Malicious Disobedience of a Lawful Order or Request of a Worker of the Police or of the People's Guard, *id.*, April 4, 1962, no. 14, Article 148. The people's guard (*narodnaia druzhina*) was formed in 1958 as a volunteer auxiliary police force.

21. Edict of the Presidium of the Supreme Soviet of the RSFSR, August 26, 1966, *Vedomosti RSFSR* (1966), no. 35, item 947. The first part of the edict replaced the Edict of the Presidium of the Supreme Soviet of the RSFSR, December 19, 1956, On Responsibility for Petty Hooliganism, *Sovetskaia Rossiia*, December 20, 1956, amended by Edict of the Presidium of the Supreme Soviet of the RSFSR, April 19, 1961, *Vedomosti RSFSR* (1961), no. 16, item 246.

22. "Arrest" (in Russian, *arest*) as a punishment for an administrative offense should not be confused with "arrest" as used in Article 127 of the Constitution of the USSR, which states that "no one may be subjected to arrest otherwise than by decree of a court or sanction of a procurator." Arrest as used in Article 127 (and in Article 11 of the 1960 RSFSR Code of Criminal Procedure) refers to detention in connection with the institution of criminal charges. Cf. *infra*, pp. 52–53.

23. See decree of the Presidium of the Supreme Soviet of the RSFSR, September 12, 1957, and the decree of the Presidium of the Supreme Soviet of the USSR, April 4, 1962, printed in *Sbornik normativnykh aktov po sovetskomu administrativnomu pravu* (Moscow, 1964), pp. 188–189, 192.

24. The antiparasite law is discussed at some length *infra*, pp. 77–81.

25. *Vedomosti RSFSR* (1970), no. 14, item 255.

can be given to the terms "criminal" and "law" in the provisions of Article 3 of the Criminal Code that "Criminal punishment shall be applied only by judgment of a court," and that "only a person guilty of committing a . . . socially dangerous act provided for by law [*zakon*] shall be subject to criminal responsibility and punishment." The possibility of establishing noncriminal offenses, nonpenal sanctions, and nonjudicial sanctioning procedures, and of doing so by administrative decree (*postanovlenie*) rather than by act of the legislature (*zakon*), threatens to give Article 3 a tautological character.

Apart from administrative confinement as a sanction for the commission of an offense, there exists in Soviet law (as in the law of other countries, including the United States) provision for administrative confinement as a form of medical treatment. If the question of mental illness arises with respect to a person charged with a crime, it is for the investigator or court to determine, on the basis of psychiatric opinion, whether such person should be relieved of criminal responsibility and whether he should be committed to a psychiatric hospital (cf. RSFSR Criminal Code, Articles 58 and 59; RSFSR Code of Criminal Procedure, Articles 188 and 403–413). If, however, no crime is charged, a person may be committed administratively by the decision of medical authorities alone. In recent years charges have been made in the Soviet unofficial press (*samizdat*, literally "self-published") and in letters to Soviet authorities, copies of which have been published outside the Soviet Union, that a number of persons who expressed opposition to various features of the Soviet political system were sent to psychiatric hospitals, whether by decision of investigators or judges in criminal cases or by administrative decision without the institution of criminal charges. In 1970 the prominent biologist Zhores Medvedev, who had published abroad a condemnation of Soviet restrictions on freedom of science, was confined in a psychiatric hospital for several months and was released after a storm of protest both inside and outside the Soviet Union.[26]

With the above qualifications and limitations, the two codes here presented in translation, together with the Law on Court Organization, contain all the basic rules of Soviet (RSFSR) criminal law and procedure as well as the definitions of all crimes and the limits of punishment applicable to such crimes. Any person (whether or not a Soviet citizen) who is charged with the commission of a crime (as that word is defined in Soviet law) on the territory of the RSFSR, any citizen of the RSFSR who is charged with the commission of a crime outside the terri-

26. See Zhores and Roy Medvedev, *A Question of Madness* (London, 1971). Cf. *The Internment of Soviet Dissenters in Mental Hospitals* (Cambridge, England, n.d.). Cf. *infra*, p. 88.

Reports published in the West that healthy persons have been placed in Soviet psychiatric hospitals have been termed "absurd" and a "preposterous fiction" by the Director of the Psychiatric Institute of the USSR Academy of Medicine. See Izvestia, October 24, 1971, p. 4 (article by K. Briantsev). In January 1972, V. K. Bukovsky was convicted of circulating anti-Soviet propaganda under Article 70 of the RSFSR Criminal Code, chiefly on the ground that he had, with anti-Soviet intent, spread false reports that political dissidents of sound mind were committed to psychiatric hospitals and were there subjected to abuse. The court is said to have denied defense counsel's request to call as witnesses persons who had been committed to psychiatric hospitals, on the theory that such persons would not be competent to testify. The Times, London, Feb. 7, 1972, p. 1. See *infra*, chap. 5, notes 18, 34, 35.

tory of the RSFSR (whether or not within the confines of the Soviet Union), and, where so provided for by international treaty, any person (whether or not a Soviet citizen) who is charged with the commission of a crime anywhere (whether or not within the confines of the Soviet Union), is subject to trial under the RSFSR Law on Court Organization, according to the procedure established in the RSFSR Code of Criminal Procedure, for acts declared criminal by the RSFSR Criminal Code.

RELATION OF THE RSFSR CODES TO USSR LAW

One who thinks of federalism only in American terms is apt to have difficulty in understanding the relation between the RSFSR codes, which are "republican" law enacted by the Supreme Soviet of the RSFSR, and the criminal law enacted by the Supreme Soviet of the USSR, which is "all-union" law. The USSR Constitution does, on the one hand, declare that "the sovereignty of the union republics is restricted only within the limits specified in Article 14 of the Constitution of the USSR," and that "beyond those limits each union republic exercises state authority independently" (Article 15). Thus it would appear that the all-union authority is limited to those powers expressly enumerated in Article 14, and that powers not delegated to the all-union authority are reserved to the republics. However, the powers expressly granted by Article 14 to the all-union authority are extremely broad. They include responsibility not only for the protection of state security, the development of Soviet military strength, and other traditional tasks of central governments, but also the direction of the entire Soviet economy on the basis of a state economic plan. For implementation of such all-union responsibilities, the Constitution vests the supreme legislative power of the USSR in the Supreme Soviet of the USSR, whose laws are binding throughout the territory of the USSR. It also provides that in the event of a contradiction between all-union and republican law, the former shall prevail.[27]

The USSR Constitution specifically mentions criminal law, criminal procedure, and court organization in Article 14, which provides for the enactment by the Supreme Soviet of all-union "fundamental principles" (*osnovy*, literally "foundations") in those fields. Nothing is said in the Constitution, however, concerning the power of the Supreme Soviet to enact specific laws (*zakony*) or basic statutes (*polozheniia*) relating to particular crimes or particular types of crimes. It has been argued that the express reference to fundamental principles excludes any power to enact specific criminal laws or basic criminal statutes.[28] The contention rests on the maxim, *lex specialis derogat legi generali*; that is, the special reference to fundamental principles of criminal law and procedure is taken as limiting the character of the criminal legislation that the Supreme Soviet of the USSR may constitutionally enact. If this argument were sound, the anomalous situation would exist whereby the all-union authority extends to the protection of the state frontiers, but no laws could be enacted making it a crime to violate the frontiers – either by the republics (since protection of the frontiers is beyond

27. Constitution of the USSR, Articles 14, 19, 20, 32.
28. Feldbrugge, *supra*, note 16, p. 59.

their competence) or by the all-union authorities (since by hypothesis they could only enact fundamental principles of criminal law and not individual criminal statutes). To an American lawyer, at least, such reasoning would seem to founder on Article 32 of the USSR Constitution, which declares that "the legislative power of the USSR shall be exercised exclusively by the Supreme Soviet of the USSR," and Article 31, which grants to the Supreme Soviet of the USSR the power to "exercise all rights vested in the Union of Soviet Socialist Republics under Article 14 of the Constitution." "Legislative power" would surely seem to include the power to enact specific criminal laws.

Moreover, Article 2 of the RSFSR Criminal Code expressly provides that all-union laws establishing responsibility for "crimes directed against the interests of the USSR" shall be applicable in the RSFSR prior to their inclusion in the RSFSR Criminal Code.

The promulgation of criminal "codes," however, as contrasted with "fundamental principles" and individual laws or basic statutes, is left by the USSR Constitution to the 15 union republics. This is not expressly stated in the Constitution, but it is clearly indicated by its legislative history, as will appear in the next section of this chapter.

In any event, in accordance with Article 14, the Supreme Soviet of the USSR enacted, in December 1958, Fundamental Principles of Criminal Legislation of the USSR and the Union Republics, Fundamental Principles of Criminal Procedure of the USSR and the Union Republics, and Fundamental Principles of Court Organization of the USSR and the Union Republics.[29] At the same time it enacted a USSR Statute (*Polozhenie*) on Crimes Against the State and a USSR Statute on Military Crimes,[30] as well as a USSR Statute on Military Tribunals.[31] In addition, it has enacted on many occasions throughout its history individual laws making particular acts criminally punishable. As stressed above, all of its enactments are binding throughout the territory of the USSR.

In considering the relation between the RSFSR codes and all-union law, it is necessary to note certain features of the Soviet judicial system. Each republic has its own system of courts, culminating in a republican supreme court. In addition to the republican courts, there is the Supreme Court of the USSR, which, except for the military tribunals, is the only all-union court. The Supreme Court of the USSR has power to reverse the decisions of republican supreme courts which violate all-union law. Finally, the military tribunals (called *tribunaly*, "tribunals," not *sudy*, "courts") are set up not within the republics as such but within the nine military districts into which the USSR is divided. Decisions of military tribunals may also be reviewed by the Supreme Court of the USSR.

A more detailed discussion of the judicial system is postponed to a later section

29. *Supra*, notes 2, 11; *Osnovy zakonodatel'stva o sudoustroistve Soiuza SSR, soiuznykh i avtonomnykh respublik* (Fundamental Principles of Legislation on the Court Organization of the USSR and of Union and Autonomous Republics), *Vedomosti SSSR* (1959), no. 1, item 6, is translated in Foreign Languages Publishing House, *supra*, note 11, and in *CDSP*, March 11, 1959, p. 8.

30. *Supra*, note 4.

31. Izvestia, December 26, 1958, p. 5. The term *polozhenie* used for this type of statute has the connotation of a more comprehensive regulation than the usual statute (*zakon*).

of this introduction. What is relevant at this point is the fact that the republican courts have jurisdiction over crimes generally, and that the applicable law is contained in the republican codes; however, since much of that applicable law, including its fundamental principles, is all-union law, the supervision of the Supreme Court of the USSR is required to maintain uniformity and to preserve all-union legal policy.

All-union law is also protected by the Procuracy of the USSR, which is responsible for the prosecution of criminals and which, in addition, exercises a supervisory function with respect to the courts to the extent that it may protest judicial decisions to higher judicial authorities and ultimately, as a last resort, to the Presidium of the Supreme Soviet of the USSR. A more detailed discussion of the Procuracy is also postponed to a later section of this introduction, but it is important to note here that the Procuracy is an all-union organization entirely independent of republican legislative or administrative control.

Finally, all-union law and legal policy is protected by the Communist Party of the Soviet Union, which, under Article 126 of the Constitution of the USSR, is "the leading core of all organizations of the working people, both social and state." The party criticizes the work of legal officials at all levels, and is ultimately responsible for their nomination and removal from office. However, party organizations and party officials are not supposed to dictate judicial decisions in particular cases. Thus in an article published in 1963 in a leading party journal it is stated: "Interference of any kind whatsoever by party agencies in the settlement of specific legal matters is impermissible."[32]

THE CODES OF THE OTHER UNION REPUBLICS

Although the RSFSR is by far the largest of the union republics as measured both by population and by land area, nevertheless some 45 percent of the people of the Soviet Union reside in the other 14 union republics, each of which has enacted its own criminal code, code of criminal procedure, and law on court organization.[33]

32. "All are Equal Before the Law," *Partiinaia zhizn'*, 1963, no. 2, pp. 50–52, translated in *CDSP* March 13, 1963, p. 10. There have been similar warnings in the past. Cf. V. P. Radkov, *Sotsialisticheskaia zakonnost' v sovetskom ugolovnom protsesse* (Moscow, 1959), pp. 152–153, translated in J. N. Hazard, I. Shapiro, and P. B. Maggs, *The Soviet Legal System: Contemporary Documentation and Historical Commentary* (Dobbs Ferry, N.Y., 1969), part I, p. 60. Cf. 1960 RSFSR Code of Criminal Procedure, Article 16, which states: "Judges and people's assessors shall decide criminal cases on the basis of law in conformity with socialist legal consciousness under conditions excluding outside pressure upon them."

33. The Criminal Codes and Codes of Criminal Procedure of the other union republics were adopted on the following dates: Uzbek SSR, May 21, 1959; Kazakh SSR, July 22, 1959; Georgian SSR, December 30, 1959; Azerbaidzhan SSR, December 8, 1960; Ukrainian SSR, December 28, 1960; Belorussian SSR, December 29, 1970; Kirgiz SSR, December 29, 1960; Latvian SSR, January 6, 1961; Estonian SSR, January 6, 1961; Armenian SSR, March 7, 1961; Moldavian SSR, March 24, 1961; Lithuanian SSR, June 26, 1961; Tadzhik SSR, August 17, 1961; Turkmen SSR, December 22, 1961.

Laws on Court Organization were enacted in the following republics on the following dates: Uzbek SSR, May 21, 1959; Kazakh SSR, July 22, 1959; Belorussian SSR, November 20, 1959; Latvian SSR, November 27, 1959; Moldavian SSR, April 16, 1960; Kirgiz SSR, May 25, 1960; Lithuanian SSR, June 8, 1970; Georgian SSR, June 25, 1960; Turkmen SSR,

Despite a high degree of uniformity imposed by all-union legislation, and despite political control from the central party and governmental agencies, the criminal codes of the various republics differ considerably both with respect to what is criminal and with respect to punishment.[34] Some of these differences reflect the diversity of cultural, religious, and historical developments and of geographic conditions in the various republics. Most, however, are the result of differences in the nature and quality of legal science in the different republics – that is, differences in the ideas, abilities, and degree of independence of the jurists. Some of the variations in the codes are inconsequential, whereas others appear to be inconsistent with the unifying purpose of the USSR Fundamental Principles of Criminal Legislation.

Certain acts are criminal in some republics, but not in others. Chapter Eleven of the RSFSR Criminal Code on "Crimes Constituting Survivals of Local Customs," dealing with such matters as blood feuds, sale of brides, and polygamy, has no counterpart in any of the other republican codes. The crimes listed in Chapter Eleven are generally not punishable at all in the European parts of the USSR, though a number of them (e.g., homicide in pursuance of a blood feud, payment for a bride) are included in the special parts of the criminal codes of various individual Central Asian and Caucasian republics. Other differences that reflect local problems are found in the articles of the criminal codes dealing with sex offenses and family relations. There are dozens of other differences, however, which have no such logical basis. For example, compelling a person to be a co-author or joint inventor is a crime in all except the Ukrainian, Kirgiz, and Turkmen republics.

There are many variations in the definitions of particular criminal acts. For example, in some republics the "malice" in the crime of malicious hooliganism can consist in the infliction of bodily harm, while in other republics mere infliction of bodily injury does not in itself constitute "malice." This difference in definition results in a serious discrepancy in the application of Article 10 of the USSR Fundamental Principles, which provides that offenders between the ages of 14 and 16 may be punished for malicious hooliganism but not for ordinary hooliganism.

A number of basic terms are defined differently in the criminal codes of various republics, including "an official," "an especially dangerous recidivist," and others.

There are substantial differences in the punishments allotted to the same crimes in different republics. For example, intentional homicide is punishable under the RSFSR Criminal Code by deprivation of freedom for three to ten years, under the Lithuanian code from three to twelve years, under the Kirgiz, Tadzhik, and Turkmen codes from five to twelve years, under the Armenian code from five to

June 29, 1960; Ukrainian SSR, June 30, 1960; Estonian SSR, August 19, 1960; Azerbaidzhan SSR, December 8, 1960; Tadzhik SSR, January 5, 1961.

34. For a comparison of the RSFSR and Uzbek Criminal Codes of 1926, see George Ginsburg and George Mason, "Soviet Criminal Law Reform: Centralized Uniformity versus Local Diversification," in G.O.W. Mueller, ed., *Essays in Criminal Science* (South Hackensack, 1961), pp. 409–444. On the RSFSR Criminal Code of 1960 and the Latvian Criminal Code of 1961, see Zigurds L. Zile, "Soviet Federalism in Criminal Law: A Case Study," in A. Sprudzs and A. Rusis, eds., *Res Baltica* (Leyden, 1968), pp. 152–159.

ten years, under the Moldavian code from five to twelve years with or without an additional period of exile up to five years. The maximum penalties for speculation as a form of business or on a large scale are seven years in the RSFSR, eight years in the Latvian SSR, ten years in the Turkmen SSR, and ten years with resettlement and confiscation of property in the Armenian SSR. One recent study has shown that, on the whole, the Special Part of the Latvian criminal code contains punishments less harsh than those of the RSFSR code for equivalent offenses, except in the area of crimes against personal property of citizens, where the sanctions in the Latvian code are more severe.[35]

The differences in the criminal procedure codes are much less significant, because of the much greater specificity of the USSR Fundamentals of Criminal Procedure. However, the procedure codes vary in length from 356 to 424 articles. There are a number of organizational differences. For instance, some codes have a separate chapter on juvenile offenders, while most distribute the articles dealing with juvenile offenders throughout the code. There are a number of differences in the times at which certain procedural actions may be taken. There are significant differences in the range of crimes that are punishable only at the instance of the victim and in the procedures for dealing with such crimes. Neither these nor other differences, however, have a major effect upon the scope of procedural protection offered to the accused.[36]

35. Zile, *op cit.*, p. 157. The differences in punishments in the various republican criminal codes may most easily be studied by using T. P. Shurakov, compiler, *Alfavitnopredmetnyi ukazatel' k sborniku "Ugolovnoe zakonodatel'stvo Soiuza SSR i soiuznykh respublik"* (Moscow, 1963). See also V. D. Men'shagin and others, *Osobennosti ugolovnykh kodeksov soiuznykh respublik, Sbornik stat'ei* (Moscow, 1963); M. P. Karpushin, "O nekotorykh voprosakh sootnosheniia obshchesoiuznogo i respublikanskogo ugolovnogo zakonodatel'stva," *Sovetskoe gosudarstvo i pravo* (1965), no. 4, p. 65. The republican codes are collected in F. I. Kalinychev, ed., *Ugolovnoe zakonodatel'stvo Soiuza SSR i soiuznykh respublik*, 2 vols. (Moscow, 1962).

36. The differences may be most easily compared through use of L. N. Smirnov, ed., *Sopostavitel'naia tablitsa statei osnov ugolovno-protsessual'nykh kodeksov soiuznykh respublik, sbornik stat'ei* (Moscow, 1962). The republican codes are collected in F. I. Kalinychev, ed., *Zakonodatel'stvo ob ugolovnom sudoproizvodstve Soiuza SSR i soiuznykh respublik*, 2 vols. (Moscow, 1963).

2 The History of the Codes: A Chronology

The first Soviet Constitution, that of the Russian Socialist Federated Soviet Republic (RSFSR), adopted on July 10, 1918, gave to the All-Russian Congress of Soviets and the All-Russian Central Executive Committee of Soviets jurisdiction over "all questions of state significance, such as . . . state legislation, judicial organization and procedure, civil and criminal legislation, etc." (Article 49(n)).[1] The 1918 Constitution made no mention of codes or other systematic statements of the criminal law. In December 1919 the People's Commissariat of Justice of the RSFSR issued a set of "Leading Principles [*Rukovodiashchie nachala*] of Criminal Legislation of the RSFSR," which was a very short statement, in 27 articles, of basic rules concerning crime and punishment, stages of commission of crimes (attempt and preparation), types of punishment, and a few other matters.[2] Apart from the "Leading Principles," Soviet criminal law and procedure in this first period of the Soviet state was contained in a host of separate decrees, including a variety of decrees on the courts and court organization.[3]

The New Economic Policy, introduced in 1921, stimulated intensive efforts to systematize and codify Soviet law generally, including civil law, labor law, family law and land law as well as criminal law and procedure. Accordingly, in 1922 the RSFSR enacted a Criminal Code[4] and a Statute on Court Organization[5] and in 1923 a Code of Criminal Procedure.[6] Further impetus to legal systematization and codification was provided by the formation, in December 1922, of a Union of Soviet Socialist Republics (consisting of the RSFSR and the Ukrainian, Belorussian and Transcaucasian Republics) and by the adoption, in January 1924, of a USSR Constitution. The 1924 USSR Constitution – like the present USSR Constitution – left the codification of criminal and civil law to the individual republics, while giving to the supreme agencies of authority of the USSR jurisdiction over "the establishment of fundamental principles [*osnovy*] of court

1. *SU* (1918), no. 51, item 582. This is the official collection of laws of the Council of People's Commissars prior to the formation of the Union of Soviet Socialist Republics.
2. Decree of the People's Commissariat of Justice, December 12, 1919, *SU* (1919), no. 66, item 590.
3. See generally J. N. Hazard, *Settling Disputes in Soviet Society: The Formative Years of Legal Institutions* (New York, 1960), pp. 1–127.
4. *SU* (1922), no. 15, item 153.
5. *SU* (1922), no. 69, item 902.
6. *SU* (1923), no. 7, item 106.

organization and procedure as well as of civil and criminal legislation of the Union" (Article 1 (o)). In accordance with this provision, in October 1924 the Central Executive Committee (predecessor of the Presidium of the Supreme Soviet) of the USSR enacted "Fundamental Principles [*Osnovnye nachala*] of Criminal Legislation of the USSR and the Union Republics," consisting of 39 articles, "Fundamental Principles of Criminal Procedure of the USSR and the Union Republics," consisting of 32 articles, and "Fundamental Principles of Court Organization of the USSR and the Union Republics," consisting of 24 articles.[7] The all-union legislation was far less detailed than the 1922 RSFSR Criminal Code, the 1923 Code of Criminal Procedure, and the 1922 Statute on Court Organization, which consisted of 232, 465, and 134 articles, respectively.

Largely as a result of changes introduced by the 1924 all-union Fundamental Principles of Criminal Legislation, a new RSFSR Criminal Code, consisting of 205 articles, was enacted on November 22, 1926, to take effect on January 1, 1927.[8] (The 1923 RSFSR Code of Criminal Procedure and the 1922 Statute on Court Organization were not replaced.) Other republics adopted their own codes and statutes on court organization, which were designed to be consistent with (and which reproduced) the all-union fundamental principles.

In December 1936 a new USSR Constitution was adopted, which provided that the highest agencies of authority of the USSR should have jurisdiction over "legislation on judicial organization and procedure; criminal and civil codes" (Article 14(u)). This meant that the dual system of all-union "fundamental principles" of judicial organization, criminal law, and criminal procedure, on the one hand, and republican codes on the other, was to be abandoned in favor of a system of all-union codes in these areas of law. (The dual system was retained, under the 1936 Constitution, in other areas of law – namely, education, health, and labor). However, at the time of the adoption of the 1936 Constitution, no all-union criminal and criminal procedure codes were in existence, and therefore the existing republican criminal and criminal procedure codes continued to be in effect pending the adoption of all-union codes. In fact, all-union codes were never adopted, although several drafts of such codes were prepared and discussed. An all-union Law on Court Organization was, however, enacted in 1938,[9] which replaced the 1924 Fundamental Principles of Court Organization, and rendered obsolete many of the provisions of the republican judiciary laws, including the 1923 RSFSR Statute on Court Organization.

In February 1957 Article 14 of the Constitution was amended to provide for the enactment of all-union "fundamental principles" (*osnovy*) of court organization, criminal law and criminal procedure;[10] that is, the provisions of Article 1(o) of the 1924 Constitution were, in effect, restored, and, with respect to criminal law and criminal procedure, the situation that had existed since 1924 was once again given Constitutional sanction.

7. *SZ* (1924), no. 24, items 205 and 206; no. 23, item 203.
8. *SZ* (1926), no. 80, item 600.
9. Law of August 16, 1938, *Vedomosti SSSR*, September 5, 1938, no. 11, p. 2.
10. Law of February 11, 1957, *Vedomosti SSSR* (1957), no. 4, item 63.

In December 1958 the Supreme Soviet of the USSR, as indicated above, enacted Fundamental Principles of Court Organization, of Criminal Legislation, and of Criminal Procedure, which replaced the 1924 Fundamental Principles of Criminal Legislation and of Criminal Procedure and the 1938 Law on Court Organization; and in October 1960 the Supreme Soviet of the RSFSR enacted a new Criminal Code, a new Code of Criminal Procedure, and a new Law on Court Organization, to take effect January 1, 1961, which replaced the 1926 RSFSR Criminal Code and the 1923 Code of Criminal Procedure, and what was left, after the 1938 all-union law, of the 1923 RSFSR Statute on Court Organization. The other 14 union republics also adopted their own criminal codes, codes of criminal procedure, and laws on court organization.

To recapitulate in tabular form the developments described above, we may list the most important pieces of legislation as follows:

On criminal law:

1. Leading Principles of Criminal Law of the RSFSR (1919);
2. Criminal Code of the RSFSR (1922);
3. Fundamental Principles of Criminal Legislation of the USSR and the Union Republics (1924);
4. Criminal Code of the RSFSR (1926);
5. Fundamental Principles of Criminal Legislation of the USSR and the Union Republics (1958);
6. Criminal Code of the RSFSR (1960).

On criminal procedure:

1. Code of Criminal Procedure of the RSFSR (1923);
2. Fundamental Principles of Criminal Procedure of the USSR and the Union Republics (1924);
3. Fundamental Principles of Criminal Procedure of the USSR and the Union Republics (1958);
4. Code of Criminal Procedure of the RSFSR (1960).

On court organization:

1. Statute on Court Organization of the RSFSR (1922);
2. Fundamental Principles of Court Organization of the USSR and the Union Republics (1924);
3. Law on Court Organization of the USSR and the Union Republics (1938);
4. Fundamental Principles of Judicial Organization of the USSR and the Union Republics (1958);
5. Law on Court Organization of the RSFSR (1960).

3 Major Changes Reflected in the 1960 Criminal Code

If we compare the RSFSR 1926 Criminal Code and 1923 Code of Criminal Procedure, as originally enacted, with the 1960 Codes, or with the 1958 Fundamental Principles upon which the 1960 Codes were based, we find drastic differences both in style and content, together with some important similarities. Many of the differences, however, reflect changes that were introduced into the older codes themselves by specific legislative enactments in the 1920's, 1930's, 1940's and 1950's, and by the development of Soviet legal science in those decades. For a quarter of a century the older codes, although still in force, had been obsolete in much of their terminology and in many of their provisions. Thus it would be a mistake to attribute all the reforms of 1958 and 1960 to the reaction against Stalin in the years after his death in 1953.

Nevertheless, the 1958 and 1960 reforms do take some of their character from the revulsion against Stalinist terror and Stalinist theories. In the first place, although Stalin had called for new codes from 1936 on, it had proved impossible to prepare such codes while he lived, and one may surmise that one reason for that was the difficulty of reconciling Stalin's emphasis on the need for "stability of laws" with his insistence upon the use of terror against political enemies, and indeed, against potential enemies. In addition, his death, and the attack launched by his successors against his cruel and arbitrary methods, were probably needed to release the energy for law reform that remained latent during his lifetime. Beyond that, however, the 1958 and 1960 reforms in the fields of criminal law and procedure are, at many points, specifically directed against abuses which were characteristic of the Stalin era.

Conceivably, the reaction against the excesses of Stalin's rule could have taken the form of a new reception of prerevolutionary Russian and contemporary Western legal norms and institutions. Such a reception had taken place in the early 1920's, when the apocalyptic and nihilistic period of War Communism (1917–1921) gave way to the "strategic retreat" of the New Economic Policy (1921–1928); at that time Soviet jurists, in drafting their codes, consciously looked to prerevolutionary Russian and Western models, although they made many changes in those models. The draftsmen of the post-Stalin codes of criminal law and procedure, however, state that they did not look abroad but built upon their own Soviet experience, attempting to preserve its positive values and at the same time to correct its mistakes. Corroboration of this may be found in the fact that the codes give little internal evidence of prerevolutionary Russian or other non-Soviet influence, except as such influence had already been embodied in Soviet legislation and Soviet legal thought. Of course, the draftsmen of the new codes were in general familiar with non-Soviet legal systems, and especially with the prerevolutionary Russian law, and no doubt they also wished to create codes that would reflect credit upon them abroad as well as at home. Yet it is important for the non-Soviet student of the codes to recognize that they are based in the first instance upon the Soviet legal tradition that had developed – in considerable part, to be sure, on prerevolutionary Russian and Western foundations – over a period of more than forty years. As will become apparent in the following account of the major changes wrought by the codes, their framers weighed the failures and successes of more than a generation of experience and sought to establish the best results of that experience rather than to imitate the codes of other countries or, on the other hand, to create something entirely new. The codes must therefore be judged, in the first instance, by their place within the Soviet legal tradition; only then may proper comparisons be made between that legal tradition and others.

Some of the most important differences between the 1960 Criminal Code and the 1926 Criminal Code, as originally enacted, are reflected in Article 3 of the 1960 Criminal Code, which states that no person may be subjected to criminal responsibility and punishment unless he has committed a crime, and which defines a crime as a socially dangerous act provided for by law; in Article 7, which further limits the concept of crime to socially dangerous acts provided for by the Special Part of the Criminal Code; and in Article 6, which states that a law establishing the punishability of an act or increasing the punishment shall not have retroactive force. Thus the social danger of the person and of the act is not enough, under the 1960 Code, to justify the imposition of criminal punishment; there must also be a crime, that is, a violation of a specific provision of the Special Part of the Code.

In contrast, the 1926 Criminal Code made social danger itself, and not violation of a specific provision of the Special Part of the Code, the key to judicial sanctioning. Moreover, in some cases punishment was based on the social danger of the *person,* rather than of the *act* he committed.

Article 7 of the 1926 Code provided:

> With regard to persons who have committed socially dangerous acts or who represent a danger because of their connection with a criminal environment or because of their past activity, measures of social defense of a judicial-correctional, medical, or medico-educational character shall be applied.

Thus a person who committed no act whatever but who merely had a "connection with a criminal environment" or who had engaged in "past activity" which caused him to "represent a danger" could be sentenced by a court under the 1926 Code, as originally enacted. ("Measures of social defense of a judicial-correctional nature" was the 1926 Code's euphemism for criminal sanctions imposed by a court; the term "punishment" was not used at all.)

It is consistent with Article 7 of the 1926 Criminal Code, and characteristic of the spirit of that Code, that under Article 58-11 "active deeds or active struggle against the worker class or against the revolutionary movement carried on by a responsible or secret official (undercover agent) under the tsarist system or under counterrevolutionary governments during the Civil War" were made punishable by death by shooting, or, if there were mitigating circumstances, by deprivation of freedom for five to ten years. Moreover, it was also provided that, at the discretion of the court, the statute of limitations could be suspended in such cases.[1]

Also the 1926 Code contained no provision similar to Article 6 of the 1960 Criminal Code denying retroactive effect to a law establishing the punishability of an act or increasing the punishment for it.

Moreover, under the 1926 Code, a person who committed a socially dangerous act not specifically provided for in the Code was subject to criminal responsibility under the doctrine of analogy. Article 16 of the 1926 Criminal Code stated:

> If any socially dangerous act is not directly provided for by the present Code, the basis and limits of responsibility for it shall be determined by application of those articles of the Code which provide for crimes most similar to it in nature.

This article reflected the concept of the 1926 Code that the terms "socially dangerous act" and "crime" are synonymous. Indeed, the first reference to socially dangerous acts, in Article 1 of the Code, is followed by the word "crimes" in parentheses, and thereafter the two terms are used interchangeably.[2] Thus *any* socially dangerous act was a crime; and a socially dangerous act was defined as "any act or omission that is directed against the Soviet system *or* that violates the legal order established by the worker-peasant power during the period of transition to the communist system."[3]

Coupled with the breadth of application of the 1926 Criminal Code was its emphasis upon protection of the political order established by the Bolshevik Revolution. This, in turn, led to a very sharp division between political and nonpolitical crimes. Article 46 of the 1926 Code provided:

> The crimes dealt with in this code are classified as follows:
> a. Those directed against the foundations of the Soviet system established in the USSR by the power of the workers and peasants, and therefore considered to be the most dangerous;
> b. All other crimes.

The first category was reflected primarily in Article 58 of the Code, entitled "Counterrevolutionary Crimes," but it also found reflection in other parts of the Code as well. Punishments for all kinds of crimes directed against the foundations of the Soviet system were, in general, much heavier than punishments for other

1. 1926 RSFSR Criminal Code, Article 14, note 2.
2. Cf. 1926 RSFSR Criminal Code, Articles 2, 3, 4, 6 and 7.
3. *Id.*, Article 6 (emphasis added).

crimes. The death penalty was applicable only to crimes against the state. Moreover, it was an aggravating circumstance of any crime, resulting in a heavier sentence, that it was committed "with the object of restoring bourgeois rule" or that it "might have harmed the interests of the state or of the working people, even though the crime was not specifically directed against the interests of either" (Article 47(a)). Also it was a mitigating circumstance of any crime that it was committed "in order to defend against infringement the Soviet power [or] the revolutionary legal order" (Article 48(a)). Finally, it is characteristic of the 1926 Code that it included as one of the applicable punishments "Declaring the convicted person to be an enemy of the working class" (Article 20(a)).

Counterrevolutionary crimes themselves were defined in the broadest terms. Under Article 58-1 an act was said to be counterrevolutionary if it was "directed to the overthrow, subversion, or weakening of the power of the worker-peasant Soviets," *or* if it was "directed toward rendering aid to that part of the international bourgeoisie which does not recognize the equality of rights of the Communist system and seeks to overthrow it . . ." *or,* even if it was not specifically directed toward the above-mentioned goals, if it constituted a "conscious attack against the basic achievements of the proletarian revolution." Moreover, participation in any organization carrying on activity of the kind indicated in Article 58-1 was made a counterrevolutionary crime punishable by death or, under mitigating circumstances, by deprivation of freedom with strict isolation for five to ten years with confiscation of property. Even if the participant was unaware of the ultimate purpose of the organization, he was punishable by deprivation of freedom for three to ten years with confiscation of property (Articles 58-2, 58-4, 58-5, 58-6). The Code also established the concept of "economic counterrevolution," consisting of an "action against the normal activity of state agencies and enterprises or against the adequate utilization of them," committed for counterrevolutionary purposes (Article 58-7).

Other counterrevolutionary crimes listed in the 1926 Code, as originally enacted, included the transfer, or collection for purpose of transfer, to any person, of economic information not subject to publication, whether or not it constituted a specially protected state secret (Article 58-10); "any kind of assistance" in the most serious counterrevolutionary crimes, even when not connected directly with the given crime and even when the person giving assistance was not aware of the counterrevolutionary purpose of the crime, was made punishable by deprivation of freedom from one to ten years (Article 58-12); "propaganda and agitation" was made punishable as a counterrevolutionary crime if it called for a "breakdown of Soviet power by force or treachery or by active or passive opposition to the worker-peasant government" (Article 58-13) or if it was carried on "for the purpose of rendering aid to the international bourgeoisie" (Article 58-17); it was also a counterrevolutionary crime to "invent and circulate for counterrevolutionary purposes false rumors or unverified information which could . . . discredit the [state] power" (Article 58-18).

Three months after the adoption of the 1926 Criminal Code a new all-union law on counterrevolutionary crimes was enacted, which was incorporated into the RSFSR Code on June 6, 1927, as a new Article 58. The new law rearranged, and in some cases reworded, the old Article 58. In addition, it appended to Article 58-1 the provision that "By virtue of the international solidarity of the interests of the working people, the same actions [listed in the first paragraph of Article 58-1] shall be deemed counterrevolutionary if they are directed against any other working people's state even though it does not belong to the USSR." Also, under the 1927 revision it was made a separate counterrevolutionary crime to "render aid to social groups and organizations that are under the influence of that part of the international bourgeoisie that does not recognize the equality of rights of the Communist system" (Article 58-4). In addition, the maximum penalty for failure to report a counterrevolutionary crime was increased from deprivation of freedom up to one year to deprivation of freedom from one to ten years (Article 58-12). The various older provisions on counterrevolutionary propaganda and agitation were unified in a single article, which was even more vague and sweeping than those it replaced, being applicable to statements containing a call not only to subvert or overthrow the Soviet power but also, alternatively, to "weaken" it, and covering not only the making of such statements but also, alternatively, the possession of literature containing them (Article 58-10). The earlier provision on "economic counterrevolution" was amended, and the term itself was eliminated (Article 58-7). The crime of "terrorist acts" against representatives of Soviet power or against persons active in revolutionary worker-peasant organizations was carried over into the 1927 law (Article 58-8).

In addition to counterrevolutionary crimes, the 1926 Criminal Code contained, in Article 59, as amended in 1927, provisions relating to a large number and variety of "Crimes Against the Administrative Order that are Especially Dangerous to the USSR." These were also classified as Crimes Against the State, and included mass disorders, attacks by armed bands, theft of firearms from the army, damaging of railways, violation of international flight regulations, evasion of military service, counterfeiting, forgery of commercial paper, smuggling, violation of the Statute on the Foreign Trade Monopoly, violation of foreign-exchange regulations, and others. These crimes did not require counterrevolutionary intent or direct intent to overthrow the Soviet power. Many of them, nevertheless, were made punishable by death, if committed under especially aggravating circumstances.[4]

If one adds to the multisectioned Articles 58 and 59 the following Chapter II, entitled "Other Crimes Against the Administrative Order," containing Articles 60–108, and Chapter III, entitled "Official Crimes" (that is, crimes by officials), containing Articles 109–127, then one may say that more than half the Special Part of the 1926 Criminal Code dealt directly with the political and administrative aspects of Soviet life. To this might be added Chapter IX, on "Military Crimes," and Chapter V, on "Violations of Regulations on the Separation of Church and State," leaving less than one third of the code to what would correspond in other systems to "private crimes" (Chapter IV on "Economic Crimes," Chapter VI on "Crimes Against the Life, Health, Freedom, and Dignity of the Person," Chapter VII on "Crimes Against Property," Chapter VIII on "Violations

4. *Id.*, Articles 59-2 paragraph 1, 59-4, 59-6, 59-8 paragraph 2, 59-9, 59-10.

of the Rules of Public Health, Security, and Order," and Chapter X on "Crimes Constituting Survivals of Kinship Life").

In addition to the breadth of application of the 1926 Criminal Code and its strong orientation toward protection of the Soviet system against political and public crimes, mention must be made of certain other features of the Code, which commended themselves to many liberals of the 1920's as manifesting a new "socialist" attitude toward criminal law. These features were the leniency of punishment for nonpolitical crimes, the emphasis upon correction of offenders, and the large amount of discretion given to the courts both in determining whether to convict and in determining the measure of punishment – a discretion to be exercised in the light of the social danger of the actor and of the act. These features, like the breadth of application and the political orientation of the Code, reflected a Leninist conception of the educational function of law in a socialist society, which was combined, in the Criminal Code, with ideas drawn from the Italian sociological or positivist school of criminology represented especially by Enrico Ferri.[5]

The Italian sociological school considered delinquency to be primarily the product of social and physical circumstances, rather than of the moral guilt of the actor. The actor's freedom of will was denied, or at least minimized, and at the same time the moral values of society were considered to be relative rather than absolute. Ferri's definition of crime was in terms of acts that "disturb the conditions of existence and shock the average morality of a given people at a given moment." He viewed punishment as "protective measures" taken by society against such acts.[6]

To this philosophy which, as we have seen, is strongly reflected in the terminology, at least, of the 1926 RSFSR Criminal Code, Leninist thought added a faith in the power of the socially conscious members of a socialist society (and especially the Communist Party leadership) to influence, guide, train, and mold the character of others – through law, as well as through other means.[7] Thus a high degree of impatience with "enemies of the working people" whose crimes were "directed against the foundations of the Soviet system" could be combined with a high degree of patience toward those who did not oppose the Soviet system and whose acts, though criminal, did not threaten its foundations.

Many provisions of the 1926 Criminal Code reflected this patience. Article 6 not only included the language quoted earlier, defining a socially dangerous act as one which either is directed against the Soviet system *or* violates the legal order, but also contained the following note:

> An act shall not be considered a crime if, although formally containing the indicia of some article of the Special Part of the present Code, it nevertheless,

5. See Enrico Ferri, *Criminal Sociology* (New York, 1896). The Soviet jurists who drafted the Criminal Code did not publicly admit their indebtedness to Ferri, but privately they acknowledged that his work greatly influenced them.

6. *Id.*, pp. 145ff.

7. See N. A. Beliaev and V. S. Smirnov, "V. I. Lenin ob ubezhdenii i prinuzhdenii v sotsialisticheskom obshchestve," in G. I. Petrov, ed., *V. I. Lenin o gosudarstve i prave* (Leningrad, 1961), p. 49.

by virtue of its clear insignificance and the absence of harmful consequences, is deprived of a socially dangerous character.

Moreover, Article 8 provided:

> If a concrete act which constituted, when it was committed, a crime according to Article 6 of the present Code has lost, at the time of investigation or consideration of it in court, its socially dangerous character as a consequence of a change in the criminal law or solely by virtue of the fact that the social-political situation has changed, or if the person who committed it cannot, in the opinion of the court, at that time be deemed socially dangerous, then such act shall not entail the application of a measure of social defense to the person who committed it.

In accordance with the same philosophy, the purposes of "measures of social defense" were declared by Article 9 of the 1926 Code to be threefold:

> a. The prevention of new crimes by persons who have committed them,
> b. Influencing other unstable members of society, and
> c. Adjustment of those who have committed crimes to the conditions of community life of the working people's state.

To this was added:

> Measures of social defense may not be applied for the purpose of causing physical harm or suffering or lowering human dignity and shall not have as their object retribution [*vozmezdie*] or chastisement [*kara*].

Thus the elements of moral guilt and moral condemnation were omitted both from the terminology of the criminal law and from the purposes stated to underlie criminal law.

The removal of moral fault did not, however, signify a decreased concern with the personal responsibility of the offender, since this bears closely on his danger to society. Indeed, the 1926 Criminal Code excluded absolute criminal liability, providing in Article 10 that "measures of social defense of a judicial-correctional character" may be applied to persons who have committed socially dangerous acts only when such acts were committed by them intentionally or negligently. In addition, persons who committed crimes in a condition of chronic mental illness or temporary mental derangement or other pathological condition were not subject to criminal responsibility, provided they were unable to realize the significance of their actions or to control them (Article 11).

Further, the 1926 Criminal Code continued the prerevolutionary Russian tradition of providing in the code a list of aggravating and mitigating circumstances to be taken into consideration in selecting the particular punishment ("measure of social defense") (Articles 47 and 48). A crime committed from "mercenary or other base motives," for example, was more severely punishable than a crime committed without such motives. The 1926 Code further provided that in exceptional circumstances the court could impose a measure of social defense less severe than the minimum prescribed in the relevant article of the Special Part (Article 51). The court could also give a "conditional" (that is, suspended) sentence (Article 53), although, strangely enough, there was no provision in the code for parole.

The Special Part of the 1926 Code, as has already been indicated, provided far more lenient penalties for nonpolitical crimes than for political. (By "political crimes," in this context, is meant crimes against the state and serious crimes against the administrative order.) The death penalty was reserved for the most serious political crimes and for certain military crimes. Prisons were abolished and all sentences of deprivation of freedom were to be served in "correctional labor colonies" (with or without strict isolation), with a maximum term of ten years. Thus the maximum penalty for intentional homicide (other than intentional homicide committed by military personnel under especially aggravating circumstances) was ten years' deprivation of freedom (Article 136); intentional homicide committed without aggravating circumstances was punishable by deprivation of freedom for a term not exceeding eight years (Article 137); and intentional homicide committed in a state of strong mental agitation suddenly provoked as a result of force or gross insult on the part of the victim was punishable by deprivation of freedom up to five years or "compulsory tasks" up to one year (Article 138). (The term "compulsory tasks" was changed to "correctional labor tasks" in 1933, and that in turn to "correctional tasks" in the 1958 Fundamental Principles and the 1960 Criminal Code. Prior to 1958 it usually signified, in the case of wage earners, a deduction from monthly wages up to 25 percent up to one year. The maximum is now 20 percent.)

Similarly, infliction of bodily injury upon another, infliction of blows, kidnapping, rape, insult, defamation, theft, robbery, embezzlement, fraud, and similar crimes against the person or against personal (that is, nonsocialist) property, were subject, under the 1926 Code as originally enacted, to extremely mild penalties, judged in comparison with the penalties attached to crimes against the state under Soviet law, or judged in comparison with the penalties attached to crimes against the person or private property in many Western countries. Theft of personal property committed for the first time was punishable by deprivation of freedom up to three months, and if repeated, up to six months (Article 162). Even large-scale theft of state property was only punishable by deprivation of freedom up to five years (Article 162).

In connection with the socialist features of the original 1926 Criminal Code mention must also be made of the broad scope of the concepts of "official crimes" and (to a lesser extent) "economic crimes." The concept of an "official," under Articles 109-111 of the 1926 Code, covered almost all employees of state, cooperative, and social organizations, and their responsibility was defined in the widest possible language to include abuse, excess, and neglect of their duties, neglect being punishable even though no material loss was caused thereby. Penalties for embezzling or losing social property and for certain forms of theft of state or social property, as well as economic mismanagement generally, were also imposed upon officials (Articles 116, 129, 128), and violation of labor laws by employers received extensive coverage (Articles 133-135).

Finally, the 1926 Criminal Code, following the 1922 Code, established the crime of "hooliganism," which was defined as "mischievous actions, accompanied by a clear disrespect toward society" (Article 74) and was included among "Especially Dangerous Crimes Against the Administrative Order" (Chapter II of the Code). The penalty for a first offense was deprivation of freedom up to three months; if the actions took place in a fight or disorder or were repeated, or were persistent despite the warning of agencies of public order, or were "exceptionally cynical or insolent," they were punishable by deprivation of freedom up to two years. The term "hooliganism," derived from the name of a notorious Irish family that lived in London in the nineteenth century, had become popular among Russian legal scholars before the revolution as a characterization of lawless, disorderly, and purposeless misconduct. It was only introduced into legislation, however, by the 1922 Criminal Code, whose definition of the crime was carried over into the 1926 Code. It was, and continues to be, the most frequently committed crime of all those listed in the Code, according to Soviet specialists in criminal law.[7a]

The 1926 Criminal Code was a product of the psychology and politics of the period of the New Economic Policy. It was a halfway house between the prerevolutionary Russian legal tradition, whose revival had become necessary owing to the bankruptcy of War Communism, and the period of Planned Economy which was inaugurated in 1928. The introduction of the First Five-Year Plan at the end of 1928 meant not only the end of the NEP and the beginning of rapid forced industrialization, but also the violent collectivization of agriculture. At the same time, Stalin, from 1928 on, began to consolidate his personal rule and to impose a system of terror upon the Soviet people. These developments had important repercussions upon criminal law, both in theory and in practice.

Developments in the Period from 1929 to 1936. The tendency of Soviet legal developments during the period from 1929 to 1936 was to carry much further both the repressive features of the 1926 Criminal Code and its emphasis upon the flexibility of the criminal law.

The increased emphasis upon repression manifested itself especially in two pieces of all-union legislation, the Law on Protection of Property of State Enterprises, Collective Farms and Cooperatives and on the Strengthening of Social (Socialist) Ownership, of August 7, 1932,[8] and an amendment of June 8, 1934, to the Law on Crimes Against the State.[9]

By the law of August 7, 1932, "social ownership" (*obshchestvennaia sobstvennost'*), or "socialist ownership" (*sotsialisticheskaia sobstvennost'*), including state, collective farm and cooperative ownership, was declared to be "sacred and inviolable," and persons "infringing" it were "to be considered as enemies of the people." Specifically, the law imposed the death penalty on persons guilty of

7a. Cf. Walter D. Connor, *Deviance in Soviet Society: Crime, Delinquency, and Alcoholism* (N.Y. and London, 1972), p. 150. Regrettably, Professor Connor's book did not appear in time to be used in writing the present introduction.

8. *SZ* (1932), no. 62, item 360.

9. *SZ* (1934), no. 33, item 255.

stealing goods being transported by rail or water as well as persons guilty of stealing collective farm or cooperative property, unless the act was committed under mitigating circumstances, in which case the minimum penalty was deprivation of freedom for ten years with confiscation of their entire property. Stealing of social property was stated to be "equivalent to a crime against the state." Although the 1932 law, which was introduced primarily to overcome resistance to the collectivization of agriculture, did not specifically make punishable the stealing of state property as such (as contrasted with "collective farm" and "cooperative" property) other than goods in transport, it was in fact applied to theft of all kinds of state property, apparently on the basis simply of the title of the law and its preamble. Indeed, the law was extensively interpreted to include destruction of state property and even failure to protect state property.[10] It is important to note that the law of August 7, 1932, introduced for the first time into Soviet criminal law the theoretical distinction between the stealing of socialist property and the theft of the property of individual citizens; and that the law was placed in the official text of the RSFSR Criminal Code as an annotation to Article 58 on counterrevolutionary crimes.

It was characteristic of the law of August 7, 1932, that it also imposed deprivation of freedom from five to ten years "with confinement in a concentration camp" upon "kulak and other antisocial elements" who used force or threats against collective farms or collective farmers.[11] Confinement in a "concentration camp" for five to ten years was also imposed by another 1932 law which created the new crime of "speculation," defined as "the buying up and resale of products of agriculture and mass consumption, by private persons for a profit" (USSR law of August 22, 1932, introduced into the RSFSR Criminal Code as Article 107).

The law of June 8, 1934, which was incorporated into Article 58 of the RSFSR Criminal Code on July 20, 1934, introduced for the first time into Soviet law the traditional prerevolutionary Russian term "betrayal of the Motherland" (*izmena rodine*), generally translated as "treason." Treason was defined as including espionage committed by a Soviet citizen, the giving out of military or state secrets, going over to the enemy, and fleeing the country, and was made punishable by death with confiscation of property, or, if committed under mitigating circumstances, by deprivation of freedom for ten years with confiscation of property. The 1934 law also introduced the collective responsibility of adult members of the household of members of the armed forces who deserted: such persons were subject to "exile to remote regions of Siberia for five years," even

10. These interpretations were not expressly based on the doctrine of analogy but were apparently considered to be implicit in the law itself and in supplementary legislation. Cf. the law of January 30, 1933, *SZ*, no. 6, item 41, and the decree of the People's Commissariat of Justice, July 8, 1933, quoted in the official text of the 1934 edition of the 1926 RSFSR Criminal Code, p. 108.

11. The term "concentration camp" first appeared in Soviet legislation in the decree of the RSFSR Council of People's Commissars of September 5, 1918, on the Red Terror. See *SU* (1918), no. 65, item 710. The second use of it was in the law of August 7, 1932. It appeared for the third time in the law of August 22, 1932, on the Struggle Against Speculation. See *SZ* (1932), no. 65, item 375. The author has not found the term in later Soviet legislation. It is not clear in what respects, if any, "concentration camps" were distinguished from "correctional labor camps," which were introduced in Soviet legislation by USSR laws of 1929 and 1930 and an RSFSR law of 1930. See *infra*, note 14.

though they knew nothing of the desertion and did not assist it in any way. In addition, very severe penalties were introduced for counterrevolutionary crimes committed by persons in military service. It is of some interest that the 1934 law reintroduced the term "punishment" (*nakazanie*) instead of "measures of social defense of a judicial-correctional character," and that in 1936 the term "prison" (*tiurma*) was restored and confinement in prison was authorized for the most serious crimes.[12]

Other harsh criminal laws of this period include:

(1) a law of 1929 declaring that officials who defect – or who had defected, for the law was expressly made applicable retroactively – are "outside the law" and punishable by death;[13]

(2) a law of 1929 establishing "correctional labor camps in remote regions of the USSR" and "general places of confinement" as the two forms of deprivation of freedom and providing that persons sentenced for three years or more should serve in the correctional labor camps;[14]

(3) a law of 1930 revising the minimum term of deprivation of freedom from one day, as it was formerly, to one year;[15]

(4) the 1932 law on speculation mentioned above;

(5) a law of 1934 imposing severe penalties (five to ten years' deprivation of freedom) upon economic officials for negligent release of goods of poor quality from industrial enterprises;[16]

(6) a law of 1934 imposing severe penalties (up to ten years' deprivation of freedom) for deception of purchasers by false weights and measures;[17]

(7) a law of 1935 increasing the maximum punishment for hooliganism to five years, coupled with judicial extension of hooliganism under the doctrine of analogy;[18]

(8) a law of 1935 lowering the age of criminal responsibility to 12 for a series of crimes against the person and against property and making all measures of punishment applicable to minors.[19] However, of the crimes listed, the only one for which the death penalty might have been applicable was theft of social property under the law of August 7, 1932, which excluded the death penalty where there were mitigating circumstances, and minority was included in the Criminal Code as a mitigating circumstance.

Together with the sharp increase in the severity of criminal sanctions, especially

12. *SZ* (1936), no. 44, item 370.

13. *SZ* (1929), no 76, item 732.

14. *SZ* (1929), no. 72, item 686; cf. *SZ* (1930), no. 22, item 248; *SU* (1930), no. 26, item 344. Prior to the 1929 law all sentences of deprivation of freedom were served in "correctional labor colonies," with or without strict isolation. Under the 1929 and 1930 laws, correctional labor colonies remained as "general places of confinement" for persons sentenced to deprivation of freedom for less than three years.

15. *SU* (1930), no. 26, item 344, amending Article 28 of the RSFSR Criminal Code.

16. *SU* (1934), no. 9, item 51;

17. *SU* (1934), no. 35, item 216.

18. *SU* (1935), no. 14, item 146; 1931 and 1932 RSFSR Supreme Court decrees extending hooliganism by analogy are quoted in the official 1934 text of the Criminal Code at p. 125.

19. *SZ* (1935), no. 19, item 155.

for theft of social property and counterrevolutionary crimes, Soviet criminal law in the early 1930's experienced a sharp decline in the stability of its provisions. Indeed, the very idea that law should have stability was itself attacked. Under the leadership of E. B. Pashukanis, Soviet legal theory at that time proclaimed that in a period of rapid transition to socialism, the law should have maximum mobility and should be merged with policy preparatory to its complete "dying out."[20] The People's Commissar of Justice, N. V. Krylenko, proposed that the Special Part of the Criminal Code be eliminated altogether.[21] New criminal codes were drafted (but not enacted) in those years which reflected the theories of Pashukanis and Krylenko; the 1926 Criminal Code was considered to be obsolete and infected with the "bourgeois" ideas of the period of the NEP.

The direct attack upon the 1926 Criminal Code by leading Soviet jurists was supplemented by a more insidious indirect attack by the political leadership. The 1930's were years of mass repression systematically carried out by agencies of state security. The collectivization of agriculture in the early 1930's resulted in large-scale deportations and executions of recalcitrant peasants, often by administrative decree. From 1934 on, the Special Board (*Osoboe soveshchanie*, or OSSO) of the People's Commissariat of Internal Affairs (NKVD), operating outside both the Criminal Code and the Code of Criminal Procedure, sentenced hundreds of thousands, at least, and probably millions, to labor camps in a secret, administrative procedure. The three-man Special Board – colloquially called "the troika" – was one of the chief instruments of the mass purges that wracked Soviet society, and especially the Communist Party and the intelligentsia, from 1934 to 1938, and of the individual purges thereafter.[22]

Developments in the Period from 1936 to 1953. A crucial turning point, however, occurred in 1936, when socialism was officially declared to have been achieved. Now the period from 1917 to 1936 was said to have been the "first stage of development of the Soviet state," and the second "socialist" stage was announced as an intermediate period between the first stage and the final "com-

20. Pashukanis had preached the dying out of law under socialism ever since the mid-1920's. In 1930 he recanted certain parts of his theory, in answer to various criticisms, but at the same time reaffirmed its main points and added a new emphasis on the immediate replacement of "law" by "policy" and on the need for "maximum elasticity" and "maximum mobility" of law during the era of the Five-Year Plans. From 1930 to 1936 Pashukanis headed the Institute of Socialist Construction and Law of the USSR Academy of Sciences and was recognized as the leading figure of Soviet legal thought. In 1936 and early 1937 Pashukanis renounced most of his principal theories, apparently in an unsuccessful effort to save his life. See H. J. Berman, *Justice in the USSR*, rev. ed. (Cambridge, Mass., 1963), pp. 26–29, 41–43, 53ff.

21. See N. V. Krylenko, *Revoliutsionnoe pravo* (Moscow, 1933). Krylenko, like Pashukanis, built in the 1930's on ideas he had developed in the 1920's. Krylenko was head of the People's Commissariat of Justice of the RSFSR in the early 1930's and was named People's Commissar of Justice of the USSR in 1936. In 1938 he was denounced as a traitor and counterrevolutionary and he disappeared. In the 1960's both Pashikanis and Krylenko were "rehabilitated," in the sense that the charges of treason for which they had been condemned were repudiated and some of their works have been praised, although their more radical ideas mentioned in the text continue to be rejected.

22. We shall return to a discussion of the Special Board in the context of Soviet criminal procedure. See *infra*, p. 48 ff.

munist" stage. Despite the continuation of the terror against those suspected of opposition to Stalin, and an increase in criminal penalties for certain counterrevolutionary crimes, a new doctrine of "socialist legality" was proclaimed for the nonpolitical sphere. Stalin, in his 1936 Report on the Draft Constitution, stated, "We need stability of laws now more than ever," and the phrase "stability of laws" became a slogan for restoring the prestige of the NEP codes, on the one hand, and for eliminating some of the more radical conceptions upon which they were based, on the other. In one field of law after another, conservative and even conventional doctrines and practices were restored under the rubric of "socialism." The theory of the "dying out" of law under socialism was denounced. A. Ia. Vyshinsky, who replaced Pashukanis as the dean of Soviet jurisprudence, proclaimed that law in a socialist society must be, to some extent at least, independent of both politics and economics; that socialist law represents "the will of the whole people"; and that while the Soviet state must continue to pursue a ruthless repression of "class enemies," strict legality must be maintained in those spheres of social and economic life in which the political factor was itself stabilized. The liquidation of Pashukanis and Krylenko as counterrevolutionaries perfectly symbolized the Stalinist dualism of terror and law.

The dualism had profound effects upon criminal law. As has already been indicated, the new Stalin Constitution, adopted in December 1936, called for the enactment of new all-union codes of criminal law and criminal procedure. Pending their adoption, the older codes were declared to remain in force – as against the earlier Krylenko drafts, which were now denounced for their excessive flexibility. At the same time, the language of the older codes was transformed, and many of their provisions were reinterpreted. Also, although the new all-union codes were not forthcoming, the 1938 USSR Law on Court Organization reflected the newer jurisprudence and it, together with the 1936 Constitution, was used by the courts as authority for repudiating some, though by no means all, of the more obnoxious features of the NEP codes.

Among the most important changes introduced into Soviet substantive criminal law in the period from 1936 to Stalin's death in 1953 were the following:

(1) The terminology of socially dangerous acts and measures of social defense, though it remained in the Criminal Code, was replaced in statutes, court decisions and legal literature by the terminology of crimes and punishments.[23]

(2) The element of moral guilt was emphasized as having critical importance in determining whether the accused in a criminal case should be convicted and what sentence should be applied to him (within the limits set by law). Whereas the 1926 Criminal Code, as we have seen, spoke only of social danger of the person

23. Cf. law of August 8, 1936, On Amendment of the Fundamental Principles of Criminal Legislation of the USSR and the Union Republics, *SZ* (1936), no. 44, item 370, which uses the term "crimes" instead of "socially dangerous acts"; law of October 2, 1937, *SZ* (1937), no. 66, item 297, which uses the term "criminal punishment" instead of "measure of social defense"; Law on Court Organization, August 16, 1938, *Vedomosti SSSR* (1938), no. 11, p. 1, in which the terms "crime" and "criminal punishment" are used; Decree of the Plenum of the Supreme Court of the USSR, June 26, 1942, in *Sbornik deistvuiushchikh postanovlenii plenuma i direktivnykh pisem Verkhovnogo suda SSSR 1924–1944 gg.* (Moscow, 1946), p. 108; I. T. Goliakov, ed., *Ugolovnoe pravo, osobennaia chast'* (Moscow, 1943).

and of the act, the post-1936 Soviet jurisprudence spoke also of the person's freedom of will and of the moral quality of his act.[24]

(3) Whereas the purposes of punishment, as defined by the 1926 Code, excluded retribution and chastisement, the post-1936 jurisprudence declared that one of the purposes of punishment, or at least one of the essential features of punishment, was the moral condemnation of the act and the infliction of suffering upon the guilty person. The emphasis upon the punitive aspect of criminal sanctions found concrete expression in the extension of the maximum duration of deprivation of freedom from ten years, as it was previously, to twenty-five years.[25]

(4) The post-1936 Soviet jurisprudence interpreted many of the provisions of the 1926 Code that defined particular crimes in terms of intentional acts as requiring not merely a knowledge that the given results would occur ("indirect intent") but also a specific desire to bring about those results ("direct intent"). In December 1938 the Plenum of the Supreme Court of the USSR overruled a 1928 Supreme Court ruling which had permitted conviction for certain counterrevolutionary crimes even though the accused had no desire to undermine the Soviet power.[26] This ruling, coming after the reaction against the excesses of the mass purges of 1936–1938, marked a return to a narrower reading of the code provisions on counterrevolutionary crimes. In this connection it should be mentioned that in 1943 and 1947 laws were passed which made the divulging of state secrets punishable as a separate offense; previously this had been punished as treason or espionage even in the absence of counterrevolutionary intent. Similarly with respect to economic crimes and crimes by Soviet officials, the Soviet courts after 1936 emphasized the requirements of specific intent. They held, for example, that the sale of goods by a person at a price higher than that which he paid for them does not constitute the crime of speculation unless the goods were originally purchased for the purpose of resale at a profit;[27] that to be guilty of the crime of theft of state property the accused must be shown to have known that the property was state property and to have intended to steal it;[28] and that the crime of abuse of official position should be more narrowly construed.[29]

(5) In contrast to the 1926 Code, which had defined negligence by an "object-

24. Moral fault as a *conditio sine qua non* of criminal responsibility was emphasized especially in the textbook on criminal law issued under the auspices of the USSR Ministry of Justice in 1948. See V. D. Men'shagin, ed., *Ugolovnoe pravo, obshchaia chast'* (Moscow, 1948), p. 305ff.

25. *SZ* (1937), no. 66, item 297. Cf. Article 18 of the 1924 Fundamental Principles of Criminal Legislation of the USSR and the Union Republics, *SZ* (1924), no. 24, item 205.

26. Decree of the Plenum of the USSR Supreme Court, December 31, 1938, *Sbornik deistvuiushchikh postanovlenii plenuma Verkhovnogo suda SSSR 1924–1957 gg* (Moscow, 1958), p. 5.

27. Cf. decrees of the Plenum of the Supreme Court of the USSR of December 31, 1938, and September 20, 1946, in *Sbornik deistvuiushchikh postanovlenii plenuma Verkhovnogo suda SSSR 1924–1957 gg.* (Moscow, 1958), p. 28; I. T. Goliakov, ed., *supra*, note 23, p. 351; A. A. Gertsenzon, ed., *Ugolovnoe pravo, chast' osobennaia* (Moscow, 1951), p. 307.

28. Cf. I. T. Goliakov, ed., *supra*, note 23, p. 91; A. A. Gertsenzon, ed., *supra*, note 27, p. 149.

29. Cf. *ibid.*, p. 329, and decree of the Plenum of the USSR Supreme Court of December 8, 1946, there cited.

ive" standard (what the accused *should* have foreseen, that is, what was reasonably foreseeable under the circumstances), Soviet courts and writers after 1936 defined negligence by a "subjective" standard (what the accused should *and could* have foreseen, that is, what it was reasonable *for him* to foresee, in the light of his own capacities, education, and the like.)[30]

(6) Article 7 of the 1926 Criminal Code, which provided that measures of social defense of a judicial-correctional nature could be applied to persons solely on the ground that they "represent a social danger because of their connection with a criminal environment or because of their past activity," was declared by the Supreme Court of the USSR in 1946 to have been repealed by the 1938 Law on Court Organization, on the ground that that law gave courts the power to apply punishment to various types of criminals (traitors, murderers, thieves, and the like) and said nothing about any judicial power to apply punishment to persons who had not committed crimes.[31] It is a measure both of the boldness of the Supreme Court in making this ruling and of its weakness that the same doctrine was never applied to negate the provision of Article 58-1c that made innocent relatives of a deserter from the armed forces liable to Siberian exile for five years.[32]

(7) The doctrine of analogy, embodied in Article 16 of the 1926 Criminal Code, came under strong attack at the hands of Soviet legal writers, and in the late 1930's the courts gave it a restrictive interpretation.[33] During the war, the doctrine of analogy was applied broadly, on the ground that war conditions prevented the enacting of necessary criminal legislation, but in the postwar period it was once more restricted. It was stressed that an act could not be punished by analogy unless it was proscribed by the General Part of the Criminal Code; that is, it must have been a socially dangerous act, committed intentionally or negligently. Further, it could not be punished by analogy if it was proscribed by a provision of the Special Part – that is, the doctrine of analogy could not be applied to increase (or decrease) the punishment for an act already made punishable by the code. Decisions of lower courts in which Article 16 was applied were scrutinized with great care by the Supreme Court of the USSR and there was a strong body of opinion, expressed in legal literature, that the doctrine of analogy should be repealed.[34]

(8) By an edict of May 26, 1947, the Presidium of the USSR Supreme Soviet

30. Cf. decree of the Plenum of the Supreme Court of the USSR of June 7, 1939, and ruling of the Judicial Division for Criminal Cases of the Supreme Court of the USSR of May 22, 1948, cited in V. M. Chkhikvadze, ed., *Sovetskoe ugolovnoe pravo, chast' obshchaia* (Moscow, 1952), pp. 238–239, and discussion pp. 235–237.

31. Decree of the Plenum of the Supreme Court of the USSR, July 12, 1946, *id.*, p. 55.

32. The statement in the text is not less valid by virtue of the fact that punishment of the relatives of deserters may well have been an "administrative," rather than a "criminal" punishment. Article 58-1c declared that relatives who conspired in the desertion "shall be punished" by certain measures, and that relatives who had no part in it "are subject to exile" up to five years. It may be that subjection of innocent relatives to exile was at the discretion of administrative, rather than judicial, authorities.

33. Cf. decrees of the Plenum of the Supreme Court of the USSR of 1937 and 1939 cited in V. M. Chkhikvadze, ed., *supra*, note 30, p. 121.

34. Cf. V. D. Men'shagin, *supra*, note 24, pp. 227–232.

abolished the death penalty for all crimes.[35] However, on January 12, 1950, the death penalty was restored but only for traitors, spies, subversives, and saboteurs.[36]

(9) By an edict of June 4, 1947, the law of August 7, 1932, which imposed the death penalty for stealing of social (socialist) property, was repealed and replaced by a new law, which imposed a penalty of seven to ten years' deprivation of freedom for the stealing, misappropriation, or embezzlement of state property, and a penalty of ten to twenty-five years for the same offenses if committed for a second time, or by an organized group, or in large amounts.[37] The penalties for the stealing of collective farm and cooperative property were slightly less severe. Previously, in 1940, a penalty of one year's imprisonment had been introduced for petty theft committed in enterprises or institutions.[38]

(10) Penalties for crimes against personal property and for rape were increased. On June 4, 1947, the minimum of three months' deprivation of freedom for theft of personal property was increased to five years,[39] and on January 4, 1949, the penalty for rape, which had been deprivation of freedom from one to five years, was increased to deprivation of freedom from ten to fifteen years.[40]

(11) Perhaps the most important new crime which was created in the post-1936 period was that of unauthorized quitting by a worker or employee, which by edict of June 26, 1940, was made punishable by two to four months' imprisonment.[41] This law, enacted expressly as a wartime measure, was retained until 1956. In 1951, however, the criminal sanctions of the law were apparently repealed and Comrades' Courts were given jurisdiction over violators.[42] Another harsh wartime law that remained in force in the postwar period was the edict of February 10, 1941, which made it a punishable offense, as a "disguised stealing of socialist property," for the director of a state economic enterprise to sell, exchange or release surplus equipment or materials, with punishment of two to five years' confinement in prison.[43] Among other important pieces of criminal legislation in this period was the law of June 27, 1936, making it a crime to undergo or perform an abortion except in certain cases (as when the mother had a serious disease which could be passed on to the child, or the mother's or the child's life would be endangered by permitting the birth);[44] and the edict of

35. *Vedomosti SSSR* (1947), no. 17, p. 1.
36. *Id.* (1950), no. 3, p. 1.
37. *Id.* (1947), no. 19, p. 1.
38. *Id.* (1940), no. 28, p. 2.
39. *Id.* (1947), no. 19, p. 1.
40. *Moskovskii bol'shevik*, January 4, 1949; the edict is published in the official text of the 1957 edition of the RSFSR Criminal Code at p. 127.
41. *Id.* (1940), no. 20. p. 1.
42. See H. J. Berman, "Soviet Law Reform – Dateline Moscow 1957," *Yale Law Journal*, 66:1202 n. 45 (1957). The 1951 Statute on Comrades' Courts was issued by Decree No. 2520 of the Council of Ministers of the USSR of July 14, 1951, published only in *Khronologicheskoe sobranie zakanov Litovskoį SSR, ukazov presidiuma verkhovnogo soveta i postanovlenii pravitel'stva Litovskoi SSR*, vol. III: *1951–1952* (Vilna, 1958), pp. 313–315 – a collection of Lithuanian laws.
43. *Vedomosti SSSR* (1941), no. 8, p. 1.
44. *SZ* (1936), no. 34, item 309.

August 10, 1940, increasing the penalty for less serious hooliganism from a maximum of three months' deprivation of freedom to imprisonment for one year, while at the same time limiting it to "hooligan acts committed in enterprises, institutions and public places."[45]

The Post-Stalin Reforms. Stalin's death in March 1953, as has already been indicated, released the movement for a more substantial law reform than that which had taken place in the last sixteen years of his reign. In criminal law this was immediately apparent, for in the first edict of the new government, a broad amnesty was declared for many classes of prisoners and it was promised that there would be a relaxation in the law relating to official and economic crimes.[46] The promised changes did not come immediately, however. Instead, the first major piece of criminal legislation undertaken by Stalin's successors was the extension of the death penalty, on April 30, 1954, to intentional homicide committed under aggravating circumstances[47] – a reform which was no doubt welcomed by many Soviet citizens who were aroused by brutal murders and by the reappearance of the murderers after serving for ten years or a portion thereof.

The way was prepared in September 1953 for a liberalization and rationalization of Soviet criminal law, and for enactment of the long-awaited new criminal code, by the abolition of the Special Board of the Ministry (former People's Commissariat) of Internal Affairs. This was a necessary step toward ending the Stalinist dualism of law and terror. It must be seen in the context of reforms of criminal procedure and the strengthening of the Procuracy and of the courts, all of which will be discussed in subsequent sections of this introduction.

In the field of substantive criminal law, the following steps were taken:

(1) On August 5, 1954, pregnant women were relieved of criminal responsibility for illegal abortions, and on November 23, 1955, the 1936 law prohibiting abortions was entirely repealed and they were authorized to be performed in hospitals and other medical institutions.[48]

(2) An edict of January 10, 1955, on petty stealing of state or social property imposed very light penalties for a first offense (correctional tasks for six months to one year or deprivation of freedom for three months), and deprivation of freedom for one to two years for a second offense.[49] (Under the 1947 law, mentioned above, the minimum penalty for stealing state or social property was seven years' deprivation of freedom, although under Article 51 of the 1926 Criminal Code the court could reduce the sentence in any case below the legally established minimum on the ground of exceptional circumstances.)

(3) On May 13, 1955, the 1941 law punishing the sale, exchange, or release of surplus equipment by directors of state economic enterprises was repealed.[50]

45. *Vedomosti SSSR* (1940), no. 28, p. 2.
46. Edict of March 27, 1953, *id.* (1953), no. 4, p. 1.
47. *Id.* (1954), no. 11, item 221.
48. *Id.* (1954), no. 15, item 334; (1955), no. 22, item 425.
49. RSFSR Criminal Code, 1957, ed., p. 109.
50. *Vedomosti SSSR* (1955), no. 8, item 193.

(4) On April 25, 1956, the law making it a crime for a worker or employee to quit without permission was repealed.[51]

(5) On December 20, 1956, "petty hooliganism" was made punishable by detention ("arrest") from three to fifteen days, whereas previously the minimum penalty was imprisonment for a year.[52]

(6) On April 28, 1956, the USSR Council of Ministers issued a new and milder list of information constituting state secrets.[53]

(7) In February and March 1957, substantial changes were made in the Statute on Military Crimes (discussed below).[54]

Changes Introduced by the Fundamental Principles of Criminal Legislation of the USSR and the Union Republics. With the enactment of the Fundamental Principles in December 1958, the following changes were introduced in Soviet substantive criminal law:

(1) By provisions identical with Articles 3, 7, and 6 of the 1960 RSFSR Criminal Code, discussed above, the scope of criminal law was limited to punishment for acts specifically proscribed by laws in force at the time of their commission, under the principle of *nullum crimen, nulla poena, sine lege.*[55] Thus the notorious doctrine of analogy was finally eliminated from Soviet criminal law (although strong traces of it reappeared in the Statute on Comrades' Courts, which is considered to be outside the criminal law).

(2) The emphasis on strict legality reflected in Articles 3, 6, and 7 was reinforced by new definitions of the purposes of criminal law and of criminal punishment. Article 1 of the 1926 Criminal Code stated: "The criminal legislation of the RSFSR has as its tasks the protection of the socialist state of workers and peasants and the legal order established therein from socially dangerous acts (crimes) . . ." In contrast, Article 1 of the 1958 Fundamental Principles of Criminal Legislation states: "The criminal legislation of the USSR and the union republics has as its tasks the protection of the Soviet social and state system, of socialist property, of the person and rights of citizens, and of the entire socialist legal order from criminal infringements." The word "entire" suggests that the social and state system is considered to be part of the legal order. Also the addition of "the person and rights of citizens" is important. Further, the correction and re-education of convicted persons in the spirit of "strict compliance with the laws" is listed as one of the tasks of punishment (Article 20). At the same time

51. *Vedomosti SSSR* (1956), no. 10, item 203.

52. See *Sovetskaia Rossiia*, December 20, 1956.

53. Compare the Decree on Responsibility for Disclosure of State Secrets and for Loss of Documents Containing State Secrets, Disclosure of Which Shall be Punished by Law, Izvestia, June 10, 1947 (translated in H. J. Berman and M. Kerner, *Documents on Soviet Military Law and Administration*, Cambridge, Mass., 1955) with the decree of the Council of Ministers of the USSR of April 28, 1956, printed in V. D. Men'shagin and B. A. Kurinov, *Nauchno-prakticheskii kommentarii k zakonu ob ugolovnoi otvetstvennosti za gosudarstvennye prestupleniia*, 2nd. rev. ed. (Moscow, 1961), pp. 27-28.

54. See *Vedomosti SSSR* (1957), no. 5, item 100; no. 8, item 221.

55. The corresponding articles of the USSR Fundamental Principles of Criminal Legislation and the RSFSR Criminal Code are listed *infra*, Appendix I.

it is declared that punishment "constitutes" a chastisement (*kara*) for a committed crime, although such chastisement is not listed as a "purpose" of punishment. The older language of "measures of social defense" is entirely abandoned. Also the language of "the worker-peasant state" and of "counterrevolutionary" crimes and "restoration of the bourgeois state" is eliminated.

(3) The age of criminal responsibility was raised from 12 to 14 for the most serious crimes and from 12 to 16 for lesser crimes (Article 10).

(4) Complicity in a crime, which formerly could be committed by negligence as well as intentionally, was limited to intentional joint participation in the commission of the (specific) criminal act (Article 17).

(5) Concealment of a criminal or a crime when not promised in advance of the crime, which previously had been considered a form of complicity, was made punishable only in cases specially provided for by law (Article 18).

(6) The following types of punishment were eliminated: (a) deprivation of political and civil rights, (b) banishment from the USSR, (c) being declared an enemy of the working people or an enemy of the people (cf. Article 21).

(7) The death penalty was limited (as it had been under the 1926 Code, but not after 1935) to persons 18 years of age or older; in addition it was excluded in the case of a crime committed by a woman who was pregnant at the time of the commission of the crime and execution of the death sentence was forbidden in the case of a woman pregnant at the time execution is scheduled (Article 22). (As under Article 22 of the 1926 Code, the death sentence may also not be imposed upon a woman who is pregnant at the time of sentencing.) Under Article 11 a mentally ill person may not be executed or otherwise punished until he recovers.

(8) Deprivation of freedom was reduced from a maximum of twenty-five years to a maximum of fifteen years and, for minors under 18, to a maximum of ten years.

(9) Juveniles sentenced to deprivation of freedom were required to be sent to special labor colonies for juveniles (Article 23).

(10) Exile and banishment were limited to five years (Article 24).

(11) Persons under 18 at the time of the commission of a crime and pregnant women and women with dependent children under 8 years of age could not be exiled or banished (Article 24).

(12) The concept of the "especially dangerous recidivist," upon whom heavier penal sanctions may be imposed, was introduced (Article 23).

(13) Confiscation of property, as a punishment for crime, was limited in its application to cases of crimes against the state and certain grave crimes committed with mercenary motives (Article 30).

(14) In the list of circumstances that mitigate criminal responsibility (Article 33), reference to defense against infringements of Soviet power or the revolutionary legal order was replaced by reference to defense against a socially dangerous infringement. Also new mitigating circumstances were added: prevention by the guilty person of harmful consequences of the crime, voluntary compensation for damage or elimination of harm caused, and sincere admission of guilt or voluntary surrender to the authorities. However, commission of a crime under the

influence of strong mental agitation, which had formerly been a mitigating circumstance, was limited to cases in which agitation is provoked by unlawful actions of the victim; and commission of a crime for the first time, which had formerly been a mitigating circumstance, was limited to cases in which the first offense resulted from a fortuitous concurrence of circumstances and does not present a great social danger. There are, in addition, other minor differences between the list of mitigating circumstances in the 1958 Fundamental Principles and that of the previous Soviet criminal law.

(15) In the list of circumstances that aggravate criminal responsibility (Article 34), reference to the commission of a crime for the purpose of restoring the bourgeois power was omitted from the 1958 Fundamental Principles. Added to the list of aggravating circumstances were the causing of grave consequences by the crime; commission of the crime against a young person, a person advanced in years, or a helpless person; incitement of a minor to commit crimes or involvement of a minor in the commission of a crime; commission of the crime by exploiting a condition of public disaster, by means dangerous to the community, or in connection with the utilization of a source of heightened danger by a person in a state of intoxication; denouncing a person known to be innocent; and commission of a new crime by a person taken on surety during the term of surety or within a year after its expiration. (Surety – in Russian, *poruka* – is a form of probation, introduced in the late 1950's, in which an accused or convicted person is placed in the care of a social organization or of a collective of fellow-workers or neighbors or of a specific individual or individuals, for re-education and correction.)

(16) More liberal provisions were introduced for the parole of convicted persons who by their exemplary behavior and honest attitude toward labor prove that they have reformed (Article 44).[56]

(17) More liberal rules were introduced for expunging of the criminal record, because of subsequent good behavior, of a person sentenced to deprivation of freedom for more than three years (Article 47).

Changes Introduced by the Statute on Crimes Against the State. The USSR Statute on Crimes Against the State, enacted in December 1958 at the same session of the USSR Supreme Soviet at which the Fundamental Principles of Criminal Legislation were enacted, and incorporated into the Special Part of the 1960 RSFSR Criminal Code as Chapter One, introduced several changes in the prior law:

(1) The phrase "counterrevolutionary crimes" was eliminated, and crimes formerly denominated as counterrevolutionary were classified either as "Especially Dangerous Crimes Against the State" or as "Other Crimes Against the State."

(2) An act directed toward "the subversion or weakening . . . of the basic economic, political and ethnic conquests of the proletarian revolution" (Article

56. Article 44 is incorporated in Articles 53 and 54 of the RSFSR Criminal Code. Prior legislation on correctional labor camps provided for early release of prisoners on the basis of the amount of work ("labor-days") done by them in the labor camp.

58-1 of the 1934 law on counterrevolutionary crime) was no longer as such punishable, although "agitation or propaganda carried on for the purpose of subverting or weakening the Soviet authority" and "defaming the Soviet state and social system" remained criminal offenses (1960 RSFSR Criminal Code, Article 70).

(3) Giving out a military or state secret was no longer considered to be treason or espionage unless the secret was transmitted to a foreign state; and divulgence of a state secret, in the absence of indicia of treason or espionage, was made a separate crime limited to persons to whom such information had been entrusted or had become known because of their position or work (Article 75).[57]

(4) "Rendering aid to a foreign state carrying on hostile activity against the USSR" and "conspiracy for the purpose of seizing power" were added to the list of treasonable acts (Article 64) but "rendering aid to that part of the international bourgeoisie which . . . seeks to overthrow the Communist system, or to social groups . . . under the influence of such bourgeoisie" was no longer considered to be a crime.

(5) The crime of "terrorist acts," which had previously been interpreted to include any violent act against a state or Party official, or indeed, his close relatives, whatever the motive, was restricted to murder or serious bodily injury of the official himself, committed for the purpose of overthrowing or weakening the Soviet authority (Article 66).

(6) What came to be called "wrecking" (*vreditel'stvo*), defined as the "subversion" (*podryv*) of state industry, transport, trade, the monetary system, etc., which had previously been punishable by death, was made punishable by deprivation of freedom for eight to fifteen years, with possible additional exile for two to five years (Article 69).

(7) Although the older law of sabotage (*diversiia*) was retained (Article 68), so-called *kontrrevolutsionnyi sabotazh,* which had been defined as "deliberate nonperformance by anyone of particular obligations . . . for the specific purpose of weakening the authority of the government and the activity of the state apparatus," and which had been punishable by deprivation of freedom for not less than one year and in extreme cases by death, was eliminated.

Changes Introduced by the Statute on Military Crimes. A new comprehensive statute on military crimes was enacted in December 1958, at the same session of the Supreme Soviet of the USSR at which the Fundamental Principles of Criminal Legislation and the USSR Statute on Crimes Against the State were enacted. The 1958 USSR Statute on Military Crimes, which was later reproduced in Chapter Twelve of the Special Part of the 1960 RSFSR Criminal Code, incorporated the 1957 amendments to the older (1927) USSR Statute on Military Crimes, with some changes and additions. The general character of the reforms in this branch of the law is apparent from the following list of changes:

(1) Whereas the 1927 Statute had punished failure by a serviceman to carry

57. This and the following references are to articles of the RSFSR Criminal Code which are identical with provisions of the USSR Statute on Crimes Against the State.

out an order, without distinguishing between intentional and negligent failure, the 1958 Statute made the distinction and characterized intentional failure to carry out an order as insubordination (Article 238).[58] In addition, it substantially reduced the punishment for unintentional (that is, negligent) failure to carry out an order (Article 239).

(2) Whereas the 1927 Statute had characterized unwarranted absence for more than twenty-four hours as desertion, with punishment of five to ten years, and, in wartime, death with confiscation of property, the 1958 Statute (following the 1957 amendments) defined desertion as abandonment of a military unit, or failure to report for duty, for the purpose of evading military service (Article 246). It also reduced substantially the punishment for desertion (Article 247).

(3) Whereas the 1927 Statute had made unwarranted absence for more than two hours a criminal offense, the 1958 Statute (following the 1957 amendments) requiredan absence of more than twenty-four hours (Article 245). In addition, the punishments for unwarranted absence for varying periods of time were substantially reduced (Article 245).

(4) The 1958 Statute introduced the crime of "forcible actions against a superior in connection with performance by him of his military duties" (Article 242), and at the same time reduced the maximum punishment for insult by forcible action, committed against a superior, from deprivation of freedom for twenty-five years, as it had been under the prior law, to deprivation of freedom for five years (Article 243).

(5) Surrender of military forces by a commander, or abandonment to the enemy of military equipment or other means of conducting war, had been punishable under the 1927 Statute if it was "contrary to military rules." In practice this often meant that the commander was required to get permission of higher authorities in order to escape criminal liability. Under the 1958 Statute a commander is liable for surrender of military forces or abandonment of military equipment to the enemy only when such is "not required by the combat situation" (Article 261).

(6) The 1927 Statute had made it a crime for a serviceman to evade performance of military duties "on the pretext of religious or other convictions." This provision was omitted from the 1958 Statute which, however, made refusal by a serviceman to perform military duties punishable generally (Article 249). Evasion of mobilization, which had been a crime under the 1927 Statute, was omitted from the 1958 Statute since it is committed by civilians rather than by persons in military service and is covered by the Statute on Crimes Against the State (Article 81).

(7) Abuse or neglect of authority by a commander or military official had been punishable under the 1927 Statute even if committed without unworthy motives and even if no serious consequences occurred, provided that the offender knew that serious consequences could occur. The 1958 Statute required either un-

58. This and the following references are to articles of the RSFSR Criminal Code which are identical with provisions of the USSR Statute on Military Crimes.

worthy motives or substantial harm or that the offense be committed systematically (Article 260).

(8) Under the 1958 Statute the death penalty could no longer be applied, as it could under the 1927 Statute, for negligent failure to carry out an order in wartime, for dissipation or loss of military property in wartime, and for divulgence of a state secret. In addition, whereas the death penalty had formerly been the sole applicable punishment in many instances, under the 1958 Statute, where it is provided for, it is always an alternative measure of punishment, to be applied at the discretion of the court (Articles 238, 240, 242, 247–249, 251, 255, 257, 260–264, 266, 267).

(9) Disciplinary punishment was made applicable to two offenses under the 1958 Statute which formerly had been punishable criminally: threatening a superior and violation of rules for performing duty at radiotechnical posts (Articles 241, 257). At the same time, disciplinary punishment is not applicable under the 1958 Statute, as it was formerly, to intentional failure to carry out an order (insubordination), refusal to perform military duty, and intentional destruction or damage of military property.

(10) Maximum terms of deprivation of freedom were reduced in twelve instances in the 1958 Statute, as compared with the 1927 Statute. However, for graver crimes such as maiming, intentional destruction of military property, and voluntary surrender into captivity, the terms of deprivation of freedom were somewhat increased (Articles 249, 251, 264). Desertion was made punishable somewhat more severely than under the 1957 amendments, though less severely than under the 1927 Statute (Article 247).

Changes Introduced by the 1960 Criminal Code. The Fundamental Principles of Criminal Legislation, the Statute on Crimes Against the State, and the Statute on Military Crimes, enacted in December 1958, were expressly applicable to all the union republics and were therefore included in the RSFSR Criminal Code adopted by the RSFSR Supreme Soviet in October 1960. The RSFSR Criminal Code also included amendments to the all-union laws that were introduced by the USSR Supreme Soviet in the intervening twenty-two months. The Fundamental Principles were incorporated as the General Part of the RSFSR Criminal Code; the USSR Statute on Crimes Against the State was reproduced as Chapter One of the Special Part of the Code (Articles 64–88); the USSR Statute on Military Crimes was reproduced as Chapter Twelve of the Special Part (Articles 237–269). The remainder of the Special Part – Chapters Two to Eleven – introduced the following major changes in Soviet criminal law:

(1) A new arrangement of chapters was introduced, intended to signify a new order of importance. The Special Part of the 1926 Code had the following table of contents:

1. Crimes Against the State (Articles 58-1 to 58-14 and 59-1 to 59-13);
2. Other Crimes Against the System of Administration (Articles 60 to 108-1);
3. Official Crimes (Articles 109 to 121);
4. Breach of Rules of Separation of Church from State (Articles 122 to 127);
5. Economic Crimes (Articles 128 to 135).

6. Crimes Against the Life, Health, Freedom and Dignity of the Person (Articles 136 to 161);

7. Property Crimes (Articles 162 to 178);

8. Breach of Rules Protecting Public Health, Social Security and Order (Articles 179 to 192 (a));

9. Military Crimes (Articles 193-1 to 193-31);

10. Crimes Constituting Survivals of Tribal Life (Articles 194 to 205).

In contrast, the 1960 RSFSR Criminal Code moved Crimes Against the System of Administration from second to ninth place, Official Crimes from third to seventh place, and Economic Crimes from fifth to sixth place. It moved Crimes Against the Person from sixth to third place, and added, in fourth and fifth places, two new chapters involving personal rights: Political and Labor Rights of Citizens and Personal Property of Citizens. (Crimes Against the Separation of Church from State are treated in the 1960 Code as Crimes Against the Political and Labor Rights of Citizens.) It also added a new chapter on Crimes Against Justice.

These changes reflect the increased importance assigned to the protection of personal rights as contrasted with the protection of the system of political and economic administration. It should be noted that the arrangement of the chapters of the Code and the inclusion of a particular provision within one chapter or another are more than matters of style; they affect the interpretation of the law and express a policy binding upon the courts in individual cases.

(2) The 1960 Code, as originally enacted, was, on the whole, far more lenient in its sanctions than the previous law. The reduction of the maximum period of deprivation of freedom for any crime from twenty-five years to fifteen years (Article 24) was accompanied by a general reduction of penalties, especially for the less serious offenses. In addition, the Code empowered the courts to transfer a wide variety of minor offenses, previously criminally punishable, to social organizations for the application of measures of social pressure (warning, reprimand, a small fine, and others). However, a general policy of increased penalties for recidivists also found expression in many provisions of the Special Part of the Code.

(3) Very substantial changes were made in the law relating to the stealing of state or social property. In the first place, the penalties were greatly reduced: for example, the previous minimum penalty of seven years' deprivation of freedom for ordinary theft of state property was reduced to three months' deprivation of freedom or correctional tasks, and the previous maximum penalty of ten years was reduced to three years (Article 89 paragraph 1). In addition, the traditional Russian distinctions between secret stealing (*krazha*), and open stealing (*grabiozh*),[59] and assault with intent to rob (*razboi*), which had been eliminated under the 1932 law on stealing social property as well as under the 1947 laws on stealing state or social property and on stealing personal property, were restored (Articles 89–91, 144–146). Also, with respect to state and social property, for the first time careful distinctions were made between stealing, extortion, appropria-

59. We depart in this instance from the Library of Congress system of transliteration, which would result in the spelling *grabezh*. The accent is on the second syllable.

tion, intentional and negligent destruction or damaging, and failure to take adequate measures to protect against stealing, damaging, or destruction (Articles 92-93, 94, 95, 97-99).

(4) The chapter on crimes against life, health, freedom, and dignity of the person introduced a variety of changes. The number of types of circumstances rendering intentional homicide more severely punishable (Article 102) was considerably increased and, even apart from the death sentence (which was introduced in 1954 for intentional homicide committed under aggravating circumstances), the penalties for intentional homicide were increased. A broader criminal liability was introduced for failure to aid a person in danger of death (Article 127); under the older law, liability for failure to render aid was confined to persons who were obligated to care for the victim (1926 Criminal Code, Article 156). Another important change was the introduction of rather severe penalties for defamation combined with an accusation of the commission of a crime against the state or other grave crimes (Article 130 paragraph 3).

(5) The chapter on Crimes Against the Political and Labor Rights of Citizens introduced for the first time the crimes of obstruction of the exercise of equal rights of women, violation of secrecy of correspondence, and violation of the inviolability of a citizen's dwelling space. It also reworded the definition of various other crimes that previously had been placed in other chapters of the code.

(6) The chapter on Crimes Against the Personal Property of Citizens in general reduced the penalties for such crimes in comparison with the 1947 law on stealing personal property, though it increased the penalties against repeaters of such crimes (cf. Article 145 *et seq.*) A new provision was introduced to protect the property of associations not constituting socialist organizations (for example, religious associations) (Article 151).

(7) The 1960 Code carried over from the earlier law the concept of "economic crimes," as distinct from "property crimes." Such economic crimes chiefly concern the functioning of industry and agriculture. The penalty for issuing industrial goods of poor quality was substantially reduced (under a 1940 law, the punishment had been deprivation of freedom from five to eight years), and liability was confined to cases in which such goods were issued repeatedly or on a large scale (Article 152). The crime of "uneconomic activity" *(beskhoziaistvennost')*, consisting of a "wrongful or unconscientious attitude toward the task entrusted to them on the part of persons in charge of state or social institutions or enterprises or their deputies, resulting in squandering of or irreplaceable damage to the property of the institution or enterprise" (Article 128 of the former Code) was eliminated; however, a parallel provision was introduced into the chapter on Crimes Against Socialist Property (Article 100). Also the crime of malicious nonfulfillment of contracts concluded by private persons with state or social institutions (Article 131 of the former Code) was eliminated.

(8) Probably the most important change introduced by the Special Part of the 1960 Criminal Code was the limitation of liability for official crimes (Chapter Seven) to persons who are engaged in executive activities (Article 170, Note). Under the earlier law, any state employee who was guilty of intentional or negligent misconduct in the performance of his duties was subject to prosecution for

"abuse" or "excess" or "neglect" of "official position." Furthermore, various types of official crimes specified in the 1926 Criminal Code (for example, the discrediting of the authority of state agencies in the eyes of the working people, by an official, even though his acts were not connected with his official duties (Article 113)) are omitted from the 1960 Code. The penalties for official crimes were substantially reduced.

(9) The 1960 Code included in its chapter on Crimes Against Justice many provisions that had been treated in the earlier Code as Official Crimes and Crimes Against the Administrative Order. There were, however, some new provisions. The crime of concealment (not promised in advance) was limited to concealment of certain specified crimes (Article 189); previously concealment, though after the fact, was a form of complicity in any type of crime (1926 Criminal Code, Article 17). The crime of failure to report a crime, previously limited to failure to report certain crimes against the state and assault with intent to rob, was extended to a wide variety of other crimes as well (Article 190).

(10) In accordance with the general policy of the 1960 Criminal Code, the chapter on Crimes Against the System of Administration reduced penalties for many offenses. Resisting a representative of authority, formerly punishable by deprivation of freedom from one to ten years (1926 Criminal Code, Article 73), was made punishable in the 1960 Code by deprivation of freedom from three months to three years or by correctional tasks or by a fine (Article 191). Publicly insulting a representative of state authority in connection with performance of his duties (Article 192) was no longer punishable by deprivation of freedom as it had been under the 1926 Criminal Code (Article 76), but only by correctional tasks or a fine or application of social pressure. The punishment for unwarranted appropriation of the title or authority of an official was reduced from a maximum of two years' deprivation of freedom (1926 Criminal Code, Article 77) to a maximum of one year's deprivation of freedom (Article 194). The crime of income tax evasion (1926 Criminal Code, Article 60) was eliminated altogether.

(11) Chapter Ten of the 1960 Code, entitled Crimes Against Public Security, Public Order, and Health of the Population, contains a miscellany of crimes, many of which were previously placed in other categories. The crime of hooliganism (Article 206), which in practice is said to be the most frequently committed of all the crimes listed in the Code, was defined more or less as it was in the 1926 Code (Article 74), but it was now divided into petty hooliganism, ordinary hooliganism, and malicious hooliganism, with penalties ranging from correctional tasks or a fine for the first type, to deprivation of freedom up to one year for the second, and deprivation of freedom up to five years for the third. The former law (from 1940 on) imposed a single penalty: imprisonment for a year.

Threat of homicide, of infliction of grave bodily injuries, or of destruction of property (Article 207) has no counterpart in previous law. Similarly, systematically engaging in vagrancy or in begging (Article 209) was an entirely new crime in 1960. Also the imposition of heavy penalties for causing injury or death by automobile (Articles 211, 212) was new, and resulted in the anomaly that negligent homicide is punishable, as a maximum, only by deprivation of freedom up to three years (Article 114), unless it is committed by driving a motor vehicle in violation of highway regulations, in which case it is punishable by deprivation of freedom up to ten years (Article 212). Another crime newly introduced into Soviet law by the 1960 Criminal Code was that of creating or leading or drawing minors into a group which, under the guise of preaching religious beliefs, causes harm to health or sexual dissoluteness (Article 227). This broad provision – rendered still broader by subsequent amendment – is no doubt to be read partly in the light of Article 143, which was carried over from the earlier law (1922 Criminal Code, Article 127), making it a crime to obstruct the performance of religious rites insofar as they do not violate public order and are not accompanied by infringement of the rights of citizens.

(12) Finally, Chapter Eleven of the 1960 Criminal Code, applicable to those non-European areas of the RSFSR where more primitive family relations still exist, substituted the phrase "survivals of local customs" for the phrase "survivals of kinship life" in the corresponding chapter of the 1926 Criminal Code, and omitted several minor provisions contained in the 1926 Code, but otherwise was virtually the same.

4 Major Changes Reflected in the 1960 Code of Criminal Procedure

Although a new RSFSR Criminal Code was adopted in 1926 to replace the 1922 Code and to reflect changes introduced by the 1924 all-union Fundamental Principles of Criminal Legislation, the 1923 RSFSR Code of Criminal Procedure survived the 1924 all-union Fundamental Principles of Criminal Procedure and continued in force until 1960. However, many of its provisions became obsolete long before its final repeal. Like the 1960 Criminal Code, the 1960 Code of Criminal Procedure builds not only upon its predecessor as originally enacted but also upon the changes introduced in the interim, especially upon principles established by the 1938 Law on Court Organization, and, of course, upon the reforms introduced after Stalin's death in 1953, including, above all, the all-union Fundamental Principles of Criminal Procedure of 1958.

The 1923 Code of Criminal Procedure established a system of preliminary investigation, indictment, trial, judgment and appeal, similar in its broad outlines to that of prerevolutionary Russia and of most Continental European countries. That system, in contrast to the system of English and American criminal procedure, provides for the investigation of major crimes by an impartial official, called in Russian an investigator (*sledovatel'*), who, like the French *juge d'instruction* or the German *Untersuchungsrichter,* examines the accused and the witnesses and prepares the materials on which the indictment is based. The indictment lists the evidence against the accused contained in the record of the preliminary investigation, which record is available to be studied by the accused. Thus the accused knows in advance all the witnesses and all the evidence to be used against him. On the other hand, in contradistinction to the privilege against self-incrimination as it is traditionally understood in the United States, a suspect or accused who refuses to answer incriminating questions put to him by the investigator (or by the prosecutor or court during trial) subjects himself to the possibility that adverse inferences will be drawn from such refusal. He cannot legally be compelled to answer; Soviet law expressly prohibits the use of force, and neither the investigator nor the court has the power to punish a suspect or accused for contempt. (A witness, on the other hand, may be prosecuted for refusing to answer questions even though the answers might incriminate him.) At trial, the prosecutor is required to prove the charges contained in the indictment on the basis of the evidence contained in the record of the preliminary investigation. The fact that the accused admits his guilt does not eliminate this requirement; such an admission is only to be weighed with the other evidence in the case.[1]

It is important to note that in Soviet as in prerevolutionary Russian and Continental European criminal procedure, the question of the civil liability to compensate for harm caused by the criminal act may be tried together with the question of criminal liability; that is, a victim of the crime may appear in the criminal case as a civil plaintiff, and the court may award him damages at the same time that it sentences the accused. Thus the Criminal Code is a source of tort law as well as of criminal law. However, the victim of a crime may, alternatively, bring a civil suit independently of the criminal case, under the Code of Civil Procedure, for vindication of his rights under the Civil Code.

The 1923 RSFSR Code of Criminal Procedure, as amended in the 1920's and 1930's, departed, however, from the Continental European model in many important respects. These departures fall into several different categories. Some of them permitted repressive measures to be taken speedily and secretly against persons suspected of political opposition to the regime. Others made it easier to prosecute and convict the guilty, regardless of the type of crime committed, though at the same time creating the potentiality of serious abuse of the rights of the innocent. Still others introduced a high degree of informality, flexibility and "popularity" in court proceedings – elements which could work to the benefit as well as to the detriment of the accused, depending on the type of case. Some of these features that are more or less peculiar to Soviet criminal procedure survived the 1938 Law on Court Organization, and some have survived the 1958 Fundamental Principles of Criminal Procedure and the 1960 RSFSR Code; others have been renounced.

In the following pages we shall present some of the principal characteristics of the 1960 Code, indicating their relation to the earlier legislation.

(1) **Regulation of Arrest and Investigation by State Security Agencies and Elimination of Their Power to Impose Criminal Punishment.** The 1923 Code of Criminal Procedure contemplated a system of investigation of crimes either (a) in less important cases, by an "inquiry" (*doznanie*), conducted by the regular police (*militsiia*) as well as by a wide variety of other organizations, including state security agencies, or (b) in more important cases, by a "preliminary investigation" (*predvaritel'noe sledstvie*), conducted by investigators of the Procuracy or by investigators of the state security agencies. Article 107 of the 1923 Code

1. In comparing the effect of an admission of guilt in Soviet criminal procedure (and that of other countries of Europe) with its effect in English or American, one must distinguish between such an admission and a "plea" of guilty. The latter, in English and American law, results in a verdict of guilty, usually followed by a hearing on the sentence. (In many states a plea of guilty is not permitted in cases of capital crimes.) In Soviet criminal procedure the accused does not "plead" at all, in the technical sense; he is asked at the beginning of the trial whether or not he acknowledges his guilt, but his answer has only evidentiary and not procedural significance. It should be kept in mind also that in Soviet procedure, in comparison with English and American, no sharp distinction is made between issues of fact and issues of law. The three-judge court decides both types of issues, and the verdict and sentence are joined in a single act, called the *prigovor*, which is translated in this volume (following the language of the Model Penal Code of the American Law Institute) as "judgment."

stated that procurators shall exercise general supervision over the activities of the agencies of police inquiry. In 1924 an amendment to Article 107, in the form of a Note added to it, provided that the procedure and supervision of police inquiries conducted by the agencies of state security (then called OGPU) "shall be regulated by a special statute." Also Article 104, dealing with arrest, provided that the system of arrests carried out by agencies of state security "shall be determined by special rules." Finally, a 1929 law, introduced into the Code as an addition to Article 108, provided that the types of cases subject to preliminary investigation by the agencies of state security "shall be determined by special rules." Such "special statute" and "special rules" governing inquiries, arrests, and investigations by the state security agencies were never published, except for very short and sweeping laws enacted in 1922.[2] Thus the courts and the Procuracy had no control over inquiries, arrests, and investigations by the state security agencies. If the latter decided to bring an accused to trial in court, they simply submitted the case to the court and presented to the Procuracy, as the prosecuting arm, the results of their investigation. This is what happened in the great public purge trials of the late 1930's.[3]

The situation described above was changed by the 1960 RSFSR Code of Criminal Procedure, which provides, in effect, that detention and investigation by the agencies of state security are governed by the same rules that govern detention and investigation by the agencies of internal affairs (that is, the *militsiia,* or police) or other agencies of inquiry and by the investigators of the Procuracy – namely, the rules laid down by the Code itself (cf. Articles 117, 125, 127). Moreover, the 1960 Code provides that preliminary investigation by all investigators, including investigators of the agencies of state security, shall be under the supervision of the Procuracy (cf. Articles 127 paragraph 2, 130, 133 paragraph 2, 211ff.). In addition, the new Code limits the types of crimes subject to investigation by the agencies of state security (Article 126 paragraph 3).[4]

An even more serious lacuna in the 1923 Code of Criminal Procedure was the absence of any provision excluding the application of criminal punishment by nonjudicial agencies. In fact, from the earliest years of the Soviet regime administrative boards of the state security agencies had wide powers of trial and

2. *SU* (1922), no. 16, item 160; no. 51, item 646; no. 65, item 844. These laws established the GPU (State Political Administration) of the NKVD (People's Commissariat of Internal Affairs) as successor to the Cheka, with power of arrest, search, seizure, detention, banishment, sentence to "forced labor camps," and death by shooting, for various counterrevolutionary and other crimes.

3. There were three public trials: "the trial of the sixteen" (Zinoviev, Kamenev, Smirnov, Mrachkovsky, and others) in August 1936, "the trial of the seventeen" (Piatakov, Radek, and others) in January 1937, and "the trial of the twenty-one" (Rykov, Bukharin, Krestinsky, Rakovsky, Yagoda, and others) in March 1938. Marshal Tukhachevsky and a group of the highest generals were tried secretly in 1937. Verbatim reports of the public trials were published in English translation in Moscow. See People's Commissariat of Justice of the USSR, *The Case of the Trotskyite-Zinovievite Terrorist Centre* (Moscow, 1936); *id., Report of Court Proceedings of the Anti-Trotskyite Centre* (Moscow, 1937); *id., Report of Court Proceedings of the Anti-Soviet "Bloc of Rights and Trotskyites"* (Moscow, 1938). R. C. Tucker and S. F. Cohen, eds., *The Great Purge Trial* (1965), contains an edited version of the transcript of the 1938 trial.

4. On changes enacted in 1961 and thereafter, see *infra,* Chapter 5.

punishment. In 1934 a "Special Board" (*Osoboe soveshchanie*, or OSSO) of the People's Commissariat of Internal Affairs (NKVD) was established, with power to exile, banish, and impose deprivation of freedom in a corrective labor camp upon persons "deemed to be socially dangerous."[5] Trial by the Special Board was secret; there was no right to counsel; often the accused himself was not present. The trial was considered to be not a judicial but an administrative proceeding; it was not governed by the Code of Criminal Procedure – and there was no RSFSR or USSR code or statute governing administrative procedure.

In 1955 it was stated informally to foreigners, and in January 1956 it was semi-officially announced in the leading Soviet law journal, that the Special Board of the Ministry of Internal Affairs (MVD, successor to the NKVD, OGPU, GPU, and Cheka) had been abolished in September 1953.[6] Other references to its abolition have appeared subsequently from time to time and there has been no sign of its existence. However, no legislative act or administrative decree effectuating the abolition has been published.

With the enactment of the Fundamental Principles of Criminal Procedure in December 1958, it was thought by many both within and without the Soviet Union, that the reestablishment of such an institution as the Special Board was prohibited. This was the significance attached to Article 7 of the Fundamental Principles, reproduced in Article 13 of the 1960 RSFSR Code of Criminal Procedure, stating: "Justice in criminal cases shall be administered only by courts. No one may be deemed guilty of committing a crime or subjected to criminal punishment except by judgment of a court." In no previous Soviet legislation had such language occurred; the 1938 Law on Court Organization stated, as the 1936 Constitution also states, that justice shall be administered by the courts, but the word "only" is not added.

The interpretation of Article 13 of the Code as excluding the imposition of penal sanctions by administrative action, without the protection of the Code of Criminal Procedure, suffered a setback, however, with the enactment of the RSFSR antiparasite law in 1961 and with the extension of the jurisdiction of Comrades' Courts. Judging by the arguments used to justify the antiparasite law, discussed in the next chapter, it would seem that, from a legal point of view, the state security agencies could once again be given the powers formerly exercised by the Special Board of the Ministry of Internal Affairs, without amendment of the Fundamental Principles of Criminal Procedure or of the 1960 Codes, provided that no "crime" were charged.

(2) Elimination of Trial of Serious Counterrevolutionary Crimes by Military Tribunals in a Special Secret and Summary Procedure. The Stalin regime was not content to leave to the Special Board of the state security agencies the trial of persons suspected of political opposition. On July 10, 1934, jurisdiction in cases of treason, espionage, terrorist acts, and sabotage was given to the Military Division of the Supreme Court of the USSR and to the military tribunals of military

5. *SZ* (1934), no. 36, items 283, 284; (1935), no. 11, item 84. Cf. *supra*, note 2.
6. *N.Y. Times*, December 16, 1955; *Sovetskoe gosudarstvo i pravo* (1956), no. 1, p. 3.

districts.[7] The Special Board of the state security agencies continued to exercise a parallel jurisdiction. On December 1, 1934, a special procedure was established for investigation and trial of cases of terrorist acts (including participation in terrorist organizations): the investigation of such cases was to be concluded within a period of not more than ten days, the indictment ("conclusion to indict") was to be handed to the accused twenty-four hours before trial, the case was to be heard without the participation of the defendant or his counsel, appeal from the judgment and submission of petitions for mercy were forbidden, and the death sentence was to be carried out immediately upon rendering of the judgment.[8] This macabre piece of legislation was followed on September 14, 1937, by a slightly less gruesome law applicable to cases of wrecking and sabotage; in such cases the conclusion to indict was to be handed to the accused twenty-four hours before trial, appeal was forbidden, and the death sentence was to be carried out immediately upon rejection of a petition of mercy by the condemned man.[9] The 1937 law preserved in form, at least, the right of the defendant to be present and to have counsel, a right established by Article 111 of the 1936 USSR Constitution. However, Article 111 was apparently not applied to trials under the special procedures established by the law of December 1, 1934.

The laws of December 1, 1934, and September 14, 1937, subsequently introduced into the RSFSR Code of Criminal Procedure as a special chapter at the end, embracing Articles 466 to 473, were repealed by the Supreme Soviet of the USSR on April 19, 1956.[10] In addition, the 1958 Statute on Military Tribunals limits the jurisdiction of military tribunals over civilians to cases of espionage and cases of complicity in military crimes. Under the 1958 Fundamental Principles of Criminal Procedure and under the 1960 RSFSR Code of Criminal Procedure, all types of crimes (including military crimes) are subject to trial under the same rules of procedure.

(3) Restriction of the Power to Confine Accused Persons Under Guard Prior to Trial. The 1923 Code, as amended in 1929, provided that the preliminary investigation was to terminate within two months from the time it was commenced, but that that period could be extended by a month with the authorization of the regional procurator, and that in exceptional cases it could be extended indefinitely by the Procurator of the Republic; in addition, the Procurator of the Republic could establish a general extension of the time limit for particular areas of the republic when local conditions so required (Article 116). Thus the Procuracy could set its own time limits for the preliminary investigation. Moreover, the 1923 Code provided that confinement of the accused under guard could be continued as long as the investigation lasted (unless the only reason for such confinement was to prevent the accused from hindering the establishment of the truth, in which case it could not continue for more than two months or, with the procurator's approval, three months) (Articles 158, 159, 145).

7. *SZ* (1934), no. 36, item 284.
8. *SZ* (1934), no. 64, item 459; cf. *SU* (1935), no. 2, item 8.
9. *SZ* (1937), no. 61, item 266; cf. *SU* (1938), no. 3, item 38.
10. *Vedomosti SSSR* (1956), no. 8, item 193.

These powers of indefinite confinement of accused persons under guard were finally removed by the 1958 Fundamental Principles of Criminal Procedure, which limit the length of confinement of accused persons during investigation to two months, in some cases six months, and in exceptional cases, with the permission of the Procurator General of the USSR, nine months (Article 34; contained in the 1960 RSFSR Code of Criminal Procedure as Article 97). Under the 1960 RSFSR Code of Criminal Procedure (Article 133) the preliminary investigation is ordinarily limited to two months, but may be prolonged to four months, or, with the permission of the RSFSR Procurator, the Chief Military Procurator or the Procurator General of the USSR, may be extended indefinitely. Thus the confinement may not continue beyond nine months, but the investigation may continue thereafter.

Neither the 1923 Code nor the 1960 Code gives the accused the right to have visitors or to send or receive letters or telephone calls during confinement under guard. In short, at the discretion of the Procuracy he may be held incommunicado for nine months.

(4) Powers of Detention of Persons Prior to Accusation. The 1923 RSFSR Code of Criminal Procedure empowered agencies of inquiry (including the police, agencies of state security, the chief administration of fire protection, agencies of financial, sanitary, technical, trade, and labor inspection, government institutions and individual officials) to detain a person suspected of the commission of a crime in order to prevent his escape (Article 100). Such detention could last for twenty-four hours prior to notification of the Procuracy, and the Procuracy was given an additional forty-eight hours to determine whether or not to "confirm or vacate the arrest" (Article 104). If the "arrest" was confirmed by the procurator, the suspect could be held longer only if he was declared to be an accused (Article 145) — that is, only if charges were formally brought against him.

Thus a person suspected of committing a crime could be held incommunicado for seventy-two hours before being accused. The term "arrest" (*arest*) — which has a variety of meanings in Soviet law[11] — was applied to such preventive detention in Article 104, although elsewhere it was simply called detention (*zaderzhanie*). The power of "arrest" under Article 104 does not seem to have been affected by Article 127 of the USSR Constitution of 1936, which prohibited "arrest" without the sanction (that is, authorization) of the court or Procuracy; apparently this was taken to include a subsequent, and not only a prior, authorization. In addition, arrest by agencies of state security continued to be subject to unpublished rules.

There was an additional loophole in the 1923 Code provisions: Article 145, which provided that measures of restraint (as distinct from preventive detention under Article 100) could be applied only after the suspect became an accused, also contained the following sentences: "In exceptional instances measures of restraint may be applied to persons before presentation of the accusation to them. In these instances the presentation of the accusation must take place not

11. Cf. *supra*, Chapter 1, note 21.

later than fourteen days after the day on which measures of restraint were adopted." Thus at the discretion of the Procuracy, a person who, seventy-two hours after he was first detained, became an accused could be kept under guard, in exceptional cases, an additional fourteen days, without being informed of the charges against him (that is, without "presentation of the accusation").

The 1960 RSFSR Code of Criminal Procedure retains the maximum seventy-two hour period of confinement prior to accusation – that is, twenty-four hours for the agency of inquiry to notify the Procuracy, and forty-eight hours for the Procuracy to determine whether or not to initiate a criminal case (Article 122). It also contains provision for confinement of suspects up to ten days without presentation to them of the accusation, in exceptional cases (Article 90), provided the sanction of the Procuracy or of a court is obtained (Articles 96 and 11). In addition, the distinction between "arrest" (*arest*) as a measure of restraint of accused persons and "detention" (*zaderzhanie*) of suspects prior to accusation is now codified in Article 178 of the Criminal Code, which imposes heavier sanctions upon illegal arrest than on illegal detention.

(5) Establishment of Right to Counsel during the Preliminary Investigation. A critical question for all Continental European systems of criminal procedure is that of the extent to which suspects in the preliminary investigation are entitled to the protection of counsel. In some European countries counsel have been excluded on the ground that they are likely to interfere with the investigation, and in some they have been permitted to be present with their clients but not to participate actively in the proceedings. In other European countries counsel are given a more active role in the preliminary investigation. Under the 1923 RSFSR Code of Criminal Procedure counsel were excluded entirely from the preliminary investigation. Only after the indictment was finally issued and a trial ordered did the right to counsel attach.

The question of right to counsel during the preliminary investigation was hotly debated by Soviet jurists during the years prior to the adoption of the Fundamental Principles of Criminal Procedure in 1958. The Fundamental Principles (Article 22) introduced the followimg compromises:

(a) Defense counsel was permitted to appear in the preliminary investigation at the moment that the investigator decided that he had taken all the necessary measures of investigation preliminary to his "conclusion to indict." At that moment the investigator was required to show the accused "all the materials of the case" – that is, the entire record of the preliminary investigation. Under Article 47 of the 1960 RSFSR Code of Criminal Procedure, the accused must then be informed of his right to defense counsel, who may thereupon consult with the accused alone and may examine the materials of the case. Defense counsel may challenge the investigator or other officials in the case (procurator, experts, interpreters). He may also petition for supplementary investigation. When the case is transferred from the investigator to the procurator, for his approval of the investigator's conclusion to indict, defense counsel may submit petitions to the procurator. He may also submit petitions to the single judge or to the administrative session of the court that reviews the conclusion to indict and decides whether or not finally to bring the accused person to trial (Articles 51, 63, 64, 66, 67, 202, 204, 221–223).

(b) Article 22 of the Fundamental Principles and Article 47 of the Code, as originally enacted, also provided that minors and persons who are mentally or physically defective have the right to counsel from the moment that they are presented with an accusation by the investigator. Such presentation of the accusation takes place at or near the beginning of the preliminary investigation.

A 1971 all-union statute expanding the right to counsel in the preliminary investigation is discussed in Chapter 5.

(6) Control of Preliminary Investigation by the Procurator. In Western Europe it is generally considered an essential guarantee of the impartiality of the preliminary investigation that it be conducted independently of the prosecuting arm and subject to the control of the courts. This means that the French *juge d'instruction* or the German *Untersuchungsrichter* is (theoretically, at least) not subject to the influence of the prosecuting arm in determining whether or not to indict; it also means that any abuses of the rights of the accused by the *juge d'instruction* or *Untersuchungsrichter* may be appealed to the courts.

Similar features characterized the prerevolutionary Russian system of criminal procedure after the reforms of 1864. The Soviet regime, however, to a certain extent restored the Russian Procuracy as it existed prior to the 1864 reforms. The law of 1922 reestablishing the Procuracy gave it very wide powers, including the power to supervise the preliminary investigation of crimes. At the same time, however, investigators were officials of the courts and the courts were given important powers over their activities. The 1923 RSFSR Code of Criminal Procedure, as originally enacted, gave the courts the power to terminate, suspend, or reopen a preliminary investigation (Articles 203, 205). In addition, the Code provided (Article 6):

> Every judge and every procurator who discovers within the boundaries of his jurisdiction or district that someone is kept under guard without a lawful decree of the authorized agencies or beyond the term established by law or by court judgment shall be obliged immediately to liberate such person incorrectly deprived of freedom.

Similarly Article 7 of the 1923 RSFSR Code of Criminal Procedure provided that either the judge or the procurator was bound to release persons confined in an improper place or under improper circumstances.

These provisions permitted an appeal to the courts *or* to the Procuracy against improper conduct of investigators in the course of the preliminary investigation.

However, in 1929 the power to terminate, suspend, or reopen a preliminary investigation was taken away from the courts and transferred to the Procuracy, and in 1930 the investigators were made officials of the Procuracy. In addition, under the 1938 Law on Court Organization the courts were not given the powers set forth in Articles 6 and 7 of the Code of Criminal Procedure, and those articles were therefore considered to have lost their force.

Soviet jurists state that control over the investigation by the court proved ineffective, since it was practically impossible for the courts to supervise the investigation or for the accused to complain to the court against abuses by the investigator until the investigation was completed. The procurator, on the other hand, is in the same office, so to speak, with the investigator and is in some respects his administrative superior, although the investigator's appointment, promotion, and dismissal are controlled by higher procurators. The procurator has more opportunity than a judge has to observe the investigator in action, and the investigator is more likely to transmit complaints of the accused to the procurator than to a court. In addition, the Procuracy is more than just a prosecuting arm; it supervises legality generally and is the most independent of all Soviet legal agencies. It has more prestige than the judicial branch, and, in some ways, more authority.

The 1958 Fundamental Principles of Criminal Procedure and the 1960 RSFSR Code of Criminal Procedure do not restore the power of the courts to supervise the lawfulness of the detention of persons by the investigator (or by the Procuracy or the police). Such power of supervision remains vested in the Procuracy.

The 1958 Fundamental Principles and the 1960 Code do, however, purport to increase somewhat the independence of the investigator with respect to the indictment. Article 30 of the Fundamental Principles (Article 127 of the Code) affirms that decisions with respect to the course of the investigation shall be taken "independently" by the investigator, and that in the event that the investigator disagrees with the instructions of the procurator concerning whether or not a person should be accused, or concerning the nature of the crime, the scope of the accusation, or whether the case should be terminated or transferred to the court for issuance of the indictment, he (the investigator) may submit the case to a higher procurator, with his written objections to such instructions. The higher procurator may not order the investigator to indict.

It is apparent, however, that these and other provisions purporting to strengthen the hand of the investigator are not designed to create an investigating arm independent of the prosecuting arm. Such independence is foreclosed by the administrative superiority of the Procuracy over the investigator. Moreover, under the 1960 Code, as under the 1923 Code, the investigator's decision to indict is subject to reversal by the procurator, and the investigator's decision not to indict is not final, since the procurator may transfer the case to another investigator. In fact, the procurator may, in his discretion, conduct the preliminary investigation (or any part of it) himself (Article 211(2)(c)).

The fact that the procurator may control the procedure leading to indictment does not seem strange to Americans, especially in those states where a person may be indicted on information of the prosecutor. The Soviet system of procedure prior to trial, however, like that of Continental European countries, purports to secure an indictment only after an impartial investigation; the indictment therefore carries more weight, psychologically, at trial. Thus it may seem to strengthen the prosecution's hand unduly to put it in control of the investigation. Yet as will become more apparent from our subsequent discussion of the courts and of the Procuracy in Chapters 6 and 8, the Soviet procurator is more than a prosecutor, and under Soviet conditions, despite the real danger of abuse, there may be no better alternative, from the point of view of the rights of the accused, than to leave the preliminary investigation under procuratorial control.

(7) Elimination of Power of Trial Court to Exclude Defense Counsel, Witnesses, and Oral Argument, and to Decide on the Basis of Evidence not Presented at the Trial. The 1923 Code of Criminal Procedure gave to the accused ample procedural rights in cases tried in the people's courts, but introduced severe restrictions upon his rights in cases tried in higher courts, including provincial (*gubernskie*) courts, supreme courts of autonomous republics, and the Supreme Court of the RSFSR. Moreover, under Article 26 of the Code the provincial and higher courts had a very broad original jurisdiction over crimes against the state, crimes against the administrative order, official crimes, and serious economic and other crimes – crimes covered by some 67 articles of the Special Part of the Criminal Code. In addition, the procedure for trial in the provincial courts was also applicable in military tribunals (which had jurisdiction over certain counterrevolutionary crimes, as indicated above, as well as jurisdiction over all crimes committed by military personnel).

Under Articles 381 and 382 of the 1923 Code, the provincial courts sitting as courts of first instance could, at their discretion, exclude the prosecutor and defense counsel or other representative of the accused from the trial. In addition, under Articles 391–397 the provincial courts were permitted to exclude witnesses who had testified in the preliminary investigation, to terminate the questioning of witnesses to rely in making their decisions on evidence not considered at the trial, and to refuse to hear the oral arguments of the parties.

The exclusion of defense counsel under Articles 381 and 382 was considered to be repealed by Article 111 of the 1936 USSR Constitution (and the corresponding Article 115 of the RSFSR Constitution), which guaranteed the right to counsel. There was no indication, however, that the denial of right to counsel in cases of terrorist acts, discussed above, was considered to be repealed by Article 111; also defense counsel were excluded, under Article 381 of the 1923 Code, in cases tried by military tribunals during World War II.

Although the 1938 USSR Law on Court Organization substantially changed the court system, a large part of Section Four of the 1923 RSFSR Code of Criminal Procedure entitled "Proceedings in Provincial Courts and Tribunals" (Articles 380–433), remained applicable in the regional and other higher courts as well as in the military tribunals.[12] In addition, the original jurisdiction of the regional and other higher courts continued to expand.

In 1950 the Plenum of the Supreme Court of the USSR ruled that Article 396 of the 1923 Code, permitting the regional (or other higher) court, sitting as a court of first instance, to rely upon evidence not considered at the trial, contradicted Article 23 of the all-union Fundamental Principles of Criminal Procedure

12. The replacement of "provinces" (*gubernye*) by "regions" (*oblasti*) and "territories" (*kraia*) in the late 1920's rendered the term "provincial court" obsolete. However, the articles of the Code of Criminal Procedure applicable to provincial courts were simply carried over to regional and territorial courts.

adopted in 1924 and was therefore invalid.[13] Article 23 expressly requires the judgment of a court to be based on evidence considered at the trial. It is characteristic of the state of Soviet criminal procedure in the Stalin era that it took the Supreme Court twenty-six years to call attention to this discrepancy. The 1950 ruling, however, apparently did not affect the power of the regional (or other higher) court to rely on evidence presented in the preliminary investigation, without requiring confirmation, provided that the existence of such evidence was announced – and hence "considered" – at the trial (1923 Code, Articles 391 and 395).

The 1958 Fundamental Principles and the 1960 RSFSR Code of Criminal Procedure establish a uniform trial procedure in all courts. They guarantee the right to defense counsel and the right to call defense witnesses. They forbid the court to limit the duration of oral argument, and they strengthen the requirement that the judgment be based solely on the evidence presented directly, and not merely announced, at trial (1960 RSFSR Code, Article 286).

(8) Clarification and Strengthening of the Rules Concerning the Burden of Proof of the Guilt of the Accused (Presumption of Innocence). The 1923 Code contained no provision concerning the burden of proof, and it contained only two rules concerning the evaluation of evidence: first, that the court shall not be limited by "formal proofs" but shall have the power to receive or demand any kind of evidence (Article 57), and second, that the court shall evaluate the evidence "according to its inner conviction based on the consideration of all the circumstances of the case in their totality" (Article 319). Many Soviet jurists, however, in commenting on the Code, stated that it is presupposed by the entire system of Soviet criminal procedure that the burden of proof of the guilt of the accused rests on the prosecution and that the accused is not required to prove his innocence. Indeed, in contrast with the usual rule in American courts, even the admission of his guilt by the accused did not necessarily dispense with the requirement of a trial.[14] In the words of a ruling of the USSR Supreme Court in 1950, "the data of the preliminary investigation must be considered and verified by the court . . . and judgments may be founded on such data only."[15]

Nevertheless, certain doubts were cast on these doctrines, especially in the 1930's. The most serious challenge to them came in cases of counterrevolutionary crimes. Although Soviet legal writings of the time did not so state, the theory was apparently held that in such cases the accusation itself was a sufficient basis for conviction, and in addition, the confession of the accused was adequate proof of guilt, since (it was said) nobody would confess to such crimes if he were not guilty! Moreover, the 1923 Code gave the court the power – though not the duty – to dispense with further proof in any case if the accused admitted his guilt (Article 282).

Perhaps the most serious open breach in the doctrine that the burden of proof

13. The decree is quoted in the official text of the 1953 edition of the RSFSR Code of Criminal Procedure at page 102.

14. See *supra*, note 1.

15. *Supra*, note 13.

rests on the prosecution was contained in a 1934 ruling of the Plenum of the USSR Supreme Court that under the law of August 7, 1932, on stealing social property, the causing of shortages was to be treated as stealing unless it was proved that the property was not appropriated by the accused and used in his own interests.[16] Other less open breaches in the doctrine may be seen in the special summary procedures applied to cases of certain counterrevolutionary crimes (discussed above), whereby the accused was in effect deprived of the opportunity to rebut the charges against him.

The notion that the accused may be found guilty unless he proves his innocence is clearly repudiated by the new Soviet legislation. In particular, the 1960 RSFSR Code of Criminal Procedure, following the 1958 USSR Fundamental Principles of Criminal Procedure, provides:

(a) that the court, procurator, investigator, or person conducting an inquiry may not transfer the obligation of proof to the accused (Article 20);

(b) that the accused has the right to present evidence (Article 46), but that it is forbidden to extract statements from him by force, threat, or other illegal measures (Article 20), and no punishment is applicable to him (as it is to others) for refusing to testify or for giving false testimony (cf. Article 282);

(c) that the judgment of the court shall be based only on evidence considered in the trial (Article 301);

(d) that the accused shall be acquitted if his participation in the commission of a crime is not proved (Article 309);

(e) that a conviction may not be based on assumptions (*predpolozheniia*, "presuppositions") but shall be decreed only if the guilt of the accused is proved in the course of the trial (Article 309);

(f) that on appeal a conviction shall be vacated and the case terminated if the findings of the court are not confirmed by evidence considered in the judicial session (Articles 342 and 344).

In the words of the first commentary on the Code:

> . . . the accused is not considered guilty under the law unless his guilt is established by the judgment of the court as a result of the thorough, complete, and objective evaluation of the proofs gathered in the case. If the accused . . . does not prove his innocence, that does not mean that he is guilty . . .[17]

In addition, the Code provides that an acknowledgment of guilt by the accused may not serve as a basis of the accusation unless it is confirmed by the totality of proofs in the case (Article 77). Apart from this restriction upon the value of confessions, the 1960 Code adds only a few qualifications to the provisions of the 1923 Code regarding the evaluation of evidence; it is expressly stated that the inner conviction of the court must be based on a thorough, complete, and objec-

16. Decree of the Plenum of the Supreme Court of the USSR, June 9, 1934, 2(a), *Sbornik deistvuiushchikh postanovlenii plenuma i direktivnykh pisem Verkhovnogo suda SSSR 1924–1944 gg.* (Moscow, 1946), pp. 5–6.

17. Leningradskii Gosudarstvennyi Universitet, *Kommentarii k ugolovno-protsessual'nomu kodeksu RSFSR 1960 g.* (Leningrad, 1962).

tive consideration of all the circumstances of the case, and must be governed by law and by socialist legal consciousness (Article 71); the rule eliminating "formal proofs" is replaced by a more precise formulation forbidding the attaching of a previously established value to any evidence (Article 71); factual data communicated by a witness may not serve as evidence unless he can show the source of his knowledge of them (Article 74); and irrelevant questions are to be excluded (Article 280).

It would appear that all that is generally meant by "presumption of innocence" in Western legal systems (or at least in Continental European legal systems) is spelled out in the 1960 Code without the use of the phrase itself. (a) The accused has no obligation to present evidence. (b) No inference of guilt may be drawn from the mere fact of indictment. (c) Evidence supporting the indictment must be presented at trial, and the judgment of the court must be based on that evidence alone. (d) The court may not "assume" that the accused is guilty. (e) If proof of his guilt is not established he may not be convicted.

Why, then, does the Code studiously omit to state *expressis verbis* that "the burden of proof of the guilt of the accused shall rest on the prosecution," and that "the accused shall be presumed to be innocent until proved guilty"?[18]

To answer this question, it is necessary to analyze the terms "proof" and "burden." To "prove" may mean to persuade or it may mean to present evidence. Indeed, in Russian the word "to prove" and the word "to present evidence" have the same root (*dokazat'*, *dokazyvat'*). A "burden" may mean a risk or it may mean an obligation. The burden of proof in criminal cases is generally understood in the United States as meaning *either* the risk that the court will not be persuaded that the accused is guilty (a risk borne by the prosecution) *or* the risk that evidence will not be produced (a risk borne by the prosecution with respect to most issues but borne by the defendant with respect to some: for example, the defendant may have the risk of not going forward with evidence of his insanity, in the sense that in the absence of such evidence he will be considered

18. Indeed, the doctrine of "presumption of innocence" was denounced as a "worm-eaten dogma of bourgeois doctrine" by one of the deputies at the session of the USSR Supreme Soviet which adopted the Fundamental Principles of Criminal Procedure. Speech by Deputy B. S. Sharkov, Pravda, December 27, 1958, p. 5; reprinted in *CDSP*, February 11, 1959, pp. 9–10. Such statements led many Western writers to charge that the presumption of innocence does not exist under Soviet law. When in 1964 the President of the Supreme Court of the USSR emphasized that an accused may not be deemed guilty until his guilt is proved in court, this was widely reported in the United States as a change in Soviet law. See A. Gorkin, "O sotsialisticheskom pravosudii," Izvestia, December 2, 1964, p. 3. In fact Soviet law had not changed in this respect between 1958 and 1965. The dispute among Soviet jurists over whether or not Soviet law recognizes a presumption of innocence has raged for several decades and is largely the result of a semantic confusion rather than a conflict over legal policy or legal philosophy, as the discussion in the text is intended to show. A contrary view is taken in George P. Fletcher, "The Presumption of Innocence in the Soviet Union," *UCLA Law Review* 15: 1203 (1968); see reply by Harold J. Berman and John B. Quigley, Jr., "Comment on the Presumption of Innocence Under Soviet Law," *id.*, pp. 1230–1239. Fletcher argues that there is an institutional conflict between the Procuracy and other branches of the legal profession, with the Procuracy opposing the presumption as inconsistent with the requirement that it must be convinced of the accused's guilt in order to support the indictment. This view, however, is refuted by the fact that leading officials of the Procuracy support the presumption and state that it exists in Soviet law.

sane, although once any evidence of insanity is produced the prosecution has the risk of nonpersuasion, in the sense that the defendant will be acquitted if the court – or jury – is not persuaded that he was sane).

Under the 1960 RSFSR Code of Criminal Procedure it is entirely clear that the accused may not be convicted if the court is not persuaded by the evidence that he is guilty. In this sense, the risk of nonpersuasion is on the prosecution. To say that the prosecution has the burden of proof would nevertheless be misleading, because of the second meaning of the word "proof" (namely, going forward with evidence) and the second meaning of the word "burden" (namely, obligation). In English and American criminal procedure, it is the prosecution that has the obligation to present evidence of the defendant's guilt with respect to almost all issues (the issue of insanity is an exception). If the prosecution presents no evidence, the defendant must be acquitted; and the prosecution cannot call the defendant as a witness (although it may, of course, cross-examine him if he takes the stand). In the Soviet system of criminal procedure, however, as in that of most European countries, evidence is elicited in the first instance by the court itself. The court calls the defendant (who is not considered to be a witness), the victim (who in Soviet procedure is also not considered to be a witness), experts (who are also not considered to be witnesses), witnesses, and others. The court first puts questions to the accused, the victim, the witnesses, the experts; the prosecutor, the victim, defense counsel, the defendant himself, may put additional questions. If, for example, it appears that a particular person saw the crime committed, and neither the prosecutor nor defense counsel asks that that person be summoned to testify, the court is obliged to summon him on its own initiative and to put questions to him; or if it appears that the accused may or may not have been in another place at the time the crime was committed, and neither the prosecutor nor defense counsel chooses to ask him whether that was so, the court itself is obliged to ask him. The procedure is in the first instance "inquisitorial"; the trial is called a "judicial investigation" (*sudebnoe sledstvie*) or an "examination" (*razbiratel'stvo*). There are, indeed, important adversary ("accusatorial") aspects (as there are important inquisitorial aspects in English and American procedure), but these do not include the risk that the prosecution will lose the case on legal grounds because of its failure to go forward with proof. *Indeed, under the 1960 Code, if the procurator decides to withdraw from the case because he reaches the conclusion, during trial, that the evidence does not establish the accused's guilt, the court is nevertheless bound to go on conducting the trial without him* (Article 248)! In the light of this rule, and of the entire system of trial procedure, an express provision to the effect that "the burden of proof rests on the prosecution" would be misleading. Not only the Soviet but other European codes as well omit any such express provision, although legal writers both in the Soviet Union and in countries of Western Europe will often state in treatises – as a general truth – that the burden of proof (*onus probandi*) rests on the accuser and not on the accused.

The RSFSR Code states that "the obligation of proof may not be transferred to the accused" (Article 20). But it does not say from whom it may not be transferred. If it did, it would have to say: from the court, the prosecution, the witnesses, experts, and other participants in the trial, all of whom have the obligation either of eliciting or of presenting evidence. Indeed, the Code expressly requires a witness not only to answer questions put to him but also to tell all he knows about the case (Article 73). Thus all participants in the trial have "the obligation of proof" – in the sense of the duty to facilitate the production of evidence – *except the accused.* It is the last phrase that the 1960 RSFSR Code of Criminal Procedure, following the 1958 USSR Fundamental Principles of Criminal Procedure, emphasizes in Article 20. The accused need not speak. If he refuses to speak, his silence alone may not convict him. These propositions, absent from the 1923 Code, are directed against the abuses of Soviet judicial procedure characteristic of the Stalin era. They express a revulsion against practices which were in violation of the spirit of the 1923 Code – against such rulings, for example, as that of the USSR Supreme Court in 1934, mentioned above, which classified causing a shortage of social property as stealing unless there was proof that the accused did not appropriate the property and use it in his own interests. In other words, if there were shortages caused by the accused and he remained silent, or spoke ineffectively, as to whether he appropriated them, he was to be convicted of stealing.

There remains the question whether the Soviet prosecutor has the obligation to persuade the court that the accused is guilty – and not merely the obligation to present evidence. Here again, Soviet (and European) concepts of the criminal trial do not match American (and English) concepts. The Soviet prosecutor does, of course, and is supposed to, present arguments to the court showing how the evidence leads to the conclusion that the accused is guilty; in this the Soviet prosecutor is no different from his American counterpart. And the Soviet court, like the American court, is not supposed to convict the accused unless it finds the evidence of his guilt to be completely convincing.[19] Yet there is a psychological difference resulting from, and reflected in, the different systems of procedure. The Soviet (and European) legal concept of persuasion seems to be different from the Anglo-American: in requiring the judge to evaluate evidence solely according to his inner conviction, the Soviet and European codes suggest that the process of reaching a conclusion is primarily one in which the evidence itself, the data presented at the trial, forms an impression of guilt or innocence on the judge's mind rather than primarily one in which the two sides compete in attempting to be persuasive and the court weighs the conflicting evidence and the competing arguments. The rejection of formal rules of exclusion of evidence and of predetermined evaluations of various kinds of evidence reinforces the idea of a free decision. The court must persuade itself, so to speak, on the basis

19. Soviet law, like other European systems, does not distinguish between degrees of proof (proof by a preponderance of the evidence, proof by clear and convincing evidence, proof beyond a reasonable doubt). In all cases, civil as well as criminal, the court must be "convinced" – and that means, according to Soviet writers, that the court must have no doubts whatsoever. Soviet jurists deny that there can be frivolous or unreasonable doubts; they state that so-called frivolous doubts are not doubts, and that the Anglo-American standard "beyond a reasonable doubt" is too vague. See M. S. Strogovich, *Material'naia istina v sovetskom ugolovnom protsesse* (Moscow, 1955), pp. 128–133. The Soviet analysis of the phrase "reasonable doubt" is handicapped by the absence in Russian of an exact equivalent for the word "reasonable." In addition, Professor Strogovich, in the work cited, fails to recognize that there is a standard of proof by clear and convincing evidence, and that the "reasonable doubt" standard goes still further than that in requiring proof of guilt.

of the evidence presented. Perhaps it may be said that European doctrine emphasizes the subjective aspect of the decision-making process ("inner conviction") and Anglo-American doctrine emphasizes the objective aspect ("weight of the evidence").

Finally, the phrase "presumption of innocence," though popular with some leading Soviet jurists, also may suggest formal rules of evidence that are alien to Soviet criminal trial procedure. Theoretically, there are no presumptions in Soviet criminal law. To this must be added the awkwardness of the phrase in Russian: *on prezumiruetsia nevinovnym* is far stronger in Russian ears than the literal equivalent – "he is presumed innocent" – is in English or American ears. Or to put it otherwise, the technical meaning of the Latin word "presumed" has penetrated more deeply into our consciousness than into the Soviet. Soviet citizens and even Soviet lawyers are apt very quickly to translate "presumed" as "considered," and to say *on schitaetsia nevinovnym* – "he is considered innocent." Indeed, in a 1946 case the Plenum of the USSR Supreme Court itself, in reversing a conviction, stated that the lower court's decision violated "the basic principles of Soviet criminal procedure, according to which any accused person is considered innocent so long as his guilt is not proved in the legally established order." Yet to say that the accused "is considered" innocent is clearly inaccurate, for the prosecutor, at least, "considers" him guilty, and so does the preliminary session of the court that confirms the indictment, while the trial court has – as yet – no opinion at all in the matter. Indeed, under Soviet law the prosecutor may not prosecute unless he is entirely convinced of the guilt of the accused; "probable cause" to believe him guilty – as in the American and some European systems – is not enough.

Nevertheless, Soviet legal scholars and Soviet courts do occasionally state without qualification that "under Soviet law the accused is considered innocent until proved guilty," and the maxim *In dubio pro reo*, signifying that all doubts must be resolved in favor of the accused, is universally accepted as an expression of Soviet legal doctrine.

It is possible that the weakness of the Latin influence upon the Russian language, and the weakness of rules of evaluation of evidence, combined with a system of trial procedure in which all participants except the accused share the obligation of eliciting or presenting evidence and there are no procedural risks of nonpersuasion – it is possible that these circumstances render the phrase "presumption of innocence" inappropriate, although to say that "there is no presumption of innocence" in Soviet law would be equally incorrect. To put it more precisely, Soviet law embodies the presumption of innocence in the general sense of that phrase but not in the technical meaning attached to it in English and American law. In any event, the RSFSR Code of Criminal Procedure seems to have gone as far as it is possible to go, in a Continental system of trial procedure, to protect the accused against a conviction supported only by accusations and without convincing proof of guilt.[20]

20. It should be noted that the phrase "presumption of innocence" (like "burden of proof") is a term found in the writings of Continental European legal scholars but not generally in Continental European criminal or criminal procedure codes or statutes.

(9) **Right of Appeal and Protection of Rights of the Accused on Appeal and on Supervisory Review.** The 1923 Code of Criminal Procedure provided for the trial of cases in the people's courts, with the right of appeal to the next higher instance (provincial courts, later renamed regional courts, or their equivalent) (Article 344). As in other European systems, either the accused or the prosecution could appeal. More important cases could be tried in first instance in the provincial (regional) or other higher courts, with right of appeal to the Supreme Court of the RSFSR (Articles 380ff., 401). However, decisions in cases tried by the Supreme Court of the RSFSR, which was given original jurisdiction in "cases of exceptional importance" (Article 449), were not subject to appeal, since there was no higher RSFSR court. Similarly, under the 1923 Statute on the Supreme Court of the USSR, that court was given original jurisdiction (both civil and criminal) in certain cases involving high officials and in "cases of exceptional importance" involving persons of more than one union republic, and its decisions in such cases were not subject to appeal.[21]

Only one appeal was permitted. Though called "cassation" (*kassatsiia*), it consisted in a review of the facts as well as the law, and indeed, the appellate court could hear new evidence; nor was the appellate court limited to affirming the decision or remanding the case for a new trial – it could also render a new decision, either increasing or reducing the sentence, or applying a different law.[22]

Alongside this system of appeals was another system of review of decisions, called "supervisory" (*v poriadke nadzora*, "by way of supervision"). Article 427 of the 1923 RSFSR Code of Criminal Procedure provided that the president of the provincial court and the provincial or district procurator had the right to remove any case tried in a people's court, during trial or thereafter, to the provincial court for consideration by way of supervision. Article 429 provided that such removal could take place without any time limits. Similarly, under Article 440, the President or Vice-President of the RSFSR Supreme Court or the RSFSR Procurator or Deputy Procurator was given the right to remove any case from any court to the RSFSR Supreme Court.

In addition, under the 1923 Statute on the Supreme Court of the USSR, that court had the power to review by way of supervision all decisions of the supreme courts of the union republics insofar as they contradicted all-union law, and to "protest" such decisions to the Presidium of the Central Executive Committee of the USSR.

21. Statute on the Supreme Court of the USSR, November 23, 1923, *SZ* (1924), no. 19, art. 183(o), Articles 2, 4.

22. The term *kassatsiia* was used in prerevolutionary Russian law, having been borrowed from French law. Under French law, *cassation* is distinguished from appeal (*appel*), being limited generally to a review of errors of law, the reviewing court having power to remand the case for retrial but generally not to dispose of it finally. An appeal, on the other hand, may be on grounds both of error of law and error of fact, and the reviewing court may finally dispose of the case. The prerevolutionary Russian law maintained the distinction between cassation (*kassatsiia*) and appeal (*zhaloba*). The Soviets kept the linguistic distinction between the two terms but confused them in practice. The confusion is now codified in the phrase "cassational appeal" (*kassatsionnaia zhaloba*); cf. RSFSR Code of Criminal Procedure, Article 325. Appeal by the prosecution is called "cassational protest" (*kassatsionnyi protest*) (*ibid.*).

Thus in contrast with the rule of only one *appeal*, a case could go *by way of supervision* from the people's court through the provincial court, supreme court of autonomous republic, RSFSR Supreme Court, and USSR Supreme Court, and ultimately to the Presidium of the Central Executive Committee. Moreover, within the higher courts there were both criminal and plenary sessions, with possibility of removal of a case from the former to the latter.

The 1958 Fundamental Principles of Criminal Procedure and the 1960 RSFSR Code of Criminal Procedure retain the dual system of appeal and review by way of supervision (Articles 325–355, 371–383). The parties are limited to one appeal (called a "cassational appeal" or, if brought by the procurator, a "cassational protest"), and decisions in cases tried originally in the RSFSR Supreme Court or in the USSR Supreme Court are "final," that is, may not be "appealed." However, all decisions may be "protested" for review "by way of supervision" either by the Procuracy or by the presidents or vice-presidents of high courts. An "appeal" is, in effect, a second trial of the case; although the defendant and witnesses are not usually permitted to testify, the procurator and defense counsel argue evidence to the court, and new written testimony may be presented. In a supervisory review the court considers questions both of fact and of law, but it confines itself to the record of the case, and defense counsel (or the accused himself) may only appear if summoned by the court (Article 377).

However, the 1960 RSFSR Code of Criminal Procedure places several important limitations on review by way of supervision: (a) protests on the grounds of lightness of the sentence, termination of the case, or acquittal, must be brought within a year (Article 373); (b) the court considering a case by way of supervision may not itself increase the punishment or apply a law governing a graver crime than the one under which the accused was sentenced (Article 380); (c) the court considering a case by way of supervision may not alter the findings of fact, the rulings on the weight of evidence, the decision of guilt or innocence, the application of law, or the sentence, but may only remand the case for retrial or a new investigation, or else reduce the sentence or else dismiss the protest (Article 380).

The 1960 Code also gives more protection to the accused who takes an appeal. The court, on appeal by the accused, may not increase the punishment or apply a law governing a graver crime (Article 353). However, the appellate judge may inform the president of the court of circumstances which may lead the president to protest the appellate decision to a higher instance by way of supervision, and in the supervisory instance the court may remand the case for retrial with instructions indicating that the sentence was too light or that a law governing a graver crime was applicable. On retrial after the supervisory review, in contrast to retrial after appeal by the accused, the court of first instance has power to increase the punishment or apply a law governing a graver crime (Article 382). Thus there remains a danger for the accused that his appeal will result – indirectly, through supervisory review of the appellate decision – in a worsening of his position.

(10) Introduction of the Concept of "Rights of the Accused" and Expansion of Such Rights at all Stages of Criminal Procedure. The 1923 RSFSR Code of Criminal Procedure contained no systematic provision concerning the rights of the accused. (Indeed, it even omitted to provide expressly for right to counsel, although that particular omission was supplied in part by the 1924 USSR Fundamental Principles of Criminal Procedure and subsequently by Article 111 of the 1936 Constitution.) The concept of "rights of the accused" was introduced in legislation only by the 1958 USSR Fundamental Principles of Criminal Procedure and the 1960 RSFSR Code of Criminal Procedure. The latter systematically states in a single article the rights of the accused: to know of what he is accused, to give explanations concerning the accusation, to present evidence, to submit petitions, to become acquainted with all materials of the case at the conclusion of the preliminary investigation, to have defense counsel, to participate in the trial, to present challenges, to bring complaints against acts and decisions of the person conducting the inquiry, the investigator, the procurator and the court, and to have the last word at the trial (Article 46).

This charter of rights of the accused is elaborated in many other articles. Article 19, guaranteeing the right to defense, expressly requires the court procurator, and person conducting an inquiry to secure the protection of the accused's personal and property rights. Articles 218–220 provide for a system of complaints against abuses of the rights of the accused by agencies of inquiry, the investigator, or the procurator. Article 58 requires the court, procurator, investigator, and person conducting an inquiry to explain to all persons participating in the case their rights and to secure to them the opportunity to realize their rights. Although these and other similar provisions have a strong foundation in the theory of leading Soviet proceduralists and also a certain foundation in previous law, the means of implementation and safeguards are now much stronger than in the past. Their new wording reflects a revulsion against the abuses of the Stalin era: the drafters of those provisions knew from bitter experience what were the evils to be guarded against.

Other new features of the 1960 Code, reflecting a similar revulsion, are the prohibition against interrogation of the accused or of witnesses at night (Articles 150, 123); the prohibition against leading questions (Article 158); the elimination of house arrest as a preventive measure (cf. 1923 Code, Article 144, with 1960 Code, Article 89); the requirement that search and seizure may be conducted only with the permission of the procurator (although such permission may be given *ex post facto*) (Articles 167, 168); the provision that participation of defense counsel is obligatory in cases of minors, persons who do not know the language in which the proceedings are conducted, co-defendants whose interests conflict (unless all refuse counsel), mentally ill and physically defective persons, and persons indicted for crimes punishable by death (Article 49); the provision that when the accused is confined under guard, the agency of inquiry, investigator, procurator, or court is obliged to take measures to protect his minor children and his property (Article 98); and many other similar provisions.

It should be noted that the 1960 Code gives the accused the right to remain silent, but it does not extend this right to other parties or witnesses, who must testify fully even at the risk of self-incrimination (cf. Article 77 with Articles 72–76). Moreover, any person – including family members, priest, physician – may be required to testify against the accused except his lawyer or a person who is physically or mentally disabled (Article 73).

Correlative with the extension of the rights of the accused is the increased emphasis on objective proof. The requirement that a confession be confirmed by other evidence (Article 77) and the prohibition against leading questions in the investigation are complemented by the introduction of a provision for conducting investigative experiments (Article 183) and by the elaborate regulation of the use of experts (Articles 72–82, 184–194, 288–290) and of real evidence (Articles 83–86, 291). Article 71 provides that no evidence shall have a previously established force, and Article 74 limits the value of hearsay evidence. These provisions reflect a repudiation of the theory – now attributed to Vyshinsky – that the confession is the *regina probationum*, "the queen of evidence," and a departure from the heavy reliance on confessions that was characteristic of Soviet criminal procedure, especially in cases of counterrevolutionary crimes, during the Vyshinsky era, whether or not he actually expressed the theory now attributed to him.[23] Under the 1960 Code, Soviet law enforcement agencies must orient themselves to the development of more scientific methods of proof.

Many of the rights of the accused contained in the RSFSR Code of Criminal Procedure are omitted from Western European codes and from English and American legislation because they are taken for granted. To the Western European jurist, especially, both the RSFSR Criminal Code and Code of Criminal Procedure may seem pedantic or casuistic in their enunciation of specific definitions, doctrines, and rules that are conventionally reserved for elaboration in treatises, textbooks, and judicial decisions. As a guide to Soviet investigators of the police and Procuracy, to prosecutors, and to judges, however, the practical significance of the technique adopted by the drafters of the RSFSR Code is very great. The systematic statement of the procedural rights of the accused, coupled with the duty to explain his rights to him at various stages in the proceedings (cf. Articles 58, 149, 272, 273, 274) is to be read against a background of thirty years of abuse and terror. Soviet jurists have learned important lessons from this bitter experience, and have sought to incorporate those lessons into a document that reflects almost every issue of criminal justice confronted by modern man. By no means all those issues are resolved in a satisfactory manner, but they are all reflected and they are all dealt with practically, within the limits imposed by a society in which crime is rampant, in which the pressures against leniency in dealing with criminals are extremely strong, and in which the level of professional legal competence is often very low.

(11) Increased Emphasis on the Educational Role of Criminal Procedure. The high degree of procedural formality and regularity characteristic of English and American criminal trials is lacking in the Soviet system of trial procedure, as it is in the systems of most European countries. The 1960 RSFSR Code of Criminal

23. The value which Stalin himself placed on confessions (at least in political cases) is evidenced by statements attributed to him at the Twentieth and Twenty-Second Party Congresses in 1956 and 1961, including Khrushchev's statement that in the case of the so-called "doctors' plot" in 1952–1953 Stalin told the Minister of State Security, "If you do not obtain confessions from the doctors we will shorten you by a head." *The Anti-Stalin Campaign and International Communism* (New York, 1956), p. 64.

Procedure, like the 1923 Code, establishes a very broad framework for the presentation of evidence, with only a few restrictions upon the power of the court to organize and administer the trial as seems most appropriate under the circumstances.

The presiding judge must open the trial by stating (and if necessary, explaining) to the accused the charges against him and asking him whether or not he admits his guilt (Article 278). The court then hears the proposals of the parties concerning, and decides on, the order of proof (Article 279). Normally, the presentation of evidence begins with the questioning of the accused by the court, and this, in turn, commences with a proposal by the presiding judge that the accused testify concerning the accusation and concerning the circumstances of the case. After questioning by the court, the accused undergoes questioning by the prosecutor, the victim, the civil plaintiff, civil defendant and their counsel, and defense counsel; thereafter, he may be questioned by other persons accused jointly with him, and by their defense counsel (Article 280). The court may put questions to the accused at any time during the trial (Article 280). Witnesses are called, and must be informed of their civil duty to tell everything they know about the case and of their criminal responsibility for refusal to give testimony or for giving false testimony; no oath is administered, but the witnesses are required to sign a statement that their obligation and responsibility were explained to them (Article 282). The witnesses are questioned by the court, the parties, and their counsel; witnesses are excluded from the courtroom prior to their appearance to testify, in order that they may not hear each other's testimony in advance (Article 283). The victim is usually questioned before the witnesses (Article 287). There are no rules of exclusion of evidence except that, as mentioned earlier, factual statements by a witness are not admissible unless he can give the source of his knowledge and irrelevant evidence is not admissible (Articles 74, 280). Experts are, in effect, officers of the court; questions submitted to them by the parties in advance of trial must first be submitted to the court in writing for its approval (Article 288); at trial they may be questioned freely, first by the court and then by the prosecutor, victim, civil plaintiff, civil defendant, their counsel, defense counsel, and accused (Article 289). Real evidence is presented, and the court may take a view of the place where the crime was committed or other places (Articles 291, 293). With the court's permission, the parties may add other evidence and then, finally, the presiding judge announces that the judicial investigation (*sudebnoe sledstvie*) is finished (Article 294).

There remains, however, another stage in the examination (*razbiratel'stvo*) of the case: the arguments of the prosecutor, of the civil plaintiff, civil defendant or their representatives, and of the defense counsel (or, if there is no defense counsel, of the accused) (Article 295). These arguments may not be terminated by the court, although the court may stop argument concerning circumstances not relevant to the case (Article 295). Each party is also permitted to make a reply argument (Article 296). The parties and their counsel may then submit written proposals to the court concerning the disposition of the case (Article 298). Thereafter the accused has the right to give the "last word," which may not be interrupted by the court or anyone else (Article 297). Immediately after hearing the last word of the accused, the court retires to a conference room in order to arrive at a judgment, which the presiding judge or an assessor subsequently announces to those present in the courtroom (Articles 299 and 318).

These provisions are not, in essence, a departure from those of the 1923 Code, and they do not deviate substantially from prerevolutionary Russian or Continental European practice. Yet behind the "European" character of the Code provisions there lies a peculiarly "Soviet" quality in the trial proceedings, as well as in the proceedings prior to trial – a quality that has persisted through the five decades of Soviet history. This quality manifests itself in the provisions for participation of representatives of "social organizations" in criminal proceedings, as well as in the provision for two laymen (people's assessors) sitting as co-judges in the three-judge trial court. We shall discuss below these two features of the Soviet trial, as examples of the "popular" element in Soviet criminal procedure. In addition, however, the informality and flexibility of the trial serve to reinforce a characteristically Soviet concept of adjudication, which is expressed by Soviet jurists in terms of the educational role of the court, and which the author has elsewhere called a "parental" concept of law.[24] This concept finds reflection in Article 3 of the 1958 USSR Fundamental Principles of Court Organization (identical with Article 3 of the 1960 RSFSR Law on Court Organization), entitled "The Tasks of Courts," which states (in part):

> By all its activity the court shall educate citizens in the spirit of loyalty to the Motherland and to the cause of communism, and in the spirit of exact and undeviating execution of Soviet laws, of a protective attitude toward socialist property, of observance of labor discipline, of an honorable attitude toward state and social duty, and of respect for the rights, honor, and dignity of citizens and for rules of socialist communal life.

A similar but much more condensed statement of the educational task of the court (and of criminal procedure in general) is found in Article 2 of the 1960 RSFSR Code of Criminal Procedure. In addition, the 1960 Code refers to the educational role of the court in various other provisions. Thus Article 243 states that the chairman of the court, in directing the judicial session, shall "secure the educational influence of the trial," and in a 1963 commentary to the Code, edited by the then Minister of Justice of the RSFSR, the following annotation is given to the quoted phrase:[25]

> This concerns above all the educational influence of the trial upon the person before the court, with respect to whom the case is being examined.
>
> But this does not exhaust the matter. The educational influence of the trial should extend also to other participants in the judicial examination and also to persons present in the courtroom.

The concept of the educational role of the trial also finds expression in the provision for transfer of a case to another court for the purpose of "securing the

24. *Justice in the USSR: An Interpretation of Soviet Law*, rev. ed. (Cambridge, Mass., 1963), especially pp. 363ff.

25. V. A. Boldyrev, ed., *Kommentarii k ugolovno-protsessual'nomu kodeksu RSFSR 1960 g.* (Moscow, 1963).

educational role of the judicial examination" (Article 44); in the requirement that the court elucidate the causes and conditions facilitating the commission of the crime and take measures to eliminate them (Article 21); in the provision for special rulings by the court addressed to directors of institutions, enterprises, and organizations, or other persons, concerning the improper conduct of citizens and the breach by them of their social duty (Article 321); and in the provision for sending a copy of the judgment, in order to increase its educational influence, to the place of work, of study, or of residence of the convicted person (Article 359).

The causes and conditions that have facilitated the commission of the crime are subject to proof during the trial (Article 68). Wide use must be made of the help of the public in bringing them to light (Article 128). Proposals for eliminating them must be made in appropriate cases (Article 140).

Perhaps the most striking provision bearing upon the educational or parental function of the court is its power to initiate criminal proceedings itself in certain instances (Articles 255 and 256). In this connection it may also be noted that the procurator has the power to institute a civil suit in a criminal case in order to protect social interests (Article 29).

Not only the trial court but also the investigator and person conducting an inquiry, at earlier stages of the proceedings, are subject to requirements similar to those listed above, especially with respect to elucidating the causes and conditions of the crime and taking measures to eliminate them.

The duty to explain to the accused his rights, which is given so large a place in the 1960 Code, is also in part a function of an educational concept of law. Similarly the provision for termination of a criminal case if the accused person is no longer "socially dangerous" (Article 6) may reflect an educational or parental concept, although it may also reflect the idea that society need not take "measures of social defense" (to use the language of the 1923 Code, which contained a provision similar to Article 6) against a person who is not dangerous.

These and other provisions designed to effectuate the educational role of criminal proceedings, although not essentially new in Soviet law and practice, receive much clearer and more detailed expression and much greater emphasis in the 1960 Code than in previous Soviet legislation. They give a special significance to the informality and flexibility of trial procedure, and they broaden considerably the concept of what is relevant to the case (cf. Article 68).

(12) Popular Participation in Criminal Proceedings. The 1958 USSR Fundamental Principles of Criminal Procedure introduced the institutions of social accuser and social defense counsel (Article 41). These persons appear in the trial as representatives of "social organizations," as distinguished from "state organizations"; such social organizations include Communist Party organizations, Komsomol (Young Communist League) organizations, trade unions, the "collective" of workers at an enterprise or institution, the "collective" of members of a collective farm, the "collective" of students, faculty and staff of an educational institution, and other groups whose membership is voluntary and which are technically not part of the state apparatus. Any social organization may petition to have its representative appear in any criminal case, either as social accuser or as social defense counsel. The social accuser or defense counsel is supposed to represent the opinion of the collective which he represents. The admission of a social prosecutor or social defender, or both, to participation in the case is decided by the administrative session of the court prior to trial (1960 RSFSR Code of Criminal Procedure, Article 228). Their rights of participation under the Code are extremely broad, extending to the presenting of evidence, questioning of parties and witnesses, presenting petitions and challenges, presenting oral argument, and giving their opinions on the law and on the sentence (Article 250; cf. Articles 228, 236, 251, 276, 288, 291, 293–298).

Other new aspects of popular participation in criminal proceedings under the 1960 Code relate to the preliminary investigation. The investigator is given the right to notify social organizations, comrades' courts, collectives of workers, and others, concerning offenses committed by persons against whom criminal proceedings have been initiated (Article 113); to enlist the aid of the public during the preliminary investigation in order to uncover the commission of a crime as well as the causes and conditions that have facilitated its commission (Article 128); and to make proposals to enterprises, institutions and social organizations concerning the taking of measures to eliminate such causes and conditions (Article 140).

In addition, the provisions for transfer of criminal cases to comrades' courts, to commissions for cases of minors, and to social organizations as sureties (cf. Articles 7–10, 95, 304) all reflect a greatly increased tendency to enlist popular participation in the administration of criminal law.

That tendency is not entirely new, however. Perhaps the most stable feature of Soviet criminal procedure has been the requirement that criminal trials be conducted by a court consisting of a presiding professional judge and two people's assessors, chosen from the general population, each of the three having equal vote. In addition, comrades' courts existed from the first days of the Revolution, though they disappeared from about 1938 to 1951 and only began once again to flourish on a large scale in 1959. The practice of issuing special rulings in criminal cases, directed to organizations that in some way bear responsibility for matters disclosed in the course of the trial, is also not a new one, though it never before had so systematic a formulation in law.

The practice of holding court in an apartment house, factory, or other place which is closely connected with circumstances of the case is not expressly authorized in Soviet legislation, although it continues to be fairly widespread. Formerly such trials were often called "demonstration trials." Today they are referred to almost exclusively as "circuit" sessions (*vyezdnye sessii*) of the court.

A discussion of the educational and popular character of Soviet criminal trial procedure must also include reference, at least, to the educational and popular character of Soviet criminal law as a whole. The point can best be made, perhaps, by the following statistics: the 1962 official texts of the RSFSR Criminal Code and Code of Criminal Procedure were published in pocket editions in 200,000 copies each, at 26 kopeks (29¢) each, and the 1964 text of the Criminal Code in 265,000 copies and of the Code of Criminal Procedure in 85,000 copies, at 27 kopeks (30¢) each.

5 Changes in the 1960 RSFSR Codes, 1961-1972

THE CRIMINAL CODE

In the first eleven years after it went into effect – more precisely, from January 1, 1961, to March 1, 1972 – the RSFSR Crimal Code underwent changes affecting 98 of its articles.[1] Many of these changes were of minor significance, but others were substantial, reflecting basic changes in policy and outlook.

Perhaps the most important changes, and certainly the greatest flurry of changes, took place very soon after the Code went into effect. On the basis of USSR legislation enacted in 1961 and 1962, 48 articles of the RSFSR Criminal Code were either amended or added in 1962 and 1963 (46 in 1962, 2 in 1963). The remaining changes were spread out over the intervening years, with the largest numbers taking place in 1965, 1966, 1968, and 1969 (11, 9, 10, and 13 articles being affected in those years, respectively). All together, from January 1, 1961, to March 1, 1972, 28 new articles were added to the original 205 articles of the Special Part, one of the original articles (Article 212) was repealed, and 52 other articles of the Special Part were changed, some more than once. Two new articles (Articles 24-1 and 53-1) were added to the 63 original articles of the General Part, and 15 other articles of the General Part were amended.

The general tendency of the amendments was to increase the penalties for a great many crimes; to introduce a series of new crimes against the state, crimes against socialist property, official crimes, economic crimes, crimes against the system of administration, and crimes against public security; and to treat recidivists and juvenile offenders more severely. On the other hand, some of the amendments went in the direction of leniency, and still others were designed simply to increase the rationality and efficiency of the criminal law.

Under the 1960 Code as originally enacted, the death penalty was applicable to the following crimes: treason (Article 64); espionage (Article 65); terrorist acts

1. The following articles were affected: 10, 23, 24, 24-1, 27, 28, 39, 44, 45, 51, 53, 53-1, 54, 55, 57, 62, 63, 64, 65, 66, 67, 68, 69, 70, 71, 77, 77-1, 78, 86, 87, 88, 88-1, 88-2, 89, 93-1, 93-2, 96, 99-1, 103, 115, 115-1, 117, 124-1, 130, 131, 142, 144, 152-1, 154, 154-1, 154-2, 156, 158, 162, 166, 167, 169, 173, 174, 174-1, 181, 186, 189, 190, 190-1, 190-2, 190-3, 191, 191-1, 191-2, 192, 192-1, 193, 197-1, 198-1, 198-2, 205-1, 206, 208, 209, 209-1, 210, 211, 211-1, 211-2, 212, 212-1, 213-1, 217, 218-1, 222, 223, 224, 225, 227, 245, 255, 257.

(Articles 66 and 67); sabotage (Article 68); organizational activity directed to the commission of especially dangerous crimes against the state, or participation in an anti-Soviet organization (Article 72); especially dangerous crimes against the state committed against another working people's state (Article 77); intentional homicide committed under aggravating circumstances (Articles 102 and 240); and certain crimes committed in time of war or in a combat situation (cf. Articles 81, 238, 240, 247–249, 255, 260–264, 266, 267). In 1961 and 1962 USSR legislation (incorporated in the RSFSR Criminal Code on July 25, 1962) extended the death penalty to the following additional crimes: actions disrupting work of correctional labor institutions (Article 77–1); making or passing counterfeit money or securities (Article 87); violation of rules on currency transactions (Article 88); stealing state or social property on an especially large scale (Article 93–1); rape (Article 117); the taking of a bribe by an official (Article 172); and "infringing" (that is, taking or attempting to take) the life of a policeman or of a people's guard (Article 191–2).

For all but one of these crimes, the death penalty remained an optional alternative punishment, applicable only in extreme cases and always at the discretion of the court; under Article 191–2, however, it is apparently mandatory if the crime is committed under any of the aggravating circumstances listed in Article 39 – unless, under Article 43, exceptional circumstances and the personality of the guilty person give a basis for assigning a milder punishment. The death penalty was not affected by any of the amendments to the Code introduced after 1962.

Another change in the direction of harsher penalties was the establishment in 1962 of an additional period of exile for two to five years as a supplementary punishment in the case of a large number of crimes, including all the especially dangerous crimes against the state (Articles 64–73). Technically, exile is not a form of deprivation of freedom; nevertheless, the effect of the change has been to raise the maximum period of punishment from fifteen to twenty years for the most serious crimes and to add an additional maximum of five years to a number of crimes punishable by deprivation of freedom for less than fifteen years. In none of the articles amended or newly introduced after 1962 was it found necessary to stipulate exile as a supplementary punishment.

A third method of increasing penalties has been to increase the minimum and/or maximum periods of deprivation of freedom or correctional tasks, or to raise the minimum and/or maximum amounts of fines to be imposed, for a wide variety of crimes (cf. Articles 88–1, 88–2, 142, 173, 174, 193, 198–1, 206, 209, 211, 223).

As important as the increased penalties are the many new crimes created after the enactment of the 1960 Code, which are easily identified because they have been inserted into their appropriate places in the Code with an additional number (Articles 77–1, 93–1, 93–2, 99–1, 124–1, 152–1, 154–1, 154–2, 174–1, 190–1, 190–2, 190–3, 191–1, 191–2, 192–1, 197–1, 198–2, 205–1, 209–1, 211–2, 212–1, 213–1, 218–1; however, Articles 88–1 and 88–2 are adapted from the original version of Articles 189 and 190, and Article 211–1 is adapted from the repealed version of Article 212). Among the most important of these new crimes are criminally wrongful use or maintenance of agricultural equipment

(Article 99–1); divulging the secret of adoption (Article 124–1); additions to, and other distortions of, accounts concerning fulfillment of plans (Article 152–1); feeding bread to cattle or poultry (Article 154–1); circulation of fabrications known to be false which defame the Soviet state and social system (Article 190–1); organization of, or active participation in, group actions which violate public order (Article 190–3); resisting or insulting a policeman or people's guard (Articles 191–1 and 192–1); violation by foreigners and stateless persons of rules for movement on Soviet territory (Article 197–1); malicious refusal to take employment and to discontinue a parasitic existence (Article 209–1); and stealing of firearms, ammunition, or explosives (Article 218–1). Articles 190–1 and 190–3 and Article 209–1 are discussed below in detail.

In many instances, however, although no newly specified crime was introduced, a change in the definition of a crime under a pre-existing article resulted in a substantial expansion of its scope. Thus in 1962 Article 227, which had originally been titled "creation of a group that causes harm to the health of citizens" and had been directed at groups that "under the guise of preaching religious doctrines" engaged in practices harmful to health or to sexual morality, was renamed and expanded to include also "active participation" in a religious group whose activity is "connected with . . . inducing citizens to refuse social activity or performance of civic duties." Similarly, Article 142, which establishes criminal liability for violating laws on the separation of church and state, but does not specify what acts constitute such a violation, was supplemented in 1966 by a decree of the Presidium of the RSFSR Supreme Soviet enumerating a series of acts that fall within the ambit of Article 142, including, on the one hand, "commission of deceptive actions for the purpose of arousing religious superstitions in the masses of the population" and, on the other hand, "denial of work in . . . or discharge from . . . an educational institution [on the basis of] attitude toward religion."[2]

2. The following actions were declared to be violations of Article 142: compulsory exaction of contributions and taxes for the benefit of religious organizations or ministers of cult; mass dissemination, or preparing for the purpose of mass dissemination, of appeals, letters, tracts, or other documents that urge nonobservance of legislation on religious cults; commission of deceptive actions for the purpose of arousing religious superstitions among the masses of the population; organization or conduct of religious meetings, processions, and other religious ceremonies that violate the social order; organization or systematic conduct of studies of religion for the instruction of minors in violation of rules established by legislation; denial of work to a citizen or a refusal to accept him in an educational institution, discharge from work or exclusion from an educational institution, deprivation of privileges and immunities to citizens established by law, or other material limitations of the rights of citizens, on the basis of their attitude toward religion. *Vedomosti RSFSR* (1966), no. 12, item 221. In an edict of the same date (March 18, 1966) the RSFSR Supreme Soviet also imposed administrative responsibility (a fine not exceeding 50 rubles) for the violation of legislation on religious cults. *Vedomosti RSFSR* (1966), no. 12, item 219.

Articles 142, 143, and 227 of the 1960 RSFSR Criminal Code superseded a special chapter "On Violations of Rules Concerning the Separation of Church from State and of School from Church" in the 1922 and 1926 RSFSR Criminal Codes, which had contained a long list of illegal actions in this sphere. Many Soviet courts assumed that the omission of such a list meant that any violation of the laws of separation of church from state and of school from church should be treated as falling within Article 142 of the 1960 Code. Soviet commentators regarded the special decree of 1966 as clarifying and narrowing the scope of Article 142 as it had been applied in judicial practice. See V. Klochkov, "Zakonodatel'stvo o

The crime of hooliganism also became broader in scope when Article 206 of the Code was amended in 1966. Petty hooliganism was made criminally punishable after administrative pressure had been applied once for this offense during the course of a year, instead of twice as was formerly the case, and the minimum penalties were increased from "correctional tasks for a term not exceeding [which means from three months to] one year or a fine not exceeding 50 rubles" to "correctional tasks for a term of [six months to one year] or a fine from 30 to 50 rubles." In addition, the definition of malicious hooliganism was broadened to include actions connected with resisting citizens who are restraining hooligan acts, and the minimum penalty for malicious hooliganism was increased from deprivation of freedom for three months to deprivation of freedom for one year. Special provision was also made for the first time for hooligan actions committed with the use of firearms, knives, brass knuckles, other side arms, or objects especially adapted to inflict bodily injury; persons convicted face deprivation of freedom for three to seven years.

Also Article 193, which makes it a crime to threaten or use force against an official or social worker, was expanded in 1966 to include force against "a citizen in connection with his participation in the restraint or prevention of a crime or antisocial offense."

A final example of the creation of new crimes without adding to the number of articles in the Code was the expansion in 1962 of the list of crimes whose concealment is itself a crime (Article 189) to include the stealing of state property by swindling, speculation under aggravating circumstances, taking or giving a bribe, and several other types of offenses.

Some of the increases in penalties and in the number and scope of crimes were no doubt a reaction against what seemed to many Soviet people, including ordinary citizens as well as political leaders, an excessive leniency in certain Code provisions as originally enacted. One example of such leniency was the original Article 103, under which intentional homicide was punishable by deprivation of freedom for a term not exceeding ten years. Since no minimum punishment was assigned under this provision, a person who intentionally killed his enemy in cold blood could, theoretically, receive a sentence of three months' deprivation of freedom (cf. Article 24); moreover, he would be eligible for parole after serving two thirds of his sentence (Article 53). Presumably few Soviet citizens were made unhappy by the 1962 amendment of Article 103, which established a minimum punishment of three years' deprivation of freedom for intentional homicide, while retaining the three months' minimum for intentional homicide committed in a state of strong mental agitation (Article 104). (Homicide committed while

religioznykh kul'takh i otvetstvennost' za ego narusheniia," *Sotsialisticheskaia zakonnost'* (1966), no. 10, pp. 36–42. However, the violations listed in the 1966 decree include some not mentioned in the earlier codes (e.g., preparing or disseminating appeals, etc., urging nonobservance of legislation on religious cults) or contain broader definitions than previous legislation (e.g., ministers were not expressly mentioned prior to 1966 in connection with compulsory contributions). In fact, Article 142 has been used as a basis of systematic repression of the "Initiative Group" (*Initsiativniki*), a large sect which has broken off from the officially recognized Baptist Church.

exceeding the limits of necessary defense remains punishable, as a minimum, by correctional tasks, under Article 105). Similarly, one would not suppose that most Soviet citizens were distressed by stricter measures taken against male juvenile offenders in 1966 and 1969 (cf. Articles 24 and 206, discussed later).

The trend toward increased severity in the Code was due in part, and perhaps primarily, to a continuing concern over the crime rate. Soviet jurists have always claimed that the crime rate has been dropping; however, no detailed crime statistics have been published since the 1920's, and this fact in itself reinforces the suspicion, shared by some Soviet citizens, that there was throughout the 1960's a persistent upward trend in criminal activity, at least insofar as major offenders and serious crimes were concerned.

At the same time, other changes reflect a renewed effort to deal more gently, and if possible by informal, nonpenal methods, with those guilty of minor offenses committed for the first time. Following the 1963 amendments to the Statute on Comrades' Courts, which substantially expanded their jurisdiction, [3] Article 51 of the Criminal Code was amended to provide that cases could be transferred to comrades' courts under Article 144 (theft), where the charge is theft of inexpensive articles of consumption and everyday life personally owned by another member of the same collective, and Article 158 (bootlegging), where the charge is making home-brewed vodka or other strong alcoholic beverage in a small quantity and without the purpose of supplying it. Article 93–2 was added to the Code in January 1965 to permit the imposition of a fine in cases of petty stealing of state or social property committed for the first time: this bridged a gap between measures of social pressure applied by comrades' courts in such cases (as provided by the 1963 amendments to the Statute on Comrades' Courts) and deprivation of freedom under Articles 89, 92, and 93 of the Criminal Code. Also Article 245 of the Criminal Code was amended in January 1965 to permit the application of the rules of the Disciplinary Code of the Armed Forces of the USSR for unwarranted absence of military personnel where there are mitigating circumstances. In addition, under the new Articles 154–1 (enacted in 1963), 197–1 and 198–2 (enacted in 1966), and 154–2 (enacted in 1970), persons may be punished only after administrative sanctions have been applied (in some instances, twice applied), unless the criminal acts were committed systematically or on a large scale. Under Article 212–1, enacted in July 1965, which introduced into the Code the crime of driving away a motor vehicle without the purpose of stealing it, the courts are given a wide latitude: for a first offense they may impose deprivation of freedom up to one year, correctional tasks up to one year, a fine of 100 rubles, or measures of social pressure.

Increased leniency is also reflected in the requirement that the crime for which an individual was once (as contrasted with twice or three times) previously sentenced to deprivation of freedom must have been of an aggravated nature in order for him to be deemed an especially dangerous recidivist when he again com-

3. See Berman and Spindler, *supra*, Chapter 1, note 18, p. 863 ff. ("Cases Considered by Comrades' Courts").

mits any of the enumerated crimes (Article 24). For example, a single prior conviction for violation of rules on currency transactions must have been under paragraph 2 of Article 88 (as a form of business or on a large scale) rather than under either paragraph 1 *or* 2, as was possible formerly, and in addition the guilty person must have been sentenced to at least five years' deprivation of freedom for his second crime. Similarly, in Article 53-1, requirements of aggravating circumstances have been added which narrow the range of criminal activities that make convicted persons ineligible for conditional early relief from punishment or replacement of punishment by milder punishment. However, conditional early relief from punishment has been made unavailable to persons convicted of malicious hooliganism with a dangerous weapon (Article 206 paragraph 2) and stealing of firearms, ammunition, and explosives when committed by assault (Article 218-1 paragraph 2). Also the new version of Article 55, adopted at the same time as Article 24-1, severely circumscribes release from punishment or replacement of punishment by milder punishment for offenders under the age of 18. On the whole, the new criteria correspond roughly to those laid down in Article 53-1 for adults.

Mention should also be made of the apparent discontinuance, or at least diminution, of the application of the death penalty in cases of large-scale currency violations, stealing of state property, and bribery. The Soviet press reported a great many such cases in 1961-64, but very few or none since the latter part of 1964. The end of this "campaign" may have been connected with the ouster of Khrushchev at that time.

The 1969 law on especially dangerous recidivists, incorporated as Article 24-1, is not only an example of the effort to stretch out the scale of severity and leniency of punishment to correspond to various gradations of criminality but is also a manifestation of a policy of characterizing offenders as a means to determine their treatment and to deter them by threat of extra penalty for future misconduct.

The original version of Article 24 relating to recidivists was ambiguous, and its provisions were often inconsistently or harshly applied. Although one could be designated an especially dangerous recidivist only by court judgment, the courts were given a very wide discretion in determining which recidivists were especially dangerous; moreover, they were not required to indicate in their written opinions the basis of such a determination. In many cases courts apparently assumed that a second offense was sufficient to invoke the article and meted out punishment accordingly, even though the defendant may have been convicted for two comparatively minor offenses.

Under the new Article 24-1 added penalties may only be imposed on a person who has previously been determined to be an especially dangerous recidivist in a separate proceeding prior to the commission of the new crime. Moreover, in determining whether a person should be deemed an especially dangerous recidivist the court must take into account not only (as before) his personality, the degree of social danger of the crimes committed, and "the circumstances of the case" but also the motives of the criminal, the extent to which he accomplished his criminal intentions, and the degree and character of his participation in the commission of the crimes. The basis of the court's decision must be explained in the judgment, and the court may not take into account a sentence for a crime committed by the accused while under 18 years of age nor a conviction canceled or quashed in the procedure established by law. If the criminal record of a person is subsequently canceled, then the designation of especially dangerous recidivist must also be removed.

Other noteworthy amendments to the Code provisions concerning punishment include narrowing Article 28 ("consequences of evasion of correctional tasks") to cover malicious evasion only, and increasing the penalty by replacing the unserved sentence with deprivation of freedom for the *same* period instead of (as before) every three days of the unserved term being replaced by one day of deprivation of freedom; making drunkenness in itself a circumstance aggravating criminal responsibility under Article 39; and requiring in Articles 44, 45, and 54 that for persons to lose the benefits of (what we call) probation and parole the commission of a new crime must be intentional, and not (as before) merely "of the same kind or of equal gravity" (which would include negligent crimes).

Finally, many changes in the Criminal Code during the 1960's were the result of the enactment of separate all-union or union-republican statutes dealing in part with law enforcement. Thus Article 63(6), concerning the treatment of juvenile offenders, was modified to empower a court to appoint a social educator pursuant to the Statute on Social Educators of Minors.[4] Malicious violation of the newly adopted Statute on Administrative Supervision by Police Agencies Over Persons Released from Places of Deprivation of Freedom was made criminally punishable in Article 198–2.[5] Changes in the General Part also were made in 1969 in connection with the adoption of Fundamental Principles of Correctional Labor Legislation of the USSR and of the Union Republics,[6] which cover virtually all aspects of the execution of punishment, and the procedure and conditions for serving punishment, ranging from the introduction of various regimens of correctional and educational labor in places of confinement to the enlisting of the public in the reform of convicted persons (cf. Articles 24, 24–1, 27, 28, 39, 44, 45, 53, 53–1, 54, 55, 57).

The Antiparasite Law. One of the significant changes in Soviet criminal law in the first decade after the adoption of the RSFSR Criminal Code was the introduction, in February 1970, of Article 209–1, incorporating as a crime what had previously constituted the "administrative offense" of "leading an antisocial, parasitic way of life."

The antiparasite laws, as they have been called in the West, were first introduced in the smaller Soviet republics in 1957, and in the major republics in

4. *Vedomosti RSFSR* (1967), no. 51, item 1239.

5. Edict of the Presidium of the Supreme Soviet of the USSR, July 26, 1966, *Vedomosti SSSR* (1966), no. 30, item 597. The Statute was amended by an edict of June 12, 1970. See *Vedomosti SSSR* (1970), no. 24, item 206.

6. *Vedomosti SSSR* (1969), no. 29, item 247. By a law of December 18, 1970, a Correctional Labor Code of the RSFSR was adopted, to take effect June 1, 1971. *Vedomosti RSFSR* (1970), no. 51, item 1220. Presumably some further changes in the RSFSR Criminal Code will be required to implement the new Correctional Labor Code.

1961.[7] The RSFSR Edict of May 4, 1961,[8] declared in its preamble that it was directed against persons "living on nonlabor income (*netrudovoi dokhod*) and enriching themselves at the expense of the state," who "engage in forbidden businesses, private enterprise, speculation and begging, who derive nonlabor income from the exploitation of personal automobiles, employ hired labor," etc. The operative part of the edict provided that persons who "avoid socially useful work," derive nonlabor income from the exploitation of land plots, automobiles, or housing, or commit "other antisocial acts which enable them to lead a parasitic way of life" (*paraziticheskii obraz zhizni*) could be tried by a court and subjected to "resettlement" (*vyselenie*, literally "ex-settlement" or "eviction") in specially designated localities for two to five years, with confiscation of property acquired by nonlabor means and with the obligation to work at the place of resettlement. The same "administrative measure," as it was called, to distinguish it from criminal punishment, could be applied by the collectives of working people of enterprises, organizations, or collective farms to persons who took jobs or were members of collective farms "only for the sake of appearances" and who in fact were committing "antisocial acts that enable them to lead a parasitic way of life." The decision of a collective was subject to confirmation by the local soviet executive committee and was not reviewable in court.

The language of the statute was so broad and vague that it came to be applied in some instances to perfectly law-abiding, hard-working people who in some way offended the authorities, including in one case a young Leningrad poet, Joseph Brodsky, whose only offense was that his poetry was politically unacceptable.[9]

Partly as a result of pressure by the higher courts to curb abuses, the 1961 edict was extensively revised in September 1965.[10] The preamble was changed to exclude the earlier references to specific nefarious activities; instead it merely referred to people who "stubbornly do not wish to work honestly and who lead an antisocial parasitic way of life." Such persons were subject to assignment — by the local soviet executive committee — to work in enterprises or construction sites located within the region, territory, or autonomous republic of their permanent residence, unless they resided in the city or region of Moscow or the city of Leningrad, in which case they were subject to resettlement and assignment to work in a special locale for two to five years. A decree of resettlement could be

7. See A. S. Shliapochnikov, "Sovetskoe zakonodatel'stvo i obshchestvernost' v borbe o paraziticheskimi elementami," *Sovetskoe gosudarstvo i pravo* (1961), no. 8, pp. 61–70.

8. *Vedomosti RSFSR* (1961), no. 26, item 371. This edict is translated in full in H. J. Berman, *Justice in the USSR: An Interpretation of Soviet Law*, rev. ed. (Cambridge, Mass., 1963), pp. 291–294.

9. The Brodsky case is discussed, and the record reproduced in part, in Samuel Kucherov, *The Organs of Soviet Administration of Justice* (Leiden, 1970), pp. 212–234. Brodsky was sentenced in March 1964 to serve five years in Arkhangelsk. He worked there as an agricultural laborer until September 1965, when he was released. See *infra*, note 10.

10. *Vedomosti RSFSR* (1965), no. 38, item 932. The amendments may have been a factor in the release of Brodsky (*supra*, note 9). It is also of interest that shortly before, in July 1965, the conviction of another celebrated "parasite," Andrei Amalrik, was reversed on appeal. See Amalrik, *Involuntary Journey to Siberia* (New York, 1970), p. 282.

rendered only by a court and only if the person concerned had not begun to work within one month after having received a warning from police agencies or a social organization.

Refusal to take a job assigned by the local soviet executive committee or evasion of resettlement ordered by a court was declared to be a criminal offense, punishable by correctional tasks up to one year with withholding of 10 percent of wages. Evasion of such correctional tasks (which in practice almost always consist of a monetary penalty payable periodically) was made punishable by deprivation of freedom under Article 28 of the Criminal Code.

The 1965 amendments were a significant improvement over the 1961 edict. The modification of the preamble excluded a variety of acts which in fact were already punishable under the Criminal Code; it thereby reduced the possibility of circumventing the Code of Criminal Procedure by charging a person with leading a parasitic existence instead of initiating criminal proceedings. The abolition of resettlement except for residents of Moscow and Leningrad was an important step in the right direction and at least gave some relief to communities which previously had been compelled to receive vagrants, prostitutes, speculators, and other refractory persons – including, occasionally, political dissidents – from afar. Moreover, the elimination of the power of collectives of working people to order the resettlement of persons who worked "only for the sake of appearances" removed the vigilante overtones of the 1961 edict. Finally, the creation of a one-month period to find work after a warning helped to reduce abuses by over-zealous police agencies or social organizations. On the other hand, the penalty of correctional tasks seems peculiarly inappropriate for the offense of refusing to take a job; presumably there are no wages to be withheld, and to assign work instead is merely to substitute the order of a court for that of the soviet executive committee.

According to informal reports from Soviet sources, the reforms of 1965 had the effect of almost eliminating parasite cases from the Soviet courts; that is, almost all persons charged with parasitism responded to administrative warnings or at least avoided criminal evasion of the order to take a job.[11] Nevertheless, there were substantial difficulties in implementing the amended law. The system of warnings was subject to abuse in that there was no requirement that such warnings be in writing; and in the case of social organizations there was often no formal record concerning the exact nature and timing of a warning. Often the police were not aware of the activities of social organizations in these matters. Moreover, while enterprises and construction sites were obliged to find work for persons assigned to them, they were not obliged to notify anyone if a person assigned to them was subsequently discharged or quit his job. It was not uncommon for "parasites" to work a week or so and then resume their previous life-style. In addition, the absence of any time-limitations on the investigation by the police or disposition by the local soviet executive committee created an irrestible

11. See author's interview with Judge L. N. Smirnov reported in the *Manchester Guardian*, August 31, 1966.

temptation to cover up all the difficulties by inordinate delays in the proceedings.[12]

Apart from problems of enforcement, there were also problems of legal principle that remained. The administrative sanction of resettlement (*vyselenie*), though restricted to residents of Moscow and Leningrad, continued to be objectionable on the grounds that it was only a disguise for the criminal sanction of banishment (*vysylka*) and that it was so much more severe than other administrative measures as to reflect a difference in quality. Obnoxious also was the imposition of criminal liability for disobedience to an administrative order.

By an edict of February 14, 1970, the antiparasite law was finally placed in the Criminal Code.[13] Now for the first time in Soviet history it was made a crime (and not merely an administrative offense) for an adult able-bodied citizen not to work. However, there are two important limitations set on this crime. First, to be guilty one must not only "avoid socially useful work" but also "lead an antisocial parasitic way of life"; this excludes a large undefined class of people, such as persons temporarily out of work, housewives, pensioners (women over 55 and men over 60), and others. Second, a procedure is established under which the shirker must be (a) officially warned by agencies of internal affairs (the police), (b) given fifteen days to find work, and (c) on failure to do so, assigned by the local soviet executive committee to work at an enterprise or construction site situated in the district of his permanent residence or in another locale within that particular region, territory, or autonomous republic. It is his failure to obey the decision of the local soviet executive committee to take the proffered employment and the continuance of his "parasitic way of life" that gives rise to criminal liability under Article 209-1 of the RSFSR Criminal Code, with punishment by deprivation of freedom up to one year or correctional tasks for the same term.

Thus the sanction of resettlement has been entirely eliminated and full control over trial and punishment has been vested in the courts, subject to all the rights and safeguards contained in the Criminal Code and Code of Criminal Procedure. Deprivation of freedom up to one year may be imposed upon a violator, but the court imposing the sentence is required to determine not only (as before) whether the accused failed to obey the administrative order to take a job but also whether he was "continuing his parasitic way of life."

Nevertheless, this is a strange sort of crime. It consists not of a specific act or omission defined by law but rather of a combination of a non-act (not working) with a status (leading a parasitic way of life). It was primarily because the original antiparasite laws conflicted with the requirement of a specific act enunciated in Article 7 of the Criminal Code (and the corresponding article of the 1958 all-union Fundamental Principles) that some leading Soviet jurists (for example, the late Professor S. A. Golunskii) believed that they should be repealed. Implicit in this objection is the broader question whether the general duty to work imposed by the Soviet Constitution can be made subject to criminal sanctions without

12. See A. Ignatov, "Otvetstvennost' za tuneiadstvo nado usilit'," *Sotsialisticheskaia zakonnost'* (1969), no. 12, pp. 34–35.
13. *Vedomosti RSFSR* (1970), no. 14, item 255.

violating fundamental human rights such as those reflected in international legislation, to which the Soviet Union adheres, prohibiting forced labor.

Legal Control of Dissent. Article 70 of the 1960 Criminal Code, on anti-Soviet agitation and propaganda, differs only slightly from the provisions on counter-revolutionary agitation and propaganda which were applicable in earlier periods of Soviet history (*supra,* pp. 23–24). Its scope is sufficiently broad to include the circulation, or indeed the mere possession, of literature containing statements defamatory of the Soviet political or social system. However, a direct (subjective) anti-Soviet intent is required; in the words of a Soviet commentary, a person is guilty of violating Article 70 only if he "knows or foresees that his acts can produce in other persons a hostile attitude to Soviet authority or instigate them to commit particular, especially dangerous crimes against the state, and he desires such result of his acts."[14] Another Soviet commentary puts the matter in these terms: To be guilty under Article 70 the actor must have a desire to undermine or weaken Soviet authority, and in the case of possession of anti-Soviet literature such possession must be for the purpose of using the literature in the future to accomplish that desire.[15]

In February 1966 two well-known Soviet writers, Andrei Sinyavsky and Yuli Daniel, were tried together and convicted of violating Article 70 of the RSFSR Criminal Code, in that they wrote and circulated books and stories containing anti-Soviet propaganda.[16] The trial raised several critical questions concerning the scope of Article 70. First, the writings had not been published in the Soviet Union, but had been secretly sent abroad to be published – which in itself is not a crime under Soviet law; however, the court interpreted Article 70 as forbidding the circulation of anti-Soviet propaganda abroad as well as at home. A second issue concerned the applicability of Article 70 to artistic works: Are statements put into the mouths of the fictitious characters of a novel to be treated as statements by the author? In one of his novels, for example, Sinyavsky portrays a grotesque character who says, among other things, that Lenin used to go out at night and bay and howl at the moon and then would go back to his writing "and his planning of the path we were to follow in life." This the presiding judge at the trial considered to be "blasphemy."[17] The defense, on the other hand, argued that all the statements made in their literary works belonged to the realm of literary creation and could not be judged by the standards applicable to political speech. Related to these two issues was a third, even more difficult, question, namely, How was the anti-Soviet intent of the writers to be determined? They denied that they had any desire to undermine or weaken Soviet authority – on the contrary, they claimed that they were loyal, patriotic citizens, seeking only to fulfill their inner need to be creative writers, and they hoped and believed that

14. Shargorodskii and Beliaev, eds., *Kommentarii k ugolovnomu kodeksu RSFSR 1960 g.* (Leningrad, 1962), p. 153 (annotation 10).

15. B. S. Nikiforov, ed., *Nauchno-prakticheskii kommentarii Ugolovnogo kodeksa RSFSR,* 2d. ed. (Moscow, 1964), p. 168 (annotation 10).

16. See Max Hayward, ed., *On Trial: The Soviet State Versus "Abram Tertz" and "Nikolai Arzhak"* (New York, 1966).

17. *Supra,* note 11.

their writings would strengthen the Soviet system by helping to eliminate the survivals of Stalinism ("the cult of personality") in Soviet life. The answer of the court to this argument was that their anti-Soviet intent could be inferred from their writings alone, and that it was confirmed by their continuing to send their manuscripts abroad even after they knew that they were being used by others, in the West, to discredit the Soviet system.

From a legal point of view the trial of Sinyavsky and Daniel was significant, first, because it was the first instance of a public trial of writers of creative fiction for anti-Soviet agitation and propaganda; second, because the defendants' insistence on their innocence provided a test of the integrity of the Criminal Code; and third, because a serious question was raised concerning the applicability of the Soviet law on dissent (Article 70) to persons whose criticism of the Soviet system is expressed in artistic terms. Can a genuinely artistic literary creation be categorized as anti-Soviet propaganda? Does a creative writer commit a crime – even under the extremely broad language of Article 70 – when his desire to portray reality leads him to write words which sharply conflict with Communist Party policy and doctrine? In such a case may one infer a political intent from the words alone?

We have mentioned the legal issues of the Sinyavsky–Daniel case – although in general we have not, in this Introduction, analyzed Soviet judicial decisions illustrating the way in which the Criminal Code is applied in practice – because of the significance of that case for the future development of the Code. Seven months after the decision (which attracted enormous attention in the Soviet Union as well as throughout the world) two new provisions were introduced into the Code which seem to have been a direct response to the legal difficulties presented by the Sinyavsky–Daniel case. These new provisions – Articles 190–1 and 190–3 – might well be termed "the Sinyavsky–Daniel law." They make it possible to convict dissenters for committing a crime against the system of administration in cases where the dissent is not motivated by an anti-Soviet intent.

Article 190–1, like Article 70, makes it a punishable offense to circulate statements defamatory of the Soviet system; in the case of Article 190–1, however, such statements, although they must be known to be false, need not be circulated for the purpose of subverting or weakening Soviet authority. Also Article 190–1 punishes preparation of such defamatory statements, but not mere possession of them. The maximum punishment is three years' deprivation of freedom, as opposed to seven (plus five years' exile) under Article 70 for a first offense in time of peace.

Article 190–3, enacted at the same time as 190–1, prohibits violation of public order by a group, either in a coarse manner or in disobedience to legal demands of representatives of authority. This provision was a response to group demonstrations that took place after the Sinyavsky–Daniel trial in support of the defendants.

Both Articles 190–1 and 190–3 (as well as 190–2, dealing with desecration of the state emblem or flag) are placed at the beginning of Chapter Nine of the Code, "Crimes Against the System of Administration." Chapter Nine is concerned with protecting the government (the Russian for "administration," *upravlenie*, and "government," *pravitel'stvo*, are very closely related) against those who resist or disobey it. Chapter Nine is to be distinguished from Chapter One, which is concerned with protecting not the government as such but the State (*gosudarstvo*), that is, the political order, the Soviet "authority" or "power" (*vlast'*), against those who are not merely recalcitrant but also disloyal.

Despite these distinctions, the wording of both Article 70 and Article 190-1 is so broad that it is possible in practice to catch almost any strong expression of political dissent within the ambit of either. In at least one case under Article 70, defense counsel argued that the accused should have been charged, at most, with violation of Article 190-1 since he intended to circulate statements within the Soviet Union but not to the anti-Soviet Western magazine which ultimately printed them.[18] This argument seems to presuppose that circulation of defamatory statements abroad (or at least to certain groups abroad) may be treated as evidence of a desire to undermine or weaken Soviet authority, whereas circulation within the Soviet Union may be treated as evidence merely of intent to infringe the system of administration. Also it may be that Article 70 is more apt to be applied to those who advocate fundamental change in the Soviet political structure such as the granting of independence to national minorities (Ukrainians, Latvians, etc.), while Article 190-1 is more apt to be applied to those who advocate change within the existing political structure (e.g., more freedom of speech, greater protection of civil rights, etc.). Judging, however, from unofficial eyewitness reports of political cases,[19] it is at least almost as easy to convict under Article 70 as under Article 190-1 or 190-3, since an anti-Soviet intent may be inferred from the defamatory character of the statement. Moreover, the argument that the accused believed the defamatory statement to be true – which is theoretically a complete defense under both Article 70 and Article 190-1 – has been ineffectual in practice, except possibly as a basis for commitment to a psychiatric hospital.[20] Soviet courts will apparently not admit that any sane Soviet citizen can honestly make a statement attacking the Soviet political or social system.

18. "Speech by Attorney B.S. Zolotukhin in Defense of Ginzburg," in Abraham Brumberg, ed., *In Quest of Justice: Protest and Dissent in the Soviet Union Today* (New York, 1970), p. 124. The fate of Vladimir Bukovsky tends to bear out this distinction. He was convicted in 1967, together with several others, for organizing a demonstration to protest the convictions of Sinyavksy and Daniel and to demand the repeal of Article 70 of the RSFSR Criminal Code. See Pavel Litvinov, *The Demonstration in Pushkin Square* (Boston, 1969). After serving a three-year sentence, he resumed his open opposition to the repression of political dissent, appearing on a Western television broadcast to accuse Soviet authorities of committing dissenters to psychiatric hospitals. In January 1972 he was charged with violation of Article 70 and sentenced by the trial court to seven years' deprivation of freedom in a labor colony and five years' exile. The Times, London, Feb. 7, 1972.

19. Most of the available information concerning Soviet political cases since 1968 derives from *A Chronicle of Current Events*, subtitled "A Journal of the Soviet Civil Rights Movement," produced bi-monthly in Moscow. As of March, 1972, 23 issues have appeared. In the Soviet Union they are circulated from hand to hand in typescript. They are published in English translation by Amnesty International, in London. Issue No. 18 (dated March 1971 and published in London in June 1971) contains a list of over 150 persons convicted or arrested for political reasons in 1969 and 1970; of these the overwhelming majority were charged under Article 70. For further references, see *infra*, notes 26-35.

20. See *infra*, notes 34 and 35; *supra*, Chapter 1, note 26.

THE CODE OF CRIMINAL PROCEDURE

From January 1, 1961, to March 1, 1972, 61 articles of the RSFSR Code of Criminal Procedure were amended, some on several different occasions, and 15 new articles were added to the original 413 articles.[21]

The most important changes were the enlargement of the jurisdiction of the agencies of state security in the preliminary investigation of crimes, the expansion of the right to counsel in the preliminary investigation, and the speeding up of pretrial proceedings in cases of hooliganism.

Shortly after the Code first entered into force, the jurisdiction of the agencies of state security in the preliminary investigation of crimes was substantially enlarged. Under Article 125 as originally enacted, preliminary investigation was entrusted to investigators of the Procuracy in all cases except those arising under Articles 64–70, 72, 73, and 79 of the Criminal Code, in which investigators of the state security agencies were given a concurrent jurisdiction. By an all-union edict of June 21, 1961, the concurrent jurisdiction of the investigators of the state security agencies was enlarged to include also cases arising under Article 75 (disclosure of a state secret), Article 76 (loss of a document containing a state secret), Article 78 (smuggling), Article 83 (illegal exit from or entry into the USSR), Article 88 (violation of rules on currency transactions), Article 189 (failure to report the most serious crimes against the state), and Article 190 (concealment of the most serious crimes against the state), as well as Article 259(a), (b), and (c) (divulgence of a military secret).[22]

Thereafter, investigators of the Ministry of Internal Affairs, that is, of the regular police (*militsiia*), were also given a jurisdiction concurrent with that of the Procuracy in the preliminary investigation of a large number of lesser crimes. Articles 125 and 126 of the Code of Criminal Procedure were amended in 1963 to reflect these new powers of the agencies of state security and of internal affairs, whose effect was to reduce somewhat the investigative authority of the Procuracy with respect to the most serious kinds of crimes on the one hand, and the least serious on the other.

A change that was originally considered but not at first adopted was the enlargement of the right to counsel during preliminary investigation. Some persons hoped that experience under the 1960 Code provision granting to minors and to persons psychologically or physically handicapped the right to counsel from the very beginning of the preliminary investigation, would demonstrate that the presence of advocates is useful not only as a protection of the procedural rights of the accused but also as a means of assisting the investigator not to indict inno-

21. The following articles were changed: 8, 10, 34, 36, 59, 67, 75, 78, 96, 102, 105, 106, 125, 126, 139, 141, 163, 170, 174, 176, 178, 179, 180, 183, 186, 200, 201, 202, 204, 228, 234, 259, 263, 264, 268, 272, 276, 277, 281, 286, 291, 293, 303, 309, 314, 315, 323, 331, 349, 357, 359, 362, 363, 364, 365, 368, 369, 374, 393, 394, 402. Articles 66-1, 96-1, 96-2, 127-1, 133-1, 141-1, 253-1, 275-1, and 414–420 were added.

22. *Vedomosti SSSR* (1961), no. 26, item 270.

cent persons. It has been reported unofficially that questionnaires showed these hopes to have been justified: In cases where lawyers were admitted at the beginning of the preliminary investigation there was a substantially lower incidence of dismissals of indictments by the court or reversals of convictions on appeal. Nevertheless, there has apparently been little support among advocates themselves for expanding the right of counsel still further, partly on the ground that it would impose too great a burden on the time of the advocates, with too little financial reward. The investigators also have an obvious vested interest in not having lawyers present to "hamper" the investigation.

Despite this indifference and, in some cases, opposition, an all-union edict was enacted in 1970 authorizing the Procuracy to permit counsel to appear from the beginning of the preliminary investigation.[23] The same edict gave a *right* to counsel from the beginning of the preliminary investigation to accused persons who do not speak the language in which the proceedings are conducted – assimilating them, in that respect, to persons who are psychologically or physically handicapped. Also in cases of persons accused of crimes for which the death penalty may be imposed, participation of defense counsel was made obligatory (and not merely, as before, an option of the accused) from the moment the accused is informed of the completion of the investigation and receives the record of the case. In February 1972, however, the right to counsel from the beginning of the investigation was withdrawn from persons who do not speak the language of the proceedings, and they were put on the same basis as persons accused of capital crimes – i.e., they are required to have counsel from the time of completion of the investigation.[23a]

Another significant change was the addition in 1966 of an entire new section entitled "Proceedings in Cases Concerning Hooliganism." Comprising seven new articles (414–420), this section creates a series of exceptions to the general rules of the Code of Criminal Procedure. The effect is to reduce the length of pretrial proceedings in the most numerous class of cases to reach the Soviet courts. Thus, for example, in cases arising under Article 206, paragraph 1, of the 1960 Criminal Code, the police or other investigative agencies are given only five days to determine the circumstances of the case and prepare other materials for referral to the court. An extension of the five-day period may be granted if the court

23. Edict of the Presidium of the Supreme Soviet of the USSR of August 31, 1970, On Introducing Changes in Articles 22 and 36 of the Fundamental Principles of Criminal Procedure of the USSR and Union Republics, *Vedomosti SSSR* (1970), no. 36, item 362. Cf. J. N. Hazard, "Expansion of the Right to a Defense Attorney under Soviet Law," International Commission of Jurists, *The Review*, no. 6 (April–June 1971), pp. 17–23.

23a. Edict of February 3, 1972, *Vedomosti SSSR* (1972), no. 6, item 51. One effect of the 1970 edict was that many foreigners had, as a matter of right, the benefit of counsel 72 hours after arrest, whereas most Soviet citizens could only rely on the procurator's discretion for such benefit. The amendment of Article 36 of the Fundamental Principles, *supra* note 23, was not affected; it consisted of requiring an administrative session of the court to issue the indictment in cases of minors and in cases of capital crimes.

returns the file of the case for additional investigation or if five days is insufficient to prepare an adequate record. However, in that event the inquiry must be complete within twenty days. Once the case is filed, it must be considered by the court within fifteen days.

The rapid pretrial procedure in cases of persons charged with hooligan actions is apparently intended – along with heavier penalties – to help deter the commission of this offense, as well as to save time for law enforcement agencies. It is argued that an exceptional procedure is justified because, in contrast to other crimes, most cases of hooliganism occur openly, in full view of the public, and do not pose difficult problems for the investigators or the courts in the collection and consideration of evidence. In fact, however, the charge of hooliganism is often brought in cases of street fights in which it is very difficult to determine whether the suspect was the aggressor or the victim.

In an effort to improve the coordination of investigative activities, the post of "chief of an investigative department" was created in late 1965 within the investigative branches of the Ministry of Internal Affairs and of the agencies of state security (Article 34). The chief of an investigative department exercises general supervisory functions over the activities of investigators in his charge and gives instructions concerning the conduct of the preliminary investigations, the prosecution of a person as an accused, the classification of a crime, etc. (Article 127-1). This provision somewhat reduces the greater independence accorded to investigators under the 1960 Code as originally enacted.

The Code of Criminal Procedure also now provides for the participation of a "specialist" in a preliminary investigation or trial (cf. Articles 59, 66-1, 67, 105, 106, 133-1, 139, 141, 170, 174, 180, 183, 186, 202, 204, 228, 253-1, 263, 268, 272, 275-1, 276, 277, 291, 293, 323).

The use of recording devices in investigative actions was not expressly authorized by the Code of Criminal Procedure in its original form. In 1965 such devices were made permissible. At the same time provisions were included to guard against their abuse in confrontations between a witness and the victim; in acquainting an accused, victim, civil plaintiff, or civil defendant with the materials of a case; in the public disclosure of a witness's or accused's testimony in court; and in preparing the record of the judicial session (cf. Articles 141, 141-1, 163, 200, 201, 264, 281, 286).

Enactment in 1969 of an all-union Statute on Persons Confined Under Guard[24] and of the all-union Fundamental Principles of Correctional Labor Legislation required numerous technical amendments of the Code of Criminal Procedure, which were introduced in 1970 (cf. Articles 96-1, 96-2, 303, 314, 315, 359, 363, 364, 365, 368, 369, 393).[25]

Also in 1970 Soviet legislators corrected several small mistakes which somehow had been overlooked when the Code was originally adopted. Thus, in articles 8, 10, and 234 the word "Commission" should not have been capitalized; in Article 176 the term *opis'* (inventory) should have been *obysk* (search); and in Article 394 the reference should have been to paragraph 2 of Article 94.

24. *Vedomosti SSSR* (1969), no. 29, item 248.
25. *Supra*, note 6.

Procedural Guarantees in Political Cases. The trial of Sinyavsky and Daniel in February 1966 (*supra*, p. 81 ff.) was the first of a long series of prosecutions of individual dissenters under Articles 70, 190-1, and/or 190-3 of the RSFSR Criminal Code (and corresponding provisions of the codes of other republics).[26] In addition, there have been many prosecutions under the same articles, and sometimes under Article 64 (treason), of adherents of various minority causes, including Ukrainian separatists, Zionists, Baptists, and others.[27] Although this is not the place for a general discussion of these trials, certain aspects of them are material to an evaluation of the Code of Criminal Procedure. On the one hand, there were many instances of charges, by the accused and by others, that Code provisions were violated, together with appeals to Soviet political and legal authorities to remedy the violations, and complaints to the United Nations and to international public opinion. On the other hand, Soviet authorities generally denied the charges and – to the extent that they admitted that such trials took place – insisted that they were properly conducted in accordance with Soviet law.

One of the most serious accusations was that the Code requirement of publicity was violated. Characteristic was the complaint of the wife of one defendant in a letter to the Chairman of the Presidium of the Supreme Soviet of the USSR, in which she stated that she and other relatives were not informed of the time and place of the trial until six or seven hours before it began; that relatives and friends of the accused were excluded from the courtroom by police; and that a well-organized group of young men, who were not even acquaintances of the accused, were admitted.[28] She received a reply from the Moscow Office of the Procuracy stating that her complaint had been duly examined and that in fact the trial "was conducted publicly, in full conformity with Article 18 of the RSFSR Code of Criminal Procedure."[29]

Some trials were allegedly held entirely *in camera*, presumably on the ground of protection of state secrets, although the accusations involved only authorship or possession of anti-Soviet literature.[30]

It has also been stated that in some cases courts refused to admit expert evidence offered in behalf of the accused, police prevented persons wishing to testify for defendants from entering the courtroom, clerks did not record the testimony of witnesses for the accused, and judges placed improper restrictions on defense counsel in the interrogation of witnesses – all in violation of Articles

26. Among the best known of these are the trials of Khaustov (February 1967); Bukovsky, Delone, and Kushev (September 1967); Galanskov, Ginzburg, Dobrovolsky, and Lashkova (January 1968); Bagitsky, Bogoraz-Daniel, Delone, Dremliuga, Fainberg, Gorbanevskaia, and Litvinov (October 1968); Grigorenko (December 1969); Gabai (January 1970); Yakhimovich (February 1970); Pimenov, Vail and Zinoveva (October 1970); Amalrik and Ubozhko (November 1970); Levitin-Krasnov (May 1971); Marchenko (September 1971); Bukovsky (January 1972). See *The New York Times Index*, 1966-1971; Abraham Brumberg, ed., *In Quest of Justice: Protest and Dissent in the Soviet Union Today* (New York, 1970); Pavel Litvinov, *The Demonstration in Pushkin Square* (Boston, 1969); *A Chronicle of Current Events*, issues 1-23 (London, 1968-1972); The Times, London, Feb. 7, 1972, p. 1. Cf. *supra*, note 19.

27. Brumberg, *op. cit.*; Michael Browne, ed., *Ferment in the Ukraine* (London, 1971); *Chronicle of Current Events*, passim; *Jews in Eastern Europe: A Periodical Survey of Events* (London), vol. iv, 1971-72, passim.

28. Litvinov, *The Demonstration in Pushkin Square* (Boston, 1969), pp. 40-41.

29. *Id.*, p. 42.

30. Browne, *op. cit.*, pp. 9-11.

243, 244, and 245 of the RSFSR Code of Criminal Procedure. In addition it has been charged that in several trials witnesses were forced to leave the courtroom after testifying, in violation of Article 283. In one case the presiding judge frequently interrupted the accused while he was attempting to make his final statement, in violation of Article 297, and indeed went so far as to call a recess, over the objection of the accused that the continuity of his final statement ("last word") was being broken.[31] In some trials the spectators admitted to the courtroom were allegedly permitted to taunt and insult the accused and witnesses, in violation of the spirit, at least, of Article 263.

In addition to alleged procedural violations in the courtroom, accused persons complained of excessive and irrelevant house searches, claiming that even the houses of witnesses and of complete outsiders were searched and that literature was confiscated which was not anti-Soviet and hence fell outside the scope of search warrants, in violation of Article 171; that books and manuscripts were confiscated without any record being made, in violation of Article 176; and that search warrants had been issued when there was no evidence to support them, in violation of Article 168. It was also charged that unlawful searches and seizures were conducted by the security police (KGB), whose participation in the investigation was in itself a violation of Article 125 of the Criminal Code in those cases where the defendants were charged with crimes provided for by Article 190–1 or 190–3 of the Criminal Code of the RSFSR, whose investigation is not within the jurisdiction of the KGB.

It has been claimed, further, that there were illegally long pretrial detentions. Some defendants, for example, were apparently held in custody for a year prior to trial,[32] although Article 97 of the RSFSR Code of Criminal Procedure declares nine months to be the absolute maxium period of confinement under guard in connection with the investigation of a case. Other violations of the law which have been alleged include "the length of interrogation exceeding permitted limits, . . . falsification of the record resulting from refusal to accept depositions in the prisoner's own hand or his amendments to the record; [and] failure to examine, or to announce the contents of, documents in court on which the indictment rested."[33] Also members of the families of accused persons have protested against intimidation and harassment of themselves and their friends, including threats of deportation, eavesdropping on conversations, and examination of private correspondence, shadowing, and the taking of photographs.

Reference has been made in an earlier chapter to the alleged abuse of psychiatric expertise to secure the commitment to mental institutions of sane persons who have been charged with anti-Soviet activities. A considerable number of such cases have been reported unofficially in some detail. In 1971 the author of an article in Izvestia denounced such reports as absurd and referred to those who accept them as "loudmouths who suffer from a pathological hatred of the Soviet system."[34]

31. Litvinov, *op. cit.*, p. 94.
32. Brumberg, *op. cit.*, p. 50, note 7.
33. Browne, *op. cit.*, p. 14.
34. Izvestia, Oct. 24, 1971, p. 4. But see *A Chronicle of Current Events*, No. 18, June

In considering the relevance of these charges to the effectiveness of the Code of Criminal Procedure, it should be kept in mind that while some of the alleged actions of the investigative agencies and of the judiciary are flagrant violations of the Code, others are not unequivocally prohibited. The specific requirements of Article 18, for example, which provides that judicial examinations must (with certain exceptions) be "open," are nowhere specified; it is possible, therefore, that the prevention of interested would-be spectators from attending certain trials, or the failure to notify relatives of an accused of the time or place of his hearing, is not considered a violation of that article. Also it is arguable that despite the language of Article 297 a judge may interrupt the final statement of the accused when that statement itself contains anti-Soviet propaganda and is therefore possibly criminal. Similarly, other articles of the Code may mean less in Soviet law than they would mean if interpreted by American standards. The objectivity required of the presiding judge under Article 243 may be limited by the further requirement of the same article that he so conduct the trial as to secure its educational influence.

At issue also is the role of the Serbskii Institute of Forensic Psychiatry, a scientific research institute which also trains psychiatrists to testify as court experts in criminal cases. Organized under the USSR Ministry of Health, it has been in existence since 1922. Many books have been published under its auspices, and it has had a distinguished record in non-political cases. In political cases, however, it has fallen under suspicion of subservience to the KGB and has been charged with using a doctrine of "incipient schizophrenia" to justify commitment to psychiatric hospitals of persons who refuse to abide by the limits of dissent laid down by the Communist Party leadership.[35]

The underlying dilemma of these cases is that the Soviet political authority seeks to legitimate its struggle against dissent by reliance upon the Criminal Code and the Code of Criminal Procedure, while the dissenters invoke the same codes to legitimate their opposition. Each side opposes the other in the name of the codes. And each side thereby accepts some limitations imposed by the codes; so far, at least, the regime is unwilling to revert to Stalinist terror, and its opponents are unwilling to espouse the cause of counterrevolution. As long as this situation remains, legality will continue to be not only a matter of crucial importance in everyday Soviet life but also a master key to Soviet politics.

1971, pp. 104–109, No. 21, August1971, pp. 273–4, 278–9, No. 19–20, September 1971, pp. 171–175, and No. 22–23, March 1972, pp. 6–10, and references cited in chap. 1, note 26.

35. See Zhores and Roy Medvedev, *supra*, chap. 1, note 26, *passim; A Chronicle of Current Events*, No. 13, April 1970, pp. 21–23 (report of letter of S. P. Pisarev to Presidium of Soviet Academy of Medical Sciences); *id.*, No. 21, August 1971, pp. 278–279 (press statement of the Committee for Human Rights, a group formed in Moscow in November 1970 consisting of Academician A. D. Sakharov and physicists A. N. Tverdokhlebov and V. N. Chalidze; see *id.*, No. 17, April 1971, pp. 45–47). On the role of the Serbskii Institute in non-political cases, see H. J. Berman, *Justice in the USSR* (rev. ed. 1963), chap. 13, and *id.*, "Law as an Instrument of Mental Health in the United States and Soviet Russia," U. of Pa. Law Rev., vol. 109 (1961), pp. 374–375. Cf. G. V. Morozov and Ia. M. Kalashnik, eds., *Forensic Psychiatry*, Introduction by David L. Bazelon, a translation of a 1967 book published under the auspices of the Serbskii Institute, in *Soviet Law and Government*, vol. 8, no. 2–3–4 (1970).

6 The Law on Court Organization

The history of the judicial system of the USSR is too long and complicated to be told in the few pages that can be allotted to it in a book devoted primarily to Soviet criminal law and procedure. Some of that history has already been indicated in the preceding pages. The present chapter will briefly recapitulate only a few of the main developments, with stress upon those features that have persisted since the early years of the Revolution, and in addition will comment on several features of the 1960 RSFSR Law on Court Organization that have special significance for criminal law and procedure.

The abolition of the prerevolutionary judicial system was proclaimed by the Bolshevik regime within a few weeks after its seizure of power in November 1917.[1] In place of the old courts, new people's courts were established and alongside these were also established revolutionary tribunals and an "extraordinary commission" (*cheka*) of the state security agency, whose task was to administer a rougher justice to persons accused of sabotage and counterrevolution.[2]

The revolutionary tribunals and the special commissions of the state security agencies stood outside the regular hierarchy of courts. Their proceedings were administrative and secret. They could not be called courts in the usual sense of that word, and the Soviet never applied the term courts (*sudy*) to them or to the "special boards" that succeeded them. They were initially created expressly as agencies of the "red terror," and they always remained that. It is in the light of this history that the abolition of the Special Board of the MVD after Stalin's death acquires its significance; for it symbolized the intention of the post-Stalin regime to establish – for the first time since 1917 – security of law in political cases.

The people's courts (*narodnye sudy*) were originally called such in order to convey the idea that they would administer a popular, or proletarian, justice, in contrast to the "bourgeois" justice of the prerevolutionary judicial system. To

1. Decree of the Council of People's Commissars of November 24, 1917, *SU* (1917), no. 4, item 50.

2. Cf. Statute on the Cheka, *SU* (1918), no. 35, item 842. The early history of Soviet courts and administrative tribunals is told in J. N. Hazard, *Settling Disputes in Soviet Society: The Formative Years of Legal Institutions* (New York, 1960), pp. 1–127. An extensive study of the entire history of the Soviet judicial system is Samuel Kucherov's *The Organs of Soviet Administration of Justice: Their History and Operation* (Leiden, 1970).

strengthen this idea, it was decided that at each trial two of the three judges – for the idea of a three-judge trial court, traditional in Europe, was never abandoned – should be laymen.[3] The two lay co-judges, called "people's assessors" (*narodnye zasedateli*), were to serve for a certain number of days annually. The system of trial courts consisting of a professional judge and two laymen has persisted in the Soviet Union from the first decree on courts of November 24, 1917.

Also the system of election of the professional judges, as well as of the assessors, has persisted from the early days, although in fact the professional judges have become, in effect, a civil service. Indeed, election of the people's judges by direct vote of the population, which was introduced in practice only in 1948,[4] coincided with an increased emphasis upon the necessity for professional legal training on the part of the judiciary; and since nominations are controlled by the Communist Party, it is an easy matter to select judges from among recent university law graduates who desire to embark upon judicial careers.

At the same time, election of judges in the Soviet Union, whether by popular vote (as in the case of people's judges) or by legislative or quasi-legislative bodies (as in the case of judges of higher courts), is a means of restricting their tenure. (It may be noted that the same word, *vybor*, "election," is used to refer to popular election of people's judges, selection of regional, city, and territorial courts by soviets of working people's deputies, which are quasi-legislative administrative agencies, and selection of supreme courts by supreme soviets, which are legislative agencies.)[5] Judges of people's courts served for three years prior to 1958, when their terms were extended – by the USSR Fundamental Principles of Court Organization – to five years; judges of higher courts have served for five years at least since the 1936 Constitution.

In addition to restrictions imposed by their relatively short tenure, judges must report on their work to their electors (whether to the popular electorate or to soviets of working people's deputies or supreme soviets), and they may be

3. Analogies may be found in the German system of trial of commercial cases by a professional judge and two laymen as well as in the similar system used in civil and criminal cases in the county courts of the state of Vermont, which differs from the Soviet chiefly in the fact that the right of jury trial is also preserved.

4. Such elections were required by the 1936 Constitution but were postponed until the passage of the Law on Court Organization in 1938 and then once again postponed until after World War II.

5. Soviet state agencies are divided into four basic types: (1) agencies of state authority (*organy gosudarstvennoi vlasti*), (2) agencies of state administration (*organy gosudarstvennogo upravleniia*), (3) courts, (4) Procuracy. Soviets on the level of the USSR (Supreme Soviet of the USSR), union republics (union republican supreme soviets), autonomous republics (supreme soviets of autonomous republics), and regions, cities, districts and villages (regional, city, district and village soviets) – all belong, technically, to the first type. However, regional, city, district and village soviets do not have power to enact laws, as the higher soviets do; and in fact they fulfill many of the functions of municipal councils in other countries, except that they also have executive committees that carry out the day-to-day tasks of local government. (The executive committees of local soviets belong to the second type of state agencies, namely agencies of state administration.) Regional and city Soviets elect (select) regional and city courts, respectively. We have called the local soviets quasi-legislative to indicate that although they belong, technically, to the category of legislative agencies, they lack the power to enact laws and in fact they fulfill administrative functions.

recalled by them prior to the expiration of their term of office (1960 RSFSR Law on Court Organization, Articles 17–19). The provision of the 1960 Law that judges shall be "independent and subordinate only to law" (Article 7), like the parallel provision of the USSR Constitution, signifies only that there should be no outside interference in the trial of particular cases; it is not intended to insulate judges against general policies of the Communist Party, expressed in "campaigns" against particular types of criminal activity and in party directives on law and law enforcement.[6]

Another feature of the Soviet judicial system that has persisted from the early years of the Revolution is the absence of clear delineation of jurisdiction in first instance as between lower and higher courts. Normally, cases are tried in first instance by people's courts. However, if a case is sufficiently important the regional court or its equivalent (territorial court, city court, court of autonomous region, court of national area, supreme court of autonomous republic), or the RSFSR Supreme Court, or the USSR Supreme Court, may try it in first instance. Each of these higher courts has a panel of people's assessors available to participate in such trials. The original jurisdiction of higher courts is discretionary and may be invoked by the procurator or by the court itself (cf. RSFSR Code of Criminal Procedure, Articles 38, 40) or in civil cases by one of the parties.

If a case is tried in a people's court there is a right of appeal to the regional (or equivalent) court, and if a case is tried in a regional (or equivalent) court there is a right of appeal to the republican supreme court. There is no right of appeal from a judgment of the RSFSR Supreme Court, since that is the highest court in the republic. However, as indicated in an earlier chapter, the Soviet lawmakers could not resist the idea of a further discretionary review of "final" judgments. Thus appellate decisions of regional courts may be reviewed "by way of supervision" (*v poriadke nadzora*) by all higher instances, up to the Supreme Court of the USSR; and the judgment of a republican supreme court in a case tried by it in first instance may also be reviewed by way of supervision.

Such review by way of supervision may take a case through a long and tortuous path. Each of the regional courts is divided into a civil and a criminal division as well as a presidium, and the presidium may review a decision of either division by way of supervision (cf. 1960 RSFSR Law on Court Organization, Articles 35, 37, 38). Also the RSFSR Supreme Court is divided into a civil and a criminal division as well as a presidium, and a decision of a division or presidium of a regional court may be reviewed by way of supervision by the criminal or civil division of the RSFSR Supreme Court (Article 52), and a decision of a division of the RSFSR Supreme Court may be reviewed by way of supervision by the Presidium of the RSFSR Supreme Court (Article 55). Thus within the republic itself a criminal case tried in a people's court may go on appeal to the criminal division of a regional court and then by way of supervision to the presidium of the regional court, thence to the Criminal Division of the RSFSR Supreme Court, and thence to the Presidium of the RSFSR Supreme Court. Thereafter it may go by way of supervision to the Criminal Division of the USSR Supreme Court and

6. Cf. *supra*, p. 14.

thence to the Plenum of the USSR Supreme Court, which is a body consisting of (a) the members of the three divisions (criminal, civil and military) of that court (b) the President and Deputy Presidents of the court, and (c) the presidents of the fifteen republican supreme courts – 31 judges in all, as of 1965. (The USSR Supreme Court has a plenum but no presidium.) As a result, cases may, and occasionally do, go through seven instances, and, if they are remanded for a new trial or a new cassational consideration, even more.

The establishment of presidia in the regional (and equivalent) courts, and of a presidium – and also a plenum – in the RSFSR Supreme Court reflected the tendency that emerged in the late 1950's to vest administrative control over lower courts in higher courts, and ultimately in the RSFSR and USSR Supreme Courts. Prior to 1956 all Soviet courts were under the general control of the USSR Ministry of Justice, which supervised their activities, criticized judges for wrong decisions, and had an important voice in their nomination and promotion. In 1956 the USSR Ministry of Justice was dissolved and many of its functions were transferred to republican ministries of justice.[7] Thereafter these, too, were dissolved (though not at first in the RSFSR), and many of their functions were inherited by juridical commissions of the republican councils of ministers. Under the 1960 RSFSR Law on Court Organization, the higher courts, and especially the RSFSR Supreme Court, were given many of the supervisory powers over lower courts that had formerly been exercised by the RSFSR Ministry of Justice, and in 1963 that Ministry was itself dissolved.[8] With the dissolution of the RSFSR Ministry of Justice, the functions of control over the lower courts was vested in the Supreme Court of the RSFSR, and the Law on Court Organization was amended accordingly (cf. Articles 20, 26, 27, 48, and 50 of the 1960 RSFSR Law on Court Organization).

In August 1970 the USSR Ministry of Justice, with republican branches, was restored.[9] A year later the functions of the restored Ministry were defined and appropriate changes were made in all-union legislation.[10] As of March 1, 1972 (the effective date of this book), RSFSR law had not yet been amended to take account of these changes; however, the all-union legislation itself had the effect of transferring to the new Ministry the functions of "organizational direction" of republican courts and military tribunals, and "direction" of the bar (*advokatura*), the notariat, and other institutions of justice – functions which had previously been vested partly in the Supreme Court of the USSR and the supreme courts of the various republics and partly in the Juridical Commission of the Council of Ministers of the USSR and the juridical commissions of the republican councils of ministers. A new provision (Article 38–1) was added to

7. *Vedomosti SSSR* (1956), no. 12, item 250.

8. *Vedomosti RSFSR* (1963), no. 15, item 289.

9. Edict of the Presidium of the Supreme Soviet of the USSR of August 31, 1970, On the Formation of a Union Republican Ministry of Justice of the USSR, *Vedomosti SSSR* (1970), no. 36, item 361; *id.*, no. 50, item 567. Cf. *Vedomosti RSFSR* (1970), no. 40, item 812.

10. Edict of the Presidium of the Supreme Soviet of the USSR of August 12, 1971, On Introducing Changes and Additions in USSR Legislation in Connection with the Formation of the Union Republican Ministry of Justice of the USSR, *Vedomosti SSSR* (1971), no. 33, item 332.

the Fundamental Principles of Legislation on Court Organization of the USSR and of Union and Autonomous Republics, which stated in part:

> The Ministry of Justice of the USSR shall:
> (a) draft proposals on questions of the organization of judicial agencies and the conducting of elections of judges and people's assessors;
> (b) direct work with cadres of judicial agencies;
> (c) check on the organization of the work of judicial agencies;
> (d) study and generalize judicial practice, coordinating this activity with the Supreme Court of the USSR;
> (e) organize the work of keeping judicial statistics.
> The Minister of Justice of the USSR shall have the right to introduce in the Plenum of the Supreme Court of the USSR proposals concerning the issuance to courts of guiding explanations on questions of the application of legislation.
> The Ministry of Justice of the USSR, ministries of justice of union and autonomous republics, and sections of justice of executive committees of regional, area, and city soviets of working people's deputies shall facilitate in all ways the carrying out of the purposes of the administration of justice and the tasks of courts, [at the same time] strictly observing the principle of the independence of judges and their subordination only to law.[11]

Also Article 1 of the 1957 Statute on the Supreme Court of the USSR was amended to replace the words "The Supreme Court of the USSR shall verify [*provodit proverku*] the application of all-union legislation by union-republican judicial agencies as well as the execution [by them] of decrees of the Plenum of the Supreme Court of the USSR" with the words "The Supreme Court of the USSR shall study the practice of the application of legislation by courts and shall issue guiding explanations to courts on questions relating to such application." In addition, the 1957 Statute on the Supreme Court of the USSR was amended to provide for participation of the Minister of Justice of the USSR in sessions of the Plenum, and the task of keeping judicial statistics was transferred from the Supreme Court to the Ministry.

Presumably, corresponding changes will eventually be made in the RSFSR Law on Court Organization, substituting certain supervisory powers of the new Ministry for those of the RSFSR Supreme Court.

Nevertheless, certain supervisory powers of the USSR Supreme Court over republican courts are retained in the new all-union legislation, and presumably parallel powers are retained by the RSFSR Supreme Court over lower RSFSR courts. The Plenum of the USSR Supreme Court retains the task of "studying and generalizing judicial practice" – that is, keeping track of the work of all the other courts – though the 1971 law provides that its work in this respect is to be coordinated with that of the Ministry of Justice. Under Article 55 of the 1960 RSFSR Law on Court Organization, a somewhat similar function of "considering . . . materials summarizing judicial practice" is assigned to the Presidium of the RSFSR Supreme Court. However, the power of the RSFSR Supreme Court

11. *Ibid.*

under Article 55 to "issue instructions and methodological directives concerning questions of the work of courts" is presumably replaced by the power of the USSR Ministry of Justice (and its RSFSR branch) to exercise "organizational direction" over the courts.

Also the Plenum of the USSR Supreme Court, under Article 9 of the 1957 Statute on the USSR Supreme Court, is empowered to issue "guiding explanations" (*rukovodiashchie raz"iasneniia)* to courts within its jurisdiction concerning the application of laws – although, once again, this power is now slightly qualified by the provision of the 1971 law (quoted above) that the Minister of Justice may make proposals with regard to such guiding explanations. The parallel power of the RSFSR Supreme Court is contained in Article 57 of the RSFSR Law on Court Organization. These explanations are entitled "decrees" (*postanovleniia*). In them the Plenum may criticize decisions and rulings of the courts and explain the meaning of code provisions and legislation. Such judicial decrees have been used to fill gaps in existing law and to revise earlier judicial policies.

The explanations of the Plenums of the USSR and RSFSR Supreme Courts are technically not treated as "interpretation" (*tolkovanie*) but rather as "application" (*primenenie*) of the law. Theoretically, and according to the USSR and RSFSR Constitutions, only the Presidia of the USSR and RSFSR Supreme Soviets have express power to "interpret" the laws. Under Article 57 of the 1960 RSFSR Law on Court Organization and Article 9 of the 1957 Statute on the USSR Supreme Court, the Plenums are empowered to make proposals to the Presidium of the RSFSR Supreme Soviet and the Presidium of the USSR Supreme Soviet, respectively, concerning "interpretation" of legislation. To an American lawyer, at least, there would appear to be no substantial difference, however, between the decrees of the Plenums on the "application" of the law and what is generally understood by "interpretation," since a statement of how a law should be applied is surely at the same time a statement of what the law means.

Finally, it may be noted that the 1960 RSFSR Law on Court Organization, following the 1958 USSR Fundamental Principles of Court Organization, includes the guarantees of the 1936 USSR Constitution concerning equality before the law (RSFSR Law, Article 5), administration of justice in accordance with the law (Article 6), public trial of cases unless otherwise provided by law (Article 12), right to defense (Article 13), and others. In addition, the 1960 Law contains several general provisions that reflect developments of the late 1950's – particularly, the provision for participation of social accusers and social defense counsel in judicial proceedings (Article 25) and the provision for direction and control of lower courts by higher courts (Article 26). All of these are general provisions that have concrete meaning only insofar as they are implemented by specific provisions of the Criminal Code and Code of Criminal Procedure and by other more detailed legislation, as well as by judicial interpretation.

The 1960 Law also provides that the RSFSR Supreme Court shall publish a "Bulletin" (Article 60); this is a monthly journal that contains selected cases decided by the Civil and Criminal Divisions, selected decisions and instructions of the Presidium of the RSFSR Supreme Court and guiding explanations of the

Plenum, as well as occasional articles by members of the court's staff and other matters. Similarly, the USSR Supreme Court publishes a bimonthly "Bulletin" containing reports of decided cases and guiding explanations of the Plenum as well as occasional articles by members of its staff and other matters. In addition, the USSR Ministry of Justice, Procuracy, and Supreme Court are responsibile for the publication of a scholarly monthly journal, *Sotsialisticheskaia zakonnost'* (Socialist Legality), and the RSFSR Ministry of Justice and Supreme Court are responsible for the publication of a scholarly semimonthly journal, *Sovetskaia iustitsiia* (Soviet Justice), both of which publish occasional reports of decided cases.

7 Military Law and Military Tribunals[1]

All crimes committed by persons in military service and by their civilian accomplices are subject to trial in permanent military tribunals, staffed by permanent military judges and located in headquarters of military units and in the various military districts of the USSR. These are not courts within the republican judicial systems but USSR courts. Their decisions are subject to review by the Military Division of the USSR Supreme Court, which also has original jurisdiction over military cases "of exceptional importance" (1958 Statute on Military Tribunals, Article 16).

Military tribunals also have jurisdiction over cases of all crimes committed by personnel of state security agencies, by officers of penal institutions, and by convoy guards of agencies of protection of public order, as well as over all cases of espionage (*id.*, Article 9). In addition the 1958 Statute provides that "in localities where, by force of exceptional circumstances, general courts are not operating, military tribunals shall consider all criminal and civil cases" (Article 10). This provision is applicable not only where martial law has been declared within the Soviet Union but also where Soviet troops are situated outside the Soviet Union.

Although military tribunals do not belong to the republican hierarchies of courts, they are governed by the republican criminal codes and codes of criminal procedure. The 1958 USSR Statute on Military Crimes is, as we have seen, included as a part of the RSFSR Criminal Code. In addition, Article 7 of the 1958 USSR Statute on Military Tribunals provides that military tribunals shall be governed by the legislation of the USSR and the legislation of union republics. This means that military tribunals must apply the substantive law of the republic in which the crime was committed and the procedural law of the republic in which the military tribunal is situated (insofar as USSR law does not govern).

Moreover, decisions of the Military Division of the USSR Supreme Court are subject to supervisory review by the Plenum of the USSR Supreme Court, and apart from review of particular cases the Supreme Court exercises supervision of

1. The Soviet system of military law and administration as it existed prior to the reforms of the later 1950's is analyzed in H. J. Berman and M. Kerner, *Soviet Military Law and Administration* (Cambridge, Mass., 1955), and basic legislation and cases are presented in Berman and Kerner, *Documents on Soviet Military Law and Administration* (Cambridge, Mass., 1955).

the work of military tribunals generally, chiefly through the President of the Military Division (1958 Statute on Military Tribunals, Articles 19 and 24). Also the military procuracy is organized within the Procuracy of the USSR and is subordinate to the Procurator General of the USSR.[2] Thus there is an integration of military and civilian law.

At the same time the personnel of military tribunals are part of the Armed Forces of the USSR under the USSR Ministry of Defense, which prior to 1970–71 shared with the President of the Military Division of the USSR Supreme Court the function of staffing and organizing the military tribunals. After the formation of the Ministry of Justice of the USSR in 1970, the 1958 Statute on Military Tribunals was amended to provide that the staffing and organization of the military tribunals as well as of the (newly formed) Administration for Military Tribunals of the Ministry of Justice shall be determined by the Ministry of Justice together with the Ministry of Defense. Other functions of the Military Division of the Supreme Court were also transferred to the Ministry of Justice and its Administration for Military Tribunals.[3] Article 24 of the Statute on Military Tribunals was amended to provide as follows:

> The Ministry of Justice of the USSR and its Administration for Military Tribunals shall carry out:
> (a) verification of the organization of the work of military tribunals;
> (b) study and generalization of the judicial practice of military tribunals, coordinating this activity with the Supreme Court of the USSR, and also organization of the work of keeping judicial statistics;
> (c) preparation jointly with the Ministry of Defense of the USSR of proposals on questions of the organization of military tribunals.

Judges of military courts of first instance must be USSR citizens on active military duty who are at least 25 years old. They are elected by the Presidium of the Supreme Soviet of the USSR for a five-year term. People's assessors must also be USSR citizens on active military duty. They are elected by open vote at general meetings of servicemen for a two-year period (1958 Statute, Articles 4 and 5).

The decisions of military tribunals of garrisons, flotillas, armies, army groups, fleets, etc., may be appealed to tribunals of the appropriate military district; decisions of tribunals of military districts sitting as courts of first instance (in more important cases) may be appealed to the Military Division of the USSR Supreme Court, which also may try cases in first instance, as indicated earlier. Appellate decisions are taken by courts sitting in benches of three professional military judges. Such appellate decisions may be reviewed only by way of supervision.

2. A new Statute on the Military Procuracy was adopted December 14, 1966, *Vedomosti SSSR* (1966), no. 50, item 1021.

3. Amendments to Articles 22, 23, 24, and 27 of the Statute on Military Tribunals were made in the Edict of the Presidium of the Supreme Soviet of the USSR of August 12, 1971, On Introducing Changes and Additions in USSR Legislation in Connection with the Formation of the Union Republican Ministry of Justice of the USSR, *Vedomosti SSSR* (1971), no. 33, item 332.

8 The Role of the Procuracy in Criminal Law and Procedure

The Soviet Procuracy is responsible, as we have seen, for the preliminary investigation of crimes – a responsibility that it shares with the state security agencies and the agencies for the protection of public order (the *militsiia*, or police); and it has sole responsibility for the prosecution of criminal cases in court. In addition, the Procuracy exercises, in the words of the USSR Constitution (Article 113), "supreme supervisory power to ensure the strict execution of the laws by all ministries and their subordinate institutions as well as by individual officials and by citizens of the USSR." It is the Procuracy's power of supervision (*nadzor*), coupled with its organizational unity and independence, which gives it its crucial importance in the Soviet system of law, and which has led some writers to suggest that it is a fourth branch of government.

Organizational Unity and Independence of the Procuracy. The Procuracy is headed by the Procurator General of the USSR, who, according to the USSR Constitution (Article 114), is appointed by the Supreme Soviet of the USSR for a term of seven years. (It may be recalled that the USSR Supreme Court is chosen by the Supreme Soviet of the USSR for a term of only five years.) The Procurator General of the USSR appoints the procurators of republics and regions (as well as of territories, autonomous republics, and autonomous regions), and the procurators of republics appoint area, district, and city procurators subject to the approval of the Procurator General (Constitution of the USSR, Articles 115 and 116). As stated in the 1955 Statute on Procuracy Supervision in the USSR, "The agencies of the Procuracy in the USSR comprise a single centralized system headed by the Procurator General of the USSR, with subordination of lower procurators to higher ones."[1] The Procurator General, in turn, is responsible only to the Supreme Soviet of the USSR and, between sessions of the Supreme Soviet, to its Presidium; the Presidium alone may vacate his orders and instructions to his subordinates (1955 Statute, Articles 7 and 8).

The significance of the administrative centralization of the Procuracy is to free it from local control in the enforcement of uniform legal policies of the central

1. Edict of May 24, 1955, *Vedomosti SSSR* (1955), no. 9, item 22, Article 5. The Statute, as amended to December 14, 1966, is translated in Harold J. Berman and John B. Quigley, Jr., *Basic Laws on the Structure of the Soviet State* (Cambridge, Mass., 1969), pp. 182–196.

authorities. It is the only Soviet governmental agency that is exempt from the principle of "dual subordination" to both local and higher authorities. The Constitution of the USSR states (Article 117): "The agencies of the Procuracy shall perform their functions independently of any local agencies whatsoever, being subordinate only to the Procurator General of the USSR." The language of the 1955 Statute (Article 2) is even stronger: "The Procurator General of the USSR and his subordinate procurators shall be obliged to watch out for (*sledit' za*) the correct and uniform application of the laws of the USSR and of union and autonomous republics, despite any kinds of local differences and against any kinds of local influences."[2]

It should be noted that although the 1955 Statute directs the Procuracy to supervise the execution of the laws and the observance of legality by various specified agencies, including ministries, it does not authorize the Procuracy to supervise the legality of acts of legislative bodies (soviets), nor does it expressly authorize the Procuracy to supervise the legality of acts of councils of ministers. In 1960 the Procuracy did successfully protest the unconstitutionality of a regulation of a council of ministers of an autonomous republic, and at least one example has been given of a protest against an order of the chairman of the council of ministers of a (smaller) union republic, but it may be doubted that it would have similar jurisdiction over the Council of Ministers of the USSR. The Procuracy is considered to be the watchdog of legality *for* the central authorities; it is not considered to be the watchdog of legality *against* the central authorities.

Perhaps it should also be stressed, in discussing the independence of the Procuracy, that it, like all other state agencies in the Soviet Union, including the courts and administrative and legislative bodies, is under the general control of the Communist Party of the Soviet Union, which, in the words of Article 126 of the USSR Constitution, "is the vanguard of the working people in their struggle to build a communist society and is the leading core of all organizations of the working people, both social and state." Protests against illegal actions of Communist Party organizations would presumably be made by the procurator only as a party member and not as an outside official.

Competence of the Procuracy. The 1955 Statute on Procuracy Supervision specifies the following duties of the Procuracy:

1. Supervision of strict execution of the laws by all ministries and departments, and their subordinate institutions and enterprises, by all executive and administrative agencies of local soviets, by cooperatives and other social organizations, and by officials and citizens;

2. Institution of criminal proceedings against persons guilty of the commission of crimes;

3. Supervision of the observance of legality by agencies of inquiry and of preliminary investigation;

2. This language goes back to Lenin, who established the Soviet Procuracy in 1922. See V. I. Lenin, "O dvoinom podchinenii i zakonnosti," in *V. I. Lenin o gosudarstve i prave* (Moscow, 1958), II, 720–724.

4. Supervision of the legality and validity of judgments, decisions, rulings, and decrees of judicial agencies;

5. Supervision of the legality of execution of judgments;

6. Supervision of observance of legality in the treatment of prisoners in places of deprivation of freedom.[3]

The first of these duties is called "general supervision." The second is not supervision at all but rather the administrative function of instituting criminal proceedings. The third is an aspect of the Procuracy's administrative responsibility for preliminary investigation. The fourth and fifth comprise the Procuracy's function of "judicial supervision," as it is called, although it is also an aspect of "general supervision." The sixth – supervision of penal institutions – was given new emphasis in 1955; it, too, is an aspect of general supervision.

The central staff of the Procurator General includes the following sections:[4]

1. General supervision;
2. Supervision of investigation by agencies of state security;
3. Supervision of judicial consideration of criminal cases;
4. Supervision of judicial consideration of civil cases;
5. Supervision of places of deprivation of freedom; and
6. Juvenile cases.

In addition, there are sections for analysis of legislation and for statistics, as well as others. The central staff also includes an investigations administration, as well as investigators for especially important cases. The Chief Military Procuracy is also part of the central staff. The Procuracy, as indicated earlier, publishes a monthly journal, "Socialist Legality," jointly with the USSR Supreme Court.

In addition, the republican, regional, and other intermediate procurators have their own staffs. Also there is at least one procurator for each of the several thousand districts into which the Soviet Union is divided, in addition to military procurators in headquarters of military districts, army groups, fleets, armies, flotillas, army corps and garrisons.

Powers of the Procuracy. In exercising general supervision, including judicial supervision and supervision of penal institutions, the Procuracy cannot generally order administrative agencies, courts, officials, or others, to do anything, or to refrain from doing anything, on the ground that it is, in the Procuracy's view, illegal. "Supervision," in the Soviet sense, is, rather, the power to "verify" (*proverit'*) acts of another and, if such verification reveals illegalities, to "protest" such illegalities, either to the offending party or to his superiors. In addition to the power of "protest" (in Russian, *protest*), supervision by the Procuracy includes the power to make "proposals" (*predstavleniia*) to state or social organizations concerning the elimination of offenses and of their causes.

3. *Supra*, note 1, Article 3. An extensive collection of protests and representations lodged by way of general supervision against the legality of governmental enactments in the Soviet Union from 1937 to 1964 has been translated by Glenn G. Morgan in *Legal Controls in the Soviet Union* (Leiden, 1966), pp. 103–286.

4. See D. A. Loeber, "The Soviet Procuracy and the Rights of the Individual against the State," *Journal of the International Commission of Jurists* 1:59 (1957).

The power of the Procuracy to protest illegalities and to make proposals for their elimination is reinforced by very strong procedural guarantees. The 1955 Statute on Procuracy Supervision states in Article 11 that procurators may demand and obtain all documents (including decrees, regulations, orders, etc.) issued by ministries and departments and their subordinate institutions and enterprises, as well as by executive and administrative agencies of local soviets, by cooperative and social organizations, and by officials, in order to verify the conformity of such documents to the law; that procurators may verify on the spot the execution of the laws, in connection with petitions, complaints, or other information concerning violations; that procurators may require ministries, departments, their subordinate institutions and enterprises, local soviets, cooperative and social organizations, as well as individual officials, to arrange audits and inspections of the activities of their respective organizations; and that they may require personal explanations from officials and citizens concerning violations of the law. In addition, Article 14 requires procurators to receive and examine petitions and complaints of citizens concerning violations of the law, to verify such petitions and complaints within a certain time, and to take measures to restore the violated rights and to protect the lawful interests of the affected citizens.

The 1955 Statute requires that a procurator's protest shall be acted upon within ten days, and that the procurator who made the protest shall be informed of the decision (Article 13). If a protest is lodged against a decision to impose an administrative penalty upon an individual, the protest stays the execution of the penalty pending consideration of the protest (Article 13). A procurator's proposal must be considered by the state or social organization to which it is addressed within one month (Article 16).

In supervising execution of laws by agencies of inquiry and of preliminary investigation, the Procuracy is required by the 1955 Statute "to strictly watch out that not a single citizen is subjected to illegal or unfounded criminal prosecution or to any other unlawful restriction of rights," as well as "to watch over the undeviating observance by agencies of inquiry and preliminary investigation of the legally established procedure of investigating crimes" (Article 17). In addition, it is provided that "A procurator shall be obliged to consider, within the time established by law, complaints addressed to him or received by him against actions of agencies of inquiry and of preliminary investigation and to inform the complainants of the decisions taken on their complaints" (Article 21).

In addition to supervising the investigation of crimes, the Procuracy also administers such investigation both through its own investigators and through other agencies of inquiry and preliminary investigation (especially, the police and agencies of state security). Article 19 of the 1955 Statute provides that a procurator shall have the right:

(1) to give agencies of inquiry and of preliminary investigation instructions concerning the investigations of crimes, concerning the choice, change or cancellation of measures of restraint relating to an accused, and also concerning discovery of concealed criminals;

(2) to require from agencies of inquiry and of preliminary investigation, for verification of a criminal case, documents, materials and other information concerning crimes that have been committed;

(3) to participate in the conduct of preliminary investigation and inquiry in criminal cases and in necessary instances personally to conduct the investigation in any case;

(4) to return criminal cases to agencies of inquiry and of preliminary investigation with his instructions concerning the conduct of a supplementary investigation;

(5) to vacate illegal and unfounded decrees of agencies of inquiry and of preliminary investigation;

(6) to remove an investigator or person conducting an inquiry, if such persons have permitted the violation of a law in the investigation of the case;

(7) to remove any case from an agency of inquiry and to transfer it to an agency of preliminary investigation, and also to transfer a case from one agency of preliminary investigation to another, for the purpose of securing the most complete and objective investigation of the case;

(8) to commission agencies of inquiry to fulfill particular investigative actions in cases being conducted by investigators of agencies of the procuracy, namely: to detain, bring in, or arrest the accused, to conduct searches and seizures, to discover concealed criminals;

(9) to terminate criminal cases on the grounds established by law.

Supervision of judicial activities by the Procuracy is also extremely broad. Procurators are authorized to participate in administrative sessions of courts (preliminary to trial) and in judicial sessions of criminal and civil cases, and to give their opinions on questions arising in the course of trials; to act as state prosecutors in criminal cases; to institute civil suits, including civil suits in criminal cases; to protest illegal and unfounded judgments, decisions, rulings, and decrees of judicial agencies; to give opinions in criminal and civil cases considered by higher courts on appeal or protest; and to supervise the execution of court judgments (Article 23). The Procuracy has the right to suspend execution of a protested judgment, decision, ruling, or decree of any court pending a decision by way of supervision (Article 27).

In addition, the Procurator General of the USSR is required to participate in sessions of the Plenum of the USSR Supreme Court (Article 28), and in the event that he considers that a decree of the Plenum does not correspond to law, to make a proposal concerning it to the Presidium of the Supreme Soviet of the USSR (Article 29). He also has the right to make proposals to the Plenum of the USSR Supreme Court concerning the issuance of guiding instructions to judicial agencies on questions of court practice (Article 30).

With respect to penal institutions, the 1955 statute provides: "Responsibility for observance of legality in places of deprivation of freedom is imposed upon agencies of the Procuracy" (Article 32). This is spelled out in provisions requiring the Procuracy "systematically to visit places of deprivation of freedom," to make detailed inspections, to suspend execution of illegal orders and regulations of the administration, to make protests, and to take measures to institute criminal or disciplinary proceedings against persons guilty of violations of legality (Article 33). Article 34 provides: "A procurator shall be obliged immediately to liberate from custody anyone illegally subjected to arrest or illegally kept under guard in places of deprivation of freedom." The Procuracy has the right to see all documents, to question persons personally, and to require personal explanations from representatives of the administration (Article 35). Complaints and petitions of prisoners must be considered by the Procuracy within the time established by law and the complainants must be informed of the decisions taken; moreover, the Procuracy is obliged to see to it that complaints and petitions of prisoners are directed by the administration to the agencies or officials to which they are addressed (Article 36). Also administrations of places of deprivation of freedom are required to fulfill – and not merely to consider – proposals of procurators concerning observance of legally established rules of confinement of prisoners (Article 37).

Significance of the Procuracy for Soviet Criminal Law and Procedure. It is apparent that the Procuracy has a significance for Soviet criminal law and procedure far beyond that which flows from its functions in the preliminary investigation and prosecution of crimes. It not only participates in the judicial process; it also supervises that process – concretely, through its power to protest individual decisions of courts, and generally through its power to make proposals for correcting abuses in the judicial system. Apart from its supervisory power with respect to the courts, the Procuracy's supervision of inquiries and preliminary investigations by the police and the state security agencies (in addition to its responsibility for the conduct of investigations by its own investigators), and its supervision of places of confinement (labor colonies and prisons), also have a very great significance for the administration of criminal law. Finally, and most important, the Procuracy's power of general supervision over the acts of state and social organizations, seen in the light of the very high degree of administrative control of Soviet economic and social life, gives it a vantage point from which to oversee the entire Soviet legal system. The procuracy is, in effect, the "inspector general" for virtually every aspect of Soviet official activity, with the two exceptions indicated earlier: its supervisory powers stop short of the center and they stop short of the Communist Party apparatus. At the same time, the Procuracy is, in effect, everyman's lawyer: anybody can complain to the Procuracy (and hundreds of thousands do complain annually) against abuses of his rights, and the Procuracy is supposed to respond to each complaint and in proper instances to take appropriate measures – whether of protest, proposal, or institution of criminal proceedings.

These powers of the Procuracy have a historical dimension that enhances them still further.[5] The Russian Procuracy was established in the early eighteenth century by Peter the Great, as "the eye of the tsar." Many of its present powers were developed in the eighteenth and early nineteenth centuries. With the establishment in 1864 of a judicial system independent of the administrative branch of government, and of a professional bar, the Russian Procuracy was shorn of many of its supervisory powers and was assimilated to the system of state attorneys in Western Europe. The Bolshevik Revolution at first abolished the Procur-

5. See H. J. Berman, *Justice in the USSR: An Interpretation of Soviet Law*, rev. ed. (Cambridge, Mass., 1963), pp. 240–241.

acy, but in 1922 Lenin brought it back, and in doing so he revived many of the functions that the Russian Procuracy had had prior to the reforms of 1864. Although there have been some changes in the structure and powers of the Soviet Procuracy since 1922, it has remained basically the same since that time. It probably has more prestige, and attracts more able young lawyers into its ranks, than any of the other branches of the Soviet legal profession, including the judiciary, the jurisconsults (legal advisers to state enterprises and institutions), and the bar (*advokatura*).

9 The Role of the Legal Profession in Criminal Law and Procedure

All Soviet legal personnel – procurators, judges, jurisconsults, advocates, law professors, legal research workers, and others – are called "jurists" (*iuristy*), as, indeed, are all persons who have received (or are receiving) a legal education. Graduates of law departments of universities or law institutes may go into any of the branches of the legal profession, depending in part on their wishes, in part on the wishes of the particular unit requiring their services, and in part on assignment by appropriate authorities. Despite the diverse types of work in which they engage, all Soviet jurists have a common professional identity, based upon their common educational background and their common concern with legality as well as upon the interlocking character of their activities.[1]

The Procuracy and the judiciary have been discussed in the two preceding chapters; it remains in this chapter to consider the practicing lawyers, particularly from the standpoint of their relation to criminal law and procedure.

There are two distinct types of practicing lawyers in the Soviet Union, the "advocate" (*advokat*) and the "jurisconsult" (*iuriskonsul't*). Jurisconsults are legal advisers to state enterprises and other institutions and organizations; their work is largely in the fields of administrative law, civil law, and labor law, rather than criminal law, although they are also concerned to prevent violations of criminal law by the organizations they serve and by the personnel thereof. Jurisconsults do not normally appear in court in criminal cases except to defend their organizations in civil suits tried in conjunction with a crime (as, for example, when a criminal case is instituted for automobile homicide, and the victim seeks compensation against the enterprise which employed the driver and which is vicariously liable for the harm caused by his acts). The number of jurisconsults in the Soviet Union has not been published, but from statistics on the total number of Soviet jurists (101,000 in 1965) it may be estimated that there are about 40,000 jurisconsults.[2]

1. See Donald D. Barry and Harold J. Berman, "The Soviet Legal Profession," *Harvard Law Review* 82:1–41 (1968). This article is reproduced with some additional pages and some deletions in H. Gordon Skilling and Franklyn Griffiths, eds., *Interest Groups in Soviet Politics* (Princeton, N.J., 1971), Chapter 9 ("The Jurists").

2. The RSFSR Model Statute on the Jurisconsult is translated in Harold J. Berman and John B. Quigley, Jr., *Basic Laws on the Structure of the Soviet State* (Cambridge, Mass., 1969), pp. 322–325.

"Advocates," who were said to number about 15,000 in the USSR as a whole in 1970 are empowered by the 1960 RSFSR Law on Court Organization "to provide defense counsel at preliminary investigations and in court, and to render other legal assistance to citizens, enterprises, institutions and organizations" (Article 23). They are organized into "colleges of advocates," which are "voluntary organizations of persons engaged in advocacy" (Article 23). Such colleges of advocates have existed since 1922 (when they were called "colleges of defenders"); in 1939 an all-union decree established colleges of advocates under the general control of the USSR Ministry of Justice operating through republican ministries of justice;[3] in 1962 various republics enacted their own statutes regulating the *advokatura* (the collective noun referring to the advocates as a body), based in part on the 1939 all-union decree. The following discussion will be concerned principally with the 1962 RSFSR Statute on the *Advokatura.*[4]

The 1962 RSFSR Statute on the *Advokatura* establishes colleges of advocates on the level of autonomous republic, territory, region, and municipality (in the cities of Moscow and Leningrad), "to perform the following functions for the benefit of citizens, enterprises, institutions, organizations, and collective farms in the RSFSR: to provide defense counsel at preliminary investigations and in court; to act as representatives in civil cases in court and *arbitrazh*; and to render any other necessary legal assistance" (Article 1). It will be noticed that the 1962 RSFSR Statute on the *Advokatura* expands somewhat the definition of functions of advocates given in Article 23 of the 1960 RSFSR Law on Court Organization, by referring to collective farms and to *arbitrazh*; the latter is a system of administrative courts established primarily for decision of contract disputes between state economic enterprises.

Article 1 of the Statute on the *Advokatura* repeats the formula of Article 23 of the Law on Court Organization, that "Colleges of advocates are voluntary organizations of persons engaged in advocacy." The phrase "voluntary organizations (*dobrovol'nye ob"edineniia*)[5] is apparently intended to distinguish colleges of advocates from state organizations and to indicate their self-governing character. Under the 1962 Statute, the general assembly of members is the "highest agency" of a college of advocates, with power to elect a governing board (presidium) and a (financial) auditing commission, to hear and approve their reports, and to "take decisions on questions concerning the work of the college of advocates" (Article 16). The general assembly must be convened at least once a year (Article 17). All advocates in the college have the right to elect and be elected to its governing

3. Decree of USSR Council of Ministers, August 16, 1939, *Sobranie postanovlenii i rasporiazhenii Pravitel'stva SSR* (1939), no. 49, item 394.

4. The statute (*Polozhenie*) is reproduced in *Sovetskaia iustitsiia* (1962), no. 15–16, pp. 31–34. It is translated with commentary by L. M. Friedman and Z. L. Zile, "Soviet Legal Profession: Recent Developments in Law and Practice," *Wisconsin Law Review* (1964), p. 32, and in Berman and Quigley, *supra*, note 2, pp. 309–321.

5. The term *ob"edinenie* means "unit" or "combine," and suggests a somewhat tighter form of organization than *obshchestvo* ("association"). However, colleges of advocates qualify as "social organizations" (*obshchestvennye organizatsii*) rather than "state organizations" (*gosudarstvennye organizatsii*), in view of their voluntary character and their inability to exercise state sanctions.

bodies, as well as to participate in the discussion of questions connected with its activities (Article 28).

The presidium, which (like the auditing commission) is elected by secret ballot for a two-year term (Article 18), has power to admit, refuse to admit, and expel members, to appoint and dismiss heads of the individual law offices into which the college of advocates is divided, and generally to direct the work of such offices (Article 19).

Also colleges of advocates, in contrast to state organizations, are exempt from the obligation of registering with the financial authorities their personnel structure, salaries of officials, wage funds, and estimated overhead expenses (Article 7).

The voluntary character of membership in a college of advocates is qualified, however, by the provision of the 1962 Statute that "Only a person who is a member of a college of advocates may engage in advocacy" (Article 4). This means that anyone who wishes to be an advocate must be a member. Under Article 12 a member has the right to withdraw from the college of advocates at any time on his own volition, but in the light of Article 4 such a withdrawal would mean the cessation of his work as an advocate. Thus the colleges of advocates are not like most bar associations as understood in the United States, but are rather comparable to the bar itself.

In addition, the self-governing character of colleges of advocates is limited by the considerable amount of control over their activities by governmental agencies. Article 5 of the 1962 Statute provides that the organization, direction, and control (in Russian, *kontrol'*, meaning supervisory rather than operative control) of the activities of colleges of advocates shall be exercised by the councils of ministers of autonomous republics or the executive committees of territorial, regional or municipal (in Moscow and Leningrad) soviets – that is, by the administrative authorities at the levels at which the colleges of advocates are organized; and that in addition, general direction and (supervisory) control over their activities shall be exercised by the RSFSR Ministry of Justice. With the abolition of the RSFSR Ministry of Justice in 1963, its function of general control over the colleges of advocates was transferred to the Juridical Commission of the RSFSR Council of Ministers. The RSFSR Minister of Justice under the 1962 Statute (Article 13), and presumably the President of the Juridical Commission of the RSFSR Council of Ministers after the abolition of the RSFSR Ministry of Justice in 1963, and since 1970 the USSR Minister of Justice,[6] is authorized to expel a member from the college of advocates for "demonstrated unsuitability for the performance of the duties of an advocate" and for "the commission of offenses that bring discredit on the title of Soviet advocate," as well as for other more specific offenses. The council of ministers of an autonomous republic or the executive committee of a territorial, regional or municipal (in Moscow and Leningrad) soviet, as well as the presidium of a college of advocates, may also expel a member on the same grounds (Article 13); but a decision of a presidium of a college of advocates to expel (or to refuse to admit) a member is subject to reversal by the aforementioned administrative authorities (Article 14).

6. *Supra*, Chapter 6, notes 8 and 9.

The system of payment for legal services is regulated by the RSFSR Ministry of Justice, according to Article 6 of the 1962 Statute (presumably by the Juridical Commission of the RSFSR Council of Ministers from 1963 to 1970, and the USSR Ministry of Justice thereafter) and must be approved by the RSFSR Council of Ministers. Decisions taken by the general assembly concerning the number of persons to be admitted to a college, and estimates of its income and expenses, are subject to the approval of the administrative body governing the territorial unit in which it is situated (autonomous republic, territory, region or city) (Article 16 (c)). Decisions of the general assembly or of the presidium that do not conform to law may be reversed by the appropriate administrative authorities (Articles 17, 20), and the choice by the presidium of its own chairman and deputy chairman is subject to their approval (Article 21).

Each of the individual law offices (*iuridicheskie konsul'tatsii*) into which a college of advocates is divided is directed by a manager appointed by the presidium of the college of advocates (Article 24). The manager is required to "distribute the work among the advocates, having regard to their qualifications and to the personal requests for their services [by clients]," and to establish their fees in accordance with the instructions issued by the RSFSR Ministry of Justice (Article 25). Fees for legal services are paid by clients to the legal consultation office, which retains a certain fixed percentage (usually about 15 percent) for its overhead expenses and that of the college of advocates and transfers the balance to the advocate who rendered the services (cf. Article 35).

With respect to the moral and social obligations of an advocate, the 1962 Statute provides (Article 30): "An advocate must be a model of strict and undeviating observance of Soviet laws, of moral purity, and of unimpeachable conduct; he shall be obliged constantly to perfect his knowledge, to increase his ideological-political level and occupational qualifications, and actively to participate in propagating Soviet law." Thus the advocate is supposed to maintain high moral and professional standards, and at the same time he is drawn into the struggle to maintain legality and respect for the "ideological-political" and the legal order. It was reported in 1961 that 53 percent of RSFSR advocates were members or candidate members of the Communist Party.[7]

In connection with the struggle to maintain respect for legality and for the legal order, it is of some interest that one of the duties of the presidium of a college of advocates is to analyze the causes of crime and other offenses against legality, on the basis of documents available in the college, and to submit appropriate proposals concerning elimination of those causes to state and social organizations (1962 Statute, Article 19 (g)). In addition, the presidium is obliged to "take measures to advance the ideological-political level and legal qualifications of members of the college, [and] to organize the participation of advocates in propagating Soviet legislation" (Article 19 (f)).

We turn, finally, to the duties of the Soviet advocate to his client. These are contained principally in four articles of the 1962 Statute. Article 31 provides:

7. K. P. Gorshenin, "Novyi zakon o sudoustroistve RSFSR," in Vsesoiuznyi Institut Iuridicheskikh Nauk, *Novoe ugolovnoe zakonodatel'stvo RSFSR* (Moscow, 1961), p. 23.

"An advocate shall be obliged to use all ways and means specified by law for the defense of rights and legal interests of citizens, enterprises, institutions, organizations, and collective farms that turn to him for legal assistance."

Article 32 forbids an advocate to handle a case when an official to whom he is related takes part in the investigation or decision of the case, when the interests of the person who requests his services conflict with those of a person to whom he has previously rendered legal services, and when he himself has participated in the case as judge, investigator, procurator, witness, person conducting an inquiry, interpreter, or witness of investigative acts.

Article 33 deals with "professional secrecy," or what in the United States is usually referred to as "the lawyer-client privilege." It provides:

> An advocate must not disclose information communicated to him by a client (*doveritel'*) in connection with legal assistance rendered in the given case.
>
> An advocate may not be interrogated as a witness concerning the circumstances of a case which have become known to him in connection with the fulfillment of the obligations of defense counsel (*zashchitnik*) in the given case.

Finally, Article 34 states: "An advocate shall not have the right to withdraw from the defense of an accused once undertaken."

It is apparent from the four articles cited above that the view sometimes expressed by Western writers to the effect that Soviet defense counsel are supposed to serve the interests of the Soviet state, regardless of the interests of their clients, is false. On the contrary, the Soviet advocate is subject to the same general dual responsibility – on the one hand to the person he is representing and on the other hand to society – as the lawyer in Western Europe, in England, and the United States, and in many other countries. Likewise, it is inaccurate to speak of the Soviet advocate as a "state employee": he is, indeed, subject to a large measure of control by administrative authorities, but both technically and substantially he is a member of an autonomous professional body that has its own traditions and is independent of the prosecutor's office (the Procuracy) as well as of the courts. Indeed, the term "state employee" is quite misleading in the Soviet context, where the state embraces so many conflicting activities that it loses significance as a basis of analysis.

The Soviet advocate's responsibility to his client in criminal cases is stressed in the 1960 RSFSR Code of Criminal Procedure, especially in Article 51 ("Duties and rights of defense counsel"), which states clearly that defense counsel is obliged to do everything legally possible to secure the acquittal of the accused or a reduction of his responsibility, and to render him necessary legal aid.

Yet it is also apparent from a study of the 1962 RSFSR Statute on the *Advokatura* that the lawyer's dual allegiance to his client and to society is more heavily weighted in favor of the latter in the Soviet system than it is in the American system and probably in most Western European systems as well. In the first place, whereas the English or American lawyer's obligation to society is expressed in the doctrine that he is an "officer of the court," the Soviet advocate (like his Continental European counterpart) is subject less to judicial control than to administrative control. Such administrative control is far more stringent in the Soviet Union than in most countries of Western Europe. The fact that he may be disbarred by regional and equivalent executive agencies and by the RSFSR Minister of Justice (or his successor) without recourse to the courts carries with it the implication that the Soviet advocate runs serious risks in opposing the administrative policies of his government. Moreover, the number of persons admitted to colleges of advocates is determined ultimately by administrative authorities; and once admitted, the Soviet advocate's mode of work, choice of clients, and fees, are much more strictly regulated by administrative authorities than in Western European countries generally or in the United States.

In addition, the secrecy of clients' communications and the lawyer-client privilege are not given as much protection by the 1962 RSFSR Statute on the *Advokatura* as might appear from a quick reading of Article 33. In the first place, Article 33 is very unclear. It speaks in the first paragraph of information communicated to an advocate by his "client," but the word "client" (*doveritel'*, literally "entruster") is used nowhere else in the Statute and is derived from the civil law relating to powers of attorney. Under the RSFSR Civil Code the "entruster" may only appoint a "trustee" (*poverennyi*) by a written authorization. If the legislator intended by Article 33 to protect any person who consults an advocate, and not merely one who has formally retained the advocate as his legal representative, the choice of the term *doveritel'* is unfortunate – all the more so in view of the fact that Soviet legal writers often use the Russian word *klient* to refer to any person who turns to a lawyer for legal advice or other assistance.

The second paragraph of Article 33, which protects against disclosure of any information (and not only information communicated by the client), binds only the "defense counsel" (*zashchitnik*), which in Soviet law refers to the advocate representing an accused person, but not to a defense attorney in a civil case and possibly not to an advocate who is consulted in a criminal case before the client is accused. Moreover, the second paragraph, which is reproduced from the RSFSR Code of Criminal Procedure (Article 72), only prohibits the interrogation of the defense counsel as a witness.

Finally, the phrase "in the given case" (*po dannomu delu*), which appears at the end of each of the two paragraphs, probably modifies "information communicated" or "circumstances that became known," but alternatively it might modify "assistance rendered" or "obligations of defense counsel." If the latter alternative is adopted, the client or accused is protected only against disclosures relating to the particular matter about which he has consulted the lawyer or the particular crime of which he is accused.

Thus it is doubtful that a client in a civil matter who disclosed to his advocate that he committed a crime would be protected by the statute against testimony by the advocate concerning such disclosure in subsequent criminal proceedings; indeed, unless a broad interpretation is given to the first paragraph of Article 33, the advocate may be criminally liable for failure to report the civil client's crime if it is serious enough to fall within those categories of crimes required to be reported by the Criminal Code. Moreover, although the second paragraph of

Article 33 forbids the advocate to testify as a witness in a criminal case involving the accused whom he is defending, concerning any circumstances of the case, it does not prohibit him (even under a broad interpretation) from reporting otherwise than as a witness those circumstances that became known to him otherwise than by communication from the accused.

In Soviet writings on the 1962 Statute, a discussion of Article 33 has been conspicuously absent. Its ambiguities may be unintended, but even so they probably reflect a division of opinion concerning how far the lawyer-client principle should be extended.

Despite these qualifications, the 1962 RSFSR Statute on the *Advokatura,* taken together with the 1960 RSFSR Code of Criminal Procedure, marks a clear and significant advance over earlier legislation in the progress of the Soviet advocate not only toward greater independence but also toward greater protection both of the rights of the accused and of the integrity of the judicial process. For prior to the 1962 Statute, Soviet legislation contained no limitations on the discretion of the Minister of Justice in disbarring an advocate; and prior to the 1960 Code (and the 1958 Fundamental Principles on which it was based) there were no express legislative provisions concerning the advocate's duties toward the accused person whom he defends, although Soviet court decisions had gone very far in implementing the 1936 Constitutional guarantee of the right to counsel. Not only is the right to counsel prior to the issuance of the indictment now secured (1960 RSFSR Code of Criminal Procedure, Articles 201–204) but also the right to counsel at trial and on appeal are amply protected (see Articles 48–51, 325, 335), and counsel's duty to do everything legally possible to secure an acquittal or a mitigation of his client's responsibility is clearly stated (Article 51).[8]

8. That these duties of defense counsel are taken seriously in practice is evidenced by the vigorous examination of witnesses and final speeches reported in many of the cases cited in Chapter 5, notes 18 and 26.

10 The Language of the Codes

Those who believe that the Bolshevik Revolution abolished the past and created a wholly new and different social system may be puzzled to find in Soviet criminal law and procedure the familiar language of rights, duties, guilt, crimes, punishments, statutes, decisions, intent, negligence, theft, fraud, homicide, court, judge, judgments, defense counsel, evidence, appeals, and hundreds of other basic terms and concepts known in all Western legal systems. Do these words mean the same thing in Russian that they mean in English? Do they mean the same thing to the Soviets that they did to their Russian forebears from whom they have been inherited? Or have they been transformed by their adaptation to a new type of social system characterized by one-party rule, planned economy, and a mobilized social order?

Contrariwise, those who suppose that the Revolution has made no new contribution to the legal ordering of society, and that its original revolutionary vision has yielded entirely, or almost entirely, either to tradition or to bureaucracy or to both, may wonder what is the significance of such words and phrases, in Soviet criminal law and procedure, as "measures of social pressure," "socialist legal consciousness," "socialist ownership," "speculation," "hooliganism," "social accuser," "social defense counsel," and dozens of other terms that have no exact counterpart in prerevolutionary Russian law or in Western law. Do these reflect a "new type of law," as Soviet writers claim, or are they merely different ways of saying the same things that other legal systems say in more traditional language? Are they, as some Western critics have suggested, only an ideological fringe on what is essentially a traditional, indeed, "neoclassical," criminal law and procedure?

Both the old and the new in the language of the Soviet codes are to be explained primarily in terms of the impact of history rather than in terms of the impact of political theory. One of the reasons for this is the fact that Marxist-Leninist political theory proved woefully weak in its understanding of law, and therefore had to yield to history – not only to the history of the prerevolutionary Russian past but also to the history of Soviet development from 1917 on. Originally, all prerevolutionary law was to be abolished, and only so much proletarian law introduced as was necessary in a period of transition to classless, "lawless" socialism. Law itself was considered "bourgeois," and therefore to the extent that it was needed by the proletarian dictatorship it would have to rely upon "bourgeois" terminology. Yet this terminology, it was thought, could be counteracted by overriding principles, and by exceptional rules and procedures, that would enable the Communist Party leadership and the state security agencies to disregard the law when it was expedient to do so, while moving toward a new utopia in which the coercions and formalities of law would gradually disappear altogether.

In addition to caring little for the idea of law, the Bolsheviks were extremely poor legal draftsmen. They lacked the ability to use the same terms consistently even when they wanted to, and they did not always want to. The 1922 and 1926 RSFSR Criminal Codes are full of unintended inconsistencies and ambiguities. They are also replete with vague, sweeping definitions of crimes in which technical legal terms are used in a popular sense, and popular terms in a technical legal sense. Similarly, the 1923 RSFSR Code of Criminal Procedure is a hodgepodge of rules and exceptions to rules. In addition, the criminal and criminal-procedure codes, as originally drafted, are dominated by programmatic statements and by a terminology that "smacked of revolution" but much of which was essentially superficial in content.

The codes of the NEP period were written hastily by a few people and were not meant to last long. At the same time, they were meant to show the world a new and revolutionary system of justice. The draftsmen took the prerevolutionary codes as models, together with Western codes, and attempted to give them a Bolshevik cast. The 1960 codes, on the other hand, were written with the greatest care, over a period of many years, with the participation of thousands of legal scholars and experienced officials of various state organizations, and after extensive public discussion in the scholarly literature and in the press. They were historical, rather than ideological, in character, in the sense that they were designed to remedy the defects of the past and to provide a foundation for future development; they were not conceived as propaganda or as a model for other countries. The draftsmen – who as legal technicians were far superior to their predecessors of the 1920's – felt no aversion to the terminology of the past, whether of prerevolutionary Russian law, earlier Soviet law, or Western law, so long as it could help them to solve the problems that they faced. Mostly they drew on the language of their own experience.

If, therefore, the language and style of the 1960 Codes are "neoclassical," or "Marxist," or "Slavic," or anything else, it is not because the draftsmen set out to create such a language or style. They did, indeed, respond to the political, economic, and other pressures of the society in which they lived and for which they were legislating, and they therefore had to satisfy the Communist Party that the codes were in the tradition of Marxist-Leninist theory as interpreted in the post-Stalin era. But in 1960 it was no longer necessary to put many revolutionary slogans in a code. The 1960 RSFSR Criminal Code and Code of Criminal Procedure are therefore written in the authentic legal language of the Soviet Union, which, like all authentic languages, builds on past experience, responds to the needs of the time, and does not consciously attempt to create a new vocabulary.

If we consider those terms and concepts of the Soviet codes that are most familiar to us, we find that some of them go far back into the history of Russian law. In Russian legal and other literature of the tenth to fourteenth centuries there appear such contemporary Soviet legal terms as "court" (*sud*), "judge" (*sud'ia*), "accuse" (*obvinit'*), "guilty" (*vinovat*), "answer" (before a court) (*otvechat'*), "case" (*delo*), "murderer" (*uboitsa*), "treason" (*izmena*), "open stealing" (*grabiozh*), "assault with intent to rob" (*razboi*), "theft" (*krad'ba*, now *krazha*), "steal" (*khishchat'*), "insult" (*oskorbit'*), "attempt" (*pokushat'sia*), "a search" (*obysk*), "witness" (*svidetel'*), "accessory" (*posobnik*), "prison" (*tiurma*), "punishment" (*kazn'*), "death penalty" (*smertnaia kazn'*), "law" (*zakon*), and others. The term "state" (*gosudarstvo*, literally "lordship") dates from the fifteenth century.

Most of the Soviet legal language of 1960, however, is of more recent vintage. Especially in the eighteenth and nineteenth centuries, the Russians built into their own language much of the legal vocabulary of the West, by finding Russian equivalents. "Ownership" (*sobstvennost'*) appeared in 1782, although the word "one's own" (*sobstvennyi*) dates from the eleventh century (cf. the French *propriété*). Similarly, as the French term *responsabilité* flourished after the French Revolution (from *répondre*, to answer) so the Russian word *otvetsvennost'* (from *otvechat'*, to answer), like the German *Verantwortlichkeit* (from *antworten*) came into vogue in the nineteenth century. The French term *entreprise* is equivalent to the German term *Unternehmung* and the Russian term *predpriiatie*, meaning a business enterprise, literally an "undertaking." Examples could be multiplied by the hundreds.

The nineteenth century in Russia was a century of law reforms and of the development, for the first time in Russian history, of a class of jurists: indeed, the Russian legal profession, especially after 1864, produced some of the best lawyers and legal minds in Europe. Not all the Russian jurists survived the Revolution, but many did, and it was they who perpetuated the Russian legal language in the new Soviet codes. Indeed, Lenin himself was a lawyer, and although he preached the nihilistic theory of the "dying out" of law under socialism, he also revived, especially during the NEP, many of the prerevolutionary Russian legal institutions, including, as indicated earlier, the Procuracy.

Because the nineteenth-century Russian system of criminal law and procedure was similar to the German and French systems, and because the Soviets have inherited that similarity, many of the terms and concepts of the Soviet codes are more easily translated into French or German than into English. We have tried to avoid, in our translation, the temptation to render Soviet legal language into American legal language where the words convey different images. Thus we have used the phrases "judicial consideration of the case" and "judicial investigation" instead of "trial" and "hearing"; "presentation of the accusation" and "conclusion to indict" instead of "arraignment" and "indictment"; "negligent homicide" and "infliction of light bodily injuries" instead of "manslaughter" and "assault and battery"; and so forth.[1] Occasionally we have departed from this rule: thus we have rendered *zashchitnik*, which is literally "defender," as "defense counsel," since the American reader might not otherwise realize that the term usually refers to the accused's lawyer (*advokat*) – though perhaps we have erred in speaking, for the sake of consistency, of the "social defense

1. Professor A.K.R. Kiralfy of London University has criticized the translation for being excessively literal in some parts. Thus he would say of punishment that it is "determined" or "inflicted" rather than "assigned" (Criminal Code, Article 37); he would avoid the more awkward phrase "unwarranted appropriation" (of the title or authority of an official) and would use instead the term "usurpation" (Article 194); also he argues for the use of "trial proceedings" and of "trial" or "hearing" instead of "judicial examination" (Chapter 21) and "judicial investigation" (Chapter 23). Professor Kiralfy also criticizes the translation of Article 227, particularly the reference to the punishment of religious activity which is "connected with" causing harm to citizens' health – the Russian phrase *sviazany s* being better rendered, in his opinion (following "quite a modest dictionary published in Moscow"), by "entailing" or "involving." "Why should the translators speak worse English than the Russians?" he asks. See Kiralfy, "Book Review," *Modern Law Review*, 31:109 (1968).

Neither Mr. Spindler nor I find these criticisms convincing. If the authors of the Code had wished to speak of "determining" punishment or "inflicting" it, they could easily have done so by use of the Russian word *opredeliat'* or *nalagat'*; instead they chose to say *naznachat'*, which means to assign, appoint, fix, set. As for "unwarranted appropriation" (*samovol'noe prisvoenie*) it says exactly what the Russian says, whereas "usurpation" might mean something a little different; moreover, the Russian is not idiomatic, so why should the English be? And to speak of a trial or a hearing instead of a judicial investigation, and of trial proceedings instead of a judicial examination, is to overlook the fact that the "trial," as we would say, is divided into separate stages, of which the judicial investigation and judicial examination are two. At best, the term "trial" or "hearing" might be used instead of "judicial consideration of the case," but this would sacrifice the distinction between the English and American emphasis on the element of contest (trial) and on the orality of the proceedings (hearing), on the one hand, and, on the other, the Russian (and Continental European) emphasis on what goes on in the minds of the judges.

Finally, with respect to Article 227, it is by no means clear that the religious activity, in order to be punishable, must "entail," in the sense of result in, the causing of harm to citizens' health. "Involving" may be as vague and ambiguous as "connected with," but it, too, suggests a causal relation which the translators were unwilling to add to the Russian original – whatever a Russian-English dictionary may say. Since one cannot tell from the Russian text how closely related the religious activity must be to the causing of harm to health, beyond being in some way "connected with" it, it seems best to give a literal rendition of the Russian. In fact, some persons have been convicted under Article 227 for religious preaching that has been only very indirectly connected with harm to others' health.

Another reviewer of the first edition, Yurii Sdobnikov, a leading Soviet translator of legal literature into English, also criticized the translation for adopting a "too literal approach." See Sdobnikov, "Translating the Criminal Code," *Anglo-Soviet Journal*, 30:27 (September 1969). Mr. Sdobnikov's carefully considered and yet spirited review is warmly appreciated by both Mr. Spindler and the writer. Nevertheless, we believe that his suggestions of a more idiomatic English rendition also lead to legal errors. Thus he asks, "What could be the purpose of saying: 'Infringing the life of a policeman'? Why not say 'an attempt on the life of' ('*posyagatelstvo na zhizn . . .*')?" The answer is that the Soviet authors of Article 191-2 did not say "attempt" (*pokushenie*) but instead used a much vaguer term, equivalent to "making an encroachment upon." In fact, it took a decision of the Supreme Court of the USSR to determine that the infringement under Article 191-2 must constitute either an attempt or the completed act in order to be punishable. The headnote of the Supreme Court case stated: "By infringement of (*posiagatel' stvo na*) the life of a policeman or people's guard . . . should be understood the homicide or attempted (*pokushenie na*) homicide of such persons." Using Mr. Sdobnikov's translation, one would have reached an absurd result.

Mr. Sdobnikov charges our translation with "a certain primitivism in the choice of words," which, he states, distorts the style of the original. He gives many examples of what he means,

counsel," who is rarely a lawyer;[2] also we have converted the present tense of most of the code provisions into the future imperative characteristic of American and English law (for example, we have written "Theft . . . shall be punished by deprivation of freedom . . ." instead of the more literal "Theft . . . is punished by deprivation of freedom . . ."), since the Russian is weak in future tenses and uses the present tense in legal provisions to convey a future imperative.[3] In almost all

---

some of which are very helpful and have led to improvements in the present edition. But most of them reflect an erroneous belief that the translation should express in English not what the Russian text says to the Russian-speaking reader but what an English-speaking author would have said if he had composed the text to start with. This belief leads Mr. Sdobnikov to take greater liberties with the Russian word-order and syntax than we believe to be justified in a translation of a code of laws. His major illustration may serve to make our point. He quotes Article 24 paragraph 8 of the Criminal Code (it has since been repealed), which he terms "as lucid and balanced a sentence as you will find in any style of Russian writing." It reads, in Russian transliteration: *Trudoustroistvo lits, osvobozhdennykh iz mest lisheniia svobody, vozlagaetsia na ispolnitel'nye komitety mestnykh Sovetov* etc. We would render this: "The arrangement of work for persons released from places of deprivation of freedom shall be the responsibility of executive committees of local soviets" etc. (In the first edition we said "organization of work of" instead of "arrangement of work for," but in the present edition we have preferred the latter phrase where the same Russian word, *trudoustroistvo*, appears, namely, in Articles 25 and 209-1.) Mr. Sdobnikov quotes our translation and then offers his own, which he believes gives "a better idea of the style of the Russian through greater fidelity to the requirements of English" (p. 30). His translation reads: "It shall be the duty of the Executive Committees of local Soviets . . . to obtain work for persons released from places of deprivation of liberty." Admittedly this is smoother, but it seems to us objectionable for three reasons.

First, it suggests a specific duty to obtain work for each person released from detention, whereas the original (*trudoustroistvo . . . vozlagaetsia*) suggests a more general responsibility to arrange for the employment of such persons. Second, by changing the original word-order the translator sacrifices something of the original thought-processes. Finally, to convert the noun-filled Russian text into verb-oriented English is to give it a quite different flavor. In general, the language of the codes is, to be sure, lucid and balanced, but it is hardly poetry. Indeed, it is considerably more ponderous and legalistic than Mr. Sdobnikov's freer translations would indicate. See also notes 3 and 4 *infra*.

2. Russian words borrowed from Western European languages have also given difficulty. Thus the Russian *kontrol'*, like the German *Kontrolle* or the French *control*, usually means supervision, or checking, or "watching over," rather than direct administration. Nevertheless, we have called it "control," since that word in English has come to have a similar meaning in many contexts, and there are other Russian words that are much closer to our "supervision" (*nadzor*) and "checking" (*proverka*). Also Americans have become used to the fact that many European languages use the word "control" in this wider sense. Another kind of translation problem arises from the occasional use of terms that have exactly the same meaning, e.g., *neostorozhnyi* and *nebrezhnyi* are defined by Soviet jurists in identical terms, and we have – not quite arbitrarily – chosen to translate the first as "negligent" and the second as "careless" (and not "wrongful" as in the first edition). We have also changed the translation of *podsudimyi* from "prisoner" (in the strict English sense of the person in the dock) to "person brought to trial" – since the former usage is a little strange for Americans. A third change from the first edition is the use of "conditional sentence" (instead of "conditional conviction") for *uslovnoe osuzhdenie*.

Despite the recommendation of one reviewer, we have not changed the translation of *ispravitel'nye raboty* from "correctional tasks" to "correctional labor" – first, because it is in the plural, and second, because "correctional labor" is more appropriately used to translate a different Russian phrase, as in "correctional labor colonies" (*ispravitel'nye-trudovye kolonii*).

3. Yurii Sdobnikov, *supra*, note 1, criticized the translation for inconsistency in this respect. He would have us use the future imperative in Articles 1, 2, and 20, for example, rather than say that the Code "has" certain tasks, or "proceeds" from certain principles, or that punishment "constitutes" a chastisement. But this, it seems to us, misses the point. The

other cases, however, we have preferred a more literal translation, despite the awkwardness that it sometimes involves. And where the Soviet style is itself unwieldy or ambiguous, we have not sought to improve it. We have preferred, for example, "Further prolongation of a period of confinement under guard may be carried out . . ." to "A period of confinement may be further prolonged . . . ," since the former literal rendition suggests that a "decree on further prolongation of the period of confinement" must be issued by competent authorities. Indeed, the style of the codes is adapted to the requirement that a "document" be issued to certify virtually every step that is taken.

Yet no matter how a translator may strive, the Russian text will inevitably have a different "ring." Sometimes that ring sounds just as strange in the ears of Soviet citizens not trained in law as it does in American ears; but on the whole, the Russian text is meaningful to the Soviet reader for whom it is intended – both lawyer and layman.

The Russian text of the codes – its vocabulary and syntax as well as its style and meaning – has three main messages. The first is the message of strict legality. The second is the message of protection of political and economic interests of the Soviet state. The third is the message of mobilization of all citizens in the struggle to eliminate crime and to build a unified society.

In speaking of these as "messages," rather than as policies, we have in mind to discuss primarily their linguistic character, rather than their political character as such, although these are, of course, two aspects of the same thing.

(1) **Strict Legality**. The 1960 codes, for very good reason, abandon many of the "modern" ideas of criminal law and penology that flourished in Western Europe and in Russia in the late nineteenth and early twentieth centuries. Sociological and psychological theories played havoc with Soviet law in the 1920's, and thereby bore a share of the blame for the excesses of Stalinism that followed. In a political and economic system such as the Soviet, where the party leadership is subject to few if any effective constitutional restraints upon its power to legislate and the weight of bureaucratism can be unbearable, the best legal safeguards against abuses consist in the traditional guarantees: no crime without a law, no

---

future imperative is used as a command; the indicative is used as a description or characterization. To state that the Code "shall have as its task" certain policies, when the Code is already in existence and its tasks are already determined, would not make sense. On the contrary, the lawmaker is saying to prosecutors, judges, and all others who will be called on to apply the Code: These *are* the tasks, policies, and principles of the Code: you *shall* do thus and so in carrying them out.

Similarly, in Article 20, the lawmaker after great debate decided to say that punishment *is* chastisement, that it *does* necessarily hurt, although it "shall be imposed" only for the purpose of correction, etc.

Mr. Sdobnikov's additional criticism of our use of the present to refer to past acts also fails to take into account the peculiar features of legislative prescriptions. In American statutory language, we say, "One who *does* A, B, and C *shall be* punished by X" – although in fact, of course, he "is" not punished until after he "has done" it. The Russian style, on the contrary, is to say, "One who *has done* A, B, and C *is* punished by X" – leaving the uninitiated with an impression of a factual description. It might, of course, be said that "One who *has done* A, B, and C *shall be* punished by X," but this is awkward because it may suggest that the punishment is to be imposed only if the act occurred before the law was passed.

punishment without a law, no crime or punishment without the judgment of a court, no crime without intent or negligence, precise definitions of specific criminal acts, no punishment except within the limits specifically stated in the dispositive part of the applicable article of the code, and similar "classical" principles. The 1960 RSFSR Criminal Code and Code of Criminal Procedure do not contain all the guarantees of strict legality that one could desire: some of the definitions of crimes (for example, anti-Soviet agitation and propaganda) remain vague and sweeping; others (for example, treason) include acts that should not be criminal at all (such as refusing to return from abroad); preparation of a crime, short of attempt, is itself equally punishable with the crime itself (Criminal Code, Article 15); a suspect may be held for ten days without presenting charges to him; an accused may be held up to nine months without being allowed to consult a lawyer or anyone else. These and many other oppressive features of the codes have been discussed in earlier chapters. Yet one of the main thrusts of the codes is toward protection of the rights of citizens against prosecution for innocent acts, or for crimes more serious than those they actually committed, as well as against arbitrary methods of criminal investigation and trial; and this is manifested in the plain and often ponderous style of the codes as well as in their basically conservative legal policies. Elegance and subtlety are sacrificed to the blunt statement of principles and rules. In this connection it may be noted that the draftsmen have adopted the technique of labeling each of the articles – a practice that is not unique but is nevertheless unusual in the tradition of European codification. This, too, adds to the plainness and directness of the style.

Connected with the blunt style of the codes is their casuistic character, as compared with many other modern European codes. In the modern European tradition, a criminal code should be very general, stating broad doctrines in the General Part and listing only the basic elements of specific crimes in the Special Part. The detailed explanation of the meaning of terms is to be left to legal scholars and to the courts. European jurists would consider it to be a stylistic defect of the RSFSR Criminal Code, for example, that it defines accessories to a crime by listing examples of the forms that being an accessory may take, instead of stating the idea implicit in the concept of being an accessory (Article 17). Similarly, to European jurists it would seem out of place to include provisions on "concealment" and "failure to report" in the General Part (Articles 18, 19), since they are in fact crimes provided for by the Special Part (Articles 88-1, 89-1, 189, 190). Also it is not in the modern Western European tradition to present an exhaustive list of aggravating circumstances (Article 39). Indeed, the RSFSR Criminal Code gives another and slightly different list of aggravating circumstances that make up the separate crime of "intentional homicide under aggravating circumstances" (Article 102). Such attempts at specificity may seem to cause confusion and inconsistency; for example, motives of hooliganism aggravate intentional homicide but not intentional infliction of grave bodily injury (cf. Articles 39, 102, 108).

Similarly, many of the provisions of the Special Part make punishable specific acts that are only instances of more general crimes. For example, four different forms of intentional homicide are provided (Articles 102–105). Also the articles on crimes against socialist property are defined with elaborate qualifications and in many special forms that from a theoretical point of view might better be treated under general principles (cf. Article 91).

Not only the RSFSR Criminal Code but also the RSFSR Code of Criminal Procedure may surprise the European jurist by its specificity. It is not usual for such a code to give a long list of the rights of the accused, as the RSFSR code does, or to define the obligations of proof. The European would expect to find in a treatise, but not in a code, the statement that "no assumptions" are to be made by the court with respect to the guilt or innocence of the accused.

The English or American lawyer may not be troubled by such casuistry (as the Europeans would call it), since he is somewhat less concerned with doctrinal consistency in law, and is more used to the juxtaposition of general principle and concrete case. However, we should judge the style, as well as the content, of the Soviet codes neither by Western European nor by American standards. The Soviet codes bear the scars of the defects and injustices of previous Soviet law. They often include provisions that may appear superfluous to a foreigner but that are necessary in order to make it clear that the previous Soviet rule has been rejected. For example, the 1926 Criminal Code defined complicity in such a way as to include concealment after the fact; it may therefore have made sense to redefine concealment in the General Part of the 1960 Criminal Code and to list various types of accessories if, as was the case, the draftsmen proposed to limit responsibility for complicity so as to exclude concealment after the fact. Similar historical and practical considerations explain many other elements of the Soviet codes that would otherwise appear anomalous. Above all, the Soviet codes are addressed to investigators, procurators, and judges who are accustomed to rely on specific written texts to support their decisions, and who must often cite those specific texts in procedural documents, in order to satisfy their superiors. This may be thought a weakness, but it also has its virtues since it limits the leeway of the law enforcement agencies and provides a basis for the citizen's precious right of complaint. Thus in the Soviet context, casuistry, though it sometimes misfires, is an element of legality.

(2) Protection of State Political and Economic Interests. The high degree of protection of state interests in the 1960 RSFSR Criminal Code and Code of Criminal Procedure is manifested not only in the broad definitions of, and severe punishments for, crimes against the state, crimes against state ownership, official crimes, economic crimes, and others, but also in the language of the codes and their style. In comparison with the earlier codes, the emphasis on the protection of the state has been diminished; in addition, greatly increased emphasis has been placed upon protection of the person, personal ownership, and of the political and labor rights of citizens. Nevertheless the state remains amply protected. Among the tasks of the Criminal Code, stated in Article 1, the protection of the Soviet social and state system and of socialist property is given first place. Crimes against the state are also placed first in the Special Part of the Code, and include a wide variety of acts that would be otherwise classified in other legal systems.

Crimes against socialist property come next, and include 15 separate crimes. Not only the prominence given to the protection of state political and economic interests, but also the language of the individual crimes suggests a difference in quality between Soviet law and older legal systems in this regard. "For the purpose of undermining or weakening Soviet authority," "collection of information on assignment from a foreign intelligence service," "terrorist acts," "the killing of a representative of a foreign state for the purpose of provoking . . . international complications," "the spreading of epidemics or epizootics," "wrecking," "slanderous fabrications which defame the Soviet state and social system," "propagandizing of war," "crimes against another working people's state," "propaganda or agitation for the purpose of arousing hostility or dissension of races or nationalities," "banditry," "mass disorders," "criminally wrongful use or maintenance of agricultural equipment," "unconscientious attitude toward protection of state or social property," "crimes against state or social property of other socialist states" – these are examples not only of a Soviet legal policy but also of a Soviet legal language. Some of the older Soviet language of "counterrevolutionary crimes," "enemy of the people," and the like, has been eliminated: the emphasis today is less on the gains of the proletarian revolution than on the power and prestige of the Soviet state. Yet the links between the state and the social system and between the Soviet state and other revolutionary states, are maintained.

The language of Soviet economic crimes also reflects the state's responsibility for the economic order. "Issuing poor-quality, nonstandard, or incomplete industrial products," "additions to and distortions of accounts concerning fulfillment of plans," "private entrepreneurial activity," "speculation," "buying up bread to feed to cattle or poultry" – are crimes characteristic of a centrally planned economy of the Soviet type. Here, too, Soviet criminal law has developed its own language.

One feature of that language has, in fact, proved too subtle to warrant a distinction in the English translation: *pokhishchenie*, an ancient Russian term which we have translated as "stealing" (and also, in Article 125 of the Criminal Code, as "abduction"), is used in the form of *khishchenie* when it is applied to the stealing of state or social property. In nonlegal speech, *khishchenie* suggests not merely a particular wrongful taking or abduction but plunder or pillage. In law, the difference between the two words is more precise. Both mean "stealing" in a general sense, and, indeed, *khishchenie* in the title of Articles 88 and 89 is defined as including *pokhishchenie* in the body of those articles. However, *khishchenie* also includes appropriation (*prisvoenie*) or embezzlement (*rastrata*) of state or social property by one to whom it has been lawfully entrusted (Article 92), whereas *pokhishchenie* does not include such appropriation or embezzlement; unless the embezzler of personal property was guilty of swindling (*moshennichestvo*) in taking possession of the property or acquiring a right to it (Article 147), he apparently is guilty of no crime and the victim is relegated to a civil remedy. Thus *khishchenie* involves an interference with the right of ownership, whether or not the accused had lawfully acquired possession of the property, while *pokhishchenie* implies an unlawful taking of possession.

(3) Mobilization of Society. The policies of strict legality and of protection of the political and economic interests of the state are related to a third policy, namely, the mobilization of all Soviet citizens for the struggle to eliminate crime and to create a unified social order; and that third policy, like the first two, is reflected in the language and style of the codes. It is characteristic of Soviet legal thought that Article 1 of the RSFSR Criminal Code defines the "tasks" of Soviet criminal law, and Article 2 of the RSFSR Code of Criminal Procedure defines the "tasks" of Soviet criminal procedure; and that these tasks include not merely legal tasks but social tasks – in the words of Article 2 of the Code of Criminal Procedure, "the rooting out of crime [and] the education of citizens in the spirit of unswerving execution of Soviet laws and of respect for the rules of socialist community life." Although such programmatic statements are far less prominent and far less flowery in the 1960 codes than in the earlier codes, they are nevertheless implemented far more effectively, especially in the Code of Criminal Procedure. The language of "measures of social pressure" (*vozdeistvie*, "action upon," is translated as "pressure," since it is slightly stronger than *vliianie*, "influence") as distinct from criminal sanctions, of "suretyship (*poruka*) of social organizations," of participation of "social accusers" and "social defense counsel" in criminal trials, of notification of state and social organizations concerning conditions facilitating the commission of crimes and measures recommended for correcting such conditions – is new language, though it carries forward the emphasis upon the educational role of criminal law that has existed from the early years of Soviet history. This concept is also reflected in the Criminal Code, which retains the older rule that a person who has committed a crime may be freed from punishment if he has "ceased to be socially dangerous," but at the same time introduces very severe penalties for "especially dangerous recidivists"; which makes specific provision for transfer of cases of minor crimes to "comrades' courts"; and which defines many crimes in terms that embody the Soviet concern not only to punish antisocial conduct but also to remove antisocial attitudes.

Despite their teleological emphasis upon the enlisting of all citizens in the struggle to eliminate crime and create a unified social order, the 1960 codes do not create the general appearance of being "propagandistic" or "ideological." They do not expressly manifest either the doctrine of the eventual "dying out" of state and law, or the doctrine of the subservience – until that time – of the individual to the state. State, law, and personal rights are all treated as ultimate goals, so far as the language and style of the codes are concerned. Only occasionally are there examples of guile – as in the reference to the applicability of the death penalty "as an exceptional measure of punishment, until its complete abolition," and even in that example, the language makes a concession to those who could discourage the application of the death penalty, and gives them something in the Code on which to rely. On the whole, even the teleological and educational (or parental) aspect of the codes is expressed in legal language, rather than in the language of revolution.

Yet this legal language differs considerably from the language of traditional criminal law and procedure as known in the West. It is a legal language that does not make a sharp distinction between law and society or between law and morality, but treats law primarily as a social process for confirming personal morality and for actively directing it to specific social ends.[4]

4. It may be appropriate here to respond more generally to the thoughtful critique of the translation of the Criminal Code made by Yurii Sdobnikov in reviewing the first edition of this book (notes 1 and 3 *supra*).

Since Mr. Sdobnikov is himself a highly qualified translator, his comments are greatly appreciated. I propose to reply in the same spirit in which he wrote, at the beginning of his review, that "since my remarks in this review tend to be mainly critical, I should like to make it clear that they are not intended as an attack but rather as a small contribution to . . . pioneer work . . . in a difficult field." It is especially gratifying that Mr. Sdobnikov considers that the translation on the whole succeeds in giving the reader "not only the meaning but also the flavour of the Russian text."

Mr. Sdobnikov takes issue with some 30 or 40 translation choices, some of which recur frequently in the book. As indicated in note 1 of this chapter, Mr. Spindler and I have adopted some of his suggestions in the present edition. The main point of the present note, however, is not to express agreement or disagreement concerning specific translations, but to reply to Mr. Sdobnikov's charge that "a rather condescending view of Soviet law seeps through" into the translation generally.

Most of the examples he gives to support this charge reflect differences of opinions concerning shades of meaning of various English words, uses of the definite and indefinite article, etc. Here, despite his proficiency in English, Mr. Sdobnikov is at a certain disadvantage. Other examples reflect the translators' deficiencies in Russian; and here we are in debt to Mr. Sdobnikov. However, a few of the most important, or at least the most interesting, differences are more political than linguistic.

Thus Mr. Sdobnikov would translate *lishenie svobody* as "deprivation of liberty" rather than "deprivation of freedom," since it "means being deprived of the liberty to come and go as you please, being the narrower framework within the larger context of freedom." For the reader who does not know Russian, it should be pointed out that that language (like French, German, and most other languages) has only one word, *svoboda*, for both "liberty" and "freedom," so that the issue here is which of the two English words conveys to the reader of the translation what is conveyed to the reader of the original by the one Russian word. Mr. Sdobnikov seems to be saying that the reader of the original understands *lishenie svobody* in the narrower sense, as deprivation of the liberty to come and go as you please, a restriction primarily on physical mobility. In fact, "liberty" does not always have this more restricted meaning, as is exemplified in Patrick Henry's famous words, "Give me liberty or give me death!" But assuming his distinction between the two words is valid, does not penal detention involve deprivation of freedom in a broader sense as well? The prisoner's whole life is regimented. Society has condemned him. Is Mr. Sdobnikov saying, however, that he still has his inner freedom, his freedom to think, dream, love, pray? Such spiritual freedom surely remains. Nevertheless, it cannot help but be affected, and we are inclined to retain the phrase "deprivation of freedom" to characterize a type of criminal punishment which removes a person from his family, his community, and his work, and subjects him to a rigorous discipline of manual labor, a greatly reduced diet, and forced association with other outcasts.

On a less philosophical plane, Mr. Sdobnikov agrees with the translators' principle that idiomatic English terms should be avoided where the Soviet terms have special meanings and the English idiom would therefore mislead, but he considers that this principle has been violated in several important instances. Thus he is pleased that the supreme legislative body in the Soviet Union is referred to in the translation as the Supreme Soviet, and not as Parliament (or Congress), and he approves of the policy of avoiding (for the most part) such terms as "sentence," "verdict," "trial," "burden of proof," "indictment," etc., which have no exact parallels in Russian. But he wishes that this policy had been carried further, and especially that it had been applied to *militsiia*, which is translated throughout as "police," and to *ssylka* and *vysylka*, which are translated in Articles 25 and 26 as "exile" and "banishment," respectively.

Soviet jurists and the Soviet press are particularly sensitive to the translation of *militsiia*. They contend that the Soviet officials who perform functions similar to those of the police in nonsocialist countries behave so differently in carrying out those functions that the two should not be confused. It is quite true that neither Mr. Spindler nor I share this view. We can see no important differences, very generally speaking, between the ways in which the Moscow or Leningrad *militsiia* behave and the ways in which the police in Boston or London or Paris behave; or at least, between the ways in which they are supposed to behave; or at the very least, between the ways in which they would be supposed to behave in similar circumstances. But even if that view were wrong, to leave the term in the original Russian, or to translate it as "militia," would bring to the American reader's mind the picture of our national guard or other reserve army.

The Soviet objection to characterizing the Soviet *militsiia* as "police" is apparently based on a translation fallacy. The objection is to the connotations of the non-Russian word "police" when translated back into Russian as *politsiia.* The latter term refers to the prerevolutionary Russian police, which Soviet usage distinguishes from the postrevolutionary Soviet *militsiia.* The answer to this problem is for the Soviet reader to retranslate the foreign word *police,* as used in this text, not as "politsiia" but as "militsiia."

With regard to exile and banishment, Mr. Sdobnikov has two objections: first, that both words are obsolete in English law, and second, that the two are synonymous in English (whereas in Russian *ssylka* restricts a person *to* a certain area and *vysylka* restricts him *from* a certain area). Therefore, he says, the two Russian words should not be translated at all but left in the original. The first objection, however, seems wholly irrelevant; we do not have to confine ourselves to English (or American) *legal* terms – if we did, we would have to leave a very large part of the codes untranslated. The second objection is more substantial. We could perhaps have referred to *ssylka* as "first-degree exile" and *vysylka* as "second-degree exile." It seemed best, however, to use two different, albeit synonymous, English words to refer to two very similar, though not identical, Soviet forms of punishment. The very fact that the English words no longer have a technical legal meaning justifies, we believe, our stretching them for purposes of the translation.

The Criminal Code of the RSFSR

October 27, 1960, as Amended to March 1, 1972

GENERAL PART

SPECIAL PART

General Part

Chapter One: General Provisions

Article 1. Tasks of RSFSR Criminal Code. The RSFSR Criminal Code has as its tasks the protection of the Soviet social and state system, of socialist property, of the person and rights of citizens, and of the entire socialist legal order, from criminal infringements.

For carrying out these tasks the RSFSR Criminal Code determines which socially dangerous acts are criminal, and establishes the punishments applicable to persons who have committed crimes.

Article 2. RSFSR Criminal Code and All-Union Criminal Legislation. The RSFSR Criminal Code proceeds from the principles and general provisions established by the Fundamental Principles of Criminal Legislation of the USSR and Union Republics.

All-union laws concerning criminal responsibility for crimes against the state and military crimes and also all-union laws which determine responsibility for other crimes directed against the interests of the USSR shall be included in the present Code. Prior to their inclusion in the RSFSR Criminal Code, all-union criminal laws shall be directly applied on the territory of the RSFSR.

The General Part of the Code shall extend both to acts specified in the present Code and to acts for which responsibility is provided by all-union laws not yet included in the present Code.

Article 3. Basis of Criminal Responsibility. Only a person guilty of committing a crime, that is, who intentionally or negligently commits a socially dangerous act provided for by law, shall be subject to criminal responsibility and punishment.

Criminal punishment shall be applied only by judgment of a court.

Chapter Two: Limits of Operation of Criminal Code

Article 4. Operation of Present Code with Respect to Acts Committed on Territory of RSFSR. All persons who commit crimes on the territory of the RSFSR shall be subject to responsibility in accordance with the present Code.

In the event that crimes are committed on the territory of the RSFSR by diplomatic representatives of foreign states and other citizens who, in accordance with prevailing laws and international agreements, are not subject to criminal jurisdiction in Soviet judicial institutions, the question of their criminal responsibility shall be decided by diplomatic means.

Article 5. Operation of Present Code with Respect to Acts Committed Outside Boundaries of USSR. Citizens of the USSR who commit crimes abroad shall be subject to responsibility in accordance with the present Code if criminal proceedings are instituted against them or they are brought to trial on the territory of the RSFSR.

Persons without citizenship who are situated in the RSFSR and who have committed crimes beyond the boundaries of the USSR shall bear responsibility on the same basis.

If the persons specified in paragraphs one and two of the present article have undergone punishment abroad for the crimes committed by them, a court may accordingly mitigate the assigned punishment or may completely relieve the guilty person from serving the punishment.

For crimes committed by them outside the boundaries of the USSR, foreigners shall be subject to responsibility in accordance with Soviet criminal laws in instances provided for by international agreements.

Article 6. Operation of a Criminal Law in Time. The criminality and punishability of an act shall be determined by the law prevailing at the time of the commission of that act.

A law eliminating the punishability of an act or reducing a punishment shall have retroactive force, that is, it shall extend also to acts committed before its promulgation.

A law establishing the punishability of an act or increasing a punishment shall not have retroactive force.

Chapter Three: Crime

Article 7. The Concept of Crime. A socially dangerous act (an action or an omission to act) provided for by the Special Part of the present Code which infringes the Soviet social or state system, the socialist system of economy, socialist property, the person, or the political, labor, property or other rights of citizens, or any other socially dangerous act provided for by the Special Part of the present Code which infringes the socialist legal order, shall be deemed a crime.

An action or an omission to act shall not be a crime, although it formally contains the indicia of an act provided for by the Special Part of the present Code, if by reason of its insignificance it does not represent a social danger.

Article 8. Intentional Commission of a Crime. A crime shall be deemed to be committed intentionally if the person who commits it is conscious of the socially dangerous character of his action or omission to act, foresees its socially dangerous consequences, and desires those consequences or consciously permits them to occur.

Article 9. Commission of Crime Through Negligence. A crime shall be deemed to be committed through negligence if the person who commits it foresees the possibility of the occurrence of the socially dangerous consequences of his action or omission to act but frivolously counts on their being prevented, or if he does not foresee the possibility of the occurrence of such consequences although he should and could foresee them.

Article 10. Responsibility of Minors. Persons who have attained the age of 16 years before the commission of a crime shall be subject to criminal responsibility.

Persons from 14 to 16 years of age who commit crimes shall be subject to criminal responsibility only for homicide (Articles 102–106), intentionally inflicting bodily injuries causing an impairment of health (Articles 108–111, 112 paragraph one), rape (Article 117), assault with intent to rob [*razboi*] (Articles 91 and 146), theft [*krazha*] (Articles 89 and 144), robbery [*grabiozh*] (Articles 90 and 145), malicious hooliganism (Article 206 paragraphs two and three), intentionally destroying or damaging state or social property or the personal property of citizens, with grave consequences (Articles 98 paragraph two, and 149 paragraph two), or intentionally committing actions that can cause a train wreck (Article 86).

If a court finds that a person who, while under the age of 18 years, has committed a crime not representing a great social danger can be reformed without application of criminal punishment, it may apply to such person compulsory measures of an educational character which do not constitute a criminal punishment (Article 63).

Under the conditions in paragraph three of the present article, the minor may be relieved of criminal responsibility and punishment and sent to a commission for cases of minors for consideration of the question of applying to him compulsory measures of an educational character.

[*Ved.* (1966), no. 32, item 769, Edict August 4, 1966.] *

Article 11. Nonimputability. A person shall not be subject to criminal responsibility who at the time of committing a socially dangerous act is in a state of nonimputability, that is, cannot realize the significance of his actions or control them because of a chronic mental illness, temporary mental derangement, mental deficiency, or other condition of illness. Compulsory measures of a medical character may be applied to such a person by order of the court.

Also, a person shall not be subject to punishment who commits a crime while in a state of imputability but before the rendering of judgment by the court contracts a mental illness which deprives him of the possibility of realizing the significance of his actions or of controlling them. Compulsory measures of a medical character may be applied to such a person by order of the court, but upon recovery he may be subject to punishment.

Article 12. Responsibility for Crime Committed in State of Intoxication. A person who commits a crime while in a state of intoxication shall not be relieved of criminal responsibility.

Article 13. Necessary Defense. Although falling within the category of an act provided for in the Special Part of the present Code, an action shall not constitute a crime if it is committed in necessary defense, that is, in protecting the interests of the Soviet state, social interests, or the person or rights of the defender or of another person against a socially dangerous infringement by causing harm to the infringer, provided that the limits of necessary defense are not exceeded.

*This reference, inserted by the translators, indicates that Article 10 was amended by an Edict of the Presidium of the Supreme Soviet of the RSFSR dated August 4, 1966, which may be found in *Vedomosti* ("Journal") of the Supreme Soviet of the RSFSR (1966), no. 32, item (*stat'ia*) 769. Comparison with the provision as it stood prior to that time shows that the only change is in line 8 of the second paragraph, where paragraph three of Article 206 is added.

The limits of necessary defense shall be deemed to be exceeded if the defense is clearly disproportionate to the character and danger of the infringement.

Article 14. Extreme Necessity. Although falling within the category of an act provided for in the Special Part of the present Code, an action shall not constitute a crime if it is committed in extreme necessity, that is, in order to eliminate a danger which threatens the interests of the Soviet state, social interests, or the person or rights of the given person or of other citizens, if in the given circumstances such danger cannot be eliminated by other means and if the harm caused is less significant than the harm prevented.

Article 15. Responsibility for Preparation of Crime and for Attempted Crime. Acquiring or arranging the means or instruments, or other intentional creation of conditions for the commission of a crime, shall be deemed preparation of a crime.

An intentional action immediately directed toward the commission of a crime shall be deemed an attempted crime, provided the crime is not brought to completion for reasons independent of the will of the guilty person.

Punishment for preparation of a crime and for attempted crime shall be assigned in accordance with the article of the Special Part of the present Code which provides for responsibility for the given crime.

In assigning punishment the court shall take into account the character and degree of social danger of the actions committed by the guilty person, the degree to which the criminal intention is carried out, and the causes by reason of which the crime is not brought to completion.

Article 16. Voluntary Refusal to Commit a Crime. A person who voluntarily refuses to bring a crime to completion shall be subject to criminal responsibility only in the event that the act he in fact commits comprises some other crime.

Article 17. Complicity. The intentional joint participation of two or more persons in the commission of a crime shall be deemed complicity.

Together with the perpetrators of a crime, the organizers, instigators, and accessories shall be deemed accomplices.

A person who directly commits a crime shall be deemed a perpetrator.

A person who organizes the commission of a crime or directs its commission shall be deemed an organizer.

A person who incites to the commission of a crime shall be deemed an instigator.

A person who contributes to the commission of a crime by advice, instructions, furnishing the means, or eliminating obstacles, and also a person who promises beforehand to hide the criminal, the instruments and means of committing the crime, traces of the crime, or articles criminally acquired, shall be deemed an accessory.

The degree and character of participation of each of the accomplices in the commission of a crime must be taken into account by the court in assigning punishment.

Article 18. Concealment. When not promised in advance, the concealment of a criminal as well as of instruments and means of committing a crime, of traces of a crime, or of articles criminally acquired shall entail responsibility only in instances specially provided for by the Special Part of the present Code.

Article 19. Failure to Report. Failure to report a crime reliably known to be in preparation or to have been committed shall entail criminal responsibility only in instances specially provided for by the Special Part of the present Code.

Chapter Four: Punishment

Article 20. Purposes of Punishment. Punishment not only constitutes a chastisement for a committed crime but also has the purpose of correcting and reeducating convicted persons in the spirit of an honorable attitude toward labor, of strict compliance with the laws, and of respect toward socialist communal life; it also has the purpose of preventing the commission of new crimes both by convicted persons and by others.

Punishment does not have as a purpose the causing of physical suffering or the lowering of human dignity.

Article 21. Kinds of Punishment. The following punishments may be applied to persons who commit crimes:

(1) Deprivation of freedom;
(2) Exile;
(3) Banishment;
(4) Correctional tasks without deprivation of freedom;
(5) Deprivation of the right to occupy specified offices or to engage in specified activity;
(6) Fine;
(7) Dismissal from office;
(8) Imposition of the duty to make amends for harm caused;
(9) Social censure;
(10) Confiscation of property;
(11) Deprivation of military or special rank.

Punishment in the form of assignment to a disciplinary battalion may also be applied to persons in military service for a regular term.

Article 22. Basic and Supplementary Measures of Punishment. Deprivation of freedom, correctional tasks without deprivation of freedom, social censure, and assignment to a disciplinary battalion constitute basic measures of punishment.

Exile, banishment, deprivation of the right to occupy specified offices or to engage in specified activity, fine, dismissal from office, and imposition of the duty to make amends for harm caused may be applied either as basic or as supplementary punishments.

Confiscation of property and deprivation of military or special rank may be applied only as supplementary punishments.

Article 23. Death Penalty as Exceptional Measure of Punishment. As an exceptional measure of punishment, until its complete abolition, the death penalty by shooting may be applied for crimes against the state in the instances provided for by the USSR Law "On Criminal Responsibility for Crimes Against the State"; for intentional homicide under the aggravating circumstances indicated in the articles of the criminal laws of the USSR and of the present Code which establish responsibility for intentional homicide; or for certain other especially grave crimes in individual instances specially provided for by legislation of the USSR.

Persons who have not attained the age of 18 years before the commission of a crime and women who are pregnant at the time of the commission of a crime or at the moment judgment is rendered may not be condemned to death. The death penalty may not be applied to a woman who is pregnant at the moment the judgment is executed.

[*Ved.* (1962), no. 29, item 449, Edict July 25, 1962.]

Article 24. Deprivation of Freedom. Deprivation of freedom shall be prescribed for a term of three months to ten years; or for especially grave crimes and for especially dangerous recidivists in instances provided for by the Special Part of the present Code, for a term not exceeding fifteen years.

In the assignment of punishment to a person who before the commission of a crime has not attained the age of 18 years, the term of deprivation of freedom may not exceed ten years.

Punishment in the form of deprivation of freedom shall, in accordance with the judgment of the court, be served in correctional labor colonies of general, reinforced, strict, and special regimens or in a prison and also in educational labor colonies of general and reinforced regimens.

Punishment in correctional labor colonies shall be served by men:

sentenced for the first time to deprivation of freedom for crimes that do not appear grave, in colonies of general regimen;

sentenced for the first time to deprivation of freedom in instances provided by Note II to the present article (except especially dangerous crimes against the state), in colonies of reinforced regimen;

convicted of especially dangerous crimes against the state (Articles 64–73) or who have previously served punishment in the form of deprivation of freedom, in colonies of strict regimen;

deemed especially dangerous recidivists, in colonies of special regimen.

Punishment in correctional labor colonies shall be served by women sentenced to deprivation of freedom: deemed especially dangerous recidivists or convicted of especially dangerous crimes against the state (Articles 64–73), in colonies of strict regimen; other women condemned to deprivation of freedom, in colonies of general regimen.

Punishment in educational labor colonies shall be served:

by minors of the male sex sentenced for the first time to deprivation of freedom for crimes that do not appear grave and also by minors of the female sex, in colonies of general regimen;

by minors of the male sex who have previously served punishment in the form of deprivation of freedom or have been sentenced to deprivation of freedom for grave crimes provided for by Note III to the present article, in colonies of reinforced regimen.

Regardless of the character and degree of social danger of the crime committed, the personality of the guilty person, and any other circumstances of the case, the court may, with an indication of reasons for the decision taken, assign deprivation of freedom to convicts not deemed especially dangerous recidivists in correctional labor colonies of any type other than colonies of special regimen; and to minor convicts of the male sex, to educational labor colonies of general regimen in lieu of colonies of reinforced regimen.

Deprivation of freedom in the form of confinement for the whole term of punishment or for a part thereof may be assigned to persons who have committed grave crimes in instances provided for by Note II to the present article, and also to especially dangerous recidivists.

Any change in the type of correctional labor institution assigned to a convicted person shall be made by the court on the grounds and in the procedure established by legislation of the USSR and RSFSR.

Note I. Deleted.

Note II. The following shall be deemed grave crimes: especially dangerous crimes against the state (Articles 64–73), banditry (Article 77), actions disrupting the work of correctional labor institutions (Article 77–1), mass disorders (Article 79), damaging of routes of communication and means of transport (Article 86), making or passing of counterfeit money or securities (Article 87), violation of rules for currency transactions (Article 88), stealing of state or social property on a large scale (Articles 89 paragraph three, 90 paragraph three, 92 paragraph three, 93 paragraph three) or on an especially large scale (Article 93–1), open stealing under aggravating circumstances (Articles 90 paragraph two, 145 paragraph two), assault with intent to rob (Articles 91 and 146, intentional destruction or damaging, under aggravating circumstances, of state or social property or personal property of citizens (Articles 98 paragraph two, 149 paragraph two), intentional homicide (Articles 102 and 103), intentional infliction of grave bodily injury (Article 108), rape (Article 117), speculation under aggravating circumstances (Article 154 paragraph two), exceeding of authority or official powers under aggravating circumstances (Article 171 paragraph two), taking or giving of a bribe or acting as an intermediary in bribery (Articles 173, 174, 174–1), instituting of criminal proceedings against a person known to be innocent, under aggravating circumstances (Article 176 paragraph two), rendering of a judgment, decision, ruling or decree known to be unjust, resulting in grave consequences (Article 177 paragraph two), compelling to give testimony under aggravating circumstances (Article 179 paragraph two), infringing the life of a policeman or people's guard (Article 191–2), malicious or especially malicious hooliganism (Article 206 paragraphs two and three), stealing of firearms, ammunition or explosives, committed by means of an assault with intent to rob (Article 218–1 paragraph three), insubordination under aggravating circumstances (Article 238 subsections "b" and "c"), resisting a superior or compelling him to violate official duties (Article 240), forcible actions against a superior

(Article 242), desertion (Article 247), intentional destruction or damaging of military property under aggravating circumstances (Article 251 subsections "b" and "c"), violations of rules for performing military watch (Article 257 subsections "a", "c," and "d").

Note III. Punishment in educational labor colonies of reinforced regimen shall be served by minors of the male sex sentenced to deprivation of freedom for the following grave crimes: banditry (Article 77), intentional commission of actions causing a train wreck (Article 86), stealing of state or social property or personal property of citizens (Articles 91 and 146), intentional destruction or damaging of state or social property or personal property of citizens, resulting in grave consequences (Articles 98 paragraph two, 149 paragraph two), intentional homicide (Articles 102 and 103), rape under aggravating circumstances (Article 117 paragraphs two and three), infringing the life of a policeman or people's guard in connection with his official or social activity for protection of public order (Article 191-2), malicious or especially malicious hooliganism (Article 206 paragraphs two and three), stealing of firearms, ammunition or explosives by means of an assault with intent to rob (Article 218-1 paragraph three).

[*Ved.* (1969), no. 47, item 1361, Edict November 14, 1969.]

Article 24-1. Especially Dangerous Recidivist. The following may, in accordance with the judgment of a court, be deemed an especially dangerous recidivist:

(1) A person previously sentenced to deprivation of freedom for an especially dangerous crime against the state (Articles 64-73), banditry (Article 77), making or passing counterfeit money or securities under aggravating circumstances (Article 87 paragraph two), violation of rules for currency transactions under aggravating circumstances (Article 88 paragraph two), stealing of state or social property on an especially large scale (Article 93-1), assault with intent to rob for the purpose of taking possession of state or social property or personal property of citizens under aggravating circumstances (Articles 91 paragraph two, 146 paragraph two), intentional homicide provided for by Articles 102 and 103 (except homicide by a mother of her newborn baby) and subsection "c" of Article 240, rape committed by a group of persons or resulting in especially grave consequences as well as rape of a minor (Article 117 paragraph three), infringing the life of a policeman or people's guard (*druzhinnik*) in connection with his official or social activity for protection of public order (Article 191-2), who again commits any one of the enumerated crimes and is sentenced to deprivation of freedom for a term of not less than five years;

(2) A person two times previously, in any sequence, sentenced to deprivation of freedom for an especially dangerous crime against the state (Articles 64-73), banditry (Article 77), mass disorders (Article 79), making or passing of counterfeit money or securities (Article 87), violation of rules for currency transactions (Article 88), stealing of state or social property under aggravating circumstances (Articles 89 paragraphs two and three, 90 paragraphs two and three, 92 paragraphs two and three, 93 paragraphs two and three, 93-1), assault with intent to rob for the purpose of taking possession of state or social property or personal property of citizens (Articles 91 and 146), intentional homicide provided for by

Articles 102 and 103 (except homicide by a mother of her newborn baby) and subsection "c" of Article 240, intentional infliction of grave bodily injury (Article 108), rape (Article 117), theft, open stealing or swindling committed under aggravating circumstances (Articles 144 paragraph two, 145 paragraph two, 147 paragraphs two and three), speculation under aggravating circumstances (Article 154 paragraph two), taking of a bribe (Article 173), infringing the life of a policeman or people's guard in connection with his official or social activity for protection of public order (Article 191-2), especially malicious hooliganism (Article 206 paragraph three), stealing of firearms, ammunition or explosives under aggravating circumstances (Article 218-1 paragraphs two and three), making, acquiring or keeping narcotics for the purpose of marketing as well as marketing such substances (Article 224 paragraph one), who again commits any of the enumerated crimes and is sentenced to deprivation of freedom for a term exceeding three years;

(3) A person three or more times previously, in any sequence, sentenced to deprivation of freedom for malicious hooliganism (Article 206 paragraph two) or for crimes enumerated in subparagraph 2 [above] of the present article, who again commits malicious hooliganism or any one of the crimes enumerated in subparagraph 2 of paragraph one of the present article and is sentenced to deprivation of freedom;

(4) A person serving punishment in the form of deprivation of freedom for any one of the crimes enumerated in subsections 2 and 3 [above] of the present article who again commits an intentional crime and is sentenced to deprivation of freedom for a term of not less than five years.

In considering the question of whether a person should be deemed an especially dangerous recidivist, the court shall take into account the personality of the guilty person, the degree of social danger of the crimes committed, the motives therefor, the degree of implementation of the intended crime, the degree and character of participation in the commission of the crimes, and other circumstances of the case. Reasons for the decision of the court must be given in the judgment.

At the time of deciding the question whether a person should be deemed an especially dangerous recidivist, account shall not be taken of a conviction for a crime committed by such person before he was 18 years of age or a conviction which has been canceled or removed in a procedure established by law.

The deeming of a person to be an especially dangerous recidivist shall be rescinded at the time of cancellation of his conviction.

The articles of the Special Part of the present Code providing for responsibility for the commission of a crime by an especially dangerous recidivist shall be applied in instances when, in the procedure established by law, a person was deemed an especially dangerous recidivist before the commission of the given crime.

[*Ved.* (1969), no. 47, item 1361, Edict November 14, 1969.]

Article 25. Exile. Exile shall consist in the removal of a convicted person from the place of his residence, with obligatory settlement in a certain locality.

Exile may be assigned either as a basic or as a supplementary punishment for a term of two to five years. Exile as a supplementary punishment may be applied only in instances specially indicated in articles of the Special Part of the present Code.

The arrangement of work for exiles shall be the responsibility of executive committees of local soviets of working people's deputies.

Exile shall not be applied to persons who have not attained the age of 18 years before the commission of a crime, to pregnant women, and to women who have dependent children under the age of 8 years.

The procedure, places, and conditions for serving exile shall be established by legislation of the USSR and RSFSR.

Article 26. **Banishment.** Banishment shall consist in the removal of a convicted person from the place of his residence, with prohibition against living in certain localities.

Banishment may be assigned as a basic or as a supplementary punishment for a term of two to five years. Banishment as a supplementary punishment may be applied only in instances specially indicated in articles of the Special Part of the present Code.

Banishment shall not be applied to persons who have not attained the age of 18 years before the commission of a crime, to pregnant women, and to women who have dependent children under the age of 8 years.

The procedure and conditions for banishment shall be established by legislation of the USSR and RSFSR.

Article 27. **Correctional Tasks Without Deprivation of Freedom.** Correctional tasks without deprivation of freedom shall be assigned for a term of one month to one year and shall be served, in accordance with the judgment of the court, either at the place of work of the convicted person or in any other place determined by the agencies in charge of application of correctional tasks, but in the convicted person's district of residence.

Deductions from the wages of a person condemned to correctional tasks without deprivation of freedom shall be made at a rate established by the judgment of the court within the limits of 5 to 20 percent of the wages, and shall be transferred to the state.

For persons deemed incapable of working, the court may replace correctional tasks by a fine, social censure, or imposition of the duty to make amends for the harm caused.

The procedure for serving correctional tasks without deprivation of freedom shall be established by legislation of the USSR and RSFSR.

Under conditions of a convicted person's conscientious work and exemplary conduct in the period of serving correctional tasks without deprivation of freedom, after he has served such punishment the court may, upon the petition of a social organization or collective of working people, include the time of serving correctional tasks without deprivation of freedom in general job seniority.

[*Ved.* (1969), no. 47, item 1361, Edict November 14, 1969.]

Article 28. **Consequences of Malicious Evasion of Correctional Tasks Without Deprivation of Freedom.** In the event that a person sentenced to correctional tasks without deprivation of freedom maliciously evades serving the punishment, the court may replace the unserved term of correctional tasks by punishment in the form of deprivation of freedom for the same term.

[*Ved.* (1969), no. 47, item 1361, Edict November 14, 1969.]

Article 29. Deprivation of Right to Occupy Specified Offices or to Engage in Specified Activity. Deprivation of the right to occupy specified offices or to engage in specified activity may be assigned by the court as a basic or supplementary punishment for a term of one to five years.

This punishment may be assigned in instances when, because of the character of the crimes committed by the guilty person in his office or when engaging in specified activity, the court deems it unfeasible to preserve his right to occupy specified offices or to engage in specified activity.

When this punishment is assigned as supplementary to deprivation of freedom, it shall extend to the entire time of serving the deprivation of freedom and, in addition, for the term established by the judgment. If deprivation of the right to occupy specified offices or engage in specified activity is assigned as supplementary to another kind of basic punishment, then the term shall be calculated from the moment the serving of the basic punishment is commenced.

Article 30. Fine. A fine is a monetary exaction imposed by the court in instances and within limits established by appropriate articles of the Special Part of the present Code.

The amount of a fine shall be established in accordance with the gravity of the crime committed, taking into account the financial position of the guilty person.

In the event that it is impossible to exact a fine, the court may decree that it be replaced by correctional tasks without deprivation of freedom, with 10 rubles of the fine to count as one month of correctional tasks, but for not more than one year of correctional tasks.

Replacement of a fine by deprivation of freedom and of deprivation of freedom by a fine shall not be permitted.

Articles not subject to confiscation may not be levied upon in exacting a fine.

Article 31. Dismissal from Office. Dismissal from office may be applied by a court in the event that it is deemed unfeasible to leave the convicted person in the office occupied by him.

Article 32. Imposition of Duty to Make Amends for Harm Caused. Execution of the duty to make amends for harm caused shall consist in direct elimination, by one's own resources, of the harm caused, or in compensation, with one's own means, for material loss, or in a public apology before the victim or before members of the collective in a form prescribed by the court.

Punishment in the form of imposing the duty of directly eliminating, by one's own resources, the harm caused may be assigned in the event that the court, taking into account the character of the harm caused, deems that the guilty person is capable of directly eliminating it in the indicated manner.

Punishment in the form of imposing the duty to compensate for material loss may be assigned if the amount of the loss caused does not exceed 100 rubles.

Punishment in the form of imposing the duty of publicly apologizing before the victim or members of the collective may be assigned if there has been an infringement of personal integrity or dignity or a violation of the rules of socialist communal life, not causing material loss.

If the convicted person fails to fulfill his duty to make amends for the harm caused within the period established by the court, the court may replace this punishment by correctional tasks, or a fine, or dismissal from office, or social censure. In such event, and also in the event that material loss is caused in an amount of more than 100 rubles, compensation for loss caused to the victim shall be effected by way of civil proceedings.

Article 33. **Social Censure.** Social censure shall consist in a public expression by the court of censure of the guilty person and, if necessary, in bringing this to the notice of the public through the press or other means.

Article 34. **Assignment of Persons in Military Service Who Commit Crimes to Disciplinary Battalion and Replacement of Correctional Tasks by Detention in Guardhouse.** Assignment to a disciplinary battalion for a term of three months to two years may be applied to persons in military service for a regular term who commit crimes, in instances provided by law and also in those instances where the court, taking into consideration the circumstances of the case and the personality of the convicted person, finds it appropriate to apply, instead of deprivation of freedom for a term not exceeding two years, assignment to a disciplinary battalion for the same term.

Correctional tasks without deprivation of freedom shall be replaced for persons in military service by detention in the guardhouse for a term not exceeding two months.

Article 35. **Confiscation of Property.** Confiscation of property shall consist in the compulsory transfer to state ownership, without compensation, of all or part of the property constituting the personal ownership of the convicted person. If part of the property is confiscated, then the court must indicate what part of the property is confiscated or list the confiscated articles.

Articles necessary for the convicted person and for persons dependent on him shall not be subject to confiscation, in accordance with the list given in the appendix to the present Code.

Confiscation of property may be assigned only for crimes against the state and grave mercenary crimes in instances specified in articles of the Special Part of the present Code.

At the time of confiscation of the property, the state shall not be responsible for debts and obligations of the convicted person if they have arisen after the taking of measures for the preservation of the property by agencies of inquiry, investigative or judicial agencies or, in any event, without the consent of such agencies.

With respect to claims subject to satisfaction out of the confiscated property, the state shall be responsible only within the limits of the assets; with respect to the order of preference of satisfying claims, the rules established by the RSFSR Code of Civil Procedure shall be observed.

Article 36. **Deprivation of Military and Other Ranks, and also of Orders, Medals, and Honorary Titles.** Upon conviction for a grave crime a person who has a military or special rank may be deprived of such rank by the judgment of the court.

Upon conviction for a grave crime of a person who has been awarded an order or medal or upon whom an honorary title has been conferred by the Presidium of the USSR Supreme Soviet, or by the Presidium of the Supreme Soviet of the RSFSR or other union republic or autonomous republic, or upon whom a military or other rank has been conferred by the Presidium of the USSR Supreme Soviet, by the USSR Council of Ministers, or by the Council of Ministers of the RSFSR or other union republic, the court in rendering judgment shall decide the question of the appropriateness of submitting a proposal to the body which has awarded the order or medal to the convicted person or conferred the rank upon him, to deprive the convicted person of the order or medal or honorary title or military or other rank.

Chapter Five: Assignment of Punishment and Relief from Punishment

Article 37. **General Principles for Assignment of Punishment.** A court shall assign punishment within the limits established by the articles of the Special Part of the present Code which provide for responsibility for a committed crime, in strict accordance with the provisions of the Fundamental Principles of Criminal Legislation of the USSR and Union Republics and of the General Part of the present Code. At the time of assigning punishment the court, guided by socialist legal consciousness, shall take into consideration the character and degree of social danger of the committed crime, the personality of the guilty person, and the circumstances of the case which mitigate or aggravate responsibility.

Article 38. **Circumstances Mitigating Responsibility.** In assignment of punishment the following shall be deemed circumstances mitigating responsibility:

1. Prevention by the guilty person of harmful consequences of the crime committed or voluntary compensation for loss inflicted or elimination of harm caused;
2. Commission of the crime as a result of the concurrence of grave personal or family circumstances;
3. Commission of the crime under the influence of a threat or compulsion or by reason of material, occupational, or other dependence;
4. Commission of a crime for the first time, as a result of a fortuitous concurrence of circumstances, if such crime does not represent a great social danger;
5. Commission of the crime under the influence of strong mental agitation provoked by unlawful actions of the victim;
6. Commission of the crime in defense against a socially dangerous infringement, although the limits of necessary defense are exceeded;

7. Commission of the crime by a minor;
8. Commission of the crime by a pregnant woman;
9. Sincere repentance or giving oneself up, as well as actively facilitating the exposure of the crime.

In assigning punishment the court may also deem other circumstances as mitigating responsibility.

Article 39. Circumstances Aggravating Responsibility. In assignment of punishment the following shall be deemed circumstances aggravating responsibility:

1. Commission of the crime by a person who has previously committed any kind of crime.

The court shall have the right, depending on the character of the first crime, not to accord it the significance of an aggravating circumstance;

2. Commission of the crime by an organized group;
3. Commission of the crime from mercenary or other base motives;
4. The causing of grave consequences by the crime;
5. Commission of the crime against a young person, a person advanced in years, or a helpless person, and also against a person in material, occupational, or other dependence on the guilty person;
6. Instigation of minors to the commission of the crime or drawing minors into participation in the crime;
7. Commission of the crime in a manner especially cruel or humiliating for the victim;
8. Commission of the crime by exploiting a condition of public disaster;
9. Commission of the crime in a manner involving general danger;
10. Commission of a crime by a person in a state of intoxication. The court shall have the right, depending on the character of the crime, not to deem this a circumstance aggravating responsibility;
11. Denouncing a person known to be innocent;
12. Commission of a new crime by a person taken on surety during the term of surety or within a year after expiration of such term.

[*Ved.* (1969), no. 47, item 1361, Edict November 14, 1969.]

Article 40. Assignment of Punishment Where Several Crimes Have Been Committed. If a person is deemed guilty of the commission of two or more crimes provided for by different articles of the Special Part of the present Code, and has not been convicted of any of them, the court, having assigned a punishment separately for each crime, shall determine a final aggregate punishment by absorbing the less severe punishment in the more severe or by fully or partially cumulating the punishments within the limits established by the article which provides for the more severe punishment.

To the basic punishment may be joined any of the supplementary punishments provided by the articles of the Special Part of the present Code which establish responsibility for those crimes the person has been found guilty of committing.

Punishment shall be assigned in accordance with the same rules if, after judgment is rendered in a case, it is established that the convicted person is guilty of yet another crime, committed by him before the judgment has been rendered in the first case. In such event, a punishment fully or partially served under the first judgment shall be counted in the term of punishment.

Article 41. Assignment of Punishment Under Several Judgments. If, after a judgment is rendered but before the punishment is fully served, the convicted person commits a new crime, the court shall join the unserved part of the punishment under the previous judgment fully or partially to the punishment assigned under the new judgment.

In cumulation of punishments in the procedure provided by the present article, the overall term of punishment must not exceed the maximum term established by the present Code for a given kind of punishment. In cumulation of punishments of deprivation of freedom, the overall term of punishment must not exceed ten years, or it must not exceed fifteen years for crimes for which the punishment of deprivation of freedom is permitted by the present Code for a term of more than ten years.

In cumulation of punishments of deprivation of freedom and detention in a disciplinary battalion, one day of deprivation of freedom shall correspond to one day of detention in a disciplinary battalion.

In cumulation of punishments of deprivation of freedom and exile, banishment, or correctional tasks, one day of deprivation of freedom shall correspond to three days of exile, banishment, or correctional tasks.

Judgments of deprivation of freedom plus a fine, or of correctional tasks plus a fine, shall be executed independently.

Article 42. Method of Determining Terms of Punishment. Terms of deprivation of freedom, detention in a disciplinary battalion, exile, banishment, correctional tasks, as well as deprivation of the right to occupy specified offices or to engage in specified activity, shall be calculated in months and years, and terms of detention in the guardhouse shall be calculated in twenty-four-hour periods and months.

In replacement or cumulation of punishments the calculation of the aforementioned punishments in days shall be permitted.

Article 43. Assignment of Milder Punishment Than That Provided by Law. If the court, taking into consideration the exceptional circumstances of a case and the personality of the guilty person, deems it necessary to assign a punishment less than the lowest limit provided by law for the given crime or to resort to another, milder type of punishment, it may permit such mitigation but shall be obliged to indicate its reasons.

Article 44. Conditional Sentence. When assigning the punishment of deprivation of freedom or correctional tasks, if the court, taking into consideration the circumstances of the case and the personality of the guilty person, becomes convinced that it would be inappropriate for the guilty person to serve the assigned punishment, it may decree the conditional nonapplication of punishment to the guilty person, but it shall be obliged to indicate in the judgment the reasons for the conditional sentence. In such event, the court shall decree that the judgment not be executed if in the course of the probation period determined by the court the convicted person does not commit a new intentional crime.

The probation period shall be set by the court for a duration of one to five years.

When there is a conditional sentence, supplementary punishments, with the exception of a fine, may not be assigned.

Taking into consideration the circumstances of the case, the personality of the guilty person, and also the petitions of social organizations or the collective of workers, employees, or collective-farm workers at the guilty person's place of work concerning his conditional sentence, the court may transfer the conditionally sentenced person to such organizations or to the collective for reeducation and correction.

If the court applies a conditional sentence in the absence of the aforementioned petitions, it may impose on a particular collective of working people, or on a person, with their consent, the duty to supervise the conditionally sentenced person and to carry on educational work with him.

Upon petition of a social organization or collective of working people entrusted with supervising a conditionally sentenced person, the court may reduce the probation period established by the judgment. The question of reducing the term of probation may be presented upon the expiration of not less than half of such term.

The court which renders judgment shall carry out registration of conditionally sentenced persons and general control of their conduct.

[*Ved.* (1969), no. 47, item 1361, Edict November 14, 1969.]

Article 45. Assignment of Punishment to Conditionally Sentenced Person in Event of his Commission of New Intentional Crime. In the event that a conditionally sentenced person during the term of probation commits a new intentional crime, for which he is sentenced to deprivation of freedom, the court shall assign him punishment in accordance with the rules provided by Article 41 of the present Code.

[*Ved.* (1969), no. 47, item 1361, Edict November 14, 1969.]

Article 46. Stay of Execution of Judgment of Person in Military Service or Subject to Military Service in Wartime. In wartime the execution of a judgment of deprivation of freedom rendered against a person in military service or a person subject to call-up or mobilization may be stayed by the court until the termination of military operations, with assignment of the convicted person to active duty. The court in such instances may also stay the execution of supplementary punishments.

If a convicted person assigned to active duty shows himself to be a steadfast defender of the socialist Motherland, then, upon petition of the appropriate military command, the court may relieve him from punishment or replace the punishment by another, milder punishment.

In the event of commission of a new crime by a person as to whom execution of a judgment has been stayed, the court shall join the punishment previously assigned to the new punishment in accordance with the rules provided by Article 41 of the present Code.

Article 47. Deducting Preliminary Confinement. The court shall deduct preliminary confinement from the term of punishment at the rate of one day for one day when sentencing to deprivation of freedom or assignment to a disciplinary battalion, and at the rate of one day for three days when sentencing to correctional tasks, exile, or banishment.

When assigning other measures of punishment, the court, taking into consideration preliminary confinement, may accordingly mitigate the punishment or completely relieve the guilty person from serving the punishment.

Article 48. Period of Limitation for Instituting Criminal Proceedings. Criminal proceedings may not be instituted against a person if the following periods have elapsed from the day of his commission of the crime:

(1) one year from the day of committing any of the crimes provided for by Articles 94, 96, 97, 112 paragraph two, 131, 143, 158 paragraph one, 165, 166, 182, 192, 197, 198, 200, 207, 209;

(2) three years from the day of committing a crime for which, under the present Code, deprivation of freedom for a term of not more than two years or a punishment not connected with deprivation of freedom may be assigned, other than crimes provided for by the articles indicated in subsection 1;

(3) five years from the day of committing a crime for which, under the present Code, deprivation of freedom for a term not exceeding five years may be assigned;

(4) ten years from the day of committing a crime for which, under the present Code, a more severe punishment than deprivation of freedom for a term of five years may be assigned.

The running of the period of limitation shall be interrupted if before expiration of the aforementioned terms the person commits a new crime for which under the present Code deprivation of freedom for a term of more than two years may be assigned. Calculation of the period of limitation in such instance shall begin from the moment of commission of the new crime.

The running of the period of limitation shall be suspended if the person who has committed a crime hides from investigation or trial. In such instances the running of the period of limitation shall be resumed from the moment the person is apprehended or gives himself up. In connection therewith, criminal proceedings may not be instituted against a person if fifteen years have elapsed from the time of commission of the crime and the period of limitation has not been interrupted by the commission of a new crime.

The question of applying the period of limitation to a person who commits a crime for which, under the law, the death penalty may be assigned shall be resolved by the court. If the court does not find it feasible to apply the period of limitation the death penalty may not be imposed but shall be replaced by deprivation of freedom.

Article 49. Period of Limitation for Execution of Judgment of Conviction. A judgment of conviction shall not be executed if it has not been executed in the following periods, counting from the day the judgment has taken legal effect:

(1) three years, in the event of a sentence to deprivation of freedom for a term not exceeding two years or a punishment not connected with deprivation of freedom;

(2) five years, in the event of a sentence to deprivation of freedom for a term not exceeding five years;

(3) ten years, in the event of a sentence to a more severe punishment than deprivation of freedom for a term of five years.

The running of the period of limitation shall be interrupted if the convicted person evades serving the punishment or, before expiration of the term, commits a new crime for which the punishment of deprivation of freedom for a term of not less than one year or exile or banishment for a term of not less than three years may be assigned by a court. The calculation of the period of limitation in the event of commission of a new crime shall begin from the moment of its commission, and in the event of evasion of serving the punishment it shall begin from the moment the convicted person gives himself up for serving the punishment or from the moment of apprehension of a convicted person in hiding. In connection therewith, a judgment of conviction may not be executed if fifteen years have elapsed from the time it was rendered and the period of limitation has not been interrupted by the commission of a new crime.

The question of applying the period of limitation to a person condemned to death shall be resolved by the court. If the court does not find it feasible to apply the period of limitation, the death penalty shall be replaced by deprivation of freedom.

Article 50. Relief From Criminal Responsibility and Punishment. A person who commits a crime may be relieved from criminal responsibility if it is deemed that by the time of the investigation or of the consideration of the case in court, as a result of a change in the situation, the act committed by the guilty person has lost its socially dangerous character or the person has ceased to be socially dangerous.

A person who commits a crime may be relieved from punishment if it is deemed that by reason of his subsequent irreproachable conduct and honorable attitude toward labor he may not, by the time of consideration of the case in court, be considered socially dangerous.

Article 51. Relief From Criminal Responsibility With Transfer of Case to Comrades' Court. A person may be relieved from criminal responsibility and punishment and the case transferred for consideration by a comrades' court if he commits for the first time any of the following acts provided for by the Special Part of the present Code:

(1) intentional infliction of light bodily injury or beatings not resulting in impairment of health (Article 112 paragraph two), the circulating in a collective of false fabrications which defame a member of the collective (Article 130 para-

graph one), insult (Article 131), theft of inexpensive articles of consumption and everyday life found in the personal ownership of citizens, if the guilty person and the victim are members of one collective (Article 144 paragraph one), making home-brewed vodka or other strong alcoholic beverages made at home, committed without the purpose of supplying and in a small quantity (Article 158 paragraph one);

(2) any other act for which the application of measures of social pressure is permitted in accordance with an article of the Special Part of the present Code;

(3) another petty crime if, because of the nature of the act committed and the personality of the guilty person, he may be corrected with the help of measures of social pressure without application of punishment.

[*Ved.* (1965), no. 27, item 670, Edict July 3, 1965.]

Article 52. Relief From Criminal Responsibility With Release of the Guilty Person on Surety. If, under the circumstances of the case, the crime committed by the person and the person himself do not represent a great social danger and if the act of the guilty person has not resulted in serious consequences and he has sincerely repented, then upon petition of a social organization or collective of working people such person may be relieved from criminal responsibility and punishment and released on surety for reeducation and correction to the social organization or collective of working people which has submitted the petition.

A person who has previously been convicted of the commission of an intentional crime or who has already been released on surety may not be released on surety.

Also, a person who does not consider himself guilty or who for any reasons insists on consideration of the case in court may not be released on surety.

If a person taken on surety has, in the course of a year, not justified the trust of the collective, has violated his promise to prove his correction by exemplary conduct and honorable labor, does not subordinate himself to norms of socialist communal life, or has left the labor collective for the purpose of evading social pressure, then the social organization or collective of working people that has taken him on surety shall render a decision to renounce the surety and shall refer such decision to the Procuracy or the court for consideration of the question of instituting criminal proceedings against the guilty person for the crime in connection with the commission of which he has been released on surety.

Article 53. Conditional Early Relief From Punishment and Replacement of Punishment by Milder Punishment. Conditional early relief from punishment or replacement of the unserved part of the punishment by a milder punishment may be applied to persons sentenced to deprivation of freedom, exile, banishment, correctional tasks, or assignment to a disciplinary battalion, other than persons enumerated in Article 53-1 of the present Code.

Conditional early relief from punishment or replacement of the unserved part of the punishment by a milder punishment may be applied to a convicted person only if by exemplary conduct and an honorable attitude toward labor he has proved his correction.

Conditional early relief from punishment and replacement of the unserved part of the punishment by a milder punishment may be applied to convicted persons by the court at the place of serving punishment upon the joint proposal of the agency charged with execution of the punishment and the supervisory commission of the executive committee of the local soviet of working people's deputies; and for a person serving punishment in a disciplinary battalion, upon the proposal of the command of the disciplinary battalion.

Conditional early relief from punishment or replacement of the unserved part of the punishment by a milder punishment may be applied after the actual serving by the convicted person of not less than half of the assigned term of punishment.

Conditional early relief from punishment or replacement of the unserved part of the punishment may be applied after the actual serving of not less than two thirds of the assigned term of punishment to:

(1) persons sentenced for an intentional crime to deprivation of freedom for a term not exceeding three years;

(2) persons who have previously served punishment in places of deprivation of freedom for an intentional crime and before the expunging or removal of the record of conviction have again committed an intentional crime for which they are sentenced to deprivation of freedom;

(3) persons who at the time of serving punishment in places of deprivation of freedom have committed an intentional crime for which they are sentenced to deprivation of freedom.

At the time of conditional early relief from punishment or replacement of the unserved part of the punishment by a milder punishment, the convicted person may be freed also from supplementary punishments in the form of exile, banishment, deprivation of the right to occupy specified offices or to engage in certain activity.

In the replacement of the unserved part of deprivation of freedom by exile, banishment, or correctional tasks, [these three types of punishment] may be assigned to the limits of the terms established by law for such types of punishment and must not exceed the unserved term of deprivation of freedom.

In applying conditional early relief from punishment or replacement of the unserved part of the punishment by a milder punishment, the court may impose on a particular collective of working people, with its consent, the duty to supervise a person granted conditional early relief during the unserved part of the term of punishment assigned by the court or a person the unserved part of whose punishment is replaced by a milder punishment, and to carry on educational work with him.

[*Ved.* (1969), no. 47, item 1361, Edict November 14, 1969.]

Article 53-1. Nonapplication of Conditional Early Relief From Punishment and Replacement of Punishment by Milder Punishment. Conditional early relief from punishment and replacement of the unserved part of the punishment by a milder punishment shall not be applied:

(1) to an especially dangerous recidivist;

(2) to a person previously sentenced to deprivation of freedom for an intentional crime, to whom conditional early relief from punishment or replacement of the unserved part of a punishment by a milder punishment has been applied, if such person has, before expiration of the unserved term of punishment, again committed an intentional crime for which he is sentenced to deprivation of freedom;

(3) to a person convicted of an especially dangerous crime against the state (Articles 64–73), banditry (Article 77), actions disrupting work of correctional labor institutions (Article 77–1), making or passing of counterfeit money or securities under aggravating circumstances (Article 87 paragraph two), violation of rules on currency transactions under aggravating circumstances (Article 88 paragraph two), stealing of state or social property on an especially large scale (Article 93–1), assault with intent to rob for the purpose of taking possession of state or social property or personal property of citizens under aggravating circumstances (Articles 91 paragraph two, 146 paragraph two), intentional homicide under aggravating circumstances (Articles 102 and 240 subsection "c"), rape committed by a group of persons or resulting in especially grave consequences as well as rape of a minor (Article 117 paragraph three), taking or giving of a bribe or acting as an intermediary in bribery under aggravating circumstances (Articles 173 paragraph two, 174 paragraph two, 174–1 paragraph two), infringing the life of a policeman or people's guard in connection with his official or social activity for protection of public order, under aggravating circumstances (Article 191–2), especially malicious hooliganism (Article 206 paragraph three), stealing of firearms, ammunition or explosives by means of an assault with intent to rob (Article 218–1 paragraph three).

[*Ved.* (1969), no. 47, item 1361, Edict November 14, 1969.]

Article 54. Assignment of Punishment for Commission of New Intentional Crime by Person Granted Conditional Early Relief. In the event of the commission of a new intentional crime during the unserved part of the punishment by a person granted conditional early relief, for which he is sentenced to deprivation of freedom, the court shall assign him punishment in accordance with the rules provided by Article 41 of the present Code. In connection therewith the court may join to a basic punishment a supplementary measure of punishment assigned under the first judgment.

[*Ved.* (1969), no. 47, item 1361, Edict November 14, 1969.]

Article 55. Conditional Early Relief From Punishment and Replacement of Punishment by Milder Punishment for Persons Who Have Committed Crime When Under the Age of 18 Years. Conditional early relief from punishment or replacement of the unserved part of the punishment by a milder punishment may be applied to persons sentenced to deprivation of freedom or correctional tasks for crimes committed when under the age of 18 years.

Conditional early relief from punishment or replacement of the unserved part of the punishment by a milder punishment may be applied to a convicted person for a crime committed when under the age of 18 years only if he has proved his correction by exemplary conduct and an honorable attitude toward labor and instruction.

Conditional early relief from punishment and replacement of the unserved part of the punishment by a milder punishment shall be applied by the court at the place of serving punishment to the convicted person upon the joint proposal of the agency charged with execution of the punishment and the commission for cases of minors or the supervisory commission of the executive committee of the local soviet of working people's deputies.

Conditional early relief from punishment or replacement of the unserved part of the punishment by a milder punishment may be applied to a convicted person for a crime committed when under the age of 18 years, after the actual serving of not less than one third of the assigned term of punishment.

Conditional early relief from punishment or replacement of the unserved part of the punishment by a milder punishment may be applied after the actual serving of not less than one half of the assigned term of punishment to:

(1) persons sentenced to deprivation of freedom for a term of not less than five years for an intentional crime committed while under the age of 18 years;

(2) persons who have previously served punishment in places of deprivation of freedom for an intentional crime and who, before the expunging or removal of the record of conviction, have again, while under the age of 18 years, committed an intentional crime for which they are sentenced to deprivation of freedom;

(3) persons who, while under the age of 18 years and during the serving of punishment in places of deprivation of freedom, have committed an intentional crime for which they are sentenced to deprivation of freedom.

Conditional early relief from punishment or replacement of the unserved part of the punishment by a milder punishment may be applied after the actual serving of not less than two thirds of the assigned term of punishment to:

(1) persons who have previously been sentenced to deprivation of freedom for an intentional crime, to whom conditional early relief from punishment or replacement of the unserved part of the punishment by a milder punishment has been applied, if such persons while under the age of 18 years and before the expiration of the unserved tem of punishment have again committed an intentional crime for which they are sentenced to deprivation of freedom;

(2) persons convicted of a crime committed while under the age of 18 years: banditry (Article 77), assault with intent to rob for the purpose of taking possession of state or social property or personal property of citizens, under aggravating circumstances (Articles 91 paragraph two, 146 paragraph two), intentional homicide under aggravating circumstances (Article 102), rape committed by a group of persons or resulting in especially grave consequences, as well as rape of a minor (Article 117 paragraph three), infringing the life of a policeman or people's guard in connection with his official or social activity for the protection of public order, under aggravating circumstances (Article 191–2), especially malicious hooliganism (Article 206 paragraph three), stealing of firearms, ammunition or explosives by means of an assault with intent to rob (Article 218–1 paragraph three).

In the replacement of the unserved part of deprivation of freedom by correctional tasks they shall be assigned to the limits of the terms established by law for such type of punishment and must not exceed the unserved term of deprivation of freedom.

In applying a conditional early relief from punishment or replacement of the unserved part of the punishment by a milder punishment, the court may impose on a particular collective of working people or on a person, with their consent, the duty to supervise a person granted conditional early release during the unserved part of the term of punishment assigned by the court or a person the unserved part of whose punishment is replaced by a milder punishment, and to carry on educational work with him.

In the event that during the unserved part of the punishment a person to whom conditional early relief from punishment was applied while he was under the age of 18 years commits a new intentional crime for which he is sentenced to deprivation of freedom, the court may assign him punishment in accordance with the rules provided by Article 41 of the present Code.

[*Ved.* (1969), no. 47, item 1361, Edict November 14, 1969.]

Article 56. Relief From Serving Punishment. Relief of a convicted person from serving punishment and also mitigation of a punishment that has been assigned, except relief from punishment or mitigation of punishment by way of amnesty or pardon, may be applied only by a court in the instances and in accordance with the procedure indicated by law.

Article 57. Expunging of Record of Conviction [*sudimost'*]. The following shall be deemed not to have a record of conviction:

(1) persons relieved from punishment by reason of Articles 49 and 50 of the present Code;

(2) persons who have served punishment in a disciplinary battalion or who have been relieved early therefrom, and also persons in military service who have served punishment in the form of detention in the guardhouse instead of correctional tasks;

(3) persons conditionally sentenced, if in the course of the probation period they do not commit a new crime;

(4) persons sentenced to social censure, imposition of the duty to make amends for harm caused, dismissal from office, fine, deprivation of the right to occupy specified offices or to engage in specified activity, or correctional tasks, if in the course of one year after serving the punishment they do not commit a new crime;

(5) persons sentenced to deprivation of freedom for a term not exceeding three years or to exile or banishment, if in the course of three years after serving the punishment (basic and supplementary) they do not commit a new crime;

(6) persons sentenced to deprivation of freedom for a term exceeding three years but not more than six years, if in the course of five years after serving the punishment (basic and supplementary) they do not commit a new crime;

(7) persons sentenced to deprivation of freedom for a term exceeding six years but not more than ten years, if in the course of eight years after serving the punishment (basic and supplementary) they do not commit a new crime;

(8) persons sentenced to deprivation of freedom for a term exceeding ten years, if in the course of eight years after serving the punishment (basic and supplementary) they do not commit a new crime and if, in addition, the court has established that the convicted person has been corrected and that there is no necessity to consider him as having had a record of conviction.

If a person sentenced to deprivation of freedom, after serving the punishment, by exemplary conduct and an honorable attitude toward labor proves his correction, then upon the petition of social organizations the court may remove the record of his conviction before expiration of the terms indicated in the present article.

If a person has been granted an early relief from punishment in a procedure established by law, the period for expunging the record of conviction shall be calculated on the basis of punishment actually served from the moment of being relieved from serving punishment (basic and supplementary). If the punishment is replaced by a milder punishment, the term actually served shall be calculated in accordance with the rules provided by Article 47 of the present Code.

If a person who has served punishment again commits a crime prior to the expiration of the period for expunging the record of conviction, the running of the period for expunging the record of conviction shall be interrupted. The period for expunging the record of conviction for the first crime shall be calculated anew after the punishment (basic and supplementary) for the latter crime is actually served. In such instances the person shall be considered convicted of both crimes prior to the expiration of the period for expunging the conviction for the graver of them.

[*Ved.* (1969), no. 47, item 1361, Edict November 14, 1969.]

Chapter Six: Compulsory Measures of a Medical and Educational Character

Article 58. Application of Compulsory Measures of Medical Character to Mentally Ill Persons. The following measures of a medical character may be applied by a court to persons who have committed socially dangerous acts while nonimputable or who have committed such acts while imputable but who, before judgment is rendered or during the serving of punishment, have contracted a mental illness depriving them of the possibility of realizing the significance of their actions or of controlling them:

(1) commitment to a general psychiatric hospital;

(2) commitment to a special psychiatric hospital.

Article 59. Commitment to Psychiatric Hospital. Compulsory treatment in a general psychiatric hospital may be applied by the court to a mentally ill person who by reason of his mental condition and the character of the socially dangerous act he has committed is in need of hospitalization and compulsory treatment.

Commitment to a special psychiatric hospital may be assigned by the court for a mentally ill person who by reason of his mental condition and the character of the socially dangerous act he has committed represents a special danger for society.

Persons committed to a special psychiatric hospital shall be kept in conditions of a reinforced supervision that excludes the possibility of their commission of a new socially dangerous act.

Article 60. Assigning, Changing, and Terminating Application to Mentally Ill Persons of Compulsory Measures of Medical Character. If the court deems it necessary to assign a compulsory measure of a medical character, its choice of the type of measure shall depend on the mental illness of the person and the character and degree of social danger of the act committed by him.

In the event of the person's recovery or of such a change in the character of the illness that the necessity for applying such measures disappears, termination of the application of compulsory measures of a medical character shall be effected by the court in accordance with the opinion of a medical institution.

A change in the type of compulsory measure of a medical character shall also be effected by the court in accordance with the opinion of a medical institution.

If the court does not deem it necessary to apply to a mentally ill person compulsory measures of a medical character, and likewise in the event of termination of the application of such measures, the court may transfer him to the care of his relatives or guardians, in which case medical supervision shall be obligatory.

Article 61. Deduction of Time of Application of Compulsory Measures of Medical Character. If a person who, after committing a crime or during the serving of punishment, contracts a mental illness which deprives him of the possibility of realizing the significance of his actions or of controlling them, subsequently recovers his health, the court may apply a punishment to him, if the terms of the period of limitation have not expired or there are not grounds for relieving him from criminal responsibility and punishment.

If punishment is applied to such a person after his recovery, the time during which compulsory measures of a medical character have been applied shall be deducted from the term of punishment.

Article 62. Application of Compulsory Measures of Medical Character to Alcoholics and Drug Addicts or Establishment of Curatorship for Them. In the event of the commission of a crime by an alcoholic or drug addict, and if there exists a medical opinion, a court, upon the petition of a social organization, collective of working people, comrades' court, or public health agency, or upon its own motion, may apply to such person compulsory therapy, together with punishment for the crime committed.

The aforementioned persons, if sentenced to measures of punishment not connected with deprivation of freedom, shall be subject to compulsory therapy in medical institutions with a special therapeutic and work regimen.

In the event such persons are sentenced to deprivation of freedom they shall be subject to compulsory therapy during the serving of punishment and, in case of necessity of prolonging such therapy after release from the place of deprivation of freedom, in medical institutions with a special therapeutic and work regimen.

The termination of compulsory therapy shall be effected by the court upon proposal of the medical institution in which the person is placed for cure.

In the event of the commission of a crime by a person who misuses alcoholic beverages or narcotics and thereby puts his family in a difficult material situation, the court, in addition to applying a punishment not involving deprivation of freedom for the crime committed, shall have the right, upon petition of members of his family, a trade union or any other social organization, a procurator, an agency of guardianship and curatorship, or a medical institution, to deem him to be of limited capacity. On the basis of a judgment the court shall establish a curatorship over such a person.

[*Ved.* (1968), no. 20, item 859, Edict May 8, 1968; *Ved.* (1971), no. 30, item 614, Edict July 22, 1971.]

Article 63. Application of Compulsory Measures of Educational Character to Minors. If, in accordance with paragraph three of Article 10 of the present Code, a court finds it appropriate not to apply criminal punishment to a minor who has committed a crime, it may assign the following measures of an educational character:

1. Imposition of the duty to make an apology to the victim either publicly or in another form determined by the court;
2. Issuance of a reprimand or severe reprimand;
3. Warning;
4. Imposition on a minor who has attained 15 years of age of the duty to compensate for the loss caused, if the minor has an independent wage and the amount of the loss does not exceed 20 rubles, or imposition of the duty to make good by his own labor the material loss caused, not exceeding 20 rubles; upon the causing of loss in an amount of more than 20 rubles, compensation for the loss shall be carried out by way of civil proceedings;
5. Transfer of the minor to the strict supervision of parents or persons substituting for them;
6. Transfer of the minor to a collective of working people or a social organization, with their consent, or to individual citizens at their request; the court may also deem it necessary to appoint a social educator in accordance with the Statute on Social Educators of Minors;
7. Commitment to a special medico-educational institution or educational institution for children and juveniles;
8. Assignment of the minor to an educational colony for minors.

The term, procedure, and conditions for placing minors in educational colonies and special medico-educational institutions shall be defined by the Statute on Commissions for Cases of Minors.

[*Ved.* (1968), no. 20, item 859, Edict May 8, 1968.]

Special Part

Chapter One: Crimes Against the State

I. ESPECIALLY DANGEROUS CRIMES AGAINST THE STATE

Article 64. Treason. (a) Treason, that is, an act intentionally committed by a citizen of the USSR to the detriment of the state independence, the territorial inviolability, or the military might of the USSR: going over to the side of the enemy, espionage, transmission of a state or military secret to a foreign state, flight abroad or refusal to return from abroad to the USSR, rendering aid to a foreign state in carrying on hostile activity against the USSR, or a conspiracy for the purpose of seizing power, shall be punished by deprivation of freedom for a term of ten to fifteen years with confiscation of property with or without additional exile for a term of two to five years, or by death with confiscation of property.

(b) A citizen of the USSR recruited by a foreign intelligence service for carrying on hostile activity against the USSR shall not be subject to criminal responsibility if he has committed no actions in execution of the criminal assignment received by him and has voluntarily reported to agencies of authority his connection with the foreign intelligence service.

[*Ved.* (1962), no. 29, item 449, Edict July 25, 1962.]

Article 65. Espionage. The transfer, or the stealing or collection for purpose of transfer, to a foreign state or foreign organization or its secret service, of information constituting a state or military secret, or the transfer or collection on assignment from a foreign intelligence service of any other information for use to the detriment of the interests of the USSR, if the espionage is committed by a foreigner or person without citizenship, shall be punished by deprivation of freedom for a term of seven to fifteen years with confiscation of property, with or without additional exile for a term of two to five years, or by death with confiscation of property.

[*Ved.* (1962), no. 29, item 449, Edict July 25, 1962.]

Article 66. Terrorist Act. The killing of a state or social figure or representative of authority, committed in connection with his state or social activity, for the purpose of subverting or weakening the Soviet regime [*vlast'*], shall be punished by deprivation of freedom for a term of ten to fifteen years with confiscation of property or by death with confiscation of property.

Grave bodily injury caused for the same purpose to a state or social figure or representative of authority in connection with his state or social activity shall be punished by deprivation of freedom for a term of eight to fifteen years with confiscation of property, with or without additional exile for a term of two to five years.

[*Ved.* (1962), no. 29, item 449, Edict July 25, 1962.]

Article 67. Terrorist Act Against Representative of Foreign State. The killing of a representative of a foreign state for the purpose of provoking war or international complications shall be punished by deprivation of freedom for a term of ten to fifteen years with confiscation of property, with or without additional exile for a term of two to five years, or by death with confiscation of property.

Grave bodily injury caused to the same persons for the same purpose shall be punished by deprivation of freedom for a term of eight to fifteen years with confiscation of property, with or without additional exile for a term of two to five years.

[*Ved.* (1962), no. 29, item 449, Edict July 25, 1962.]

Article 68. Sabotage. The destruction or damaging, by explosion, arson, or other means, of enterprises, structures, routes and means of transportation, means of communication, or other state or social property, or the commission of mass poisoning or the spreading of epidemics or epizootics, for the purpose of weakening the Soviet state, shall be punished by deprivation of freedom for a term of eight to fifteen years with confiscation of property, with or without additional exile for a term of two to five years, or by death with confiscation of property.

[*Ved.* (1962), no. 29, item 449, Edict July 25, 1962.]

Article 69. Wrecking. An action or omission to act directed toward the subversion of industry, transport, agriculture, the monetary system, trade, or other branches of the national economy, or the activity of state agencies or social organizations, for the purpose of weakening the Soviet state, if such act is committed by making use of state or social institutions, enterprises, or organizations, or by obstructing their normal work, shall be punished by deprivation of freedom for a term of eight to fifteen years with confiscation of property, with or without additional exile for a term of two to five years.

[*Ved.* (1962), no. 29, item 449, Edict July 25, 1962.]

Article 70. Anti-Soviet Agitation and Propaganda. Agitation or propaganda carried on for the purpose of subverting or weakening the Soviet regime [*vlast'*] or of committing particular, especially dangerous crimes against the state, or the circulation, for the same purpose of slanderous fabrications which defame the Soviet state and social system, or the circulation or preparation or keeping, for the same purpose, of literature of such content, shall be punished by deprivation of freedom for a term of six months to seven years, with or without additional exile for a term of two to five years, or by exile for a term of two to five years.

The same actions committed by a person previously convicted of especially dangerous crimes against the state or committed in wartime shall be punished by deprivation of freedom for a term of three to ten years, with or without additional exile for a term of two to five years.

[*Ved.* (1962), no. 29, item 449, Edict July 25, 1962.]

Article 71. Propagandizing of War. The propagandizing of war, in whatever form it is conducted, shall be punished by deprivation of freedom for a term of three to eight years, with or without additional exile for a term of two to five years.

[*Ved.* (1962), no. 29, item 449, Edict July 25, 1962.]

Article 72. Organizational Activity Directed to Commission of Especially Dangerous Crimes Against the State and Also Participation in Anti-Soviet Organizations. Organizational activity directed to the preparation or commission of especially dangerous crimes against the state, or to the creation of an organization which has as its purpose the commission of such crimes, or participation in an anti-Soviet organization, shall be punished in accordance with Articles 64–71 of the present Code.

Article 73. Especially Dangerous Crimes Against the State Committed Against Another Working People's State. By virtue of the international solidarity of working people, especially dangerous crimes against the state committed against another working people's state shall be punished in accordance with Articles 64–72 of the present Code.

II. OTHER CRIMES AGAINST THE STATE

Article 74. Violation of Equality of Rights of Nationalities and Races. Propaganda or agitation for the purpose of arousing hostility or dissension of races or nationalities, or the direct or indirect restriction of rights or the establishment of direct or indirect privileges for citizens depending on the races or nationalities to which they belong, shall be punished by deprivation of freedom for a term of six months to three years, or by exile for a term of two to five years.

Article 75. Divulgence of State Secret. Divulgence of information constituting a state secret by a person to whom such information has been entrusted or has become known because of his position or work, in the absence of the indicia of treason or espionage, shall be punished by deprivation of freedom for a term of two to five years.

The same act, if it results in serious consequences, shall be punished by deprivation of freedom for a term of five to eight years.

Article 76. Loss of Documents Containing State Secrets. The loss of documents containing state secrets, or of articles information concerning which constitutes a state secret, by a person to whom they have been entrusted, if the loss is a result of violation of the rules established for handling the aforementioned documents or articles, shall be punished by deprivation of freedom for a term of one to three years.

The same act, if it causes serious consequences, shall be punished by deprivation of freedom for a term of three to eight years.

Article 77. Banditry. The organization of armed bands for the purpose of attacking state or social institutions or enterprises or individual persons, or participation in such bands and in attacks committed by them, shall be punished by deprivation of freedom for a term of three to fifteen years with confiscation of property and with or without additional exile for a term of two to five years, or by death with confiscation of property.

[*Ved.* (1962), no. 29, item 449, Edict July 25, 1962.]

Article 77-1. Actions Disrupting Work of Correctional Labor Institutions. Especially dangerous recidivists or persons convicted of grave crimes who in places of deprivation of freedom terrorize convicts who have followed the road of correction, or who commit attacks on the administration, or those who for such purposes organize criminal groups or who actively participate in such groups, shall be punished by deprivation of freedom for a term of eight to fifteen years or by death.

[*Ved.* (1962), no. 29, item 449, Edict July 25, 1962.]

Article 78. Smuggling. Smuggling, that is, the illegal transfer of goods or other valuables across the state border of the USSR, committed by concealment of articles in special containers or by fraudulent utilization of customs or other documents, or on a large scale, or by a group of persons organized for engaging in smuggling, or by an official by utilization of his official position, or the smuggling of explosives, narcotics, virulent and poisonous substances, arms and military equipment, shall be punished by deprivation of freedom for a term of three to ten years with confiscation of property, with or without additional exile for a term of two to five years.

[*Ved.* (1962), no. 29, item 449, Edict July 25, 1962.]

Article 79. Mass Disorders. The organization of mass disorders accompanied by pogroms, acts of destruction, arson, and other similar actions, or the direct commission of the aforementioned crimes by participants in them, or the offering by such persons of armed resistance to authority, shall be punished by deprivation of freedom for a term of two to fifteen years.

Article 80. Evasion of Regular Call to Active Military Service. Evasion of a regular call to active military service shall be punished by deprivation of freedom for a term of one to three years.

The same act committed by means of causing oneself bodily injury or by malingering, by means of forgery of documents or by any other deception, or committed under other aggravating circumstances, shall be punished by deprivation of freedom for a term of one to five years.

Article 81. Evasion of Call-up by Mobilization. Evasion of a call-up by mobilization into the ranks of the Armed Forces of the USSR shall be punished by deprivation of freedom for a term of three to ten years.

The same act, or evasion of further calls for making up the complement of the Armed Forces of the USSR, committed in wartime, shall be punished by deprivation of freedom for a term of five to ten years or by death.

Article 82. **Evasion in Wartime of Fulfillment of Compulsory Service or Payment of Taxes.** Evasion in wartime of labor mobilization or of fulfillment of other compulsory service, or of payment of taxes, shall be punished by deprivation of freedom for a term of one to five years or by correctional tasks for a term of six months to one year.

Article 83. **Illegal Exit Abroad and Illegal Entry into the USSR.** Exit abroad, entry into the USSR, or crossing the border without the requisite passport or the permission of the proper authorities, shall be punished by deprivation of freedom for a term of one to three years.

Operation of the present article shall not extend to instances of arrival in the USSR of foreign citizens, without the requisite passport or permit, for exercise of the right of asylum granted by the Constitution of the USSR.

Article 84. **Violation of Rules for International Flights.** Flying into the USSR or out of the USSR without the requisite permit, nonobservance of the routes, landing places, air gateways, or altitude of flights indicated on the permit, or any other violation of rules of international flights, shall be punished by deprivation of freedom for a term of one to ten years or by a fine in an amount of not more than 1,000 rubles with or without confiscation of the aircraft.

Article 85. **Violation of Rules for Safe Movement and Operation of Transport.** Violation by a worker of rail, water, or air transport of rules for safe movement and operation of transport, resulting in accidents involving persons, a wreck, damage, or other serious consequences, or improper repair of means of transport, routes, or means of signaling and communication, resulting in such consequences, shall be punished by deprivation of freedom for a term of three to fifteen years.

The same acts, if they do not result in such consequences but create a known threat that such consequences will occur, shall be punished by deprivation of freedom for a term of one to three years or by correctional tasks for a term not exceeding one year.

Article 86. **Damaging of Routes of Communication and Means of Transport.** The intentional destruction or damaging of routes of communication, structures thereon, rolling stock, or vessels, means of communication or of signaling, which results in or can result in a train wreck, damage to a ship, or interference with the normal operation of transport and communication, shall be punished by deprivation of freedom for a term of three to fifteen years, with or without additional exile for a term of two to five years.

[*Ved.* (1962), no. 29, item 449, Edict July 25, 1962.]

Article 87. Making or Passing Counterfeit Money or Securities. Making for the purpose of passing, or passing, counterfeit state treasury notes, notes of the USSR State Bank, coins, state securities, or foreign currency, shall be punished by deprivation of freedom for a term of three to fifteen years with confiscation of property, with or without additional exile for a term of two to five years.

The same actions committed as a form of business shall be punished by deprivation of freedom for a term of ten to fifteen years with confiscation of property, with or without additional exile for a term of two to five years, or by death with confiscation of property.

[*Ved.* (1962), no. 29, item 449, Edict July 25, 1962.]

Article 88. Violation of Rules for Currency Transactions. Violations of rules for currency transactions, or speculation in currency or securities, shall be punished by deprivation of freedom for a term of three to eight years, with or without confiscation of property, with obligatory confiscation of the currency and securities, with or without additional exile for a term of two to five years.

Speculation in currency or securities as a form of business or on a large scale, or violation of rules for currency transactions by a person previously convicted under paragraph one of the present article, shall be punished by deprivation of freedom for a term of five to fifteen years with confiscation of property, with or without additional exile for a term of two to five years, or by death with confiscation of property.

[*Ved.* (1962), no. 29, item 449, Edict July 25, 1962.]

Article 88–1. Failure to Report Crimes Against the State. The failure to report crimes against the state that are known to be in preparation or to have been committed, provided for by Articles 64 (treason), 65 (espionage), 66 and 67 (terrorist act), 68 (sabotage), 69 (wrecking), 72 (organizational activity directed at commission of especially dangerous crimes against the state or participation in an anti-Soviet organization), 77 (banditry), 87 (making or passing of counterfeit money or securities) of the present Code, shall be punished by deprivation of freedom for a term of one to three years or by correctional tasks for a term of six months to one year.

[*Ved.* (1962), no. 29, item 449, Edict July 25, 1962.]

Article 88–2. Concealment of Crimes Against the State. When not promised in advance, the concealment of crimes against the state provided for by Articles 64 (treason), 65 (espionage), 66 and 67 (terrorist act), 68 (sabotage), 69 (wrecking), 72 (organizational activity directed at commission of especially dangerous crimes against the state or participation in an anti-Soviet organization), 77 (banditry), 78 (smuggling), 87 (making or passing of counterfeit money or securities), 88 (violation of rules for currency transactions) of the present Code, shall be punished by deprivation of freedom for a term of one to five years with or without additional exile for a term of two to five years, or by exile for a term not exceeding five years.

[*Ved.* (1962), no. 29, item 449, Edict July 25, 1962.]

Chapter Two: Crimes Against Socialist Ownership

Article 89. Stealing of State or Social Property, Committed by Theft [*Krazha*]. The secret stealing of state or social property (theft) shall be punished by deprivation of freedom for a term not exceeding three years or by correctional tasks for a term not exceeding one year.

Theft committed repeatedly or by a group of persons in accordance with a preliminary agreement or by the application of technical means shall be punished by deprivation of freedom for a term not exceeding six years.

Theft committed by an especially dangerous recidivist or on a large scale shall be punished by deprivation of freedom for a term of five to fifteen years with or without confiscation of property.

Note: A crime specified in Articles 89, 90, 92, and 93 shall be deemed to be repeated if it is committed by a person who has previously committed any one of the crimes provided for by these articles or by Articles 77, 91, 93-1, or 144–147 of the present Code.

[*Ved.* (1962), no. 29, item 449, Edict July 25, 1962.]

Article 90. Stealing of State or Social Property, Committed by Open Stealing [*Grabiozh*]. The open stealing of state or social property (open stealing), committed without force, shall be punished by deprivation of freedom for a term not exceeding four years or by correctional tasks for a term not exceeding one year.

Open stealing combined with force that is not dangerous for life or health, or committed by a group of persons in accordance with a preliminary agreement, or committed repeatedly, shall be punished by deprivation of freedom for a term not exceeding seven years.

Open stealing committed by an especially dangerous recidivist or on a large scale shall be punished by deprivation of freedom for a term of six to fifteen years with or without confiscation of property.

Article 91. Assault With Intent to Rob [*Razboi*] **for the Purpose of Taking Possession of State or Social Property.** An attack for the purpose of taking possession of state or social property, combined with force that is dangerous for the life or health of the person subjected to the attack, or with the threat of application of such force (assault with intent to rob), shall be punished by deprivation of freedom for a term of three to ten years with or without confiscation of property.

The same actions, if they are committed:

(a) by a group of persons in accordance with a preliminary agreement;

(b) by the application of weapons or other articles used as weapons;

(c) with the causing of grave bodily injuries;

(d) by an especially dangerous recidivist;

(e) by a person who has previously committed assault with intent to rob for the purpose of taking possession of state or social property or personal property of citizens, or who has previously committed banditry; or

(f) if such actions are directed at taking possession of state or social property on a large scale;

shall be punished by deprivation of freedom for a term of six to fifteen years with or without exile and with or without confiscation of property.

Article 92. Stealing of State or Social Property, Committed by Appropriation or Embezzlement or by Abuse of Official Position. The appropriation or embezzlement of state or social property which has been entrusted to the guilty person, or the taking possession of state or social property for a mercenary purpose through abuse by an official of his office, shall be punished by deprivation of freedom for a term not exceeding four years, or by correctional tasks for a term not exceeding one year, or by deprivation of the right to occupy specified offices or to engage in specified activity.

The same actions committed repeatedly or by a group of persons in accordance with a preliminary agreement shall be punished by deprivation of freedom for a term not exceeding seven years with or without deprivation of the right to occupy specified offices or to engage in specified activity.

Actions provided for by paragraphs one or two of the present article, which have caused serious loss to the state or to a social organization, shall be punished by deprivation of freedom for a term of six to fifteen years with or without confiscation of property and by deprivation of the right to occupy specified offices or to engage in specified activity.

Article 93. Stealing of State or Social Property, Committed Through Swindling. The taking possession of state or social property through deception or abuse of trust (swindling) shall be punished by deprivation of freedom for a term not exceeding three years or by correctional tasks for a term not exceeding one year.

Swindling committed repeatedly or by a group of persons in accordance with a preliminary agreement shall be punished by deprivation of freedom for a term not exceeding six years.

Swindling causing serious loss to the state or to a social organization or committed by an especially dangerous recidivist shall be punished by deprivation of freedom for a term of five to fifteen years with or without confiscation of property.

Article 93-1. Stealing of State or Social Property on an Especially Large Scale. The stealing of state or social property on an especially large scale, regardless of the manner of stealing (Articles 89–93), shall be punished by deprivation of freedom for a term of eight to fifteen years with confiscation of property, with or without exile, or by death with confiscation of property.

[*Ved.* (1962), no. 29, item 449, Edict July 25, 1962.]

Article 93-2. Application of Fine for Stealing of State or Social Property. The stealing of state or social property through theft (Article 89), appropriation, embezzlement, abuse of official position (Article 92), or swindling (Article 93), committed for the first time and on a small scale, if according to the circumstances of the case and taking into account the personality of the guilty person the application of measures of punishment provided by the indicated articles is not necessary, shall be punished by a fine in an amount not exceeding three times the cost of what was stolen.

[*Ved.* (1965), no. 4, item 83, Edict January 16, 1965.]

Article 94. Causing of Property Damage Through Deception or Abuse of Trust. The causing of property damage to the state or to a social organization through deception or abuse of trust, in the absence of the indicia of stealing, shall be punished by deprivation of freedom for a term not exceeding one year, or by correctional tasks for the same term, or by deprivation of the right to occupy specified offices or to engage in specified activity, or by dismissal from office, or shall entail application of measures of social pressure.

Article 95. Extortion of State or Social Property. A demand that state or social property or right to property be transferred under threat of force against a person responsible for the management or protection of such property, of force against his near ones, of circulating defamatory information concerning him or his near ones, or of destruction of their property (extortion), shall be punished by deprivation of freedom for a term not exceeding four years.

Article 96. Petty Stealing of State or Social Property. The petty stealing of state or social property through theft, appropriation, embezzlement, abuse of official position, or swindling, committed by a person to whom, according to the circumstances of the case, measures of social pressure cannot be applied, shall be punished by deprivation of freedom for a term not exceeding six months, or by correctional tasks for a term not exceeding one year, or by a fine not exceeding 50 rubles.

The same act committed for a second time or by a person who has previously committed the stealing of state or social property or personal property of citizens, provided for by Articles 89 to 93-1 and 144–147 of the present Code, shall be punished by deprivation of freedom for a term not exceeding two years or by a fine not exceeding 100 rubles.

[*Ved.* (1965), no. 4, item 83, Edict January 16, 1965.]

Article 97. Appropriation of State or Social Property Found by or Accidentally in Possession of Guilty Person. The appropriation of valuable property known to belong to the state or to a social organization, which has been found by or has accidentally come into the possession of the guilty person, shall be punished by deprivation of freedom for a term not exceeding six months or by correctional tasks for a term not exceeding one year, or shall entail application of measures of social pressure.

Article 98. Intentional Destruction or Damaging of State or Social Property. The intentional destruction or damaging of state or social property shall be punished by correctional tasks for a term not exceeding one year, or by a fine not exceeding 100 rubles, or by imposition of the duty to make amends for the harm caused.

The intentional destruction or damaging of state or social property, committed through arson or in any other manner involving general danger, or resulting in loss of human life or causing serious loss or any other grave consequences, or the intentional destruction or substantial damaging of large tracts of forest through arson, shall be punished by deprivation of freedom for a term not exceeding ten years.

Article 99. Negligent Destruction or Damaging of State or Social Property. The negligent destruction or damaging of state or social property, resulting in loss of human life or any other grave consequences, and also the destruction or substantial damaging of large tracts of forest as a result of careless handling of fire or other sources of heightened danger, shall be punished by deprivation of freedom for a term not exceeding three years, or by correctional tasks for a term not exceeding one year.

Article 99-1. Criminally Careless Use or Maintenance of Agricultural Equipment. The criminally careless use or maintenance of tractors, automobiles, combines, or any other agricultural machinery belonging to state farms, collective farms, or to other state or cooperative organizations, which results in damage or breakage, or the dismantling of such machinery, shall be punished by deprivation of freedom for a term not exceeding one year or by correctional tasks for the same term.

The same acts committed repeatedly or causing serious loss shall be punished by deprivation of freedom for a term not exceeding three years.

[*Ved.* (1962), no. 29, item 49, Edict July 25, 1962.]

Article 100. Unconscientious Attitude Toward Protection of State or Social Property. An unconscientious attitude toward his duties on the part of a person charged with protection of state or social property, resulting in the stealing, damaging, or destroying of such property on a large scale, in the absence of the indicia of an official crime, shall be punished by deprivation of freedom for a term not exceeding two years, or by correctional tasks for a term not exceeding one year, or by social censure.

Article 101. Crimes Against State or Social Property of Other Socialist States. Crimes against state or social property of other socialist states, committed with respect to property situated on the territory of the RSFSR, shall be punished in accordance with the articles of the present chapter.

Chapter Three: Crimes Against Life, Health, Freedom, and Dignity of the Person

Article 102. Intentional Homicide Under Aggravating Circumstances. Intentional homicide

a. from mercenary motives;

b. from motives of hooliganism;

c. committed in connection with the victim's performance of his official or social duty;

d. committed with special cruelty;

e. committed in a manner dangerous for the life of many persons;

f. for the purpose of concealing another crime or facilitating its commission, or in conjunction with rape;

g. of a woman known by the guilty person to be pregnant;

h. of two or more persons;

i. committed by a person who has previously committed intentional homicide, with the exception of homicide as provided for by Articles 104 and 105 of the present Code;

j. committed because of a blood feud;

k. committed by an especially dangerous recidivist;

shall be punished by deprivation of freedom for a term of eight to fifteen years, with or without exile, or by death.

Article 103. **Intentional Homicide.** Intentional homicide committed without the aggravating circumstances stated in Article 102 of the present Code shall be punished by deprivation of freedom for a term of three to ten years.

[*Ved.* (1962), no. 29, item 449, Edict July 25, 1962.]

Article 104. **Intentional Homicide Committed in State of Strong Mental Agitation.** Intentional homicide committed in a state of sudden strong mental agitation provoked by force or grave insult on the part of the victim, or provoked by any other unlawful actions of the victim, if these actions result or could result in grave consequences for the guilty person or his near ones, shall be punished by deprivation of freedom for a term not exceeding five years or by correctional tasks for a term not exceeding one year.

Article 105. **Homicide Committed While Exceeding Limits of Necessary Defense.** Homicide committed while exceeding the limits of necessary defense shall be punished by deprivation of freedom for a term not exceeding two years or by correctional tasks for a term not exceeding one year.

Article 106. **Negligent Homicide.** Homicide committed by negligence shall be punished by deprivation of freedom for a term not exceeding three years or by correctional tasks for a term not exceeding one year.

Article 107. **Incitement to Suicide.** The incitement of a person who is economically or otherwise dependent on the guilty person to commit suicide or to attempt suicide, by cruel treatment of the victim or systematic lowering of his personal dignity, shall be punished by deprivation of freedom for a term not exceeding five years.

Article 108. **Intentional Infliction of Grave Bodily Injury.** The intentional infliction of bodily injury dangerous for life or resulting in loss of sight, of hearing, or of any organ, or in loss by an organ of its functions, or in mental illness or any other impairment of health, joined with persistent loss of at least one third of the capacity to work, or when it results in an interruption of pregnancy or permanent disfigurement of the face, shall be punished by deprivation of freedom for a term not exceeding eight years.

The same actions, if they cause the victim's death or assume the character of torment or torture or are committed by an especially dangerous recidivist, shall be punished by deprivation of freedom for a term of five to twelve years.

Article 109. **Intentional Infliction of Less Grave Bodily Injury.** The intentional infliction of bodily injury not dangerous for life and not causing the consequences provided for in Article 108 of the present Code, but provoking a lengthy impairment of health or a significant persistent loss of at least one third of the capacity to work, shall be punished by deprivation of freedom for a term not exceeding three years or by correctional tasks for a term not exceeding one year.

The same actions, if they assume the character of torment or torture or are committed by an especially dangerous recidivist, shall be punished by deprivation of freedom for a term not exceeding five years.

Article 110. **Intentional Infliction of Grave or Less Grave Bodily Injury While in State of Strong Mental Agitation.** The intentional infliction of grave or less grave bodily injury while in a state of sudden strong mental agitation provoked by force or grave insult on the part of the victim, or provoked by any other unlawful actions of the victim, if such actions result or could result in grave consequences for the guilty person or his near ones, shall be punished by deprivation of freedom for a term not exceeding two years or by correctional tasks for a term not exceeding one year.

Article 111. **Infliction of Grave or Less Grave Bodily Injury While Exceeding Limits of Necessary Defense.** The infliction of grave or less grave bodily injury while exceeding the limits of necessary defense shall be punished by deprivation of freedom for a term not exceeding one year or by correctional tasks for the same term.

Article 112. **Intentional Infliction of Light Bodily Injury or Beatings.** The intentional causing of light bodily injury or infliction of beatings resulting in an impairment of health of short duration or an insignificant persistent loss of the capacity to work shall be punished by deprivation of freedom for a term not exceeding one year or by correctional tasks for the same term.

The same actions not resulting in the consequences stated in paragraph one of the present article shall be punished by deprivation of freedom for a term not exceeding six months, or by correctional tasks for the same term, or by a fine not exceeding 50 rubles, or shall entail application of measures of social pressure.

Article 113. **Torture.** The systematic infliction of beatings or other actions which assume the character of torture, if they do not result in the consequences stated in Articles 108 and 109 of the present Code, shall be punished by deprivation of freedom for a term not exceeding three years.

Article 114. Negligent Infliction of Grave or Less Grave Bodily Injury. The negligent infliction of grave bodily injury shall be punished by deprivation of freedom for a term not exceeding two years or by correctional tasks for a term not exceeding one year.

The negligent infliction of less grave bodily injury shall be punished by correctional tasks for a term not exceeding one year or by social censure.

Article 115. Infecting With Venereal Disease. Deliberately placing another person, through sexual relations or other actions, in danger of infection with venereal disease shall be punished by deprivation of freedom for a term not exceeding two years or by a fine not exceeding 100 rubles.

The infecting of another person with a venereal disease by a person who knows that he has such disease shall be punished by deprivation of freedom for a term not exceeding three years or by correctional tasks for a term not exceeding one year.

Actions provided for by paragraph two of the present article, committed by a person previously convicted of infecting another person with venereal disease, and also the infecting of two or more persons or of a minor, shall be punished by deprivation of freedom for a term not exceeding five years.

[*Ved.* (1971), no. 42, item 881, Edict October 20, 1971.]

Article 115-1. Refusing Treatment for Venereal Disease. Refusing treatment for venereal disease after a warning given by a health agency shall be punished by deprivation of freedom for a term not exceeding two years, or by correctional tasks for a term not exceeding one year, or by a fine not exceeding 100 rubles.

[*Ved.* (1971), no. 42, item 881, Edict October 20, 1971.]

Article 116. Illegal Performance of Abortion. The illegal performance of an abortion by a doctor shall be punished by deprivation of freedom for a term not exceeding one year, or by correctional tasks for the same term, or by deprivation of the right to engage in medical activity.

The performance of an abortion by a person not having a higher medical education shall be punished by deprivation of freedom for a term not exceeding two years or by correctional tasks for a term not exceeding one year.

Actions provided for by paragraphs one and two of the present article, if committed repeatedly or resulting in the death of the victim or any other grave consequences, shall be punished by deprivation of freedom for a term not exceeding eight years.

Article 117. Rape. Rape, that is, sexual relations by application of physical force or threats or by taking advantage of the helpless condition of the victim, shall be punished by deprivation of freedom for a term of three to seven years.

Rape in conjunction with the threat of homicide or of causing grave bodily injury or committed by a person who has previously committed rape shall be punished by deprivation of freedom for a term of five to ten years.

Rape committed by a group of persons or by an especially dangerous recidivist or resulting in especially grave consequences, or the rape of a minor, shall be punished by deprivation of freedom for a term of eight to fifteen years with or without additional exile for a term of two to five years, or by death.

[*Ved.* (1962), no. 29, item 449, Edict July 25, 1962.]

Article 118. Compelling a Woman to Enter into Sexual Intercourse. The compelling of a woman to enter into sexual intercourse or to satisfy sexual desire in any other form by a person upon whom the woman is dependent economically or occupationally shall be punished by deprivation of freedom for a term not exceeding three years.

Article 119. Sexual Relations With a Person Who Has Not Attained Puberty. Sexual relations with a person who has not attained puberty shall be punished by deprivation of freedom for a term not exceeding three years.

The same actions in conjunction with satisfaction of sexual desire in perverted forms shall be punished by deprivation of freedom for a term not exceeding six years.

Article 120. Depraved Actions. Depraved actions with respect to minors shall be punished by deprivation of freedom for a term not exceeding three years.

Article 121. Pederasty. Sexual relations of a man with another man (pederasty) shall be punished by deprivation of freedom for a term not exceeding five years.

Pederasty committed by application of physical force or threats, or with respect to a minor, or by taking advantage of the dependent condition of the victim, shall be punished by deprivation of freedom for a term not exceeding eight years.

Article 122. Malicious Evasion of Payment for Support or Maintenance of Children. The malicious evasion by parents of payment, in accordance with a court decision, of the means for maintenance of minor children or of maintenance of adult children incapable of working who are dependent on them, shall be punished by deprivation of freedom for a term not exceeding one year, or by exile for a term not exceeding three years, or by correctional tasks for a term not exceeding one year.

Article 123. Malicious Evasion of Rendering Aid to Parents. The malicious evasion of payment, in accordance with a court decision, of the means for maintenance of parents incapable of working shall be punished by correctional tasks for a term not exceeding one year or by social censure or shall entail application of measures of social pressure.

Article 124. Abuse of Duties of Guardianship. The abuse of a guardianship for mercenary purposes or the leaving of a ward without supervision and necessary aid shall be punished by deprivation of freedom for a term not exceeding two years or by correctional tasks for a term not exceeding one year.

Article 124–1. Divulgence of Secret of Adoption. The divulgence of a secret of adoption against the wish of the adopter shall be punished by correctional tasks for a term not exceeding one year or by a fine not exceeding 50 rubles or by social censure.

[*Ved.* (1970), no. 22, item 441, Edict May 21, 1970.]

Article 125. Abduction or Substitution of Infant. The abduction of another's infant or the substitution of an infant, committed for mercenary purposes or from other base motives, shall be punished by deprivation of freedom for a term not exceeding seven years.

The same actions committed in the absence of the indicia stated in paragraph one of the present article shall be punished by deprivation of freedom for a term not exceeding one year or by correctional tasks for the same term.

Article 126. Illegal Deprivation of Freedom. The illegal deprivation of freedom shall be punished by deprivation of freedom for a term not exceeding six months, or by correctional tasks for the same term, or by social censure.

The same act committed in a manner dangerous for the life or health of the victim or in conjunction with causing him physical suffering shall be punished by deprivation of freedom for a term not exceeding three years.

Article 127. Leaving in Danger. The failure to render aid which is necessary and is clearly required immediately to a person in danger of death, if such aid could knowingly be rendered by the guilty person without serious danger to himself or to other persons, or the failure to inform the appropriate institutions or persons of the necessity to render aid, shall be punished by correctional tasks for a term not exceeding six months or by social censure or shall entail application of measures of social pressure.

Knowingly leaving without aid a person in danger of death who is deprived of the possibility of taking measures for self-preservation by reason of his youth, old age, illness, or generally because of his helplessness, in instances where the guilty person is able to render aid to the victim and is under an obligation to take care of him or has himself placed him in danger of death, shall be punished by deprivation of freedom for a term not exceeding two years or by correctional tasks for a term not exceeding one year.

Article 128. Failure to Render Aid to Sick Person. The failure to render aid to a sick person without valid reasons by a person obliged by law or by a special rule to render it shall be punished by correctional tasks for a term not exceeding one year, or by a fine not exceeding 100 rubles, or by social censure, or shall entail the application of measures of social pressure.

The same act, if it results or it is known that it could result in the death of the sick person or any other grave consequences for him, shall be punished by deprivation of freedom for a term not exceeding two years with deprivation of the right to engage in professional activity for a term not exceeding three years.

Article 129. Failure of Captain of Vessel to Render Aid to Victims of Disaster. The failure of the captain of a vessel to render aid to persons perishing at sea or on any other water route, if such aid could be rendered without serious danger to his vessel, its crew and passengers, shall be punished by deprivation of freedom for a term not exceeding two years or by correctional tasks for a term not exceeding one year, with or without deprivation of the right to occupy the office of captain.

Article 130. Defamation. Defamation, that is, the circulating of fabrications known to be false which defame another person, shall be punished by deprivation of freedom for a term not exceeding one year, or by correctional tasks for the same term, or by a fine not exceeding 50 rubles, or by imposition of the duty to make amends for the harm caused, or by social censure, or shall entail the application of measures of social pressure.

Defamation in a work printed or reproduced by other means, or committed by a person previously convicted of defamation, shall be punished by deprivation of freedom for a term not exceeding three years or by correctional tasks for a term not exceeding one year.

Defamation combined with an accusation of commission of a crime against the state or other grave crime shall be punished by deprivation of freedom for a term not exceeding five years.

[*Ved.* (1962), no. 29, item 449, Edict July 25, 1962.]

Article 131. Insult. Insult, that is, the intentional lowering of the honor and dignity of a person, expressed in indecent form, shall be punished by correctional tasks for a term not exceeding six months, or by a fine not exceeding 50 rubles, or by social censure, or shall entail the application of measures of social pressure.

Insult in print or insult inflicted by a person previously convicted of insult shall be punished by correctional tasks for a term not exceeding one year or by a fine not exceeding 100 rubles.

[*Ved.* (1962), no. 29, item 449, Edict July 25, 1962.]

Chapter Four: Crimes Against Political and Labor Rights of Citizens

Article 132. Obstruction of Exercise of Right to Vote. The obstruction through force, deception, threat, or bribery of the exercise by a USSR citizen of the right to vote shall be punished by deprivation of freedom for a term not exceeding one year.

Article 133. Forgery of Voting Documents or Incorrect Tallying of Votes. The forgery of voting documents or the knowingly incorrect tallying of votes, or the violation of the secrecy of voting, committed by a member of an electoral commission or by another official, shall be punished by deprivation of freedom for a term not exceeding three years or by correctional tasks for a term not exceeding one year.

Article 134. Obstruction of Exercise of Equal Rights of Women. The obstruction of a woman from participating in state, social, or cultural activity, thereby substantially violating the woman's equal rights, if combined with force or threat of application of force, shall be punished by deprivation of freedom for a term not exceeding two years or by correctional tasks for a term not exceeding one year.

Article 135. Violation of Secrecy of Correspondence. The violation of the secrecy of citizens' correspondence shall be punished by correctional tasks for a term not exceeding six months, or by a fine not exceeding 30 rubles, or by social censure.

Article 136. Violation of Inviolability of Citizens' Dwelling Space. An illegal search, illegal eviction, or other illegal actions violating the inviolability of citizens' dwelling space, shall be punished by deprivation of freedom for a term not exceeding one year, or by correctional tasks for the same term, or by a fine not exceeding 50 rubles, or by dismissal from office.

Article 137. Violation of Legal Rights of Trade Unions. The obstruction of the legal activity of trade unions or their agencies shall be punished by correctional tasks for a term not exceeding one year, or by a fine not exceeding 100 rubles, or by dismissal from office.

Article 138. Violation of Labor Legislation. The illegal dismissal of a working person from work for personal motives, the failure to execute the decision of a court concerning his reinstatement at work, or any other intentional substantial violation of labor legislation, committed by an official of a state or social enterprise or institution, shall be punished by correctional tasks for a term not exceeding one year or by dismissal from office.

Article 139. Refusal to Employ or Dismissal of Pregnant Woman or Nursing Mother. The refusal to employ or the dismissal from work of a woman because of her pregnancy, as well as the refusal to employ or the dismissal from work of a mother who is nursing, for that reason, shall be punished by correctional tasks for a term not exceeding one year or by dismissal from office.

Article 140. Violation of Rules for Protection of Labor. The violation by an official of rules of technical safety, industrial sanitation, or other rules for the protection of labor, if such violation could result in accidents involving persons or other grave consequences, shall be punished by deprivation of freedom for a term not exceeding one year, or by correctional tasks for the same term, or by a fine not exceeding 100 rubles, or by dismissal from office.

The same violations resulting in bodily injuries or loss of the capacity to work shall be punished by deprivation of freedom for a term not exceeding three years or by correctional tasks for a term not exceeding one year.

Violations stated in paragraph one of the present article resulting in the death of a person or grave bodily injuries to several persons shall be punished by deprivation of freedom for a term not exceeding five years.

Article 141. Violation of Authors' and Inventors' Rights. The issuance under one's own name of another's scientific, literary, musical, or artistic work, or any other appropriation of the authorship of such a work, or the illegal reproduction or distribution of such a work, or the compelling of someone to be a co-author, shall be punished by deprivation of freedom for a term not exceeding one year or by a fine not exceeding 500 rubles.

The public disclosure of an invention before it is registered without the inventor's consent, the appropriation of the authorship of an invention, the compelling of someome to be a co-inventor, or the appropriation of the authorship of a rationalization proposal, shall be punished by deprivation of freedom for a term not exceeding one year, or by correctional tasks for the same term, or by a fine not exceeding 500 rubles.

Article 142. Violation of Laws on Separation of Church and State and of Church and School. The violation of laws on the separation of church and state and of school and church shall be punished by correctional tasks for a term not exceeding one year or by a fine not exceeding 50 rubles.

The same acts committed by a person previously convicted of violation of laws on the separation of church and state and of school and church, as well as organizational activity directed to the commission of such acts, shall be punished by deprivation of freedom for a term not exceeding three years.

[*Ved.* (1966), no. 12, item 220, Edict March 18, 1966).]

Article 143. Obstruction of Performance of Religious Rites. The obstruction of the performance of religious rites, insofar as they do not violate public order and are not accompanied by infringement of the rights of citizens, shall be punished by correctional tasks for a term not exceeding six months or by social censure.

Chapter Five: Crimes Against Personal Ownership of Citizens

Article 144. Theft [*Krazha*]. The secret stealing of personal property of citizens (theft) shall be punished by deprivation of freedom for a term not exceeding two years or by correctional tasks for a term not exceeding one year.

Theft committed repeatedly, or by a group of persons in accordance with a preliminary agreement, or by the application of technical means, or causing significant loss to the victim, shall be punished by deprivation of freedom for a term not exceeding five years.

Theft committed by an especially dangerous recidivist shall be punished by deprivation of freedom for a term of four to ten years.

Note: A crime specified in Articles 144, 145, and 147 shall be deemed to be repeated if it is committed by a person who has previously committed any one of the crimes provided for by these articles or by Articles 77, 89 to 93-1, and 146 of the present Code.

[*Ved.* (1962), no. 29, item 449, Edict July 25, 1962.]

Article 145. Open Stealing [*Grabiozh*]. The open stealing of personal property of citizens (open stealing) shall be punished by deprivation of freedom for a term not exceeding three years or by correctional tasks for a term not exceeding one year.

Open stealing committed repeatedly, or by a group of persons in accordance with a preliminary agreement, or combined with force that is not dangerous for the life or health of the victim, or causing significant loss to the victim, shall be punished by deprivation of freedom for a term not exceeding seven years.

Open stealing committed by an especially dangerous recidivist shall be punished by deprivation of freedom for a term of five to ten years.

Article 146. Assault With Intent to Rob [*Razboi*]. An attack for the purpose of taking possession of personal property of citizens, combined with force that is dangerous for the life or health of the victim or with the threat of application of such force (assault with intent to rob), shall be punished by deprivation of freedom for a term of three to ten years.

The same actions, if they are committed:

(a) by a group of persons in accordance with a preliminary agreement;

(b) by the application of weapons or other articles used as weapons;

(c) with the causing of grave bodily injuries;

(d) by an especially dangerous recidivist;

(e) by a person who has previously committed assault with intent to rob for the purpose of taking possession of state or social property or personal property of citizens, or who has previously committed banditry;

shall be punished by deprivation of freedom for a term of six to fifteen years with or without exile, with or without confiscation of property.

Article 147. Swindling. The taking possession of personal property of citizens or the acquisition of a right to property through deception or abuse of trust (swindling) shall be punished by deprivation of freedom for a term not exceeding two years or by correctional tasks for a term not exceeding one year.

Swindling committed repeatedly or by a group of persons in accordance with a preliminary agreement shall be punished by deprivation of freedom for a term not exceeding four years.

Swindling causing significant loss to the victim or committed by an especially dangerous recidivist shall be punished by deprivation of freedom for a term of three to ten years.

Article 148. Extortion. A demand that personal property of citizens or right to property, be transferred, or the commission of any actions concerning property, under threat of force against the person of the victim or of his near ones or under threat of publicly disclosing defamatory information concerning them or of destruction of their property (extortion) shall be punished by deprivation of freedom for a term not exceeding three years or by correctional tasks for a term not exceeding one year.

Article 149. Intentional Destruction or Damaging of Personal Property of Citizens. The intentional destruction or damaging of personal property of citizens, causing significant loss to the victim, shall be punished by correctional tasks for a term not exceeding six months with or without imposition of the duty to make amends for the harm caused, or by a fine not exceeding 100 rubles with or without imposition of the duty to make amends for the harm caused.

The intentional destruction or damaging of personal property of citizens, committed through arson or in any other manner involving general danger, or resulting in loss of human life or any other grave consequences, shall be punished by deprivation of freedom for a term not exceeding eight years.

Article 150. Negligent Destruction or Damaging of Personal Property of Citizens. The destruction or damaging of personal property of citizens as a result of negligent handling of fire, which causes loss of human life or any other grave consequences, shall be punished by deprivation of freedom for a term not exceeding one year.

Article 151. Crimes Against Property of Associations Not Constituting Socialist Organizations. Crimes against the property of associations not constituting socialist organizations, committed with respect to property situated on the territory of the RSFSR, shall be punished in accordance with the articles of the present chapter.

Chapter Six: Economic Crimes

Article 152. Issuance of Poor-Quality, Nonstandard, or Incomplete Products. The issuance from an industrial enterprise, repeatedly or on a large scale, of products of poor quality or not conforming with standards or technical conditions, or of incomplete products, by the director, chief engineer, or head of the department of technical control, or by persons occupying other offices who fulfill the duties of the persons listed, shall be punished by deprivation of freedom for a term not exceeding three years, or by correctional tasks for a term not exceeding one year, or by dismissal from office.

Article 152-1. Additions to and Other Distortions of Accounts Concerning Fulfillment of Plans. Additions to state accounts or the presentation of other intentionally distorted accounting data concerning the fulfillment of plans, as antistate actions inflicting harm on the national economy of the USSR, shall be punished by deprivation of freedom for a term not exceeding three years.

[*Ved.* (1962), no. 29, item 449, Edict July 25, 1962.]

Article 153. Private Entrepreneurial Activity and Activity as Commercial Middleman. Private entrepreneurial activity by utilization of state, cooperative, or other social forms shall be punished by deprivation of freedom for a term not exceeding five years with confiscation of property or by exile for a term not exceeding five years with confiscation of property.

Activity as a commercial middleman carried on by private persons as a form of business for the purpose of enrichment shall be punished by deprivation of freedom for a term not exceeding three years with confiscation of property.

Article 154. Speculation. Speculation, that is, the buying up and reselling of goods or any other articles for the purpose of making a profit, shall be punished by deprivation of freedom for a term not exceeding two years with or without confiscation of property, or by correctional tasks for a term not exceeding one year, or by a fine not exceeding 300 rubles.

Speculation as a form of business or on a large scale shall be punished by deprivation of freedom for a term of two to seven years with confiscation of property.

Petty speculation committed by a person who has previously been convicted of speculation shall be punished by deprivation of freedom for a term not exceeding one year, or by correctional tasks for the same term, or by a fine not exceeding 200 rubles with confiscation of the articles of speculation.

[*Ved.* (1962), no. 29, item 449, Edict July 25, 1962.]

Article 154–1. Buying up for Feeding to Cattle or Poultry, or Feeding to Cattle or Poultry, Bread and Other Grain Products. The buying up in state or cooperative stores of baked bread, meal, groats, or other grain products for feeding cattle or poultry, as well as feeding to cattle or poultry of baked bread, meal, groats, and other grain products, committed after imposition of a fine for such actions in an administrative procedure, or committed systematically or on a large scale, shall be punished by correctional tasks for a term not exceeding one year or by deprivation of freedom for a term of one to three years with or without confiscation of the cattle.

[*Ved.* (1963), no. 18, item 317, Edict May 6, 1963.]

Article 154–2. Buying up, Selling, and Exchanging of Currency or Securities on Small Scale. The buying up, selling, and exchanging of currency or securities on a small scale, committed by a person who for the same actions in the course of a year was twice subjected to an administrative penalty, shall be punished by deprivation of freedom for a term not exceeding one year or by correctional tasks for the same term with confiscation of the currency valuables.

[*Ved.* (1970), no. 22, item 441, Edict May 21, 1970.]

Article 155. Illegal Use of Trademarks. The illegal use of another's trademark shall be punished by correctional tasks for a term not exceeding six months or by a fine not exceeding 300 rubles.

Article 156. Deception of Purchasers. False measuring, false weighing, marking up of established retail prices, false reckoning, or any other deception of purchasers in stores or any other trade enterprises or in public eating establishments shall be punished by deprivation of freedom for a term not exceeding two years, or by correctional tasks for a term not exceeding one year, or by deprivation of the right to occupy offices in trade enterprises or public eating establishments.

The same actions committed in accordance with a preliminary agreement of a group of persons, or on a large scale, or by persons previously convicted of the same crimes shall be punished by deprivation of freedom for a term of two to seven years with or without confiscation of property, with deprivation of the right to occupy offices in trade enterprises or public eating establishments.

[*Ved.* (1965), no. 27, item 670, Edict July 3, 1965.]

Article 157. Issuance for Sale of Poor-Quality, Nonstandard, and Incomplete Goods. The issuance for sale in trade enterprises, repeatedly or in large amounts, of goods known to be of poor quality, nonstandard, or incomplete, by the manager of a store, depot, warehouse, or section, or by a marketing specialist or specialist in sorting spoiled goods, shall be punished by deprivation of freedom for a term not exceeding two years, or by correctional tasks for a term not exceeding one year, or by a fine not exceeding 100 rubles, or by deprivation of the right to occupy the offices stated.

Article 158. Illegal Making, Marketing, and Keeping of Alcoholic Beverages. The making or keeping, without the purpose of marketing, of home-brewed vodka, grape vodka, arrack, mulberry vodka, home-brewed beer, or other strong alcoholic beverages made at home, or the making, without the purpose of marketing or keeping, of equipment for their distillation, shall be punished by deprivation of freedom for a term not exceeding one year or by a fine not exceeding 300 rubles.

The making or keeping, for the purpose of marketing, of home-brewed vodka, grape vodka, arrack, mulberry vodka, home-brewed beer or other strong alcoholic beverages made at home, or the making, for the purpose of marketing, of equipment for their distillation, or the marketing of such alcoholic beverages or equipment, shall be punished by deprivation of freedom for a term of one to three years with or without confiscation of property.

[*Ved.* (1962), no. 29, item 449, Edict July 25, 1962.]

Article 159. Forgery of Marks of Postal Payment and of Transportation Tickets. The forgery of postage stamps or other marks of postal payment or of international reply coupons, or the utilizing or putting into circulation of forged postage stamps or other marks of postal payment or international reply coupons, shall be punished by deprivation of freedom for a term not exceeding two years or by correctional tasks for a term not exceeding one year.

The making or marketing, as a form of business, of forged tickets or other documents for the carriage of passengers or the transport of freight shall be punished by deprivation of freedom for a term not exceeding three years.

Article 160. Violation of Veterinary Rules. The violation of veterinary rules resulting in the spreading of epizootics or in other grave consequences shall be punished by deprivation of freedom for a term not exceeding three years or by correctional tasks for a term not exceeding one year.

Article 161. Violation of Rules Established for Combating Plant Diseases and Pests. The violation of rules established for combating plant diseases and plant pests resulting in grave consequences shall be punished by deprivation of freedom for a term not exceeding one year or by correctional tasks for the same term.

Article 162. Engaging in a Prohibited Trade. The engaging in a trade concerning which there is a special prohibition, if such act does not entail administrative liability or if it is committed after imposition of an administrative penalty for such act, shall be punished by correctional tasks for a term not exceeding one year or by a fine not exceeding 200 rubles.

The engaging in a trade concerning which there is a special prohibition, committed on a significant scale or by using hired labor, or committed by a person previously convicted of engaging in a prohibited trade, shall be punished by deprivation of freedom for a term not exceeding four years with or without confiscation of property.

[*Ved.* (1962), no. 29, item 449, Edict July 25, 1962.]

Article 163. Illegally Engaging in Fishing and Other Water-Extractive Trades. The carrying on of fishing, of catching marine animals, and of other water-extractive trades in territorial waters of the USSR, inland seas, rivers and lakes, ponds, reservoirs, and their tributary waters without an appropriate permit, or at a forbidden time, or in illegal places, or with illegal implements, methods, and devices, shall be punished by deprivation of freedom for a term not exceeding one year, or by correctional tasks for the same term, or by a fine not exceeding 100 rubles with or without confiscation of the catch, of the implements of catching, and of the means of floating with their appurtenances.

The same actions committed repeatedly or in conjunction with catching or killing of valuable species of fish or water animals or causing serious loss shall be punished by deprivation of freedom for a term not exceeding four years with or without confiscation of property.

Article 164. Illegally Engaging in Hunting of Seals and Beavers. The carrying on of the trade of hunting fur-seals and sea-beavers in the open sea or in forbidden places shall be punished by deprivation of freedom for a term not exceeding one year, or by correctional tasks for the same term, or by a fine not exceeding 1,000 rubles with confiscation of the catch, of the implements of catching, and of the means of floating with their appurtenances.

Article 165. Floating of Timber or Blasting in Violation of Rules for Protection of Fish Reserves. The floating of timber or blasting in violation of the rules established for the purpose of protecting fish reserves shall be punished by correctional tasks for a term not exceeding six months or by a fine not exceeding 200 rubles.

Article 166. Illegal Hunting. Hunting without an appropriate permit or in prohibited places or at prohibited times or with prohibited implements and methods, if such actions are committed after the application of measures of administrative pressure for such a violation, shall be punished by correctional tasks for a term not exceeding one year or by a fine not exceeding 200 rubles, with or without confiscation of the catch and of the implements for hunting.

The hunting of beasts and birds which it is entirely prohibited to hunt, or illegal hunting causing great loss, shall be punished by deprivation of freedom for a term not exceeding one year, or by correctional tasks for the same term, or by a fine not exceeding 500 rubles with or without confiscation of the catch and of the implements for hunting.

[*Ved.* (1963), no. 41, item 718, Edict October 14, 1963.]

Article 167. Violation of Rules for Mining and Surrender of Gold to the State. The violation by individual citizens of rules for mining or rules for surrendering to the state of gold or other precious metals or precious stones extracted by them from the earth shall be punished by a fine not exceeding 1,000 rubles with confiscation of what has been extracted.

The same actions causing great loss to the state shall be punished by deprivation of freedom for a term not exceeding five years with confiscation of property.

[*Ved.* (1962), no. 29, item 449, Edict July 25, 1962.]

Article 168. Intentional Damaging of Crops by Grazing and Damaging of Plantings Sheltering Fields and Other Plantings. The intentional damaging of crops by grazing or the intentional damaging of forest planting, fruit trees, and other plantings sheltering fields, causing significant loss to a collective farm, state farm, or other state or social farm, shall be punished by correctional tasks for a term not exceeding one year, or by a fine not exceeding 100 rubles, or by imposition of the duty to make amends for the harm caused.

Article 169. Illegal Felling of Timber. The illegal felling of timber in forests sheltering fields, soil, and shores, in state reservations, in forests of health resorts, in forest-parks, in forests of the green belt around cities or industrial enterprises if the loss exceeds 100 rubles, and in the remaining forests concerned in the first group if the loss exceeds 200 rubles in accordance with the tariff established for calculating the rate of exactions for loss caused by the illegal felling or damaging of timber, or the illegal felling of timber in other forests if the loss exceeds 300 rubles in accordance with the same tariff, or the felling of timber in the aforementioned forests resulting in loss on a lesser scale but committed repeatedly, shall be punished by deprivation of freedom for a term not exceeding one year, or by correctional tasks for the same term, or by a fine not exceeding 300 rubles with confiscation of what has been illegally extracted.

The illegal felling of timber in whatever kinds of forests, committed as a form of business, although for the first time, but causing great loss, shall be punished by deprivation of freedom for a term not exceeding three years or by a fine not exceeding 500 rubles with confiscation of what has been illegally extracted.

[*Ved.* (1962), no. 29, item 449, Edict July 25, 1962.]

Chapter Seven: Official Crimes

Article 170. Abuse of Authority or of Official Position. The abuse of authority or of official position, that is, the intentional utilization by an official of his official position contrary to the interests of the office, committed for mercenary or any other personal interest and causing substantial harm to state or social interests or to legally protected rights and interests of citizens, shall be punished by deprivation of freedom for a term not exceeding three years, or by correctional tasks for a term not exceeding one year, or by dismissal from office.

The abuse of authority or of official position causing grave consequences shall be punished by deprivation of freedom for a term not exceeding eight years.

Note: By officials, in articles of the present chapter, are meant persons who are permanently or temporarily exercising functions of representatives of authority, or who are permanently or temporarily occupying offices in state or social institutions, organizations, or enterprises which are connected with fulfillment of organizational-executive duties or administrative-economic duties, or who are fulfilling such duties in the aforementioned institutions, organizations, or enterprises, by special authorization.

Article 171. Exceeding of Authority or Official Powers. The exceeding of authority or official powers, that is, the intentional commission by an official of actions clearly exceeding the limits of rights and powers granted to him by law, thereby causing substantial harm to state or social interests or to legally protected rights and interests of citizens, shall be punished by deprivation of freedom for a term not exceeding three years, or by correctional tasks for a term not exceeding one year, or by dismissal from office.

The exceeding of authority or official powers, if accompanied by force, by use of weapons, or by actions which torment the victim and insult his personal dignity, shall be punished by deprivation of freedom for a term not exceeding ten years.

Article 172. Neglect. The nonperformance or improper performance by an official of his duties as the result of a careless or unconscientious attitude toward them, causing substantial harm to state or social interests or to legally protected rights and interests of citizens, shall be punished by deprivation of freedom for a term not exceeding three years, or by correctional tasks for a term not exceeding one year, or by dismissal from office.

Article 173. Taking of Bribe. The taking by an official personally or through an intermediary, in whatever form, of a bribe for performance or nonperformance, in the interests of the giver, of any kind of action which the official has a duty to perform or can perform by utilization of his official position, shall be punished by deprivation of freedom for a term of three to ten years with confiscation of property.

The same actions committed by an official who is occupying a responsible position, or who has previously been convicted of bribery or of having taken bribes repeatedly, or in conjunction with the extortion of a bribe, shall be punished by deprivation of freedom for a term of eight to fifteen years with confiscation of property and with or without exile for a term of two to five years after the serving of deprivation of freedom, or, under especially aggravating circumstances, by death with confiscation of property.

[*Ved.* (1962), no. 29, item 449, Edict July 25, 1962.]

Article 174. Giving of Bribe. The giving of a bribe shall be punished by deprivation of freedom for a term of three to eight years.

The giving of bribes repeatedly or by a person previously convicted of bribery shall be punished by deprivation of freedom for a term of seven to fifteen years with or without confiscation of property and with or without exile for a term of two to five years after the serving of deprivation of freedom.

Note: A person who gives a bribe shall be relieved of criminal responsibility if the bribe was extorted from him or if after giving the bribe he voluntarily reported its occurrence.

[*Ved.* (1962), no. 29, item 449, Edict July 25, 1962.]

Article 174-1. Acting as Intermediary in Bribery. The acting as an intermediary in bribery shall be punished by deprivation of freedom for a term of two to eight years.

The acting as an intermediary in bribery, committed repeatedly or by a person previously convicted of bribery, or by utilizing one's official position, shall be punished by deprivation of freedom for a term of seven to fifteen years with confiscation of property and with or without exile for a term of two to five years after the serving of deprivation of freedom.

[*Ved.* (1962), no. 29, item 449, Edict July 25, 1962.]

Article 175. Official Forgery. Official forgery, that is, the entering by an official, from mercenary or other personal motives, on official documents of information known to be false, the falsification, erasure, or misdating, or the composition and issuance by him of documents known to be false, or the entry in books of transactions known to be false, shall be punished by deprivation of freedom for a term not exceeding two years, or by correctional tasks for a term not exceeding one year, or by dismissal from office.

Chapter Eight: Crimes Against Justice

Article 176. Institution of Criminal Proceedings Against Persons Known to be Innocent. The institution of criminal proceedings against a person known to be innocent by a person conducting an inquiry, by an investigator, or by a procurator, shall be punished by deprivation of freedom for a term not exceeding three years.

The same actions combined with an accusation of an especially dangerous crime against the state or any other grave crime or with artificially created proof of the accusation shall be punished by deprivation of freedom for a term of three to ten years.

Article 177. Rendering of Judgment, Decision, Ruling, or Decree Known to Be Unjust. The rendering by a judge of a judgment, decision, ruling, or decree known to be unjust shall be punished by deprivation of freedom for a term not exceeding three years.

The same actions resulting in grave consequences shall be punished by deprivation of freedom for a term of three to ten years.

Article 178. Arrest or Detention Known to Be Illegal. An arrest known to be illegal shall be punished by deprivation of freedom for a term not exceeding one year.

A detention known to be illegal shall be punished by correctional tasks for a term not exceeding one year or by dismissal from office.

Article 179. Compelling to Give Testimony. The compelling to give testimony by means of application of threats or other illegal actions on the part of a person conducting an inquiry or preliminary investigation shall be punished by deprivation of freedom for a term not exceeding three years.

The same actions combined with the application of force or with humiliation of the person interrogated shall be punished by deprivation of freedom for a term of three to ten years.

Article 180. Making of Report Known to Be False. The making of a report, known to be false, of the commission of a crime shall be punished by deprivation of freedom for a term not exceeding three years or by correctional tasks for a term not exceeding one year.

The same actions combined with an accusation of an especially dangerous crime against the state or any other grave crime or with artificially created proof of the accusation, or committed for a mercenary purpose, shall be punished by deprivation of freedom for a term of two to seven years.

Article 181. Giving of Testimony Known to Be False. The giving of testimony known to be false by a witness or by the victim, or of an opinion known to be false by an expert, or of a translation known to be incorrect by an interpreter in court or in the conduct of a preliminary investigation or inquiry shall be punished by deprivation of freedom for a term not exceeding one year or by correctional tasks for the same term.

The same actions combined with an accusation of an especially dangerous crime against the state or any other grave crime or with artificially created proof of the accusation, or committed for a mercenary purpose, shall be punished by deprivation of freedom for a term of two to seven years.

[*Ved.* (1962), no. 29, item 449, Edict July 25, 1962.]

Article 182. Refusal or Evasion by Witness or Victim to Give Testimony or by Expert to Give Opinion. The refusal or evasion by a witness or victim to give testimony or by an expert to give an opinion in a judicial session or in the conduct of a preliminary investigation or inquiry, or the obstruction of the appearance of a witness or victim or the giving of testimony by him, shall be punished by correctional tasks for a term not exceeding six months, or by a fine not exceeding 50 rubles, or by social censure.

Article 183. Compelling of Witness or Victim to Give False Testimony or of Expert to Give False Opinion, or Bribing of Such Persons. The compelling of a witness, victim, or expert to give judicial or investigative agencies false testimony or a false opinion, committed by threatening such persons or their near ones with homicide, force, or destruction of property, or the bribing of a witness, victim, or expert for the purpose of inducing him to give false testimony or a false opinion, shall be punished by deprivation of freedom for a term not exceeding two years or by correctional tasks for a term not exceeding one year.

Article 184. Divulgence of Data of Preliminary Investigation or Inquiry. The divulgence of data of a preliminary investigation or inquiry without permission of the procurator, investigator, or person conducting the inquiry shall be punished by correctional tasks for a term not exceeding six months or by a fine not exceeding 50 rubles.

Article 185. Embezzlement, Alienation, or Concealment of Property Subjected to Distraint or Impounding. The embezzlement, alienation, or concealment of property subjected to distraint or impounding, committed by a person to whom such property is entrusted, shall be punished by deprivation of freedom for a term not exceeding one year or by correctional tasks for the same term.

Article 186. Escape From Place of Exile or From Medico-Labor Dispensary. The escape from a place of exile or a medico-labor dispensary, or en route to a place of exile or to a dispensary, shall be punished by deprivation of freedom for a term not exceeding one year.

[*Ved.* (1968), no. 20, item 859, Edict May 8, 1968.]

Article 187. Unwarranted Return to a Place Forbidden for Residence by One Who Has Been Banished. The unwarranted return to a place forbidden for residence by one who has been banished shall be punished by replacement of banishment with exile for the unserved term.

Article 188. Escape From Place of Confinement or From Guard. The escape from a place of confinement or from guard, committed by a person serving punishment or in preliminary confinement, shall be punished by deprivation of freedom for a term not exceeding three years.

Escape combined with force against a guard shall be punished by deprivation of freedom for a term not exceeding five years.

Article 189. Concealment of Crimes. When not promised in advance, the concealment of crimes provided for by Articles 102, 103, and 240 subsection "c" (intentional homicide), 117 paragraphs two and three (rape under aggravating circumstances), 93-1 (stealing state or social property on especially large scale), 89 paragraphs two and three and 144 paragraphs two and three (theft under aggravating circumstances), 90 paragraphs two and three and 145 paragraphs two and three (open stealing under aggravating circumstances), 91 and 146 (assault with intent to rob), 92 paragraphs two and three (stealing state or social property, committed by appropriation, embezzlement, or abuse of official position, under aggravating circumstances), 93 paragraphs two and three and 147 paragraph three (swindling under aggravating circumstances), 154 paragraph two (speculation under aggravating circumstances), 173 paragraph two, 174 paragraph two and 174–1 paragraph two (taking or giving a bribe or acting as an intermediary in bribery under aggravating circumstances), 191–2 (infringing the life of a policeman or people's guard), 211 paragraphs two and three (violation of rules of safe movement and operation of motor transport under aggravating circumstances), 218–1 paragraph three (stealing of a firearm, ammunition or explosives committed by means of an assault with intent to rob or by an especially dangerous recidivist) of the present Code shall be punished by deprivation of freedom for a term not exceeding five years or by correctional tasks for a term not exceeding one year.

The same act with respect to crimes provided for by Articles 89 paragraph one and 144 paragraph one (theft), 90 paragraph one and 145 paragraph one (open stealing), 93 paragraph one and 147 paragraphs one and two (swindling), 106 (negligent homicide), 152–1 (additions to and other distortions of accounts concerning fulfillment of plans), 173 paragraph one, 174 paragraph one, 174–1 paragraph one (taking or giving a bribe or acting as an intermediary in bribery), 188 (escape from place of confinement or from guard), 218–1 paragraphs one and two (stealing of a firearm, ammunition, or explosives) of the present Code shall be punished by deprivation of freedom for a term not exceeding two years or by correctional tasks for a term not exceeding one year.

[*Ved.* (1962), no. 29, item 449, Edict July 25, 1962; *Ved.* (1967), no. 23, item 533, Edict June 1, 1967; *Ved.* (1968), no. 26, item 1010, Edict June 19, 1968.]

Article 190. **Failure to Report Crimes.** The failure to report known crimes which are being prepared or have been committed, provided for by Articles 102, 103, and 240 subsection "c" (intentional homicide), 117 paragraphs two and three (rape under aggravating circumstances), 89 paragraph three and 144 paragraph three (theft under aggravating circumstances), 90 paragraph three and 145 paragraph three (open stealing under aggravating circumstances), 91 and 146 (assault with intent to rob), 92 paragraph three (stealing state or social property, committed by appropriation, embezzlement, or abuse of official position, under aggravating circumstances), 93 paragraph three and 147 paragraph three (swindling under aggravating circumstances), 93–1 (stealing state or social property on especially large scale), 173 paragraph two, 174 paragraph two, and 174–1 paragraph two (taking or giving a bribe or acting as an intermediary in bribery under aggravating circumstances), 191–2 (infringing the life of a policeman or people's guard), 218–1 paragraphs two and three (stealing of a firearm, ammunition, or explosives) of the present Code shall be punished by deprivation of freedom for a term not exceeding three years or by correctional tasks for a term not exceeding one year.

[*Ved.* (1962), no. 29, item 449, Edict July 25, 1962; *Ved.* (1967), no. 23, item 533, Edict June 1, 1967.]

Chapter Nine: Crimes Against the System of Administration

Article 190–1. **Circulation of Fabrications Known to Be False Which Defame Soviet State and Social System.** The systematic circulation in an oral form of fabrications known to be false which defame the Soviet state and social system and, likewise, the preparation or circulation in written, printed or any other form of works of such content shall be punished by deprivation of freedom for a term not exceeding three years, or by correctional tasks for a term not exceeding one year, or by a fine not exceeding 100 rubles.

[*Ved.* (1966), no. 38, item 1038, Edict September 16, 1966.]

Article 190–2. **Desecration of State Emblem or Flag.** The desecration of the state emblem or flag of the USSR, RSFSR, or any other union republic shall be punished by deprivation of freedom for a term not exceeding two years, or by correctional tasks for a term not exceeding one year, or by a fine not exceeding 50 rubles.

[*Ved.* (1966), no. 38, item 1038, Edict September 16, 1966.]

Article 190–3. **Organization of, or Active Participation in, Group Actions Which Violate Public Order.** The organization of, and, likewise, the active participation in, group actions which violate public order in a coarse manner or which are attended by clear disobedience of the legal demands of representatives of authority or which entail the violation of the work of transport or of state and social institutions or enterprises shall be punished by deprivation of freedom for a term not exceeding three years, or by correctional tasks for a term not exceeding one year, or by a fine not exceeding 100 rubles.

[*Ved.* (1966), no. 38, item 1038, Edict September 16, 1966.]

Article 191. **Resisting Representative of Authority or Representative of Public Fulfilling Duties of Protection of Public Order.** Resisting a representative of authority while he is performing duties entrusted to him by law, or resisting a representative of the public who is fulfilling duties for protection of public order, or compelling such person to carry out clearly illegal actions, committed by force or by threat of application of force, except in instances stated in Article 191–1 of the present Code, shall be punished by deprivation of freedom for a term not exceeding three years, or by correctional tasks for a term not exceeding one year, or by a fine not exceeding 60 rubles.

[*Ved.* (1962), no. 29, item 449, Edict July 25, 1962.]

Article 191–1. **Resisting Policeman or People's Guard [*Druzhinnik*].** Offering resistance to a policeman or to a people's guard during the performance by such person of duties imposed upon him for protection of public order shall be punished by deprivation of freedom for a term not exceeding one year, or by correctional tasks for the same term, or by a fine not exceeding 100 rubles.

The same actions, in conjunction with force or the threat of application of force, or the compelling of such persons by force or threat of force to carry out clearly illegal actions, shall be punished by deprivation of freedom for a term not exceeding five years.

[*Ved.* (1962), no. 29, item 449, Edict July 25, 1962.]

Article 191–2. **Infringing Life of Policeman or of People's Guard.** Infringing the life of a policeman or a people's guard in connection with his official or social activity for protection of public order shall be punished by deprivation of freedom for a term of five to fifteen years with or without additional exile for a term of two to five years or, under aggravating circumstances, by death.

[*Ved.* (1962), no. 29, item 449, Edict July 25, 1962.]

Article 192. Insulting Representative of Authority or Representative of Public Fulfilling Duties for Protection of Public Order. Publicly insulting a representative of authority or a representative of the public who is fulfilling duties for the protection of public order, in connection with performance by such person of duties imposed on him, except in instances stated in Article 192-1 of the present Code, shall be punished by correctional tasks for a term not exceeding one year, or by a fine not exceeding 50 rubles, or shall entail application of measures of social pressure.

[*Ved.* (1962), no. 29, item 449, Edict July 25, 1962.]

Article 192-1. Insulting Policeman or People's Guard. Insulting a policeman or a people's guard in connection with performance by such person of duties imposed on him for protection of public order shall be punished by deprivation of freedom for a term not exceeding six months, or by correctional tasks for a term not exceeding one year, or by a fine not exceeding 100 rubles.

[*Ved.* (1962), no. 29, item 449, Edict July 25, 1962.]

Article 193. Threat or Force Against Official or Citizen Fulfilling Social Duty. A threat of homicide, of infliction of grave bodily injuries, or of destruction of property by arson, against an official or a social worker, made for the purpose of terminating official or social activity or of changing its character in the interests of the person making the threat and, likewise, such a threat made against a citizen in connection with his participation in the prevention or restraint of a crime or antisocial act, shall be punished by deprivation of freedom for a term not exceeding one year, or by correctional tasks for the same period, or by social censure.

The infliction of light bodily injury or of beatings, or the commission of any other forcible actions, against an official or a social worker in connection with his official activity or fulfillment by him of his social duty and, likewise, against a citizen in connection with his participation in the prevention or restraint of a crime or antisocial act, shall be punished by deprivation of freedom for a term not exceeding three years or by correctional tasks for a term not exceeding one year.

[*Ved.* (1966), no. 32, item 769, Edict August 4, 1966.]

Article 194. Unwarranted Appropriation of Title or Authority of Official. The unwarranted appropriation of the title or authority of an official, in conjunction with the commission on such basis of any kind of socially dangerous actions, shall be punished by deprivation of freedom for a term not exceeding one year.

Article 195. Stealing or Damaging of Documents, Stamps, Seals, or Forms. The stealing, destroying, damaging, or concealing of documents, stamps, seals, or forms in state institutions and enterprises or social organizations, committed from mercenary or other base motives, shall be punished by deprivation of freedom for a term not exceeding one year, or by correctional tasks for the same term, or by a fine not exceeding 100 rubles.

The same actions committed with respect to documents, stamps, seals, or forms of special importance, or resulting in grave consequences, shall be punished by deprivation of freedom for a term not exceeding five years.

The stealing of a passport or other important personal document from a citizen shall be punished by deprivation of freedom for a term not exceeding eight months, or by correctional tasks for a term not exceeding one year, or by a fine not exceeding 80 rubles.

Article 196. **Forging, Making or Marketing of Forged Documents, Stamps, Seals, Forms.** The forging of a certificate or any other document issued by a state institution or enterprise or social organization, which grants a right or a release from duties, for the purpose of utilization of such document by the forger himself or by another person, or the marketing of such a document, or the making of forged stamps, seals, and forms of state institutions or enterprises or social organizations for the same purposes, or the marketing thereof shall be punished by deprivation of freedom for a term not exceeding two years or by correctional tasks for a term not exceeding one year.

The same actions committed systematically shall be punished by deprivation of freedom for a term not exceeding five years or by exile for the same term.

The using of a document known to be forged shall be punished by deprivation of freedom for a term not exceeding one year, or by correctional tasks for the same term, or by a fine not exceeding 30 rubles.

Article 197. **Violation of Rules of Entry into or of Living in Border Region or Border Zone.** The violation of rules of entry into or of living or registration in a border region or border zone, committed after imposition of an administrative penalty for the same violation, shall be punished by deprivation of freedom for a term not exceeding six months, or by correctional tasks for the same term, or by a fine not exceeding 50 rubles.

Article 197-1. **Violation by Foreigners and Persons Without Citizenship of Rules for Movement on Territory of USSR.** The malicious violation by foreigners and persons without citizenship of the rules for movement on the territory of the USSR, that is, a change of place of residence, a temporary departure from a place of residence, a visit to points not stated in USSR entry visas, or a deviation from the route of a journey stated in travel documents, committed without special permission therefor, if such persons have previously been twice subjected to administrative exaction for violation of the stated rules, shall be punished by deprivation of freedom for a term not exceeding one year or by correctional tasks for the same term, or by a fine not exceeding 50 rubles.

[*Ved.* (1966), no. 32, item 769, Edict August 4, 1966.]

Article 198. Violation of Passport Rules. The malicious violation of passport rules in localities where special rules of living or registration have been introduced, if such violation takes the form of living without a passport or without registration and if the person has already twice previously been subjected to an administrative penalty for such violation, shall be punished by deprivation of freedom for a term not exceeding one year, or by correctional tasks for the same term, or by a fine not exceeding 50 rubles.

Article 198-1. Evasion of Training Courses or Musters and of Military Registration by Person Subject to Military Service. The evasion of training courses or musters by a person subject to military service shall be punished by deprivation of freedom for a term not exceeding one year, or by correctional tasks for the same term, or by a fine not exceeding 30 rubles.

The same act, committed by self-infliction of any kind of injury (maiming), malingering, forgery of documents, or any other deception, or committed under other aggravating circumstances, shall be punished by deprivation of freedom for a term not exceeding three years.

The evasion of military registration by a person subject to military service if measures of administrative pressure have been previously applied to the guilty person for such an act, shall be punished by correctional tasks for a term not exceeding three months or by a fine not exceeding 20 rubles.

[*Ved.* (1962), no. 29, item 449, Edict July 25, 1962; *Ved.* (1969), no. 1, item 1, Edict December 27, 1968.]

Article 198-2. Malicious Violation of Rules of Administrative Supervision. The malicious violation of the rules provided for by the Statute on Administrative Supervision by Agencies of the Police Over Persons Released From Places of Deprivation of Freedom in order to evade supervision, if committed by a person who has been subjected to administrative pressure for the same violations twice within a year, shall be punished by deprivation of freedom for a term of six months to two years or by correctional tasks for a term of six months to one year.

[*Ved.* (1966), no. 32, item 769, Edict August 4, 1966.]

Article 199. Unwarranted Seizure of Land and Unwarranted Construction. The unwarranted seizure or unwarranted exchange, purchase, or sale of a plot of land or other actions violating the laws on the nationalization of land shall be punished by correctional tasks for a term of six months to one year or by a fine not exceeding 100 rubles.

The unwarranted construction of a dwelling or the unwarranted enlargement thereof shall be punished by correctional tasks for a term of six months to one year with confiscation of the illegally erected construction.

Article 200. Arrogation [*Samoupravstvo*]. Arrogation, that is, the unwarranted exercise, in violation of the legally established order, of one's actual or supposed right, causing substantial harm to citizens or to state or social organizations, shall be punished by correctional tasks for a term not exceeding six months, or by a fine not exceeding 50 rubles, or by social censure, or shall entail application of measures of social pressure.

Article 201. Violation of Laws on Registration of Acts of Civil Status. The concealment of circumstances which are impediments to marriage, or the furnishing of false information to agencies which register acts of civil status, shall be punished by correctional tasks for a term not exceeding one year, or by a fine not exceeding 50 rubles, or by social censure.

Article 202. Illegal Use of Insignia of Red Cross or Red Crescent. The illegal use of insignia of the Red Cross or the Red Crescent, or of the names of the Red Cross or the Red Crescent, shall be punished by correctional tasks for a term not exceeding one year, or by a fine not exceeding 100 rubles, or by social censure.

Article 203. Illegal Displaying of State Flag of USSR or of Union Republic on Merchant Vessel. The displaying of the state flag of the USSR or of a union republic on a merchant vessel which lacks the right to such flag shall be punished by deprivation of freedom for a term not exceeding one year with or without confiscation of the vessel and with or without a fine not exceeding the full value of the vessel.

Article 204. Failure to Render Aid Upon Collision of Vessel or Failure to Communicate Name of Vessel. The failure by the captain of a vessel which collides with another vessel at sea to take due measures for saving the other vessel, if such measures can be taken without serious danger for his passengers, crew, and vessel, regardless of the responsibility for failure to render aid to the crew and passengers of the vessel suffering a disaster (Article 129), shall be punished by deprivation of freedom for a term not exceeding one year, or by correctional tasks for the same term, or by a fine not exceeding 300 rubles.

The failure by the captain of a vessel to communicate to another vessel which has collided with it at sea the name and port of registration of his vessel or the places of its departure and destination despite the possibility of communicating such information shall be punished by correctional tasks for a term not exceeding three months or by a fine not exceeding 100 rubles.

Article 205. Damaging of Marine Telegraph Cable. The negligent damaging of a marine telegraph cable, if it has resulted or could result in an interruption of telegraph communication, shall be punished by correctional tasks for a term not exceeding three months or by a fine not exceeding 100 rubles.

Article 205-1. Violation of Rules for Protection of Lines of Communication. The violation of rules for the protection of lines of communication, causing damage to a cable line of interurban communication and resulting in an interruption of communication, shall be punished by deprivation of freedom for a term not exceeding one year, or by correctional tasks for the same term, or by a fine not exceeding 200 rubles.

[*Ved.* (1969), no. 43, item 1291, Edict October 17, 1969.]

Chapter Ten: Crimes Against Public Security, Public Order, and Health of the Population

Article 206. Hooliganism. Hooliganism, that is, intentional actions violating public order in a coarse manner and expressing a clear disrespect toward society, and, likewise, petty hooliganism committed by a person to whom a measure of administrative pressure for petty hooliganism has been applied within a year, shall be punished by deprivation of freedom for a term of six months to one year, or by correctional tasks for the same term, or by a fine of 30 to 50 rubles.

Malicious hooliganism, that is, the same actions distinguished in their content by exceptional cynicism or special impudence, or connected with resisting a representative of authority or representative of the public fulfilling duties for protection of public order or other citizens who are restraining hooliganistic actions and, likewise, actions which are committed by a person previously convicted of hooliganism, shall be punished by deprivation of freedom for a term of one to five years.

Actions provided for by paragraphs one or two of the present article, if committed with the use or attempted use of a firearm, a knife, brass knuckles, other sidearms, or any other objects especially adapted to the infliction of bodily injuries, shall be punished by deprivation of freedom for a term of three to seven years.

[*Ved.* (1966), no. 32, item 769, Edict August 4, 1966.]

Article 207. Threat of Homicide, of Infliction of Grave Bodily Injuries, or of Destruction of Property. A threat of homicide, of infliction of grave bodily injuries, or of destruction of property through arson, if there are grounds to apprehend the carrying out of such threat, shall be punished by deprivation of freedom for a term not exceeding six months, or by correctional tasks for a term not exceeding one year, or by social censure, or shall entail the application of measures of social pressure.

Article 208. Acquisition or Marketing of Property Known to Have Been Criminally Acquired. When not promised in advance, the acquisition of property known to have been criminally acquired shall be punished by correctional tasks for a term not exceeding six months, or by a fine not exceeding 100 rubles, or by social censure, or shall entail the application of measures of social pressure.

The same act committed on a large scale shall be punished by deprivation of freedom for a term not exceeding two years or by correctional tasks for a term not exceeding one year.

When not promised in advance, the marketing or keeping for the purpose of marketing, or the acquisition for the purpose of marketing, of property known to have been criminally acquired, shall be punished by deprivation of freedom for a term not exceeding five years or by correctional tasks for a term not exceeding one year.

Acts provided for by paragraph three of the present article, committed as a form of business or on a large scale, shall be punished by deprivation of freedom for a term not exceeding seven years with or without additional exile for a term not exceeding five years, with or without confiscation of property.

[*Ved.* (1962), no. 29, item 449, Edict July 25, 1962.]

Article 209. Systematically Engaging in Vagrancy or in Begging. Systematically engaging in vagrancy or in begging shall be punished by deprivation of freedom for a term not exceeding two years or by correctional tasks for a term of six months to one year.

The same actions committed by a person previously convicted of vagrancy or begging shall be punished by deprivation of freedom for a term not exceeding four years.

[*Ved.* (1970), no. 14, item 256, Edict February 25, 1970.]

Article 209-1. Malicious Evasion of Performance of Decision Concerning Arrangement of Work and Discontinuance of Parasitic Existence. The malicious evasion, by a person leading an antisocial form of life, of the performance of a decision of a district (or city) executive committee of a soviet of working people's deputies concerning the arrangement of work and the discontinuance of a parasitic existence shall be punished by deprivation of freedom for a term not exceeding one year or correctional tasks for the same term.

The same act committed by a person previously convicted in accordance with paragraph one of this article shall be punished by deprivation of freedom for a term not exceeding two years.

[*Ved.* (1970), no. 14, item 256, Edict February 25, 1970.]

Article 210. Drawing of Minors into Criminal Activity. The drawing of minors into criminal activity or into drunkenness, engaging in begging, prostitution, gambling, or the influencing of minors to use narcotics, or the utilizing of minors for purposes of a parasitic existence, shall be punished by deprivation of freedom for a term not exceeding five years.

[*Ved.* (1965), no. 27, item 670, Edict July 9, 1965.]

Article 211. Violation of Rules of Safe Movement or Operation of Transport by Persons Who Drive Transport Vehicles. The violation of rules of safe movement or operation of transport by a person who drives a motor transport vehicle or an urban electrical transport vehicle, a tractor or any other self-propelled machine, causing the victim less grave or light bodily injury or causing substantial material loss, shall be punished by deprivation of freedom for a term not exceeding three years or by correctional tasks for a term not exceeding one year, or by a fine not exceeding 100 rubles with or without deprivation of the right to drive transport vehicles for a term not exceeding two years.

The same actions resulting in the death or grave bodily injury of the victim shall be punished by deprivation of freedom for a term not exceeding ten years with or without deprivation of the right to drive transport vehicles for a term not exceeding five years.

Actions provided for by paragraph one [sic] of the present article resulting in the death of several persons shall be punished by deprivation of freedom for a term of three to fifteen years with or without deprivation of the right to drive transport vehicles for a term not exceeding five years.

[*Ved.* (1968), no. 26, item 1010, Edict June 19, 1968.]

Article 211-1. Driving Transport Vehicles While Drunk. The driving of a motor transport vehicle or an urban electrical transport vehicle, a tractor, or any other self-propelled machine by a person in a state of intoxication who was deprived of the right to drive for such a violation, or the driving of the said transport vehicles by a person in a state of intoxication who did not have the right to drive and who had been subjected to an administrative penalty for such a violation within one year, shall be punished by deprivation of freedom for a term not exceeding one year, or by correctional tasks for the same term, or by a fine not exceeding 100 rubles.

[*Ved.* (1968), no. 26, item 1010, Edict June 19, 1968.]

Article 211-2. Approving the Operation of Technically Defective Transport Vehicles. The approving for operation of motor transport vehicles or urban electrical transport vehicles, tractors, or any other self-propelled machines known to be technically defective, or any other coarse violation of the rules for their operation which assure safe movement, committed by a person responsible for the technical condition or operation of transport vehicles, if this results in the consequences specified in Article 211 of the present Code, shall be punished by deprivation of freedom for a term not exceeding five years, or by correctional tasks for a term not exceeding one year, or by a fine not exceeding 100 rubles with or without deprivation of the right to hold positions involving responsibility for the technical condition or operation of transport vehicles, for a term not exceeding five years.

[*Ved.* (1968), no. 26, item 1010, Edict June 19, 1968.]

Article 212. Violation of Rules of Safe Movement of Transport by Person Not a Motor Transport Worker. [Deemed to have lost its validity in view of revised Article 211.]

[*Ved.* (1968), no. 26, item 1010, Edict June 19, 1968.]

Article 212-1. Driving Away Means of Motor Transport. The driving away of means of motor transport or other self-propelled vehicles without the purpose of stealing them shall be punished by deprivation of freedom for a term not exceeding one year, or by correctional tasks for the same period, or by a fine not exceeding 100 rubles, or shall entail application of measures of social pressure.

The same actions committed a second time shall be punished by deprivation of freedom for a term not exceeding three years or by correctional tasks for a term not exceeding one year.

[*Ved.* (1965), no. 27, item 670, Edict July 9, 1965.]

Article 213. Violation of Rules Governing Transport. The violation of rules governing transport for the protection of order and safety of movement, resulting in the loss of human life or other grave consequences, shall be punished by deprivation of freedom for a term not exceeding five years.

Article 213-1. Unwarranted Needless Stopping of Train. The unwarranted needless stopping of a train by use of the stop-cock, by disconnecting the airbrake line, or by other means, resulting in the breach of the normal movement of the train, shall be punished by deprivation of freedom for a term not exceeding two years or by correctional tasks for a term not exceeding one year.

The same actions resulting in an accident involving people, a wreck, injury to rolling stock, or other grave consequences shall be punished by deprivation of freedom for a term not exceeding eight years.

[*Ved.* (1965), no. 27, item 670, Edict July 9, 1965.]

Article 214. Violation of Rules for Mining Safety. The violation of rules for mining safety causing harm to human health shall be punished by deprivation of freedom for a term not exceeding one year or by correctional tasks for the same term.

The violation of rules for mining safety resulting in loss of human life or other grave consequences shall be punished by deprivation of freedom for a term not exceeding five years or by correctional tasks for a term not exceeding one year.

Article 215. Violation of Rules When Carrying on Construction Work. The violation of construction, sanitation, or fire-prevention rules when carrying on construction work, or of rules of operating construction machinery, causing harm to human health, shall be punished by deprivation of freedom for a term not exceeding one year or by correctional tasks for the same term.

The same violation resulting in loss of human life or other grave consequences shall be punished by deprivation of freedom for a term not exceeding five years or by correctional tasks for a term not exceeding one year.

Article 216. Violation of Rules of Safety in Enterprises or Shops Where There Is Danger of Explosion. The violation of industrial and technical discipline or of rules ensuring the safety of production in enterprises or shops where there is danger of explosion shall be punished by correctional tasks for a term not exceeding one year, or by a fine not exceeding 100 rubles, or by dismissal from office.

The same actions resulting in loss of human life or other grave consequences shall be punished by deprivation of freedom for a term not exceeding seven years.

Article 217. Violation of Rules for Keeping, Utilizing, Registering, or Transporting of Explosives and Radioactive Materials or Pyrotechnical Devices. The violation of rules for the keeping, utilizing, registering, or transporting of explosives and radioactive materials or pyrotechnical devices, or the illegal sending of such materials by post or carrier, if such actions could result in grave consequences, shall be punished by deprivation of freedom for a term not exceeding one year or by correctional tasks for the same term.

The same actions resulting in grave consequences shall be punished by deprivation of freedom for a term not exceeding seven years.

[*Ved.* (1968), no. 51, item 1732, Edict December 12, 1968.]

Article 218. Illegal Carrying, Keeping, Making or Marketing of Arms or Explosives. The carrying, keeping, making, or marketing of a firearm (except a smooth-bore hunting piece), ammunition, or explosives, without an appropriate permit, shall be punished by deprivation of freedom for a term not exceeding two years, or by correctional tasks for a term not exceeding one year, or by a fine not exceeding 100 rubles.

The carrying, making, or marketing of daggers, Finnish daggers, or any other cutting weapon, without an appropriate permit, except in those localities where the carrying of a cutting weapon is an accessory of the national costume or is connected with the hunting trade, shall be punished by deprivation of freedom for a term not exceeding one year, or by correctional tasks for the same term, or by a fine not exceeding 30 rubles.

Article 218–1. Stealing of Firearm, Ammunition, or Explosives. The stealing of a firearm (except a smooth-bore hunting rifle), ammunition, or explosives shall be punished by deprivation of freedom for a term not exceeding seven years.

The same act committed repeatedly, or by a group of persons by previous agreement, or committed by a person to whom the firearm, ammunition, or explosives have been issued for official use or entrusted for safekeeping, shall be punished by deprivation of freedom for a term not exceeding ten years.

The stealing of a firearm (except a smooth-bore hunting rifle), ammunition, or explosives committed by means of an assault with intent to rob or by an especially dangerous recidivist shall be punished by deprivation of freedom for a term of six to fifteen years.

[*Ved.* (1967), no. 23, item 533, Edict June 1, 1967.]

Article 219. Careless Keeping of Firearm. The careless keeping of a firearm, thereby creating conditions for use of such weapon by another person, resulting in grave consequences, shall be punished by deprivation of freedom for a term not exceeding one year or by correctional tasks for the same term.

Article 220. Illegal Sending of Easily Flammable or Caustic Materials. The illegal sending by post or carrier of easily flammable or caustic materials resulting in grave consequences shall be punished by deprivation of freedom for a term not exceeding three years or by correctional tasks for a term not exceeding one year.

Article 221. Illegal Practice of Medicine. Engaging in the practice of medicine as a profession by a person not having the proper medical education shall be punished by deprivation of freedom for a term not exceeding one year, or by correctional tasks for the same term, or by a fine not exceeding 300 rubles, or shall entail the application of measures of social pressure.

Article 222. Violation of Rules Established for Purpose of Combating Epidemics. The violation of hygienic and antiepidemic rules, which result or could result in spreading epidemic and other contagious diseases, shall be punished by deprivation of freedom for a term not exceeding two years, or by correctional tasks for a term not exceeding one year, or by a fine not exceeding 100 rubles.

[*Ved.* (1971), no. 25, item 507, Edict June 22, 1971.]

Article 223. Pollution of Waters or Air. The polluting of rivers, lakes, or other waters or water sources with sewage water which is not purified or rendered harmless, or with garbage or refuse of industrial, communal or other enterprises, institutions or organizations, which causes or could cause harm to human health or to agricultural production or fish reserves, or the polluting of the air with refuse from manufacturing production which is harmful for human health, shall be punished by correctional tasks for a term not exceeding one year or by a fine not exceeding 300 rubles.

The same actions causing substantial harm to human health or agricultural production or entailing mass destruction of fish shall be punished by deprivation of freedom for a term not exceeding five years.

[*Ved.* (1970), no. 22, item 441, Edict May 21, 1970.]

Article 224. Making or Marketing Narcotics or Other Virulent or Poisonous Substances. The making, marketing, or keeping for the purpose of marketing, or the acquisition for the same purpose, of narcotics without a special permit therefor, shall be punished by deprivation of freedom for a term not exceeding ten years with or without confiscation of property, with obligatory confiscation of the narcotics.

The making, marketing, or keeping for the purpose of marketing, or the acquisition for the same purpose, of other virulent or poisonous substances that are not narcotics without a special permit therefor, shall be punished by deprivation of freedom for a term not exceeding two years or by correctional tasks for a term not exceeding one year with confiscation of the virulent and poisonous substances.

The violation of rules established for producing, keeping, issuing, registering, transporting, or sending of narcotics and other virulent or poisonous substances shall be punished by deprivation of freedom for a term not exceeding one year, or by correctional tasks for the same term, or by a fine not exceeding 100 rubles.

[*Ved.* (1962), no. 29, item 449, Edict July 25, 1962.]

Article 225. Growing of Opium Poppies, Indian, Southern Manchurian, or Southern Chuisk Hemp. The growing of opium poppies or Indian hemp without an appropriate permit shall be punished by deprivation of freedom for a term not exceeding two years or by correctional tasks for a term not exceeding one year with obligatory confiscation of the crops.

The growing of Southern Manchurian or Southern Chuisk hemp shall be punished by deprivation of freedom for a term not exceeding three years or by correctional tasks for a term not exceeding one year with obligatory confiscation of the crops.

[*Ved.* (1965), no. 27, item 670, Edict July 9, 1965.]

Article 226. Keeping of Dens and Pandering. The keeping of dens of debauchery, pandering for a mercenary purpose, or the keeping of dens for use of narcotics or gambling dens, shall be punished by deprivation of freedom for a term not exceeding five years with or without banishment, with or without confiscation of property, or by exile for the same term with or without confiscation of property.

Article 227. Infringement of Person and Rights of Citizens Under Appearance of Performing Religious Ceremonies. The organizing or directing of a group, the activity of which, carried on under the appearance of preaching religious beliefs and performing religious ceremonies, is connected with the causing of harm to citizens' health or with any other infringements of the person or rights of citizens, or with the inducing of citizens to refuse social activity or performance of civic duties, or with the drawing of minors into such group, shall be punished by deprivation of freedom for a term not exceeding five years or by exile for a similar term with or without confiscation of property.

The active participation in the activity of a group specified in paragraph one of the present article, or the systematic propaganda directed at the commission of acts specified therein, shall be punished by deprivation of freedom for a term not exceeding three years, or by exile for the same term, or by correctional tasks for a term not exceeding one year.

Note: If the acts of persons stated in paragraph two of the present article, and the persons themselves, do not represent a great social danger, measures of social pressure may be applied to them.

[*Ved.* (1962), no. 29, item 449, Edict July 25, 1962.]

Article 228. Making or Marketing of Pornographic Articles. The making, circulating, or advertising of pornographic writings, printed publications, pictures, or any other articles of a pornographic character, or the trading therein or the keeping thereof for the purpose of sale or dissemination shall be punished by deprivation of freedom for a term not exceeding three years or by a fine not exceeding 100 rubles with confiscation of the pornographic articles and the means of producing them.

Article 229. Desecration of Grave. The desecration of a grave or the stealing of articles in or on a grave shall be punished by deprivation of freedom for a term not exceeding three years or by correctional tasks for a term not exceeding one year.

Article 230. Intentional Destroying, Demolishing, or Damaging of Cultural Monuments. The intentional destroying, demolishing, or damaging of cultural monuments or natural objects taken under the protection of the state shall be punished by deprivation of freedom for a term not exceeding two years, or by correctional tasks for a term not exceeding one year, or by a fine not exceeding 100 rubles.

Chapter Eleven: Crimes Constituting Survivals of Local Customs

Article 231. Evasion of Reconciliation. The evasion by a slain person's relatives of refusal to engage in a blood feud with the slayer and his relatives, when the refusal is to be carried out in accordance with the procedure established by the statute on reconciliation proceedings in cases of blood feud, shall be punished by exile for a term not exceeding two years or by banishment for a term not exceeding three years.

Article 232. Payment and Acceptance of Bride Price. The acceptance of a bride price by the parents, kinsmen, or relatives by marriage of the bride, in the form of money, cattle, or other property, shall be punished by deprivation of freedom for a term not exceeding one year with confiscation of the bride price or by correctional tasks for the same term with confiscation of the bride price.

The payment of a bride price by the groom, his parents, kinsmen, or his relatives by marriage, shall be punished by deprivation of freedom for a term not exceeding one year or by social censure.

Article 233. Compelling of Woman to Enter Into Marriage or Obstruction of Entry Into Marriage. The compelling of a woman to enter into marriage or to continue marital cohabitation, or the obstructing of a woman's entry into marriage, or the abducting of her for entry into marriage, shall be punished by deprivation of freedom for a term not exceeding two years.

Article 234. Concluding of Marital Agreement With Person Who Has Not Attained Marital Age. The concluding in accordance with local customs of a marital agreement with a person who has not attained the marital age shall be punished by deprivation of freedom for a term not exceeding two years or by correctional tasks for a term not exceeding one year.

The commission in this connection of rape or the entering into sexual intercourse with a person who has not attained puberty shall entail responsibility in accordance with appropriate articles of the present Code.

Article 235. Bigamy or Polygamy. Bigamy or polygamy, that is, the cohabiting in a common household with two or several women, shall be punished by deprivation of freedom for a term not exceeding one year or by correctional tasks for the same term.

Article 236. Limits of Operation of Chapter Eleven of the Present Code. The operation of the present chapter shall extend to those autonomous republics, autonomous regions, and other localities of the RSFSR where the socially dangerous acts enumerated in the present chapter constitute survivals of local customs.

Chapter Twelve: Military Crimes

Article 237. Concept of Military Crime. Crimes provided for by the present Code against the established procedure for performing military service, committed by persons in military service, or by persons subject to military service during training courses, shall be deemed to be military crimes.

Officers, noncommissioned officers, and rank-and-file personnel of agencies of state security, as well as persons with respect to whom special indication is made in legislation of the USSR, shall bear responsibility for crimes against the established procedure for performing service in accordance with appropriate articles of the present Code.

Complicity in military crimes by persons not specified in the present article shall entail responsibility in accordance with appropriate articles of the present Code.

Article 238. Insubordination.

(a) Insubordination, that is, the open refusal to execute an order of a superior, or any other intentional failure to execute an order, shall be punished by deprivation of freedom for a term of one to five years.

(b) The same act committed by a group of persons or resulting in grave consequences shall be punished by deprivation of freedom for a term of three to ten years.

(c) Insubordination committed in wartime or in a combat situation shall be punished by death or by deprivation of freedom for a term of five to ten years.

Article 239. Failure to Execute Order.

(a) The failure to execute a superior's order, committed in the absence of the indicia specified in subsection "a" of Article 238 of the present Code, shall be punished by deprivation of freedom for a term of three months to three years.

(b) The same act committed under mitigating circumstances shall entail the application of the rules of the Disciplinary Code of the Armed Forces of the USSR.

(c) An act provided for by subsection "a" of the present article, committed in wartime or in a combat situation, shall be punished by deprivation of freedom for a term of three to ten years.

Article 240. Resisting of Superior or Compelling of Him to Violate Official Duties.

(a) The resisting of a superior or any other person performing military duties imposed on him, or the compelling of him to violate such duties, shall be punished by deprivation of freedom for a term of one to five years.

(b) The same acts committed by a group of persons or by use of weapons or resulting in grave consequences shall be punished by deprivation of freedom for a term of three to ten years.

(c) The acts provided for by subsection "b" of the present article, in conjunction with intentional homicide of a superior or any other person performing military duties or committed in wartime or in a combat situation, shall be punished by death or by deprivation of freedom for a term of five to fifteen years.

Article 241. Threatening a Superior.

(a) The threatening of a superior with intentional homicide, with the causing of bodily injuries, or with the infliction of beatings, in connection with the performance by him of his military duties, shall be punished by deprivation of freedom for a term of three months to three years.

(b) The same act under mitigating circumstances shall entail application of the rules of the Disciplinary Code of the Armed Forces of the USSR.

(c) An act provided for by subsection "a" of the present article, committed in wartime or in a combat situation, shall be punished by deprivation of freedom for a term of three to ten years.

Article 242. Forcible Actions Against Superior.

(a) The infliction of bodily injuries or beatings upon a superior in connection with the performance by him of his military duties shall be punished by deprivation of freedom for a term of two to ten years.

(b) The same act, committed in wartime or in a combat situation resulting in grave consequences, shall be punished by death or by deprivation of freedom for a term of five to fifteen years.

Article 243. Insult by Subordinate of Superior or by Superior of Subordinate.

(a) An insult by words or by nonforcible action inflicted by a subordinate on a superior or by a junior officer on a senior officer, or by a superior on a subordinate or by a senior on a junior, when at least one of them is performing military duties, shall be punished by deprivation of freedom for a term of three to six months.

(b) The same acts under mitigating circumstances shall entail application of the rules of the Disciplinary Code of the Armed Forces of the USSR.

(c) An insult by forcible action, inflicted under conditions specified in subsection "a" of the present article, shall be punished by deprivation of freedom for a term of six months to five years.

Article 244. Insult by Forcible Action Inflicted by One Person in Military Service on Another in Absence Between Them of Relationship of Subordination or Seniority.

(a) An insult by forcible action inflicted by one person in military service on another if they are not in a relationship of subordination or seniority and if at least one of them is performing military duties shall be punished by deprivation of freedom for a term of three months to one year.

(b) The same act under mitigating circumstances shall entail application of the rules of the Disciplinary Code of the Armed Forces of the USSR.

Article 245. Unwarranted Absence.

(a) The unwarranted absence from a unit or duty station by a person in military service for a regular term, or the failure to report for duty on time without valid reasons upon separation from a unit, upon assignment, upon transfer, upon return from detached service, upon return from leave, or from a medical institution, for a period of more than twenty-four hours but not more than seventy-two hours, or for a period of less than twenty-four hours but committed repeatedly in the course of three months, shall be punished by assignment to a disciplinary battalion for a term of three months to two years.

(b) The same acts committed in wartime shall be punished by deprivation of freedom for a term of two to ten years.

(c) The acts provided for by subsection "a" of the present article, committed by a person in military service who is serving punishment in a disciplinary battalion, shall be punished by deprivation of freedom for a term of one to three years.

(d) The acts provided for by subsection "a" of the present article, if committed under mitigating circumstances, shall entail application of the rules of the Disciplinary Code of the Armed Forces of the USSR.

[*Ved.* (1965), no. 27, item 670, Edict July 3, 1965.]

Article 246. Unwarranted Abandonment of Unit or Duty Station.

(a) The unwarranted abandonment of a unit or duty station by a person in military service for a regular term, or his failure to report for duty on time without valid reasons upon separation from a unit, upon assignment, upon transfer, upon return from detached service, upon return from leave, or from a medical institution, for a period of more than seventy-two hours, shall be punished by deprivation of freedom for a term of one to five years.

(b) The same acts committed in wartime shall be punished by deprivation of freedom for a term of five to ten years.

(c) Unwarranted abandonment of a unit or duty station by an officer or by a person in military service beyond the regular term, or his failure to report for duty on time without valid reasons for more than ten full days, shall be punished by deprivation of freedom for a term of one to five years.

(d) The acts provided for by subsection "c" of the present article committed in wartime, if the unwarranted absence continues for more than twenty-four hours, shall be punished by deprivation of freedom for a term of five to ten years.

Article 247. Desertion.

(a) Desertion, that is, the abandonment of a military unit or duty station by a person in military service for a regular term for the purpose of evading military service, or the failure to report for duty, for the same purpose, upon assignment, upon transfer, upon return from detached service, upon return from leave, or from a medical institution, shall be punished by deprivation of freedom for a term of three to seven years.

(b) The same acts committed in wartime shall be punished by death or by deprivation of freedom for a term of five to ten years.

(c) Desertion committed by an officer or by a person in military service beyond the regular term shall be punished by deprivation of freedom for a term of five to seven years.

(d) The same act committed in wartime shall be punished by death or by deprivation of freedom for a term of seven to ten years.

Article 248. Unwarranted Abandonment of Unit in Combat Situation. The unwarranted abandonment of a unit or duty station in a combat situation, regardless of the length of time, shall be punished by death or by deprivation of freedom for a term of seven to ten years.

Article 249. Evasion of Military Service by Maiming or Any Other Method.

(a) The evasion by a person in military service of performance of military duties by causing himself any kind of injury (maiming) or by malingering, forgery of documents, or any other deception, or a refusal to perform military duties, shall be punished by deprivation of freedom for a term of three to seven years.

(b) The same acts committed in wartime or in a combat situation shall be punished by death or by deprivation of freedom for a term of five to ten years.

Article 250. Dissipation [*Promotanie*] or Loss of Military Property.

(a) The selling, pawning, or lending, by a person in military service for a regular term, of articles of clothing or equipment issued to him for personal use (dissipation) or the loss or damage of such articles because of violation of rules for their care shall be punished by assignment to a disciplinary battalion for a term of three months to one year.

(b) The same acts under mitigating circumstances shall entail application of the rules of the Disciplinary Code of the Armed Forces of the USSR.

(c) The acts specified in subsection "a" of the present article committed in wartime or in a combat situation shall be punished by deprivation of freedom for a term of one to five years.

(d) The loss or damage of a weapon, ammunition, means of transportation, article of technical supply, or any other military property issued for use on duty, as a result of violation of the rules for their care, shall be punished by deprivation of freedom for a term of one to three years.

(e) The acts provided for by subsection "d" of the present article committed in wartime or in a combat situation shall be punished by deprivation of freedom for a term of two to seven years.

Article 251. Intentional Destruction or Damaging of Military Property.

(a) The intentional destruction or damaging of a weapon, ammunition, means of transportation, military equipment, or any other military property, in the absence of the indicia of an especially dangerous crime against the state, shall be punished by deprivation of freedom for a term of one to five years.

(b) The same act resulting in grave consequences shall be punished by deprivation of freedom for a term of three to ten years.

(c) The acts specified in subsection "b" of the present article committed in wartime or in a combat situation shall be punished by deprivation of freedom for a term of five to ten years or by death.

Article 252. Violation of Rules for Driving or Operating of Motor Vehicles. The violation of rules for the driving or operating of military, special, or transport vehicles, resulting in accidents involving persons or other grave consequences, shall be punished by deprivation of freedom for a term of two to ten years.

Article 253. Violation of Rules for Flights or Preparations for Flights. The violation of rules for flights or preparations for flights resulting in a catastrophe or other grave consequences shall be punished by deprivation of freedom for a term of three to ten years.

Article 254. Violation of Rules for Navigation. The violation of rules for navigation, resulting in the loss or serious damaging of a ship, loss of human life, or other grave consequences, shall be punished by deprivation of freedom for a term of three to ten years.

Article 255. Violation of Service Regulations for Guard Duty.

(a) The violation of service regulations for guard (watch) duty, or of orders and decrees issued in elaboration of such regulations, committed on guard duty or at posts for the protection of weapons, or of ammunition depots, or of combat technology, or of other objects having important significance, shall be punished by deprivation of freedom for a term of six months to three years.

(b) The same act under mitigating circumstances shall entail the application of rules of the Disciplinary Code of the Armed Forces of the USSR.

(c) The violation of service regulations for sentry or patrol duty entailing harmful consequences which the sentry guard (post) has been assigned to prevent shall be punished by deprivation of freedom for a term of one to five years or by assignment to a disciplinary battalion for a term of three months to two years.

(d) An act provided for by subsections "a" and "c" of the present article committed in wartime or in a combat situation shall be punished by deprivation of freedom for a term of two to seven years.

(e) The violation of rules for guard (watch) or convoy duty accompanied by the harmful consequences which the particular guard or convoy unit is established to prevent shall be punished by deprivation of freedom for a term of one to ten years.

(f) An act specified in subsection "e" of the present article committed in wartime or in a combat situation shall be punished by deprivation of freedom for a term of three to ten years or by death.

[*Ved.* (1965), no. 27, item 670, Edict July 3, 1965.]

Article 256. Violation of Rules for Performing of Border Duty.

(a) The violation of the rules for the performing of border duty by a person forming part of a detail for protecting the state border of the USSR shall be punished by deprivation of freedom for a term of one to three years.

(b) The same act under mitigating circumstances shall entail the application of the rules of the Disciplinary Code of the Armed Forces of the USSR.

(c) An act provided for by subsection "a" of the present article, resulting in grave consequences, shall be punished by deprivation of freedom for a term of three to ten years.

Article 257. Violation of Rules for Performing of Combat Lookout.

(a) The violation of the rules for the performing of combat lookout for protecting the inviolability of the land, sea, or air space of the USSR or for averting a sudden attack on the Soviet Union, committed by a person comprising part of a lookout relief of a combat unit, ship's view, post, or other lookout unit shall be punished by deprivation of freedom for a term of one to five years.

(b) The same act under mitigating circumstances shall entail the application of the rules of the Disciplinary Code of the Armed Forces of the USSR.

(c) An act provided for by subsection "a" of the present article, resulting in grave consequences, shall be punished by death or by deprivation of freedom for a term of five to fifteen years.

[*Ved.* (1965), no. 27, item 670, Edict July 3, 1965.]

Article 258. Violation of Service Regulations for Interior Duty.

(a) The violation of the service regulations for interior duty by a person forming part of the daily detail of a unit (except a guard or watch unit) shall be punished by deprivation of freedom for a term of three to six months.

(b) The same act under mitigating circumstances shall entail the application of the rules of the Disciplinary Code of the Armed Forces of the USSR.

(c) An act provided for by subsection "a" of the present article, resulting in harmful consequences, the prevention of which was part of the duty of the given person, shall be punished by deprivation of freedom for a term of six months to two years.

(d) An act provided for by subsection "c" of the present article, committed in wartime or in a combat situation, shall be punished by deprivation of freedom for a term of one to five years.

Article 259. Divulgence of Military Secret or Loss of Document Containing Military Secret.

(a) The divulgence of information of a military character constituting a state secret, in the absence of the indicia of treason, shall be punished by deprivation of freedom for a term of two to five years.

(b) The loss of documents containing information of a military character constituting a state secret, or of articles information concerning which constitutes a state secret, by a person to whom such documents or articles have been entrusted, if the loss is a result of violation of the rules established for handling the aforementioned documents or articles, shall be punished by deprivation of freedom for a term of one to three years.

(c) The acts provided for by subsections "a" and "b" of the present article, resulting in grave consequences, shall be punished by deprivation of freedom for a term of five to ten years.

(d) The divulgence of military information not subject to disclosure but not constituting a state secret shall be punished by deprivation of freedom for a term of five to ten years.

(e) An act provided for by subsection "d" of the present article under mitigating circumstances shall entail the application of the rules of the Disciplinary Code of the Armed Forces of the USSR.

Article 260. Abuse of Authority, Exceeding Authority, and Neglectful Attitude Toward Duty.

(a) The abuse by a commander or an official of his authority or official position, the omission to act or the exceeding of authority, or a neglectful attitude toward duty, committed systematically or from mercenary motives or for any other personal interest, or causing substantial harm, shall be punished by deprivation of freedom for a term of six months to ten years.

(b) The same acts under mitigating circumstances shall entail the application of the rules of the Disciplinary Code of the Armed Forces of the USSR.

(c) The acts provided for by subsection "a" of the present article, committed in wartime or in a combat situation, shall be punished by deprivation of freedom for a term of three to ten years or by death.

Article 261. Surrendering or Abandoning to Enemy of Means of Waging War. The surrender to an enemy by a commander of the military forces entrusted to him, or the abandoning to an enemy of fortifications, military equipment, or other means of waging war, when not required by the combat situation, if the aforementioned actions are not committed for the purpose of aiding the enemy, shall be punished by deprivation of freedom for a term of three to ten years or by death.

Article 262. Abandonment of Sinking Warship.

(a) The abandonment of a sinking warship by a commander who does not fulfill his official duties to the end, or by a person belonging to the ship's crew without the proper order therefor by the commander, shall be punished by deprivation of freedom for a term of five to ten years.

(b) The same act committed in wartime or in a combat situation shall be punished by death or by deprivation of freedom for a term of ten to fifteen years.

Article 263. Unwarranted Abandonment of Battlefield or Refusal to Use Weapon. The unwarranted abandonment of a battlefield or the refusal to use a weapon during combat shall be punished by death or by deprivation of freedom for a term of fifteen years.

Article 264. Voluntary Surrender into Captivity. The voluntary surrender into captivity because of cowardice or faint-heartedness shall be punished by death or by deprivation of freedom for a term of fifteen years.

Article 265. Criminal Actions of Person in Military Service as Prisoner of War.

(a) The voluntary participation, by a person in military service who is a prisoner of war, in work having military significance or in other measures known to be capable of causing loss to the Soviet Union or to states allied with it, in the absence of the indicia of treason, shall be punished by deprivation of freedom for a term of three to ten years.

(b) Force against other prisoners of war or cruel treatment of them on the part of a prisoner of war in a senior position shall be punished by deprivation of freedom for a term of three to ten years.

(c) The commission, by a person in military service who is a prisoner of war, of actions directed toward harming other prisoners of war, from mercenary motives or for the purpose of securing leniency toward himself on the part of the enemy, shall be punished by deprivation of freedom for a term of one to three years.

Article 266. Pillage. The stealing on the battlefield of things found on slain or wounded persons (pillage) shall be punished by deprivation of freedom for a term of three to ten years or by death.

Article 267. Force Against Population in Area of Military Operations. Assault with intent to rob, the illegal destruction of property, force, or the illegal removal of property under the pretext of military necessity, committed against the population in an area of military operations, shall be punished by deprivation of freedom for a term of three to ten years or by death.

Article 268. Mistreatment of Prisoners of War.

(a) The mistreatment of prisoners of war, occurring repeatedly or in conjunction with special cruelty, or directed against ill or wounded persons, or the wrongful performance of duties with respect to the sick and wounded by persons charged with their treatment and care, in the absence of the indicia of a graver crime, shall be punished by deprivation of freedom for a term of one to three years.

(b) The mistreatment of prisoners of war without the aforementioned aggravating circumstances shall entail the application of the rules of the Disciplinary Code of the Armed Forces of the USSR.

Article 269. Illegal Wearing or Abuse of Insignia of Red Cross or Red Crescent. The wearing of insignia of the Red Cross or Red Crescent in an area of military operations by persons not having the right to do so, or the abuse in wartime of the flags or insignia of the Red Cross or Red Crescent or of the color identifying transport vehicles for medical evacuation, shall be punished by deprivation of freedom for a term of three months to one year.

Appendix: List of Property Not Subject to Confiscation by Judgment of Court

The following kinds of property and articles belonging to a convicted person by right of personal ownership, or constituting his share in common property, which are necessary for him and his dependents, shall not be subject to confiscation:

1. Dwelling house and appurtenant buildings or separate parts thereof, for persons whose basic occupation is agriculture, if the convicted person and his family live permanently therein.

2. For persons whose basic occupation is agriculture, a single cow; in the absence of a cow, a single heifer; in households having neither a cow nor a heifer, a single goat, sheep, or pig; for collective-farm workers, in addition, sheep, goats, and pigs up to half the norm established for a collective-farm household by the charter for the agricultural artel, and also poultry.

In the taiga and tundra districts of the Far North – mother and young reindeer and also draught reindeer in the amount of 25 head per household.

3. Feed for cattle (if the cattle are not subject to confiscation) necessary until the harvest of new feed or until the cattle are turned out to pasture.

4. For persons whose basic occupation is agriculture, seed necessary for regular sowing.

5. Articles of household furniture, utensils, and clothes necessary for the convicted person and his dependents:

(a) clothes for each person: one summer or fall coat, one winter coat or sheepskin coat, one winter suit (for women, two winter dresses), one summer suit (for women, two summer dresses), one headgear for each season (for women, in addition, two summer kerchiefs, and one warm kerchief or shawl), other clothes and headgear in use for a long time and not having any value;

(b) footwear, underwear, bedding, kitchen and table utensils in use (with the exception of articles made of valuable materials or articles of artistic value);

(c) furniture: one bed and chair for each person, one table, one cupboard, and one trunk for the family;

(d) all children's belongings.

6. Food products in an amount necessary for the convicted person and his family until the new harvest, if the basic occupation of the convicted person is agriculture; otherwise food products and money in an aggregate amount of the extent of monthly wages of the convicted person, but not less than 100 rubles.

7. Fuel necessary for preparation of food and heating of the family living quarters during the cold season.

8. Supplies (including manuals and books) necessary for continuing the professional occupation of the convicted person, except when the convicted person is deprived by judgment of the court of the right to engage in particular activity or when the supplies have been used by him for the illegal pursuit of a trade.

9. Shares in cooperative organizations, if the convicted person is not excluded from membership in a cooperative.

10. In the event of confiscation of a convicted person's share of the common property of the peasant household (collective-farm or individual), the size of the share shall be determined after exclusion of the following property: dwelling house in which members of the household live and appurtenant buildings, seed necessary for regular sowing, one cow or, in the absence of a cow, one heifer (and, in a collective-farm household, also sheep, goats, pigs, and poultry up to half the norm established by the charter for the agricultural artel), and feed necessary for the remaining cattle.

The Code of Criminal Procedure of the RSFSR

October 27, 1960, as Amended to March 1, 1972

SECTION ONE: GENERAL PROVISIONS

SECTION TWO: INITIATION OF A CRIMINAL CASE, INQUIRY AND PRELIMINARY INVESTIGATION

Section One: General Provisions

Chapter One: Fundamental Provisions

Article 1. Legislation Concerning Criminal Proceedings. The method of conducting proceedings in criminal cases on the territory of the RSFSR shall be determined by the Fundamental Principles of Criminal Procedure of the USSR and Union Republics, by other laws of the USSR promulgated in accordance therewith, and by the RSFSR Code of Criminal Procedure.

In the conduct of a criminal case the law of criminal procedure shall be applied which was in force at the time of the inquiry, preliminary investigation, or judicial consideration of the case, respectively.

Regardless of the place where a crime is committed, proceedings in criminal cases on the territory of the RSFSR shall in all instances be conducted in conformity with the RSFSR Code of Criminal Procedure.

The method of conducting judicial proceedings established by laws of criminal procedure shall be uniform and binding in all criminal cases and for all courts, agencies of the Procuracy, of preliminary investigation, and of inquiry.

Article 2. Tasks of Criminal Proceedings. The tasks of Soviet criminal proceedings are the speedy and complete exposure of crimes, the conviction of the guilty, and the securing of the correct application of the law, so that every person who commits a crime shall be subjected to a just punishment and not a single innocent person shall be criminally prosecuted or convicted.

Criminal proceedings must facilitate the strengthening of socialist legality, the prevention and eradication of crimes, and the education of citizens in the spirit of undeviating execution of Soviet laws and respect for the rules of socialist communal life.

Article 3. Obligation to Initiate Criminal Case and Expose a Crime. A court, procurator, investigator, and agency of inquiry shall be obliged, within the limits of their competence, to initiate a criminal case in every instance in which indicia of a crime are disclosed and to take all measures provided by law for ascertaining the occurrence of the crime and the persons guilty of committing it, and for punishing them.

Article 4. Impermissibility of Prosecuting Except on Grounds and in Accordance With Procedure Established by Law. No one may be prosecuted as an accused except on the grounds and in accordance with the procedure established by law.

Article 5. Circumstances Precluding Criminal Proceedings. A criminal case may not be initiated, and if initiated shall be subject to termination:

(1) in the absence of the occurrence of a crime;

(2) in the absence, in the act, of the elements of a crime;

(3) upon the expiration of the periods of limitation;

(4) when an act of amnesty has eliminated the application of punishment for the act committed, or when the individual persons have been pardoned;

(5) with respect to a person who at the moment of committing a socially dangerous act has not attained the age at which, according to law, criminal responsibility is possible;

(6) upon reconciliation of the victim with the accused in cases which can be initiated only upon complaints of victims, except in instances provided for by Article 27 of the present Code;

(7) in the absence of a complaint by the victim, if the case can be initiated only upon his complaint, except in instances provided for by paragraph three of Article 27 of the present Code, when a procurator is granted the right to initiate a case even in the absence of the victim's complaint;

(8) with respect to a deceased person, except in instances when proceedings are necessary in order to rehabilitate the deceased or to reopen a case with respect to other persons on the basis of newly discovered circumstances;

(9) with respect to a person concerning whom under the same accusation there is a judgment of a court which has taken legal effect, or a ruling or decree of a court to terminate the case;

(10) with respect to a person concerning whom under the same accusation there is an unrevoked decree of an agency of inquiry, of an investigator, or of a procurator to terminate the case, except in instances provided for by Articles 255 and 256 of the present Code.

If circumstances stated in subsections 1, 2, 3, and 4 of the present article are disclosed during the judicial examination, the court shall bring to an end the examination of the case and shall decree a judgment of acquittal in instances provided for by subsections 1 and 2, or judgment of conviction with relief of the convicted person from punishment in instances provided for by subsections 3 and 4.

Termination of a case on the grounds stated in subsections 3 and 4 of the present article shall not be permitted if the accused objects. In such instance proceedings in the case shall be continued in the usual manner.

Article 6. Termination of Criminal Case Because of Change in Situation. A court or procurator, or an investigator or agency of inquiry with the consent of a procurator, shall have the right to terminate a criminal case if it is deemed that because of a change in the situation at the time of conducting the inquiry, preliminary investigation, or consideration of the case in court, the act committed by the guilty person has lost its socially dangerous character or the person has ceased to be socially dangerous.

Article 7. Termination of Criminal Case in Connection With Its Transfer to Comrades' Court. A court or procurator, or an investigator or agency of inquiry with the consent of a procurator, shall have the right, on the grounds stated in Article 51 of the RSFSR Criminal Code, to terminate criminal proceedings in a case and transfer it for consideration by a comrades' court.

The accused and the victim shall be notified of the termination of a case before it is transferred for consideration by a comrades' court, and shall have the right within five days to appeal from the ruling of the court or the decree of the procurator, investigator, or agency of inquiry to a higher court or higher procurator, as appropriate.

Article 8. Termination of Criminal Case in Connection With Its Transfer to Commission for Cases of Minors. A court or procurator, or an investigator with the consent of a procurator, shall have the right to terminate a criminal case against a person under the age of 18 years who has committed a crime not representing a great social danger, and to refer the case for consideration by a commission for cases of minors, if, in accordance with the circumstances of the case and facts characterizing the personality of the offender, his correction is possible without the application of criminal punishment.

The accused and his legal representative, as well as the victim, shall be notified of the termination of the case before it is transferred for consideration by the commission for cases of minors, and shall have the right within five days to appeal from the ruling of the court or the decree of the investigator or procurator to a higher court or higher procurator, as appropriate.

[*Ved.* (1970), no. 22, item 442, Edict May 21, 1970.]

Article 9. Termination of Criminal Case With Release of Guilty Person on Surety. A court or procurator, or an investigator or agency of inquiry with the consent of a procurator, shall have the right, on the grounds stated in Article 52 of the RSFSR Criminal Code, to terminate a criminal case and release on surety the person who has committed the crime, for his reeducation and correction, to an organization or collective of working people which has submitted a petition therefor.

Release on surety and termination of a case on this ground shall not be permitted with respect to a person who has previously been convicted of committing an intentional crime or who has already been released on surety.

If a person with respect to whom a criminal case is initiated does not consider himself guilty or for any reasons insists on consideration of the case in court, termination of the case and release of the person on surety shall not be permitted.

A victim shall be notified of the termination of the case and shall have the right within five days to appeal from the ruling of the court or the decree of the procurator, investigator, or agency of inquiry to a higher court or higher procurator, as appropriate.

If a person taken on surety has not in the course of a year justified the trust of the collective, has violated his promise to be corrected, and does not subordinate himself to norms of socialist society, or has left work for the purpose of evading social pressure, the social organization or collective of working people which has taken him on surety shall render a decision to renounce the surety and shall refer such decision to a court or to the Procuracy for consideration of the question of the criminal responsibility of the guilty person. In such instance the criminal case may be reopened by a ruling of an administrative session of the court or by a decree of the procurator.

Article 10. Referral of Materials Without Initiation of Criminal Case for Application of Measures of Social Pressure. In the event that a person commits a crime that is insignificant or does not represent a great social danger, and when the fact of the crime is obvious and the person who has committed it may be corrected by measures of social pressure, a court or procurator, or an investigator or agency of inquiry with the consent of a procurator, shall have the right, without initiating a criminal case, to transfer the materials for consideration by a comrades' court or a commission for cases of minors, or to release the guilty person on surety to a collective of working people or to a social organization for reeducation and correction.

[*Ved.* (1970), no. 22, item 442, Edict May 21, 1970.]

Article 11. Inviolability of Person. No one may be subjected to arrest except by decree of a court or with the sanction of a procurator.

A procurator shall be obliged to release immediately any person illegally deprived of freedom or kept under guard for more than a term provided for by law or by a judgment of a court.

Article 12. Inviolability of Dwelling Space and Secrecy of Correspondence. The inviolability of citizens' dwelling space and the secrecy of correspondence shall be protected by law.

A search where a citizen lives, the impounding of correspondence, and its seizure at postal and telegraph offices may be conducted only on the grounds and in accordance with the procedure established by law.

Article 13. Administration of Justice Only by Courts. Justice in criminal cases shall be administered only by courts. No one may be deemed guilty of committing a crime or subjected to criminal punishment except by judgment of a court.

Article 14. Administration of Justice on Basis of Equality of Citizens Before Law and Courts. Justice in criminal cases shall be administered on the basis of the equality of all citizens before the law and the courts, without regard to their social, property, or occupational status, nationality, race, or religion.

Article 15. Participation of People's Assessors and Collegiality in Consideration of Cases. Criminal cases in all courts shall be considered by judges and people's assessors elected in accordance with the procedure established by law.

The consideration of criminal cases in all courts of first instance shall be carried out by a judge and two people's assessors.

The people's assessors shall exercise equal rights with the person presiding in the judicial session in deciding all questions arising in the consideration of the case and in the decreeing of judgment.

The consideration of cases by way of cassation shall be carried out by a bench composed of three members of the court; the consideration of cases by way of judicial supervision shall be carried out by a bench composed of not fewer than three members of the court.

Article 16. Independence of Judges and Their Subordination Only to Law. In administering justice in criminal cases, judges and people's assessors shall be independent and subordinate only to law.

Judges and people's assessors shall decide criminal cases on the basis of law in conformity with socialist legal consciousness under conditions excluding outside pressure upon them.

Article 17. Language in Which Judicial Proceedings Shall Be Conducted. Judicial proceedings shall be conducted in the Russian language, but in autonomous republics, autonomous regions, or national areas, in the language of the autonomous republic, autonomous region, or national area, respectively, or in the language of the majority of the local population.

Persons who do not have command of the language in which the judicial proceedings are conducted shall be secured the right to make statements, give testimony, speak in court, and submit petitions in their own language, as well as to make use of the services of an interpreter in accordance with the procedure established by the present Code.

The accused shall be handed translations of investigative and judicial documents in his own language or in another language of which he has command, in conformity with the procedure established by the present Code.

Article 18. Publicity of Judicial Examination. The examination of cases in all courts shall be open, except in instances when this contradicts the interests of protecting a state secret.

In addition, a closed judicial examination shall be permitted, upon a reasoned ruling of the court, in cases of crimes of persons who have not attained the age of 16 years, cases of sexual crimes, or other cases for the purpose of preventing the divulgence of information about intimate aspects of the lives of persons participating in the case.

The judgments of courts shall in all cases be proclaimed publicly.

Article 19. Securing to an Accused the Right to Defense. An accused shall have the right to defense.

A court, procurator, investigator, and person conducting an inquiry shall be obliged to secure to the accused the possibility of defending himself against the accusation brought against him by the means and methods established by law, and to secure protection of his personal and property rights.

Article 20. Thorough, Complete, and Objective Analysis of Circumstances of Case. A court, procurator, investigator, and person conducting an inquiry shall be obliged to take all measures provided by law for a thorough, complete, and objective analysis of the circumstances of the case, and to expose circumstances tending both to convict and to acquit the accused, as well as those tending to aggravate and to mitigate his guilt.

The court, procurator, investigator, and person conducting the inquiry shall not have the right to shift the obligation of proof to the accused.

It shall be prohibited to solicit the accused's testimony by force, threats, or any other illegal measures.

Article 21. Exposing Causes and Conditions Facilitating Commission of the Crime. In the conduct of an inquiry, preliminary investigation, and judicial examination of a criminal case the agencies of inquiry, investigator, and court shall be obliged to expose the causes and conditions facilitating the commission of the crime, and to take measures to eliminate them.

Article 22. Right of Appeal From Actions and Decisions of Court, Procurator, Investigator, or Person Conducting Inquiry. The actions and decisions of a court, procurator, investigator, or person conducting an inquiry may be appealed, in accordance with the procedure established by the present Code, by interested citizens, institutions, enterprises, and organizations.

Article 23. Challenge of Judge, Procurator, and Other Participants in Case. A judge, people's assessor, procurator, investigator, person conducting an inquiry, secretary of a judicial session, expert, or interpreter may not participate in the conduct of a criminal case, and shall be subject to challenge, if he is personally interested in the case directly or indirectly.

Article 24. Supervision of Higher Courts Over Judicial Activity. In conformity with Article 19 of the Fundamental Principles of Criminal Procedure of the USSR and Union Republics, the USSR Supreme Court shall exercise supervision over the judicial activity of judicial agencies of the USSR operating on the territory of the RSFSR as well as of judicial agencies of the RSFSR within the limits established by law.

The RSFSR Supreme Court shall exercise supervision over the judicial activity of all judicial agencies of the RSFSR, and the supreme courts of autonomous republics shall exercise supervision over the judicial activity of courts of the respective autonomous republics.

Territorial, regional, and city courts, courts of autonomous regions, and courts of national areas shall exercise supervision over the judicial activity of district (city) people's courts of the given territory, region, city, or area.

Article 25. Procurator's Supervision in Criminal Proceedings. In conformity with Article 20 of the Fundamental Principles of Criminal Procedure of the USSR and Union Republics, supervision over the exact execution of the laws of the USSR, the RSFSR, and autonomous republics in criminal proceedings shall be exercised by the USSR Procurator General both directly and through the RSFSR Procurator and other procurators subordinate to him.

A procurator shall be obliged in all stages of criminal proceedings promptly to take measures provided by law for eliminating any violations of law, regardless of who may be the source of such violations.

A procurator shall exercise his powers in criminal proceedings independently of any agencies and officials whatsoever, being subordinate only to the law and being governed by the instructions of the USSR Procurator General.

All institutions, enterprises, organizations, officials, and citizens shall be obliged to execute decrees of a procurator rendered in conformity with law.

Article 26. Joinder and Disjoinder of Criminal Cases. There may be joined in one proceeding only cases in which several persons are accused of complicity in committing one or several crimes, or cases in which one person is accused of commission of several crimes or of concealment of such crimes or failure to report them when not promised in advance.

The disjoinder of a case shall be permitted only in necessary instances, if it will not affect the thoroughness, completeness, and objectivity of the analysis and resolution of a case.

Joinder and disjoinder of cases shall be carried out by decree of a person conducting an inquiry, investigator, or procurator, or by ruling or decree of a court.

Article 27. Criminal Cases Initiated Upon Complaint of Victim. Cases of crimes provided for by Articles 112, 130 paragraph one, and 131 of the RSFSR Criminal Code shall be initiated only upon the complaint of a victim and shall be subject to termination in the event of his reconciliation with the accused. Reconciliation shall be permitted only before the court retires to the conference room to decree judgment.

Cases of crimes provided for by Articles 117 paragraph one and 141 of the RSFSR Criminal Code shall be initiated only upon the complaint of a victim, but shall not be subject to termination because of reconciliation of the victim with the accused. Proceedings in such cases shall be conducted in the usual manner.

In exceptional instances, if a case of any crime provided for by Articles 112, 130 paragraph one, 131 and 141 of the RSFSR Criminal Code has special social significance, or if a victim, because of helpless condition, dependence on the accused, or for any other reasons is not in a position to defend his rights and legal interests, a procurator shall have the right to initiate such a case even in the absence of the victim's complaint. A case initiated by a procurator shall be referred for inquiry or preliminary investigation, and after completion of the inquiry or investigation shall be considered by a court in the usual manner. Such a case shall not be subject to termination because of the reconciliation of the victim with the accused.

A procurator shall have the right at any time to enter into a case initiated by a judge upon the complaint of a victim concerning crimes provided for by Articles 112, 130 paragraph one, and 131 of the RSFSR Criminal Code, and to support the accusation in court, if the protection of state or social interests or of the rights of citizens so requires. The entry of a procurator into a case shall not deprive a victim of the rights provided by Article 53 of the present Code, but in such instances the case shall not be subject to termination because of reconciliation of the victim with the accused.

Article 28. Significance of Decisions or Rulings of Court in Civil Cases in Resolution of Criminal Cases. A court's decision, ruling, or decree in a civil case, which has taken legal effect, shall be binding on a court, procurator, investigator, or person conducting an inquiry in criminal proceedings as to the question whether an event or action has taken place, but not with respect to the guilt of the accused.

Article 29. Civil Suit in Criminal Case. A person who has suffered material loss from a crime shall have the right in a criminal case to bring a civil suit against the accused or persons bearing material responsibility for the actions of the accused, which suit shall be considered by the court jointly with the criminal case. A civil suit in a criminal case shall be relieved from state tax.

A civil suit may be brought from the moment the criminal case is initiated until the beginning of the judicial investigation. Dismissal of a suit decreed by way of civil proceedings shall deprive the plaintiff of the right to bring the same suit again in a criminal case.

The procurator shall have the right to bring a civil suit or to support a civil suit brought by a victim, if the protection of state or social interests or of the rights of citizens so requires.

If a civil suit has not been brought, a court in decreeing judgment shall have the right on its own initiative to resolve the question of compensation for the material loss caused by the crime.

Proof in a civil suit brought in a criminal case shall be made in accordance with the rules established by the present Code.

A person who has not brought a civil suit in a criminal case, or a person whose civil suit has been left unconsidered, shall have the right to bring it by way of civil proceedings.

Article 30. Securing Compensation for Material Loss Caused by a Crime and Execution of Judgment of Confiscation of Property. If there exists sufficient information that a crime has caused material loss, the agency of inquiry, investigator, procurator, and court shall be obliged to take measures to secure the bringing of a civil suit or the possibility thereof in the future.

In criminal proceedings concerning a crime for which punishment may be applied in the form of confiscation of property, the agency of inquiry, investigator, procurator, and court shall be obliged to take measures of security against concealment of the accused's property.

Article 31. Procedure Governing Relations of Courts, Investigators, and Agencies of Inquiry With Corresponding Agencies of Other Union Republics. When it is necessary to perform particular judicial or investigative actions or to make searches on the territory of other union republics, judges, investigators, and agencies of inquiry shall, in cases conducted by them, communicate directly with the corresponding agencies of other union republics.

Judges, investigators, and agencies of inquiry of the RSFSR shall be obliged within the limits of their competence to execute the commissions of corresponding agencies of other union republics.

When it is necessary to transfer a criminal case to an agency of preliminary investigation or inquiry or to a court of another union republic, the case shall be referred through the RSFSR Procurator or the Chairman of the RSFSR Supreme Court, as appropriate.

Article 32. Procedure Governing Relations of Courts, Procurators, Investigators, and Agencies of Inquiry With Corresponding Institutions of Foreign States. The procedure governing relations of courts, procurators, investigators, and agencies of inquiry with judicial and investigative agencies of foreign states, as well as the procedure for executing commissions of the latter, shall be determined by legislation of the USSR and RSFSR and by international treaties concluded by the USSR and the RSFSR with the respective states.

Article 33. Operation of Law of Criminal Procedure With Respect to Citizens of Foreign States and Persons Without Citizenship. Judicial proceedings in cases of crimes committed by citizens of foreign states and by persons without citizenship shall be conducted on the territory of the RSFSR in conformity with the rules of the present Code.

With respect to persons possessing the right of diplomatic immunity, procedural actions provided for by the present Code shall be carried out only upon their request or with their consent. Consent for the carrying out of such actions shall be obtained through the Ministry of Foreign Affairs.

Article 34. Explanation of Certain Terms Contained in the Present Code. Terms contained in the present Code shall, if there are no special indications, have the following meaning:

(1) "Court" – USSR Supreme Court, RSFSR Supreme Court, supreme courts of autonomous republics, territorial, regional, and city courts, courts of autonomous regions, courts of national areas, district (city) people's courts, military tribunals, acting within the limits of their competence;

(2) "Court of first instance" – a court authorized to decree judgment in a case;

(3) "Cassational instance" or "second instance" – a court considering by way of cassation cases on appeals from, or protests of, judgments and rulings of a court of first instance and decrees of a judge which have not taken legal effect;

(4) "Supervisory instance" – a court considering by way of judicial supervision cases on protests of judgments, rulings, and decrees which have taken legal effect;

(5) "Judge" – people's judge; president, deputy president, or member of the court; people's assessor;

(6) "Procurator" – the USSR Procurator General, the RSFSR Procurator, procurators of autonomous republics, of territories, regions, autonomous regions, national areas, cities, and districts, their deputies and assistants, procurators of departments and administrations of the Procuracy, military procurators, acting within the limits of their competence;

(6a) "Chief of an investigative department" – the chief of an investigative administration, department, [or] division of agencies of internal affairs, [or] of state security, and his deputies, acting within the limits of their competence;

[*Ved.* (1965), no. 50, item 1243, Edict December 14, 1965; *Ved.* (1970), no. 22, item 442, Edict May 21, 1970.]

(7) "Investigator" – investigator of the Procuracy, investigator of agencies of internal affairs, investigator of agencies of state security;

[*Ved.* (1963), no. 15, item 288, Edict April 15, 1963; *Ved.* (1970), no. 22, item 442, Edict May 21, 1970.]

(8) "Legal representatives" – parents, foster parents, guardians and curators of the accused or of the victim, representatives of institutions and organizations which have charge of the accused or the victim;

(9) "Near relatives" – parents, children, foster parents, foster children, natural brothers and sisters, grandfather, grandmother, grandchildren, and also spouse;

(10) "Judgment" – a decision rendered by a court in session concerning the question of the guilt or innocence of the person brought to trial and concerning the application or nonapplication of punishment to him;

(11) "Ruling" – any decision, other than a judgment, rendered by a court of first instance in a criminal case; any decision of a court, except presidia of courts, in review of court judgments, rulings, and decrees which have taken legal effect;

(12) "Decree" – a decision taken by presidia of courts in review of court judgments, rulings, and decrees which have taken legal effect; any decision taken by a judge individually; a decision of an investigator, person conducting an inquiry, or procurator, taken in the preliminary investigation or inquiry, except a conclusion to indict;

(13) "Conclusion of the procurator" – opinion of a procurator expressed by him in court in instances provided for by law;

(14) "Criminal law" – criminal laws of the USSR, the RSFSR Criminal Code, as well as criminal codes of other union republics, when they are subject to application by agencies of inquiry, of preliminary investigation, and of the Procuracy, and by courts of the RSFSR;

(15) "Night" – from 10 p.m. to 6 a.m. local time.

Chapter Two: Jurisdiction

Article 35. Criminal Cases Within Jurisdiction of District (City) People's Courts. District (city) people's courts shall have jurisdiction over all cases except those within the jurisdiction of higher courts or military tribunals.

Article 36. Criminal Cases Within Jurisdiction of Territorial, Regional, City Courts, Courts of Autonomous Regions, and Courts of National Areas. Territorial, regional, and city courts, courts of autonomous regions, and courts of national areas shall have jurisdiction over cases of crimes provided for by Articles 64, 66–77-1, 79, 81 paragraph two, 84, 85 paragraph one, 86, 87, 88 paragraph two, 88-1 (in particular, concerning the failure to report the crimes provided for by Articles 64, 66–69 and 72), 88-2 (in particular, concerning the concealment, when not promised in advance, of crimes provided for by Articles 64, 66–69 and 72), 93-1, 102, 117 paragraph three, 152, 173 paragraph two, 176–179, 190–1, 190–2, 190–3, and 191-2 of the RSFSR Criminal Code.

[*Ved.* (1963), no. 36, item 661, Edict September 10, 1963; *Ved.* (1966), no. 38, item 1039, Edict September 16, 1966.]

Article 37. **Criminal Cases Within Jurisdiction of Supreme Courts of Autonomous Republics.** Supreme courts of autonomous republics shall have jurisdiction over cases indicated in Article 36 of the present Code.

Article 38. **Criminal Cases Within Jurisdiction of RSFSR Supreme Court.** The RSFSR Supreme Court shall have jurisdiction over cases of special complexity or of special social significance, accepted by it for trial upon its own initiative or upon the initiative of the RSFSR Procurator.

Article 39. **Criminal Cases Within Jurisdiction of Military Tribunals.** The jurisdiction of a military tribunal in criminal cases shall be determined by the Statute on Military Tribunals.

Article 40. **Right of Higher Court to Accept for Trial Criminal Case Within Jurisdiction of Lower Court.** A higher court shall have the right to accept for trial as a court of first instance any case within the jurisdiction of a lower court.

Article 41. **Territorial Jurisdiction Over Criminal Case.** A case shall be subject to consideration in the court of the district where the crime is committed. If it is impossible to determine the place of commission of the crime, the case shall be within the jurisdiction of the court of the district where the preliminary investigation or inquiry in the case is completed.

Article 42. **Determination of Jurisdiction in Combining Criminal Cases.** When one person or a group of persons is accused of committing several crimes, the cases concerning which are within the jurisdiction of courts of different kinds, a case embracing all the crimes shall be considered by the highest of such courts.

If a case in which one person or a group of persons is accused of committing several crimes is within the jurisdiction of a military tribunal with respect to at least one person or one crime, a case embracing all the persons and crimes shall be considered by the military tribunal in conformity with Article 12 of the Statute on Military Tribunals.

A case which on these or any other grounds is within the jurisdiction simultaneously of several courts of the same kind shall be considered by the court of the district where the preliminary investigation or inquiry in the case is completed.

Article 43. **Transfer of Criminal Case to Another Jurisdiction.** A judge or a court in administrative session, having established that a case which has been accepted is not within the jurisdiction of the given court, shall refer the case to another jurisdiction.

A court, having established that a case it is conducting is within the jurisdiction of another similar court, shall have the right to continue to conduct the case only in the event that it has already commenced to consider it in judicial session. If, however, a case is within the jurisdiction of a higher court or a military tribunal, it shall in all instances be subject to referral to the jurisdiction of such higher court or military tribunal.

It shall not be permitted to transfer to a lower court a case whose consideration in judicial session of a higher court has commenced.

Article 44. Transfer of Criminal Case From Court Having Jurisdiction to Another Court. In individual instances, for the purpose of the most speedy, complete, and objective consideration of a case, and also for the purpose of best securing the educational role of the judicial examination of a case, it may be transferred for consideration from one court to another similar court. Transfer of a case on such grounds shall be permitted only before its consideration in judicial session has commenced.

The question of transferring a case on the said grounds from one district (city) people's court to another within an autonomous republic, territory, region, city, autonomous region, or national area shall be resolved by the president of the supreme court of the autonomous republic, of the territorial or city court, of the court of the autonomous region, or of the court of the national area, respectively.

The question of transferring a case on the said grounds to a court of another autonomous republic, territory, region, city, autonomous region, or national area shall be resolved by the President of the RSFSR Supreme Court or by his deputy.

If there is a ruling of an administrative session on the question of transferring the case to another court, the president of an appropriate higher court may, in the event that he disagrees, protest such ruling by way of judicial supervision.

Article 45. Impermissibility of Disputes Over Jurisdiction. Disputes over jurisdiction between courts shall not be permitted. Any case referred from one court to another in the procedure provided for by Articles 43 and 44 of the present Code shall be subject to unconditional acceptance by the court to which it is referred.

Chapter Three: Participants in the Trial, Their Rights and Duties

Article 46. The Accused. A person with respect to whom, in accordance with the procedure established by the present Code, a decree to prosecute as the accused has been rendered, shall be deemed the accused.

An accused who is brought to trial shall be called a person brought to trial; an accused with respect to whom a judgment of conviction has been rendered shall be called a convicted person.

The accused shall have the right to know what he is accused of and to give explanations concerning the accusation presented to him; to present evidence; to submit petitions; to become acquainted with all the materials of the case upon completion of the preliminary investigation or inquiry; to have defense counsel from the moment provided for by Article 47 of the present Code; to participate in the judicial examination in the court of first instance; to submit challenges; and to appeal from the actions and decisions of the person conducting the inquiry, the investigator, procurator, and court.

The person brought to trial shall have the right to the last word.

Article 47.* Participation of Defense Counsel in Criminal Proceedings. Defense counsel shall be permitted to participate in a case from the moment the accused is informed of the completion of the preliminary investigation and is presented with all the proceedings of the case to become acquainted with them.

In cases of crimes of minors, as well as of persons who by reason of their physical or mental defects are not themselves able to exercise their right to defense, defense counsel shall be permitted to participate in the case from the moment the accusation is presented.

In cases in which a preliminary investigation is not conducted, defense counsel shall be permitted from the moment the accused is brought to trial.

Advocates and representatives of trade unions and of other social organizations shall be permitted to serve as defense counsel.

By ruling of the court or decree of the judge, near relatives and legal representatives of the accused, as well as other persons, shall be permitted to serve as defense counsel.

The same person may not be defense counsel for two accused persons if the interests of one of them conflict with the interests of the other.

Article 48. Engagement, Assignment, and Replacement of Defense Counsel. A defense counsel shall be engaged from among the persons specified in Article 47 of the

*Article 47 is revised by the Edicts of the Presidium of the Supreme Soviet of the USSR of August 31, 1970 (*Vedomosti SSSR*, September 9, 1970, no. 36, item 362) and of February 3, 1972 (*Vedomosti SSSR*, February 9, 1972, no. 6, item 51) amending Article 22 of the Fundamental Principles of Criminal Procedure of the USSR and the Union Republics. The amended Article 22 is set forth below with the changes italicized for the reader's convenience. As of March 1, 1972, the RSFSR Code of Criminal Procedure had not been amended to conform to the USSR edicts.

Article 22. *Participation of defense counsel in criminal proceedings.* Defense counsel shall be permitted to participate in a case from the moment the accused is informed of the completion of the preliminary investigation and is presented with all the proceedings of the case to become acquainted with them. *By decree of the procurator, defense counsel may be permitted to participate in the case from the moment the accusation is presented.*

Participation of defense counsel in the preliminary investigation and at the judicial examination shall be obligatory in cases of minors, of *deaf, dumb, and blind persons,* and of other persons who by reason of their physical or psychological defects cannot themselves exercise their right to defense. *In these situations the defense counsel shall be allowed to participate in the case from the moment of the presentation of the accusation.*

In cases of persons who do not have command of the language in which the proceedings are conducted and also of persons accused of committing crimes for which the death penalty may be imposed as a measure of punishment, the participation of defense counsel is obligatory from the moment the accused is informed of the completion of the preliminary investigation and is presented with all the proceedings of the case to become acquainted with them.

Obligatory participation of defense counsel in a case may also take place in other instances defined by legislation of union republics.

Advocates, representatives of trade unions and of other social organizations, and other persons to whom such right is given by legislation of union republics, shall be permitted to serve as defense counsel.

present Code by the accused, by his legal representative, or by other persons upon the commission or with the consent of the accused.

Upon the request of the accused the participation of defense counsel shall be secured by the investigator or court.

In those instances when participation of defense counsel selected by the accused is impossible for a long period of time, the investigator or court shall have the right to propose to the accused that he engage other defense counsel or to assign defense counsel for the accused through the college of advocates.

Article 49. Obligatory Participation of Defense Counsel. The participation of defense counsel in a judicial examination shall be obligatory in cases:

(1) in which a state or social accuser is participating;

(2) of dumb, deaf, blind, and other persons who by reason of their physical or mental defects are not themselves able to exercise their right to defense;

(3) of minors;

(4) of persons who do not have command of the language in which the judicial proceedings are conducted;

(5) of persons whose interests conflict and one of whom has defense counsel;

(6) of persons brought to trial for crimes for which the death penalty may be applied as a measure of punishment.

In instances stated in subsections 2 and 3 of the present article, participation of defense counsel is also obligatory in the preliminary investigation.

If in the instances provided for by the present article defense counsel is not engaged by the accused himself, by his legal representative, or by other persons upon his commission, the investigator or court shall be obliged to secure the participation of defense counsel in the case.

Article 50. Refusal of Defense Counsel. The accused shall have the right at any moment in the conduct of a case to refuse defense counsel. Such a refusal shall be permitted only upon the initiative of the accused himself and may not be an obstacle to the continued participation in the case of the state or social accuser or of defense counsel for other persons brought to trial.

A petition to refuse defense counsel by a minor or by an accused who by reason of his physical or mental defects is not himself able to exercise his right to defense shall not be binding on the court, investigator, or procurator, respectively.

Article 51. Duties and Rights of Defense Counsel. Defense counsel shall be obliged to make use of all means and methods of defense indicated in the law for the purpose of explaining the circumstances tending to acquit the accused or to mitigate his responsibility, and to render the accused necessary legal aid.

From the moment he is permitted to participate in a case defense counsel shall have the right to meet with the accused; to become acquainted with all the materials of the case and to copy necessary information therefrom; to present evidence; to submit petitions; to participate in the judicial examination; to submit challenges; to appeal from actions and decisions of the investigator, procurator, and court. With the permission of the investigator, defense counsel may be present during interrogations of the accused and during the conduct of any other investigative actions performed upon petition of the accused or of his defense counsel.

In instances where defense counsel is permitted to participate in a case from the moment the accusation is presented he may, in addition:

(1) be present at the presentation of the accusation and the interrogation of the accused and, with the permission of the investigator, put questions to the accused;

(2) be present when other investigative actions are carried out and, with the permission of the investigator, put questions to witnesses, victims, and experts;

(3) make written remarks in connection with the correctness and completeness of the entries in the record of an investigative action in which he has participated.

An investigator may exclude questions of the defense counsel, but shall be obliged to enter the excluded questions in the record.

An advocate shall not have the right to withdraw from the defense of an accused after he has accepted it.

Article 52. Suspect. The following shall be deemed a suspect:

1. A person detained on suspicion of committing a crime;

2. A person to whom a measure of restraint has been applied before the presentation of an accusation.

A suspect shall have the right to give explanations, submit petitions, and appeal from the actions and decisions of the person conducting the inquiry, the investigator, or the procurator.

Article 53. Victim. A person to whom moral, physical, or property harm is caused by a crime shall be deemed a victim. A citizen shall be declared a victim by decree of a person conducting an inquiry, an investigator, or a judge, or by a ruling of a court.

A citizen declared to be a victim of a crime shall have the right to give testimony in the case. The victim or his representative shall have the right to present evidence; to submit petitions; to become acquainted with the materials of the case from the moment the preliminary investigation is completed; to participate in the analysis of evidence in the judicial investigation; to submit challenges; to appeal from actions of the person conducting the inquiry, investigator, procurator, and court, as well as to appeal from the judgment or rulings of the court and decrees of the judge.

In instances provided for by paragraphs one and four of Article 27 of the present Code, the victim shall have the right to support the accusation in the judicial examination, personally or through his representative.

In cases of crimes resulting in the death of the victim, his near relatives shall have the rights provided by the present article.

Article 54. Civil Plaintiff. A citizen, institution, enterprise, or organization that has suffered material loss from a crime and has brought a claim for compensation in conformity with Article 29 of the present Code shall be deemed a civil plaintiff. One shall be declared a civil plaintiff by decree of a person conducting the inquiry, an investigator, or a judge, or by a ruling of a court.

A civil plaintiff or his representative shall have the right to present evidence; to submit petitions; to participate in the judicial examination; to request the agency of inquiry, the investigator, and the court to take measures to secure the suit brought by him; to support the civil suit; to become acquainted with the materials of the case from the moment the preliminary investigation is completed; to submit challenges; to appeal from actions of the person conducting the inquiry, investigator, procurator, and court, as well as to appeal from the judgment and rulings of the court insofar as they concern the civil suit.

The civil plaintiff shall be obliged, upon demand of the court, to present documents at his disposal connected with the suit.

Article 55. Civil Defendant. Parents, guardians, curators, and other persons as well as institutions, enterprises, and organizations which by law bear material responsibility for a loss caused by the criminal actions of the accused, may be prosecuted as civil defendants. One may be prosecuted as a civil defendant by decree of a person conducting the inquiry, an investigator, or a judge, or by ruling of a court.

The civil defendant or his representative shall have the right to object to the suit; to give explanations concerning the substance of the suit; to present evidence; to submit petitions; to become acquainted with the materials of the case, insofar as they pertain to the civil suit, from the moment the preliminary investigation is completed; to participate in the judicial examination; to submit challenges; to appeal from actions of the person conducting the inquiry, investigator, procurator, and court, as well as to appeal from the judgment and rulings of the court insofar as they concern the civil suit.

Article 56. Representatives of Victim, Civil Plaintiff, and Civil Defendant. The following may participate in the case as representatives of the victim, of the civil plaintiff, and of the civil defendant: advocates, near relatives, and any other persons authorized by law to represent in a criminal case the legal interests of the victim, civil plaintiff, or civil defendant, respectively.

Article 57. Interpreter. A person who has command of languages the knowledge of which is necessary for translation and who is assigned by an agency of inquiry, investigator, procurator, or court in an instance provided for by Article 17 of the present Code shall be an interpreter.

An interpreter shall be obliged to appear when summoned and to execute completely and exactly the translation entrusted to him.

In the event that an interpreter knowingly makes an incorrect translation he shall bear responsibility in accordance with Article 181 of the RSFSR Criminal Code. If a person assigned as an interpreter evades appearance or fulfillment of his duties, measures of social pressure may be applied to him or a monetary exaction up to 10 rubles may be imposed on him. The monetary exaction shall be imposed by the court in accordance with the procedure provided for by Article 323 of the present Code.

The rules of this article shall extend to a person who understands the signs of the dumb and deaf and who is engaged to participate in a trial.

Article 58. **Duty to Explain and Secure Rights to Persons Participating in Case.** A court, procurator, investigator, and person conducting an inquiry shall be obliged to explain to persons participating in a case their rights and to secure the possibility of exercising such rights.

Chapter Four: Circumstances Precluding Possibility of Participating in Judicial Proceedings. Challenges

Article 59. **Circumstances Barring Judge From Participating in Consideration of Criminal Case.** A judge may not participate in the consideration of a case:

(1) if he is a victim, civil plaintiff, civil defendant, or witness, or if he has participated in the given case as an expert, specialist, interpreter, person conducting the inquiry, investigator, accuser, defense counsel, legal representative of the accused, representative of the victim, civil plaintiff, or civil defendant;

(2) if he is a relative of the victim, of the civil plaintiff, of the civil defendant or of their representatives, a relative of the accused or of his legal representative, a relative of the accuser, of defense counsel, of the investigator, or of the person conducting the inquiry;

(3) if there are any other circumstances giving grounds to believe that the judge is personally interested in the case, directly or indirectly.

Persons related to each other may not be members of a court that is considering a criminal case.

[*Ved.* (1966), no. 36, item 1018, Edict August 31, 1966.]

Article 60. **Impermissibility of Repeated Participation of Judge in Consideration of Case.** A judge who has taken part in the consideration of a criminal case in a court of first instance may not participate in the consideration of the case in a court of second instance or by way of judicial supervision, or participate in a new consideration of the case in a court of first instance in the event that a judgment or ruling to terminate the case, decreed with his participation, is vacated.

A judge who has taken part in the consideration of a case in a court of second instance may not participate in the consideration of the case in a court of first instance or by way of judicial supervision, or in a new consideration of the case in a court of second instance after a ruling decreed with his participation is vacated.

A judge who has taken part in the consideration of a case by way of judicial supervision may not participate in the consideration of the same case in a court of first or second instance.

Article 61. **Challenge of Judge.** Under the circumstances stated in Articles 59 and 60 of the present Code, a judge shall be obliged to disqualify himself. On the same grounds a challenge of a judge may be submitted by the accuser, defense counsel, or person brought to trial, or by the victim, civil plaintiff, or civil defendant, or their representatives.

A challenge must be reasoned and must be submitted before the beginning of the judicial investigation. Later submission of a challenge shall be permitted only in instances when the grounds therefor become known to the person submitting the challenge after the beginning of the judicial investigation.

Article 62. **Procedure for Ruling on Challenge of Judge.** A challenge of a judge shall be ruled on by the remaining judges in the absence of the challenged judge, who shall have the right, however, to set forth publicly in advance to the remaining judges his explanation concerning the challenge of him. If there is a tie vote, the judge shall be considered excluded.

A challenge of two judges or of the entire membership of the court shall be ruled on by the court as a whole by a simple majority vote.

The question of a challenge shall be resolved by the court in the conference room.

Article 63. **Challenge of Procurator.** A procurator may not take part in a case if there exist the grounds stated in Article 59 of the present Code.

The participation of a procurator in a preliminary investigation or inquiry, or his support of the accusation in court, shall not be an obstacle to his further participation in the case.

If there exist grounds for a challenge, a procurator shall be obliged to bar himself from participating in the case. A procurator may be challenged on the same grounds by the accused or defense counsel, or by the victim, civil plaintiff, or civil defendant, or their representatives.

The question of a challenge of a procurator shall be resolved in an inquiry or preliminary investigation by a higher procurator, or in a court by the court considering the case.

Article 64. **Challenge of Investigator and Person Conducting Inquiry.** An investigator or person conducting an inquiry may not take part in the investigation of a case if there exist the grounds provided for by Article 59 of the present Code. Their participation in a previous inquiry or preliminary investigation in a given case shall not be a ground for challenge.

If there exist grounds for a challenge, an investigator or person conducting an inquiry shall be obliged to bar himself from participating in the case. They may be challenged on the same grounds by the suspect, accused, or defense counsel, or by the victim, civil plaintiff, or civil defendant, or their representatives.

The question of a challenge of an investigator or person conducting an inquiry shall be resolved by a procurator.

Article 65. **Challenge of Secretary of Judicial Session.** The rules set forth in Articles 59 and 61 of the present Code shall pertain to the secretary of the judicial session.

His previous participation in the case as secretary of the judicial session shall not be a ground for challenge.

The question of a challenge of a secretary shall be resolved by the court considering the case.

Article 66. Challenge of Interpreter. An interpreter may not take part in a case if there exist grounds provided for by Article 59 of the present Code, or in an instance when his incompetence is disclosed.

If such grounds exist, an interpreter may be challenged by the suspect, accused, defense counsel, or accuser, or by the victim, civil plaintiff, or civil defendant, or their representatives.

A person's previous participation in a case as interpreter shall not be a ground for challenging him.

The question of a challenge of an interpreter shall be resolved in an inquiry or preliminary investigation by the person conducting an inquiry, investigator or procurator, respectively, or in a court by the court considering the case.

Article 66–1. Challenge of Specialist. A specialist may not take part in a case if there exist grounds provided for by Article 67 of the present Code. Previous participation in the case as a specialist shall not be a ground for challenging a person.

The question of a challenge of a specialist shall be resolved in the procedure provided for by Article 66 of the present Code.

[*Ved.* (1966), no. 36, item 1018, Edict August 31, 1966.]

Article 67. Challenge of Expert. An expert may not take part in a case:

(1) if there exist grounds provided for by Article 59 of the present Code; his previous participation in the case as an expert shall not be a ground for challenge;

(2) if he has been or is occupationally or otherwise dependent upon the accused, victim, civil plaintiff, or civil defendant;

(3) if in the given case he has carried out an inspection, materials of which have served as a ground for initiating the criminal case;

(3a) if he has participated in the case as a specialist, except for a physician's participation as a specialist in the field of forensic medicine in an external examination of a corpse;

(4) in an instance when his incompetence is disclosed.

The question of a challenge of an expert shall be decided in accordance with the procedure provided by Article 66 of the present Code.

[*Ved.* (1966), no. 36, item 1018, Edict August 31, 1966.]

Chapter Five: Evidence

Article 68. Circumstances Subject to Proof in Criminal Case. In an inquiry or preliminary investigation and in the examination of a criminal case in court the following shall be subject to proof:

(1) the occurrence of the crime (time, place, method, and other circumstances of the commission of the crime);

(2) the guilt of the accused in committing the crime and motives for the crime;

(3) circumstances stated in Articles 38 and 39 of the RSFSR Criminal Code which influence the degree and character of the responsibility of the accused, as well as other circumstances characterizing the personality of the accused;

(4) the character and extent of loss caused by the crime.

Circumstances that have facilitated the commission of the crime shall also be subject to ascertainment.

Article 69. Evidence. Evidence in a criminal case shall be any factual data on the basis of which, in accordance with the procedure determined by law, the agencies of inquiry, investigator, and court establish the presence or absence of a socially dangerous act, the guilt of the person who has committed such act, and any other circumstances that are of significance for the correct resolution of the case.

Such data shall be established by the testimony of a witness, by the testimony of a victim, by the testimony of a suspect, by the testimony of the accused, by the opinion of an expert, by real evidence, by the records of investigative and judicial actions, and by any other documents.

Article 70. Collection of Evidence. A person conducting an inquiry, investigator, procurator, and court shall have the right in cases conducted by them to summon, in accordance with the procedure established by the present Code, any person to be interrogated or to give an opinion as an expert; to conduct views, searches, and other investigative actions provided for by the present Code; to demand that institutions, enterprises, organizations, officials, and citizens furnish articles and documents capable of establishing factual data necessary for the case; and to demand that inspections be carried out.

Evidence may be presented by a suspect, accused, defense counsel, and accuser, as well as by a victim, civil plaintiff, and civil defendant, and their representatives, and by any citizens, institutions, enterprises, and organizations.

All evidence collected in a case shall be subject to careful, thorough, and objective verification on the part of a person conducting an inquiry, investigator, procurator, and court.

Article 71. Evaluation of Evidence. A court, procurator, investigator, and person conducting an inquiry shall evaluate evidence in accordance with their inner conviction, based on a thorough, complete, and objective consideration of all the circumstances of the case in their totality, being governed by law and by socialist legal consciousness.

No evidence shall have a previously established force for the court, procurator, investigator, or person conducting the inquiry.

Article 72. Persons Summoned as Witnesses. Any person who may have knowledge of any circumstances to be established in a given case may be summoned as a witness to give testimony.

The following may not be interrogated as witnesses:

(1) defense counsel of the accused, concerning circumstances of the case which

have become known to him in connection with the fulfillment of his duties of defense counsel;

(2) a person who by reason of his physical or mental defects is incapable of correctly grasping circumstances of significance for the case or of giving correct testimony concerning them.

Participation in a case by the legal respresentatives of a victim, suspect, or accused shall not exclude the possibility of interrogation of such persons as witnesses.

Article 73. Duties of Witness. A witness shall be obliged to appear when summoned by a person conducting an inquiry, investigator, procurator, or court, and to give truthful testimony; to communicate everything known to him about the case and to reply to the questions put to him.

If a witness fails to appear without a valid reason, a person conducting an inquiry, investigator, procurator, or court shall have the right to subject him to compulsory appearance.

For refusing to give or evading the giving of testimony, a witness shall bear responsibility in accordance with Article 182 of the RSFSR Criminal Code; and for giving testimony known to be false, in accordance with Article 181 of the RSFSR Criminal Code.

Article 74. Testimony of Witness. A witness may be interrogated concerning any circumstances to be established in a given case, including the personality of the accused and the victim and his relationships with them. Factual data communicated to a witness may not serve as evidence if he cannot indicate the source of his information.

Article 75. Testimony of Victim. A victim shall be obliged to appear when summoned by a person conducting an inquiry, investigator, procurator, or court, and to give truthful testimony; to communicate everything known to him about the case and to reply to the questions put to him.

A victim may be interrogated about any circumstances to be proved in a given case, as well as about his relationships with the accused. Factual data communicated to a victim may not serve as evidence if he cannot indicate the source of his information.

If a victim fails to appear without a valid reason, an investigator, procurator, or court shall have the right to subject him to compulsory appearance.

For refusing to give or evading the giving of testimony, a victim shall bear responsibility in accordance with Article 182 of the RSFSR Criminal Code; and for giving testimony known to be false, in accordance with Article 181 of the RSFSR Criminal Code.

[*Ved.* (1963), no. 36, item 661, Edict September 10, 1963.]

Article 76. Testimony of Suspect. A suspect shall have the right to give testimony in connection with the circumstances which serve as the ground for his detention or confinement under guard, and also in connection with any other circumstances of the case known to him.

Article 77. Testimony of Accused. An accused shall have the right to give testimony concerning the accusation presented to him, or in connection with any other circumstances of the case known to him, or in connection with any other evidence in the case. An acknowledgment of guilt by the accused may become the basis for an accusation only if the acknowledgment is confirmed by the totality of evidence in the case.

Article 78. Expert Examination. An expert examination shall be assigned in instances when, in the conduct of the inquiry or preliminary investigation or during the judicial examination, special knowledge of science, engineering, art, or a trade is necessary. An expert examination shall be carried out by experts of appropriate institutions or by other specialists assigned by a person conducting an inquiry, investigator, procurator, or court. Any person possessing knowledge necessary for giving an opinion may be summoned as an expert.

The request of the person conducting an inquiry, investigator, procurator, or court that an expert be summoned shall be binding on the manager of the institution, enterprise, or organization where the expert works. The questions put to the expert and his opinion may not go beyond the limits of the special knowledge of the expert.

[*Ved.* (1966), no. 36, item 1018, Edict August 31, 1966.]

Article 79. Obligatory Conduct of Expert Examination. An expert examination shall be obligatory:

(1) to establish the causes of death and the character of bodily injuries;

(2) to determine the mental state of an accused or a suspect in those instances when doubt arises of his imputability or of his ability, at the time of the conduct of the case, to realize the significance of his actions or to control them;

(3) to determine the mental or physical state of a witness or victim in instances when doubt arises of his ability to grasp correctly circumstances of significance for the case and to give correct testimony concerning them;

(4) to establish the age of an accused, a suspect, or a victim in instances when such age is of significance for the case and documents concerning it are lacking.

Article 80. Opinion of Expert. An expert shall give an opinion in his own name on the basis of analyses carried out in conformity with his special knowledge and shall bear responsibility for the opinion given by him.

When several experts are assigned to carry out an expert examination they shall confer among themselves before giving an opinion. If the experts in one specialty arrive at a common opinion, it shall be signed by all the experts. In the event of disagreement among the experts, each expert shall give his opinion separately.

The opinion of an expert shall not be binding on the person conducting the inquiry, investigator, procurator, or court; their disagreement with an opinion must, however, be reasoned.

Article 81. Supplementary and Repeated Expert Examination. In the event of insufficient clarity or completeness of an opinion, a supplementary expert examination may be assigned, and entrusted to the same or another expert.

In the event of an unfounded opinion of an expert or of doubts of its correctness, a repeated expert examination may be assigned and entrusted to another expert or to other experts.

Article 82. Duties and Rights of Expert. An expert shall be obliged to appear when summoned by a person conducting an inquiry, investigator, procurator, or court and to give an objective opinion in accordance with the questions put to him. If a question goes beyond the limits of the special knowledge of the expert or if the materials presented to him are insufficient for giving an opinion, the expert shall inform in writing the agency which has assigned the expert examination of the impossibility of giving an opinion.

An expert shall have the right:

(1) to become acquainted with the materials of the case pertaining to the object of the expert examination;

(2) to submit petitions for supplementary materials necessary for giving an opinion;

(3) with the permission of a person conducting an inquiry, investigator, procurator, or court, to be present when interrogations or other investigative or judicial actions are conducted and to put questions to the persons interrogated pertaining to the subject of the expert examination.

In the event that an expert refuses to fulfill or evades fulfilling his duties without valid reasons, or gives an opinion known to be false, or fails to appear without valid reasons when summoned by a person conducting an inquiry, investigator, procurator, or court, the measures provided for by Article 73 of the present Code shall be applied.

Article 83. Real Evidence. Articles which have served as instruments of the crime or which retain traces of the crime, or which have been the objects of the criminal actions of the accused, as well as money and other valuables criminally acquired, and all other articles which may serve as means for discovering the crime, establishing the factual circumstances of the case, exposing the guilty, or disproving the accusation, or mitigating the guilt of the accused, shall constitute real evidence.

Article 84. Preserving Real Evidence. Real evidence must be described in detail in the records of a view, photographed if possible, and attached to the file of the case, by special decree of a person conducting an inquiry, investigator or procurator, or by ruling of a court. Real evidence must be preserved with the file of the criminal case.

If certain articles because of their bulk or for other reasons cannot be preserved with the file of a criminal case, they must be photographed and, if possible, sealed and preserved in a place indicated by the person conducting the inquiry, investigator, procurator, or court, and there must be an appropriate certificate thereof in the file of the case.

When a case is transferred from an agency of inquiry to an investigator or from one agency of inquiry or investigator to another, and also when a case is referred to a procurator or court or when a case is transferred from one court to another, real evidence shall be forwarded with the file of the case, except in the instance provided for by paragraph two of the present article.

Article 85. Periods for Preserving Real Evidence. Real evidence shall be preserved until the judgment takes legal effect or until the expiration of the period for appealing from a decree or ruling to terminate the case. In instances when a dispute concerning the right to a thing is subject to resolution by way of civil proceedings, real evidence shall be preserved until the civil decision of the court takes legal effect.

In individual instances real evidence may be returned to its owners even before the expiration of the periods indicated in paragraph one of the present article, if such is possible without detriment to the conduct of the case.

If it cannot be returned to the owner, real evidence subject to rapid deterioration shall be delivered to appropriate institutions to be used in accordance with its purpose. When necessary they shall compensate the owner with articles of the same kind and quality or shall pay the latter their value.

Article 86. Measures Taken With Respect to Real Evidence When Resolving Criminal Case. In a judgment, ruling, or decree to terminate a case the question of the real evidence must be decided, in which connection:

(1) the instruments of the crime belonging to the accused shall be subject to confiscation and shall be transferred to appropriate institutions or destroyed;

(2) things whose circulation is prohibited shall be subject to transfer to appropriate institutions or shall be destroyed;

(3) things of no value and incapable of being used shall be subject to destruction, but in the event of a petition by interested persons or institutions they may be given to them;

(4) money or other valuables criminally acquired shall, in accordance with the judgment of the court, be subject to conversion to state revenue; the remaining things shall be given to their lawful owners, but if the latter are not ascertained, they shall become state property; in the event of a dispute concerning the ownership of such things, the dispute shall be subject to resolution by way of civil proceedings;

(5) documents constituting real evidence shall remain with the file of the case during the whole period of preservation of the latter or shall be transferred to interested institutions.

Article 87. Records of Investigative and Judicial Actions. Records certifying circumstances and facts established in a view, examination, seizure, search, detention, or presentation for identification, as well as during the conduct of an investigative experiment, which are drawn up in accordance with the procedure provided by the present Code, shall constitute evidence in the criminal case.

Article 88. Documents. Documents shall constitute evidence if the circumstances and facts certified or set forth by institutions, enterprises, organizations, officials, or citizens have significance for the criminal case.

In instances when documents contain the indicia stated in Article 83 of the present Code, they shall constitute real evidence.

Chapter Six: Measures of Restraint

Article 89. Application of Measures of Restraint. If there exist sufficient grounds for supposing that an accused will hide from an inquiry, preliminary investigation, or court, or that he will hinder the establishment of the truth in a criminal case, or that he will engage in criminal activity, and also in order to secure the execution of a judgment, the person conducting the inquiry, investigator, procurator, or court shall have the right to apply to the accused one of the following measures of restraint: signed promise not to depart, personal surety, surety of social organizations, confinement under guard.

With the sanction of the procurator or in accordance with a ruling of the court, bail may be applied as a measure of restraint.

Surveillance may be applied as a measure of restraint to members of the armed forces by the command of the military units in which they are serving.

In the absence of grounds necessitating the application of a measure of restraint, an obligation shall be obtained from the accused to appear when summoned and to give notice of a change of place of residence.

Article 90. Application of Measure of Restraint Against Suspect. In exceptional instances a measure of restraint may be applied against a person suspected of the commission of a crime even before presentation to him of an accusation. In such instance the accusation must be presented not later than ten days from the moment of application of the measure of restraint. If in this period an accusation is not presented, the measure of restraint shall be canceled.

Article 91. Circumstances Considered When Selecting Measure of Restraint. When resolving the question whether it is necessary to apply a measure of restraint, as well as the question which of them shall be selected, a person conducting an inquiry, investigator, procurator, or court shall also consider, besides the circumstances indicated in Article 89 of the present Code, the gravity of the accusation, the personality of the suspect or accused, the nature of his occupational activites, his age, the state of his health, his family situation, and other circumstances.

Article 92. Decree or Ruling to Apply Measure of Restraint. A person conducting an inquiry, investigator, or procurator, shall render a reasoned decree, or the court a reasoned ruling, for the application of a measure of restraint, indicating the crime of which the given person is suspected or accused and the ground for selecting the measure of restraint. The decree or ruling shall be announced to the person with respect to whom it is rendered.

Article 93. Signed Promise Not to Depart. A signed promise not to depart shall consist in obtaining from a suspect or an accused the obligation not to absent himself from his place of residence or temporary location without the permission of a person conducting an inquiry, investigator, procurator, or court, respectively. In the event the suspect or accused violates the signed promise given by him, a more severe measure of restraint may be applied, and he must be informed of this when the signed promise is obtained.

Article 94. Personal Surety. Personal surety shall consist in the acceptance by trustworthy persons of a written obligation that they will ensure the proper conduct of a suspect or an accused and his appearance when summoned by a person conducting an inquiry, investigator, procurator, or court. The number of sureties may not be less than two.

When a signed promise of personal surety is obtained, the surety must be informed of the nature of the case for which the given measure of restraint is selected, and of his responsibility in the event that the suspect or accused commits actions for the prevention of which the measure of restraint in the form of personal surety has been applied. In such instance the court may impose on each surety either a monetary exaction up to 100 rubles in accordance with the procedure provided by Article 323 of the present Code, or measures of social pressure.

Article 95. Surety of Social Organization. The surety of a social organization shall consist in the giving of a written obligation that the social organization will ensure the proper conduct of a suspect or an accused and his appearance when summoned by a person conducting an inquiry, investigator, procurator, or court.

The social organization giving surety must be informed of the nature of the case for which the given measure of restraint is selected.

Article 96. Confinement Under Guard. Confinement under guard as a measure of restraint shall be applied, in conformity with the requirements of Article 11 of the present Code, only in cases of crimes for which punishment in the form of deprivation of freedom is provided for by law.

To persons accused of committing the crimes provided for by Articles 64–74, 75 paragraph two, 77–79, 81, 84, 85 paragraph one, 86–88, 89 paragraphs two and three, 90 paragraphs two and three, 93 paragraph three, 93-1, 98 paragraph two, 102, 103, 108, 117, 119 paragraph two, 121 paragraph two, 144 paragraphs two and three, 145 paragraphs two and three, 146, 147 paragraph three, 149 paragraph two, 154 paragraph two, 173 paragraph two, 174, 174-1, 176 paragraph two, 177 paragraph two, 179 paragraph two, 191-1 paragraph two, 191-2, 218-1 paragraphs two and three, 238 subsections "b" and "c", 240 subsections "b" and "c", 242 subsection "b", 247 subsections "b" and "d", 248, 249 subsection "b", 251 subsection "c," 255 subsection "f", 257 subsection "d", 259 subsection "c", 261, 262 subsection "b", 263-267 of the RSFSR Criminal Code, confinement under guard may be applied as a measure of restraint only on grounds of the danger of the crime.

[*Ved.* (1963), no. 36, item 661, Edict September 10, 1963; *Ved.* (1970), no. 22, item 442, Edict May 21, 1970.]

Article 96–1. Procedure for Keeping Persons Confined Under Guard. The procedure for keeping persons with respect to whom confinement under guard is selected as a measure of restraint is determined by the Statute on Preliminary Confinement Under Guard, confirmed by the Law of the USSR of July 11, 1969.

[*Ved.* (1970), no. 22, item 442, Edict May 21, 1970.]

Article 96–2. Terms for Keeping Persons Confined Under Guard in Cell of Preliminary Confinement. Persons confined under guard may be kept in a cell of preliminary confinement for not more than seventy-two hours.

If the delivery of persons confined under guard to a separate investigative cell is impossible because of distance or lack of appropriate communications, then they may be kept in a cell of preliminary confinement for up to thirty days.

[*Ved.* (1970), no. 22, item 442, Edict May 21, 1970.]

Article 97. Periods of Confinement Under Guard. Confinement under guard in connection with the investigation of a case may not continue for more than two months. Only by reason of the special complexity of the case may this period be prolonged up to three months from the day of confinement under guard by a procurator of an autonomous republic, territory, region, autonomous region, or national area, or by a military procurator of a military region or fleet, or up to six months by the RSFSR Procurator or the Chief Military Procurator. Further prolongation of a period of confinement under guard may be carried out only in exceptional instances by the USSR Procurator General for a period of not more than an additional three months.

Article 98. Measures of Care for Children of Person Confined Under Guard and Measures of Protection of his Property. An agency of inquiry, investigator, procurator, or court shall be obliged:

(1) when a person confined under guard has minor children remaining without supervision, to transfer them to the care of relatives or other persons or institutions;

(2) when a person confined under guard has property or dwelling space untended, to take measures for their protection.

The agency of inquiry, investigator, procurator, or court shall notify the person confined under guard of the measures taken.

Article 99. Bail. Bail shall consist of money or valuables deposited with a court by an accused, suspect, or other person or organization to secure the appearance of the accused or suspect when summoned by a person conducting an inquiry, investigator, procurator, or court. A record of the receipt of bail shall be drawn up and a copy of it shall be handed to the person furnishing bail.

The amount of bail shall be determined by the agency which has selected the given measure of restraint in conformity with the circumstances of the case.

When depositing bail the person furnishing bail must be informed of the nature of the case for which the given measure of restraint has been selected.

In the event that the accused or suspect evades appearing when summoned by the person carrying out an inquiry, investigator, procurator, or court, the bail shall be converted to state revenue by a ruling of the court rendered in accordance with the procedure provided for by Article 323 of the present Code.

Article 100. Surveillance by Command of Military Unit. Surveillance of an accused who is a member of the armed forces by the command of a military unit shall consist in taking measures provided for by the codes of the Armed Forces of the USSR to secure the proper conduct of the accused and his appearance when summoned by a person conducting an inquiry, investigator, procurator, or court.

The command of the military unit shall be notified of the nature of the case for which the given measure of restraint is selected.

The command of the military unit shall inform in writing the agency which has selected such measure of restraint that surveillance has been established.

Article 101. Cancellation or Change of Measure of Restraint. A measure of restraint shall be canceled when there is no further necessity for it, or shall be changed to a more severe or a milder measure when this is called for by the circumstances of the case. The cancellation or change of a measure of restraint shall be carried out by a reasoned decree of a person conducting an inquiry, investigator, or procurator, or, after the case has been transferred to a court, by a reasoned ruling of the court.

A cancellation or change of a measure of restraint selected by a person conducting an inquiry or investigator in accordance with the instructions of a procurator shall be permitted only with the sanction of the procurator.

Chapter Seven: Records, Time Periods, and Court Costs

Article 102. Obligation to Keep Record. In the conduct of investigative actions as well as in administrative and judicial sessions of courts of first instance, the keeping of records shall be obligatory.

A record may be handwritten or typed. For securing the completeness of the record, the taking of shorthand may be employed. The stenographic notes shall not be appended to the file of the case.

A record must contain an indication of the place and date of the conduct of a procedural action with designation of the time of its commencement and completion and an indication of the persons who have taken part in it. The record shall set forth the procedural actions in the order in which they have taken place, the circumstances material to the case which have been disclosed and the statements of persons who have participated in such actions.

The record shall be signed by the persons specified in the appropriate articles of the present Code. All changes, additions, and corrections entered in the record must be stipulated and certified by the signatures of such persons.

[*Ved.* (1966), no. 36, item 1018, Edict August 31, 1966.]

Article 103. Calculation of Time Periods. The time periods established by the present Code shall be calculated in hours, days, and months. In the calculation of time periods the hour and day at which time the periods begin shall not be taken into account.

In the calculation of time periods in days the time period shall expire at midnight of the last day. In the calculation of time periods by months the time period shall expire on the corresponding day of the last month, and if such month does not have a corresponding day, the time period shall end on the last day of such month. If the end of the period does not fall on a working day, the first subsequent working day shall be considered the last day.

The time period shall not be considered to have lapsed if appeals or any other documents are put in the mail before the expiration of the time period, or for persons kept under guard, if the appeal or any other document is delivered to the administration of the place of confinement before the expiration of the time period.

Article 104. Extension of Lapsed Time Period. A time period which has lapsed for a valid reason must be extended by decree of the person conducting the inquiry, investigator, or procurator, or by a ruling of the court conducting the case.

Upon the petition of an interested person the execution of a decision that is appealed after the lapse of the established time period may be suspended until resolution of the question of extending the lapsed period.

Article 105. Court Costs. Court costs shall consist of:

1. Sums paid to witnesses, victims, experts, specialists, interpreters, witnesses of investigative actions;
2. Sums spent for preserving, transmitting and investigating real evidence;
3. [Deleted] ;
4. Any other expenses incurred in the conduct of a given case.

[*Ved.* (1963), no. 36, item 661, Edict September 10, 1963; *Ved.* (1966), no. 36, item 1018, Edict August 31, 1966.]

Article 106. Compensation of Witnesses, Victims, Experts, Specialists, Interpreters, and Witnesses of Investigative Actions for Expenses Incurred. A person summoned as a witness, victim, expert, specialist, interpreter, or witness of investigative action shall retain his average wages at his place of work for the entire time he spends in connection with a summons before a person conducting an inquiry, investigator, procurator, or court. Persons who are not workers or employees shall be paid a remuneration for being taken away from their usual occupational activities. In addition, all the persons specified shall have the right to compensation for expenses incurred in connection with appearing.

An expert, specialist, or interpreter shall have the right to remuneration for fulfilling his duties except in instances when such duties have been fulfilled as part of his occupational functions.

Compensation for expenses in connection with appearing and payment of remuneration shall be made from the resources of the agencies of inquiry, preliminary investigation, or court. The method of payment and the amounts of the sums subject to payment shall be established by the RSFSR Council of Ministers.

[*Ved.* (1966), no. 36, item 1018, Edict August 31, 1966.]

Article 107. Exaction of Court Costs. Court costs shall be imposed on convicted persons or shall be assumed by the state.

In the event that a person brought to trial is found guilty, a court shall have the right to exact court costs from him. The court may also impose court costs on a person brought to trial who is found guilty but relieved of punishment.

If in a case several persons brought to trial are found guilty, the court shall decree in what proportion court costs must be imposed on each of them, taking into account the guilt, degree of responsibility, and property status of such persons.

In the event that a case is terminated or the person brought to trial is acquitted, or when the person from whom court costs must be exacted is insolvent, such costs shall be assumed by the state.

When the person brought to trial is acquitted in a case which can be initiated only upon the complaint of a victim, the court shall have the right to impose costs, in full or in part, on the person upon whose complaint the case was commenced.

The method of payment for the work of an advocate assigned to participate in a case shall be determined by the rules of Article 322 of the present Code.

Section Two: Initiation of a Criminal Case, Inquiry, and Preliminary Investigation

Chapter Eight: Initiation of a Criminal Case

Article 108. Reasons and Grounds for Initiating Criminal Case. The following shall constitute reasons for initiating a criminal case:

1. Declarations and letters of citizens;
2. Communications of trade union and Communist Youth League organizations, people's guards for the protection of public order, comrades' courts, and other social organizations;
3. Communications of institutions, enterprises, organizations, and officials;
4. Articles, notices, and letters published in the press;
5. Giving oneself up;
6. Direct discovery of indicia of a crime by an agency of inquiry, investigator, procurator, or court.

A case may be initiated only in instances when there exist sufficient data indicating the indicia of a crime.

Article 109. Requirement to Consider Declarations and Communications Concerning a Crime. A procurator, investigator, agency of inquiry, and judge shall be obliged to accept declarations and communications concerning any crime that has been committed or is in preparation and to take decisions concerning them within a period of not more than three days from the day of receiving the declaration or communication, or in exceptional instances within a period of not more than ten days.

With respect to declarations and communications that have been received, necessary materials and explanations may be demanded and received without, however, the conducting of investigative actions provided for by the present Code.

With respect to a declaration or communication that has arrived, one of the following decisions must be taken:

1. To initiate a criminal case;
2. To refuse to initiate a criminal case;
3. To transfer the declaration or communication to another investigative or judicial jurisdiction.

The person who has made the declaration shall be informed of the decision taken.

Before initiating a case with respect to crimes provided for by Articles 112, 130 paragraph one, and 131 of the RSFSR Criminal Code, a judge shall take measures to reconcile the victim with the person against whom the complaint has been made. If reconciliation has not taken place, and there exist sufficient data, the judge shall render a decree to initiate the case and to bring to trial the person against whom the complaint is made. The judge may join counterclaims in the same proceedings with the complaint of the victim.

Article 110. Declarations and Communications Concerning a Crime. The declarations of citizens may be oral or written. Oral declarations shall be entered in the record, which shall be signed by the person who has made the declaration and by the official of the agency of inquiry, investigator, procurator, or judge who has received the declaration. A written declaration must be signed by the person from whom it comes.

Responsibility for making a report known to be false must be explained to the person who makes the declaration, and a note to such effect shall be made in the record and certified by the signature of the person who made the declaration.

Communications of institutions, enterprises, organizations, and officials must be made in writing.

Article 111. Giving Oneself Up. In the event that a person gives himself up, his identity shall be established and a record shall be drawn up, in which the declaration that has been made shall be set forth in detail. The record shall be signed by the person who has given himself up and by the person conducting the inquiry, investigator, procurator, or judge who has drawn up the record.

Article 112. Procedure for Initiating Criminal Case. If there exist a reason and grounds for initiating a criminal case, a procurator, investigator, agency of inquiry, or judge shall be obliged, within the limits of his competence, to initiate a criminal case.

A procurator, investigator, agency of inquiry, or judge shall render a decree to initiate a criminal case. The decree must indicate the time, place, by whom it is drawn up, the reason and grounds for initiating the case, the article of the criminal law in accordance with whose indicia it is initiated, as well as the further routing of the case.

A copy of the decree to initiate a criminal case rendered by the investigator or agency of inquiry shall be sent immediately to the procurator.

Simultaneously with the initiation of a criminal case, measures must be taken to prevent or suppress the crime and to preserve the traces of the crime.

Article 113. Refusal to Initiate Criminal Case. In the absence of grounds for initiating a criminal case, or if there exist circumstances precluding proceedings in a case, a procurator, investigator, agency of inquiry, or judge shall refuse to initiate the criminal case.

If a declaration or communication which has been received contains data concerning an administrative or disciplinary offense or other breach of public order or of rules of socialist communal life, a procurator, investigator, agency of inquiry, or judge shall have the right to refer the declaration or communication for consideration to a social organization, comrades' court, or collective of working people, or to transfer the material received for disposition in an administrative or disciplinary procedure.

A reasoned decree of refusal to initiate a criminal case shall be rendered and the person, institution, enterprise, or social organization from which the declaration or communication has been received shall be notified thereof, and the right to appeal from such decree shall be explained to them.

A refusal to initiate a criminal case may be appealed from by the person who has made the declaration to the proper procurator or higher court, as appropriate.

Article 114. Referral of Declaration or Communication to Another Investigative or Judicial Jurisdiction. A procurator, investigator, agency of inquiry, or judge may, without initiating a criminal case, refer a declaration or communication that has been received to another investigative or judicial jurisdiction. In such instance he shall be obliged to take measures to prevent or suppress the crime, or to preserve traces of the crime.

Article 115. Referral of Case After Its Initiation. After rendering a decree to initiate a criminal case:

(1) a procurator shall refer the case for preliminary investigation or inquiry;

(2) an investigator shall begin a preliminary investigation or agency of inquiry an inquiry;

(3) a judge shall refer the case for preliminary investigation or inquiry or shall take the case for consideration by his court.

Article 116. Supervision of Procurator Over Legality of Initiation of Criminal Case. A procurator shall exercise supervision over the legality of the initiation of a criminal case.

If the case is initiated by an investigator or agency of inquiry without legal reasons and grounds, the procurator shall by his own decree vacate the decree of the investigator or agency of inquiry, thereby refusing to initiate the criminal case, or shall terminate the case if investigative actions have been conducted in it.

In the event of an unfounded refusal to initiate a case, the procurator shall by his own decree vacate the decree to such effect rendered by the investigator or agency of inquiry and shall initiate the case.

Chapter Nine: The Inquiry

Article 117. Agencies of Inquiry. The following shall constitute agencies of inquiry:

(1) agencies of the police;

(2) commanders of military units and formations and heads of military institutions, in cases of all crimes committed by members of the armed forces subordinate to them as well as by persons subject to military service while in training courses, and in cases of crimes committed by workers and employees of the armed forces in connection with the discharge of their occupational duties or within the purview of the unit, formation, or institution;

(3) agencies of state security, in cases referred by law to their jurisdiction;

(4) heads of correctional labor institutions in cases of crimes against the established procedure for performance of service committed by persons working in such institutions, and in cases of crimes committed within the purview of correctional labor institutions;

(5) agencies of state fire supervision, in cases of causing fires and of violations of rules for fire prevention;

(6) agencies of border protection, in cases of violations of the state border;

(7) captains of ocean-going vessels on long voyages and heads of polar stations during periods of absence of transportation connections with the polar station.

Article 118. Duties of Agencies of Inquiry. Agencies of inquiry shall be charged with taking necessary operative-search measures and any other measures provided for by criminal-procedure law for the purpose of discovering crimes and the persons who have committed them.

Agencies of inquiry shall also be charged with the duty to take all measures necessary to prevent and suppress crime.

The activity of agencies of inquiry shall differ depending on whether they are acting in cases for which a preliminary investigation is obligatory or in cases for which a preliminary investigation is not obligatory.

Article 119. Activity of Agencies of Inquiry in Cases for Which Preliminary Investigation is Obligatory. If there exist indicia of a crime for which a preliminary investigation is obligatory, an agency of inquiry shall initiate a criminal case and, governed by the rules of criminal-procedure law, shall conduct urgent investigative actions to establish and preserve traces of the crime: view, search, seizure, examination, detention, and interrogation of suspects, interrogation of victims and witnesses.

The agency of inquiry shall immediately inform a procurator of the discovery of the crime and of the commencement of the inquiry.

Upon performing urgent investigative actions, the agency of inquiry shall, without awaiting the instructions of the procurator or the end of the period provided for by paragraph one of Article 121 of the present Code, be obliged to transfer the case to an investigator.

After transferring a case to an investigator, the agency of inquiry may conduct investigative and search actions in connection with it only upon the commission of the investigator. In the event that it transfers to the investigator a case in which it has not appeared possible to discover who committed the crime, the agency of inquiry shall continue to take operative-search measures to ascertain the criminal and shall inform the investigator of the results.

Article 120. Activity of Agencies of Inquiry in Cases in Which Preliminary Investigation Is Not Obligatory. In cases in which a preliminary investigation is not obligatory, an agency of inquiry shall initiate the case and shall take all the measures provided by criminal-procedure law to establish the circumstances to be proved in the criminal case.

In an inquiry in a case for which a preliminary investigation is not obligatory, the agency of inquiry shall be governed by the rules established by the present Code for a preliminary investigation, with the following exceptions:

(1) defense counsel shall not participate in the inquiry;

(2) a victim, civil plaintiff, civil defendant, and their representatives shall be notified of the completion of the inquiry and of referral of the case to a procurator, but the materials of the case shall not be presented to them for examination;

(3) the rules established by paragraph two of Article 127 of the present Code shall not apply to agencies of inquiry. When there is disagreement with a commission of a procurator, the agency of inquiry shall have the right to appeal from it to a higher procurator, without suspending execution of such commission.

In cases in which a preliminary investigation is not obligatory, the materials of the inquiry shall constitute the basis for consideration of the case in court.

Article 121. Period for Conducting Inquiry. In cases for which a preliminary investigation is obligatory, the inquiry must be completed not later than ten days from the day the case is initiated.

In cases in which a preliminary investigation is not obligatory, the inquiry must be completed not later than one month from the day the criminal case is initiated, including in this period the drawing up of a conclusion to indict or a decree to terminate or suspend the case.

The period of inquiry established by paragraph two of the present article may be prolonged by the procurator exercising immediate supervision over the inquiry, but not for more than one month.

In exceptional instances the period of the inquiry in a case may be prolonged in accordance with the rules established by Article 133 of the present Code.

Article 122. Detention of Persons Suspected of Committing Crime. An agency of inquiry shall have the right to detain a person suspected of committing a crime for which punishment may be assigned in the form of deprivation of freedom, only if one of the following grounds exists:

(1) when such person is caught committing the crime or immediately after committing it;

(2) when eyewitnesses, including victims, directly indicate the given person as the one who has committed the crime;

(3) when obvious traces of the crime are discovered on the suspect or on his clothing, where he is, or in his dwelling.

If there exist other data that give grounds to suspect that a person has committed a crime, he may be detained only if he has attempted to escape, or if he does not have a permanent place of residence, or if the identity of the suspect has not been established.

An agency of inquiry shall be obliged to draw up a record of any instance of detaining a person suspected of committing a crime, with indication of the grounds and reasons for detention, and shall be obliged to give notice thereof to a procurator within twenty-four hours. The procurator shall be obliged, within forty-eight hours from the moment of receiving notification of a detention, to sanction confinement under guard or to free the person detained.

Article 123. **Summons and Interrogation of Suspect.** Summons and interrogation of a suspect shall be conducted in conformity with the rules established by Articles 145–147 and 150–152 of the present Code.

Before interrogation, a suspect's rights as provided by Article 52 of the present Code must be explained to him. It must be declared to him what crime he is suspected of committing, and a note to such effect must be made in the record of his interrogation.

If a suspect has been detained or a measure of restraint in the form of confinement under guard has been selected with respect to him, his interrogation shall be conducted immediately. If, however, it does not appear possible to conduct the interrogation immediately, the suspect must be interrogated not later than twenty-four hours from the moment of detention.

Article 124. **Completing or Suspending Inquiry.** In cases in which a preliminary investigation is obligatory, the inquiry shall end with the drawing up of a decree to refer the case to an investigator.

In cases in which a preliminary investigation is not obligatory, the inquiry shall end with the drawing up of a conclusion to indict or a decree to terminate the case. If there exists one of the grounds provided for by Article 208 of the present Code, the agency of inquiry shall terminate the case with a reasoned decree, a copy of which shall be sent to a procurator within twenty-four hours. In remaining instances a conclusion to indict shall be drawn up which, with all the materials of inquiry, shall be presented to the procurator for approval.

If there exists one of the grounds provided for by Article 195 of the present Code, the agency of inquiry shall have the right to suspend the conduct of a case in which a preliminary investigation is not obligatory. A decree shall be rendered to suspend the inquiry and a copy shall be sent to the procurator within twenty-four hours.

Chapter Ten: General Conditions for Conducting the Preliminary Investigation

Article 125. Agencies of Preliminary Investigation. Preliminary investigation in criminal cases shall be conducted by investigators of the Procuracy, and also by investigators of agencies of internal affairs and investigators of agencies of state security.

[*Ved.* (1963), no. 15, item 288, Edict April 15, 1963; *Ved.* (1970), no. 22, item 442, Edict May 21, 1970.]

Article 126. Requirement of Preliminary Investigation and Investigative Jurisdiction. A preliminary investigation shall be obligatory in all cases, with the exception of crimes provided for by Articles 96 paragraph one, 97, 112, 130 paragraph one, 131, 154-2, 158, 162 paragraph one, 163, 166, 168, 169, 197, 198–201, 206 paragraphs one and two, 209 of the RSFSR Criminal Code, for which preliminary investigation shall be conducted only in such instances when it is deemed necessary by a court or a procurator.

The conduct of a preliminary investigation shall be obligatory in all cases of crimes committed by minors or by persons who by virtue of their physical or mental defects are not themselves able to exercise their right of defense.

In cases of crimes provided for by Articles 71, 74, 77, 77–1, 80–82, 85, 99–1, 101–107, 116–120, 124, 124–1, 126–129, 130 paragraphs two and three, 132–143, 151–152–1, 160, 161, 164, 170–180, 190–1, 190–2, 190–3, 191–193, 197–1, 202–205–1, 210, 214–216, 221–223, 227, 231–235, 238–258, 259 subsections "d" and "e," 260–269 of the RSFSR Criminal Code, and in all cases of crimes committed by minors, the preliminary investigation shall be conducted by investigators of agencies of the Procuracy, and in cases provided for by Articles 64–70, 72, 73, 75, 76, 78, 79, 83, 84, 259 subsections "a," "b," and "c" of the RSFSR Criminal Code, also by investigators of agencies of state security.

In cases of crimes provided for by Articles 86, 87, 89–91, 93, 94, 95, 96 paragraph two, 98, 99, 100, 108–111, 113–115–1, 121–123, 125, 144–150, 153–154–1, 155–157, 159, 162 paragraph two, 165, 167, 186–188, 194–196, 206 paragraph three, 207, 208, 211–213–1, 217–220, 224–226, 228–230 of the RSFSR Criminal Code, the preliminary investigation shall be conducted also by investigators of agencies of internal affairs.

In cases of crimes provided for by Articles 88, 92, and 93–1 of the RSFSR Criminal Code, the preliminary investigation shall be conducted by those agencies which initiated the criminal case. If in the course of investigation of such cases official crimes (Articles 170–175 of the RSFSR Criminal Code) are established which are connected with the crimes for which the case was initiated, then they shall be investigated by the agency which initiated the case.

In cases of crimes provided for by Articles 88–1, 88–2, 181–185, 189, 190 of the RSFSR Criminal Code, the preliminary investigation shall be conducted by that agency in whose investigative jurisdiction belongs the crime in connection with which the given case was initiated.

[*Ved.* (1965), no. 50, item 1243, Edict December 14, 1965; *Ved.* (1966), no. 35, item 946, Edict August 24, 1966; *Ved.* (1966), no. 38, item 1039, Edict

September 16, 1966; *Ved.* (1970), no. 14, item 256, Edict February 25, 1970; *Ved.* (1970), no. 22, item 422, Edict May 21, 1970; *Ved.* (1971), no. 42, item 881, Edict October 20, 1971.]

Article 127. Powers of Investigator. In a preliminary investigation all decisions concerning the course of the investigation and the performance of investigative actions shall be taken by the investigator independently, except in instances when the law provides for obtaining the sanction of a procurator, and the investigator shall bear full responsibility for the lawful and prompt execution of such decisions.

In the event that the investigator disagrees with instructions of the procurator concerning the prosecution of a person as the accused, the characterization of the crime and scope of the accusation, the referral of a case in order to bring the accused to trial, or the termination of a case, the investigator shall have the right to present the case to a higher procurator with a written statement of his objections. In such instance the procurator shall either vacate the instruction of the lower procurator or entrust the conduct of the investigation in that case to another investigator.

In cases in which a preliminary investigation is obligatory, the investigator shall have the right to commence the preliminary investigation at any moment, without waiting for agencies of inquiry to perform the actions provided for by Article 119 of the present Code.

In cases investigated by him the investigator shall have the right to give to agencies of inquiry commissions and instructions concerning the conduct of search and investigative actions and to require the cooperation of agencies of inquiry in conducting particular investigative actions. Such commissions and instructions of the investigator shall be given in writing and shall be binding upon the agencies of inquiry.

All institutions, enterprises, organizations, officials, and citizens shall be bound to execute decrees of the investigator rendered in conformity with law in criminal cases conducted by him.

The investigator shall have the right to detain and interrogate a person suspected of committing a crime in accordance with the procedure and on the grounds provided by Articles 122 and 123 of the present Code.

Article 127–1. Powers of Chief of Investigative Department. The chief of an investigative department shall exercise control over the timeliness of actions of the investigators concerning the uncovering and prevention of crimes, shall take measures for the most complete, thorough, and objective conduct of the preliminary investigation in criminal cases.

The chief of an investigative department shall have the right to check criminal cases; to give to an investigator instructions concerning the conduct of the preliminary investigation, the prosecution of a person as an accused, the classification of the crime and the scope of the accusation, the referral of a case, the conduct of individual investigative activities; to transfer a case from one investigator to another; to entrust the investigation of a case to several investigators;

and also to participate in the conduct of the preliminary investigation, in so doing enjoying the full powers of an investigator.

The instructions of the chief of an investigative department concerning criminal cases shall be given to the investigator in writing and shall be binding for execution.

Appealing to a procurator from instructions received shall not suspend their execution with the exception of instances provided for by paragraph two of Article 127 of the present Code.

Instructions of a procurator in criminal cases which are given in accordance with the rules established by the present Code shall be binding for the chief of the investigative department. Appealing from such instructions to a higher procurator shall not suspend their execution.

[*Ved.* (1965), no. 50, item 1243, Edict December 14, 1965.]

Article 128. Enlisting Public to Participate in Exposing Crimes. In conducting an investigation, the investigator must make wide use of the help of the public to expose crimes and to search for the persons who have committed them, as well as to bring to light and eliminate the causes and conditions facilitating the commission of crimes.

Article 129. Commencement of Preliminary Investigation. A preliminary investigation shall be conducted only after initiation of a criminal case and in accordance with the procedure established by the present Code.

An investigator shall be obliged immediately to begin an investigation in a case initiated by him or transferred to him. If a criminal case is initiated by an investigator and accepted by him, a single decree shall be drawn up to initiate and accept the criminal case. In the event that he accepts a case initiated by a procurator or court, the investigator shall render a separate decree to accept the case. The investigator shall send copies of such decrees to the procurator within twenty-four hours.

In the event of a complex case or one of great scope, the preliminary investigation may be entrusted to several investigators. This shall be indicated in the decree to initiate the case, or a separate decree shall be rendered. One of the investigators shall accept the case and shall direct the actions of the other investigators. In such event the whole staff of investigators shall be announced to the suspect, accused, victim, civil plaintiff, and civil defendant when the right to challenge is explained to them.

Article 130. Procedure for Ruling on Challenge of Investigator. Upon receiving a declaration of challenge, an investigator shall refer it within twenty-four hours to the procurator with his explanations. If there exist the grounds stated in Article 64 of the present Code, the investigator shall be obliged to address to the procurator a declaration to bar himself from conducting the preliminary investigation in the given case.

Within three days from the moment of receiving the declaration, the procurator shall be obliged to take a decision with respect thereto. The investigative actions shall not be suspended before the procurator takes a decision.

Article 131. Requirement to Grant Petitions of Significance for a Case. An investigator shall not have the right to deny the suspect, the accused, or his defense counsel, or the victim, civil plaintiff, or civil defendant, or their representatives, the opportunity to interrogate witnesses or conduct an expert examination or other investigative actions in the collection of evidence, if the circumstances which they petition to establish may be of significance for the case. The circumstances stated in Articles 20, 21, and 68 of the present Code, and all other circumstances whose disclosure may be of significance for the correct investigation of the case, shall constitute circumstances of significance for the case.

The results of the consideration of a petition shall be communicated to the person who has submitted the petition. If the investigator denies a petition, in whole or in part, he shall be obliged to render a decree indicating the reasons for denial.

Article 132. Place of Conducting Preliminary Investigation. A preliminary investigation shall be conducted in the district where the crime was committed. For the purpose of securing the most speedy, objective, and complete investigation, it may be conducted at the place where the crime was discovered or at the place where the suspect, accused, or majority of the witnesses are located.

If an investigator ascertains that a given case is not within his investigative jurisdiction, he shall be obliged to conduct all urgent investigative actions, after which he shall be obliged to transfer the case to a procurator for referral to the proper investigative jurisdiction. The question of investigative jurisdiction over the case shall be decided by the procurator of the place where the investigation has commenced.

In the event that it is necessary to conduct investigative or search actions in another district, the investigator shall have the right to conduct them personally or to entrust their conduct to the appropriate investigator or agency of inquiry, which shall be obliged to fulfill the commission within a period of not more than ten days.

Article 133. Period for Preliminary Investigation. A preliminary investigation in a criminal case must be completed within a period of not more than two months. Such period shall include the time from the day of initiating the case until the moment the case is referred to the procurator with a conclusion to indict or with a decree to transfer the case to a court for consideration of the question of applying compulsory measures of a medical character or until the termination or suspension of the case.

The period for preliminary investigation established by paragraph one of the present article may be prolonged by a procurator of an autonomous republic, territory, region, autonomous region, or national area, or by a military procurator of a military area or fleet, but not for more than two months. Further prolongation of the period for preliminary investigation may be carried out only in exceptional instances by the RSFSR Procurator, Chief Military Procurator, or USSR Procurator General.

When a court returns a case for supplementary investigation, or when a suspended or terminated case is reopened, the period for the supplementary investigation shall be established by the procurator who exercises supervision over the investigation, within limits of up to one month from the moment of acceptance of the case. Further prolongation of the period shall be carried out on the usual grounds.

In the event that it is necessary to prolong the period of the investigation, the investigator shall be obliged to draw up a reasoned decree to such effect and to present it to the appropriate procurator before the expiration of the period for preliminary investigation.

Article 133-1. Participation of Specialist. In instances provided for by the present Code, an investigator shall have the right to summon, for participation in the conduct of an investigative action, a specialist not interested in the outcome of the case. The request of an investigator that a specialist be summoned shall be binding on the manager of the institution, enterprise, or organization where the specialist works.

Before beginning an investigative action in which a specialist is participating, the investigator shall ascertain the identity and competence of the specialist and find out his attitude toward the accused and the victim. The investigator shall explain to the specialist his rights and duties and shall warn him of his responsibility for refusing or evading the discharge of his duties, and this shall be noted in the record of the particular investigative action and shall be certified by the signature of the specialist.

The specialist shall be bound to appear upon summons; to participate in the conduct of the investigative action, using his special knowledge and skills in assisting the investigator in discovering, securing, and removing evidence; to direct the attention of the investigator to circumstances connected with discovering, securing, and removing evidence; to give explanations for the basis of actions performed by him.

The specialist shall have the right to make statements for the record connected with discovering, securing, and removing evidence.

For refusing to discharge or evading the discharge of his duties, measures of social pressure may be applied to a specialist, or a monetary exaction in an amount not exceeding 10 rubles may be imposed. A monetary exaction shall be imposed by a court in the procedure provided for by Article 323 of the present Code.

[*Ved.* (1966), no. 36, item 1018, Edict August 31, 1966.]

Article 134. Participation of Interpreter. In instances provided for by Articles 17 and 57 of the present Code, an investigator shall engage an interpreter in interrogations and other investigative actions.

Before beginning an investigative action in which an interpreter is participating, the investigator shall explain to the interpreter his duties and shall warn him of his responsibility for making a translation known to be incorrect, and this shall be noted in the record of the particular investigative action and shall be certified by the signature of the interpreter.

Article 135. Participation of Witnesses of Investigative Actions. In a view, search, seizure, examination, or other investigative action, in instances provided for by the present Code, witnesses of investigative actions shall be summoned. At least two witnesses of investigative actions shall be summoned.

Any citizens not interested in a case may be summoned as witnesses of investigative actions.

A witness of investigative actions shall be obliged to certify the fact, contents, and results of an action at which he has been present. A witness of investigative actions shall have the right to make remarks in connection with an action. Remarks of a witness of investigative actions shall be subject to being entered in the record of the particular investigative action.

Before the commencement of an investigative action in which witnesses of investigative actions participate, the investigator shall explain to them their rights and duties.

Article 136. Declaration as Victim. When he has established that a crime has caused moral, physical, or property harm to a citizen, an investigator on his own initiative or on the basis of a declaration of such person shall render a decree declaring him a victim. The investigator shall notify the victim or his representative that he has been declared a victim. At the interrogation or appearance of the victim, the investigator shall explain to him the rights provided by Article 53 of the present Code, and in an instance when the person declared a victim is also a civil plaintiff, shall explain the rights provided by Article 54 of the present Code. A note to such effect shall be made in the record of the interrogation or in the decree declaring him a victim.

Article 137. Declaration as Civil Plaintiff. When an investigator sees from the file of a case that the crime committed has caused material loss to a citizen, institution, enterprise, or organization, he shall explain to him [it] or to his [its] representatives the right to bring a civil suit, and shall draw up a record to such effect, or he shall give written notification.

In the event that a civil suit is brought, the investigator shall be obliged to render a reasoned decree declaring or refusing to declare the claimant a civil plaintiff.

A decree to declare him a civil plaintiff shall be communicated to the civil plaintiff or his representative. In the event that a civil plaintiff or his representative appears, the rights provided by Article 54 of the present Code shall be explained to him, and a note to such effect shall be made on the decree and shall be certified by the signature of the civil plaintiff or his representative.

A decree refusing to declare him a civil plaintiff shall be announced to the applicant, and a receipt obtained.

Article 138. Prosecution as Civil Defendant. If an investigator establishes that parents, guardians, curators, or other persons or institutions, enterprises, or organizations must by law bear material responsibility for a loss caused by the criminal actions of the accused, he shall render a reasoned decree to prosecute the appropriate person or institution, enterprise, or organization as a civil defendant.

The decree shall be announced to the civil defendant or his [its] representative. In this connection the rights provided by Article 55 of the present Code shall be explained to him [it], and a note to such effect shall be made in the decree and certified by the signature of the civil defendant or his [its] representative.

Article 139. Impermissibility of Divulging Data of Preliminary Investigation. The data of a preliminary investigation may be given publicity only with the permission of an investigator or procurator and only to the extent to which he deems it possible.

When necessary the investigator shall warn the witnesses, victim, civil plaintiff, civil defendant, defense counsel, expert, specialist, interpreter, witnesses of investigative actions, and other persons present at investigative actions of the impermissibility of divulging the data of the preliminary investigation without his permission. A signed promise shall be obtained from the aforementioned persons with a warning of responsibility under Article 184 of the RSFSR Criminal Code.

[*Ved.* (1966), no. 36, item 1018, Edict August 31, 1966.]

Article 140. Measures to Eliminate Causes and Conditions Facilitating Commission of Crime. When an investigation establishes causes and conditions facilitating the commission of a crime, an investigator shall submit to the appropriate enterprises, institutions, and social organizations a proposal to take measures to eliminate such causes and conditions. The appropriate enterprises, institutions, and social organizations shall be obliged, within a period of not more than a month, to consider the proposal of the investigator, to take the necessary measures, and to notify the investigator thereof.

Article 141. Record of Investigative Action. A record of an investigative action shall be drawn up by an investigator in the course of the investigative action or immediately after its completion.

The record shall indicate the place and date of the investigative action, the time of its commencement and completion, the office and last name of the person drawing up the record, the surname, first name, and patronymic, and when necessary the address, of each person participating in the investigative action, the content of the investigative action, and the material circumstances of the case disclosed in the investigative action. If in the conduct of the investigative action photographing, filming, or sound-recording has been employed, or molds and impressions of tracks have been prepared, then there must also be indicated in the record the technical media employed in the conduct of the particular investigative action, the conditions and procedure for their utilization, the objects to which such media were employed, and the results obtained. It must also be noted in the record that before technical media were employed the persons participating in the investigative action were informed thereof.

The record shall be read to all persons participating in the investigative action, and the right to make remarks for the record shall be explained to them.

The record shall be signed by the investigator, the person interrogated, interpreter, specialist, witnesses of investigative actions, and other persons, if they participate in the investigative action.

Photographic negatives and photographs, films, slides, phono-records of the interrogation, plans, diagrams, molds, and impressions of tracks made during the conduct of investigative actions shall be appended to the record.

[*Ved.* (1966), no. 36, item 1018, Edict August 31, 1966.]

Article 141-1. Employment of Sound-Recording During Interrogation. In accordance with the decision of an investigator, sound-recording may be employed during the interrogation of an accused, suspect, witness, or victim. A sound-recording may be employed also upon the request of an accused, suspect, witness, or victim.

The investigator shall take the decision concerning a sound-recording and shall inform the interrogated person thereof prior to the beginning of the interrogation.

The sound-recording must reflect the information stated in paragraph two of Article 141 of the present Code, and the entire course of the interrogation. The sound-recording of part of an interrogation, and also the repetition of testimony especially for sound-recording, shall not be permitted.

Upon the completion of the interrogation the sound-recording shall be replayed completely for the person interrogated. Additions to the sound-recording made by the person interrogated shall also be entered on the phono-record. The sound-recording shall be concluded with the statement of the person interrogated, certifying that it is correct.

Testimony received in the course of an interrogation with the employment of sound-recording shall be entered in the record in conformity with the rules of the present Code. The record of the interrogation must also contain a note concerning the employment of sound-recording and the informing of the interrogated person thereof; information concerning the technical media and the conditions of sound-recording; statements of the interrogated person concerning the employment of sound-recording; certification by the interrogated person and the investigator of the correctness of the record and the sound-recording. The phono-record shall be kept with the file of the case and upon completion of the preliminary investigation shall be sealed up.

In the event that a sound-recording of testimony is replayed in the conduct of another investigative action, the investigator shall be bound to make a note to such effect in the record of the particular investigative action.

[*Ved.* (1966), no. 36, item 1018, Edict August 31, 1966.]

Article 142. Certification of Fact of Refusal to Sign or Inability to Sign Record of Investigative Action. If the accused, suspect, witness, or other person refuses to sign the record of an investigative action, a note to such effect shall be made in the record, attested by the signature of the person conducting the investigative action.

An opportunity to give an explanation of the reasons for refusal must be granted to the person who has refused to sign the record, and this shall be entered in the record.

If by reason of physical defects one of the persons indicated in paragraph one of the present article lacks the ability to sign the record of an investigative action, a note to such effect shall be made in the record and attested by the signatures of the investigator and of the witnesses of investigative actions.

If for the same reasons the accused, suspect, witness, or victim is unable to sign the record of an interrogation, the investigator shall call in a third person, who with the consent of the person interrogated shall certify by his signature the correctness of the recording of his testimony. The investigator who has conducted the interrogation shall also sign this record.

Chapter Eleven: Presentation of the Accusation and Interrogation of the Accused

Article 143. Prosecution as the Accused. If there exists sufficient evidence to provide a basis for presenting an accusation of the commission of a crime, an investigator shall render a reasoned decree to prosecute the person as the accused.

Article 144. Decree to Prosecute as the Accused. A decree to prosecute as the accused must indicate the time and place it is drawn up; by whom the decree is drawn up; the surname, first name, and patronymic of the person prosecuted as the accused; the crime which the given person is accused of committing, with an indication of the time, place, and other circumstances of the commission of the crime, insofar as they are established by materials of the case; the criminal law which provides for the given crime.

If the accused is charged with committing several crimes which fall under the operation of different articles of the criminal law, the decree to prosecute as the accused must indicate which precise actions are imputed to the accused under each of the articles of the criminal law.

Article 145. Procedure for Summoning Accused. An accused, if at liberty, shall be summoned before an investigator by means of a summons which shall be handed to the accused with an indication of the time at which it has been handed to him, and a receipt shall be obtained from him. The summons may also be transmitted by means of a written telephone message or telegram.

The summons must indicate who has been summoned as the accused, where and before whom, the day and hour of appearance, as well as the consequences of nonappearance.

In the event that the accused is temporarily absent, the summons shall be handed to any one of the adult members of the family living with him, to the management of his apartment house or the administration at his place of work, or to the executive committee of the rural or settlement soviet of working people's deputies, for transmission to the accused, and a receipt shall be obtained.

An accused who is under guard shall be summoned through the administration of the place of confinement.

Article 146. Obligation of Accused to Appear When Summoned by Investigator. An accused shall be obliged to appear within the appointed time. The following shall be deemed valid reasons for nonappearance of the accused when summoned by an investigator:

1. Illness making it impossible for the accused to appear;
2. Late receipt of the summons by the accused;
3. Other circumstances making it impossible for the accused to appear within the appointed time.

Article 147. Compulsory Appearance of Accused. In the event an accused fails to appear without valid reason, he may be subjected to compulsory appearance.

The accused may be compelled to appear without having been previously summoned only in instances when he hides from investigation or does not have a particular place of residence.

Compulsion of the accused to appear may not be carried out at night except in instances not permitting delay.

An investigator shall draw up a decree of compulsory appearance, which shall be announced to the accused.

Compulsion to appear shall be carried out by the police upon the commission of the investigator.

Article 148. Presentation of Accusation. The presentation of an accusation must follow within forty-eight hours from the moment the decree to prosecute as the accused is rendered, or in the event of compulsory appearance, on the day of the compulsory appearance.

The accusation may be presented after the expiration of forty-eight hours if the whereabouts of the accused are not known or if he has not appeared when summoned by an investigator.

After ascertaining the identity of the accused, the investigator shall announce to him the decree to prosecute him as the accused, and shall explain the nature of the accusation. The performance of such actions shall be certified by the signature of the accused on the decree to prosecute him as the accused and by the signature of the investigator, with an indication of the time of presentation of the accusation.

In the event that the accused refuses to sign, the investigator shall certify on the decree to present the accusation that the text of the decree has been announced to the accused.

Article 149. Explanation to Accused of His Rights in Preliminary Investigation. When presenting an accusation, an investigator shall be obliged to explain to an accused his rights as provided by Article 46 of the present Code, and a note to such effect shall be made on the decree to prosecute him as the accused and shall be certified by the signature of the accused.

Article 150. Procedure for Interrogation of Accused. An investigator shall be obliged to interrogate an accused immediately after presenting the accusation to him.

Interrogation of the accused may not take place at night, except in instances not permitting delay.

The accused shall be interrogated at the place where the preliminary investigation is conducted. The investigator shall have the right, if he deems it necessary, to conduct the interrogation at the place where the accused is.

Accused persons summoned in the same case shall be interrogated separately, and the investigator shall take measures to prevent them from communicating with one another.

At the beginning of the interrogation the investigator must ask the accused whether he acknowledges himself to be guilty of the accusation presented to him, after which he shall propose that the accused give testimony concerning the substance of the accusation. The investigator shall listen to the testimony of the accused, and then if necessary shall put questions to the accused.

Article 151. Record of Interrogation of Accused. An investigator shall draw up a record of each interrogation of an accused in conformity with the requirements of Articles 141 and 142 of the present Code. The record of the interrogation shall indicate the data concerning the identity of the accused, including surname, first name, patronymic, date and place of birth, citizenship, nationality, education, family position, place of work, kind of occupation or official position, domicile, record of previous convictions, as well as other information which may appear necessary according to the circumstances of the case.

The testimony of the accused shall be entered in the record in the first person and, as far as possible, word for word; the questions put to the accused and his answers shall be recorded when necessary.

Upon completion of the interrogation the record shall be presented to the accused for him to read or, at his request, shall be read to him by the investigator. The accused shall have the right to demand additions to the record and the insertion of corrections therein. Such additions and corrections shall be required to be entered in the record.

Upon reading the record the accused shall certify with his signature the correctness of the recording of his testimony. A notation shall be made in the record before the signature of the accused indicating whether the accused has read the record personally or whether it has been read to him by the investigator.

If the record is written on several pages, the accused shall sign each page separately. All additions and corrections in the record must be certified by the signature of the accused and of the investigator.

If interrogation of the accused is conducted with the participation of an interpreter, the record of the interrogation must include an indication that the interpreter's duties have been explained to him and that he has been warned concerning responsibility for making a translation known to be incorrect, and this shall be certified by the signature of the interpreter. The record shall also note the explanation to the accused of his rights to challenge the interpreter and the statements of the accused made in this connection.

The interpreter shall sign each page of the record and the record as a whole.

The accused shall confirm with his signature at the end of the record that the translation of the record made to him orally corresponds to the testimony given by him. If the record of the interrogation has been translated in writing into another language, the translation as a whole and each separate page thereof must be signed by the interpreter and the accused.

Article 152. **Recording of Testimony by Accused in Own Hand.** After an accused gives testimony, he must be given an opportunity, in the event that he so requests, to write his testimony in his own hand, and a note to such effect shall be made in the record of the interrogation. The testimony shall be signed by the accused and the investigator.

After becoming acquainted with the written testimony of the accused, the investigator may put additional questions to him. Such questions, and the answers thereto, shall be written down in the record. The correctness of the recording of the questions and answers shall be certified by the signatures of the accused and of the investigator.

Article 153. **Removal From Office.** If in prosecuting an official as the accused it is necessary to remove him from his office, an investigator shall render a reasoned decree to such effect, which shall be subject to approval by a procurator. The decree shall be referred for execution at the place of work of the accused.

Removal from office shall be canceled by decree of the investigator when there is no further necessity for the application of such measure.

Article 154. **Changes in and Additions to Accusation.** If during a preliminary investigation grounds emerge for changing an accusation or adding thereto, an investigator shall be obliged to present a new accusation to the accused, in conformity with the requirements of Articles 143, 144, and 148 of the present Code, and shall interrogate him concerning the new accusation.

If in the course of the preliminary investigation any part of the accusation has not been confirmed, the investigator shall by his own decree terminate that part of the case, and shall notify the accused thereof.

Chapter Twelve: Interrogation of a Witness and of a Victim

Article 155. **Procedure for Summoning Witness.** A witness shall be summoned before an investigator by means of a writ which shall be handed to the witness and a receipt obtained, and in the event that he is temporarily absent it shall be handed to, and a receipt obtained from, any one of the adult members of his family or the management of his apartment house, the administration at his place of work, or the executive committee of his rural or settlement soviet of working people's deputies. The writ must indicate who shall be summoned as a witness, where and before whom, the day and hour of appearance, as well as the consequences of nonappearance. A witness may also be summoned by means of a written telephone message or telegram.

Article 156. Procedure for Summoning Witness Who Has Not Attained Age of 16 Years. Summoning as a witness a person who has not attained the age of 16 years shall be conducted through his parents or other legal representatives. No other procedure shall be permitted except when the circumstances of the case so require.

Article 157. Place of Interrogating Witness. A witness shall be interrogated at the place of conducting the investigation. An investigator shall have the right, if he deems it necessary, to conduct the interrogation where the witness is.

Article 158. Procedure for Interrogating Witness. Witnesses summoned in the same case shall be interrogated separately and in the absence of other witnesses. In this connection an investigator shall take measures to prevent witnesses in the same case from communicating with one another.

Before the interrogation the investigator shall ascertain the identity of the witness and shall explain to him his duties and warn him of responsibility for refusing to give or evading giving testimony or for giving testimony known to be false, and a note to such effect shall be made in the record, which shall be certified by the signature of the witness.

The investigator shall explain to witnesses who have not attained the age of 16 years the necessity for truthfully telling everything in the case known to them, but they shall not be warned of responsibility for refusing to give or evading giving testimony or for giving testimony known to be false.

At the beginning of the interrogation the investigator shall establish the relationship of the witness to the accused and to the victim and shall ascertain other necessary information about the personality of the person interrogated.

Interrogation concerning the substance of the case shall commence with a proposal to the witness to tell everything known to him about the circumstances in connection with which he has been summoned for interrogation; after the witness's account the investigator may put questions to him. Leading questions shall not be permitted.

Article 159. Interrogation of Minor Witness. In the interrogation of witnesses up to 14 years of age and also, at the discretion of an investigator, in the interrogation of witnesses from 14 to 16 years of age, a teacher shall be summoned. When necessary the legal representatives of the minor or his near relatives shall also be summoned.

Before the commencement of the interrogation the rights and duties of such persons shall be explained to them, and this shall be noted in the record of the interrogation.

The persons indicated shall be present at the interrogation and may, with the permission of the investigator, put questions to the witness. The investigator shall have the right to exclude a question which has been put; the excluded question must, however, be entered in the record. Upon completion of the interrogation those present shall confirm with their signatures the correctness of the recording of the testimony.

Article 160. Record of Interrogation of Witness. A record shall be drawn up concerning an interrogation of a witness, in conformity with the requirements of Articles 141, 142, and 159 of the present Code.

The testimony of the witness shall be written down in the first person and, as far as possible, word for word. The questions put to the witness, and his answers, shall be written down.

Upon completion of the interrogation the record shall be presented to the witness for him to read or, at the request of the witness, shall be read to him by the investigator. The witness shall have the right to demand additions to the record and the insertion of corrections in it. It shall be obligatory that such additions and corrections be entered in the record. Upon reading the record the witness shall certify that the testimony is correctly recorded, and a note to such effect shall be made in the record before the signature of the witness. A notation shall also be made in the record before the signature of the witness indicating whether the witness has read the record personally or whether it has been read to him by the investigator. If the record is written on several pages, the witness shall sign each page separately.

After the witness gives testimony, he must be given an opportunity, in the event that he so requests, to write his testimony in his own hand, and a note to such effect shall be made in the record of the interrogation. The testimony shall be signed by the witness and the investigator.

In the event that the interrogation has taken place with the participation of an interpreter, the record of the interrogation shall be drawn up in conformity with the rules established by Article 151 of the present Code.

Article 161. Summoning and Interrogating Victim. The rules of Articles 155–160 of the present Code shall apply to the summoning of a victim, his interrogation, and the drawing up of a record of his interrogation.

Chapter Thirteen: Confrontation and Presentation for Identification

Article 162. Confrontation. An investigator shall have the right to carry out a confrontation between two persons previously interrogated in whose testimony there are substantial contradictions.

Article 163. Procedure for Confrontation. If a confrontation is carried out with the participation of a witness and a victim, they shall be warned before the interrogation commences of responsibility for refusing to give or evading giving testimony or for giving testimony known to be false, and this shall be noted in the record.

In commencing an interrogation at a confrontation, the investigator shall ask the persons between whom the confrontation is being carried out whether they know each other and what relation they have to each other. Then it shall be proposed to the said persons in turn that they give testimony about those circumstances for the elucidation of which the confrontation is being carried out. After the giving of testimony the investigator may put questions to each of the persons interrogated. The persons between whom the confrontation is carried out may, with the permission of the investigator, put questions to each other, and a notation to such effect shall be made in the record.

The public disclosure of testimony contained in records of previous interrogations, or reproduced in a sound-recording of such testimony, by participants in a confrontation shall be permitted only after their testimony at the confrontation is given and is written down in the record.

Testimony of the persons interrogated shall be written down in the record of a confrontation in the order in which it is given. Each participant in the confrontation shall sign his testimony and each page separately.

[*Ved.* (1966), no. 36, item 1018, Edict August 31, 1966.]

Article 164. Presentation for Identification. When necessary an investigator may present a person or article to a witness, victim, suspect, or accused for identification.

Those making the identification shall be interrogated beforehand concerning the circumstances under which they have observed the particular person or article and concerning the marks or peculiarities by which they are able to make the identification.

Article 165. Procedure for Presentation for Identification. A person who is being identified shall be presented to a person making the identification together with other persons who as closely as possible resemble the person being identified. The total number of persons presented for identification must be not fewer than three. This rule shall not extend to the identification of a corpse.

Before the presentation begins it shall be proposed to the person being identified to take any place he chooses among the persons being presented, and this shall be noted in the record.

If it is impossible to present a person, the identification may be conducted by presenting his photograph together with at least three other photographs.

An article shall be presented in a group of similar articles.

If the person making the identification is a witness or victim, he shall be warned before the identification of responsibility for refusing to give or evading giving testimony or for giving testimony known to be false, and this shall be noted in the record.

It shall be proposed to the person making the identification to indicate the person or article concerning which he has given testimony. Leading questions shall not be permitted.

If the person making the identification has indicated one of the persons or articles presented to him, it shall be proposed to him to explain by what marks or peculiarities he has recognized the given person or article.

Presentation for identification shall be carried out in the presence of witnesses of investigative actions.

Article 166. Record of Presentation for Identification. A record shall be drawn up concerning a presentation for identification in conformity with the requirements of Articles 141 and 142 of the present Code. The record shall indicate information concerning the identity of the person making the identification and concerning the persons and objects presented for identification, and the testimony of the person making the identification shall, as far as possible, be set forth word for word.

Chapter Fourteen: Seizure, Search, and Impounding of Property

Article 167. Grounds for Conducting Seizure. In the event that it is necessary to remove certain articles or documents of significance for a case, and if it is known precisely where they are and who has them, an investigator shall conduct a seizure.

The seizure of documents containing information which constitutes a state secret shall be conducted only with the sanction of a procurator and in accordance with a procedure agreed upon with the director of the respective institution.

Seizure shall be conducted in accordance with a reasoned decree of the investigator.

Article 168. Grounds for Conducting Search. If an investigator has sufficient grounds to suppose that the instruments of a crime, or articles or valuables criminally acquired, or other articles or documents which may be of significance for the case, are on some premises or in any other place or are in someone's possession, he shall conduct a search to find and remove them.

A search may also be conducted for finding wanted persons, as well as corpses.

A search shall be conducted in accordance with a reasoned decree of the investigator and only with the sanction of a procurator. In instances not permitting delay a search may be conducted without the sanction of a procurator, but the procurator must be informed subsequently within one day of the search.

Article 169. Persons Present During Seizure and Search. The presence of witnesses of investigative actions shall be obligatory during the conduct of a seizure or search.

The presence of the person at whose dwelling place a search or seizure is conducted, or of adult members of his family, must be secured during the search or seizure. In the event that it is impossible for them to be present, representatives of the management of the apartment house or of the executive committee of the rural or settlement soviet of working people's deputies shall be invited.

Seizures or searches on premises occupied by institutions, enterprises, or organizations shall be conducted in the presence of a representative of the given institution, enterprise, or organization.

Persons at whose dwelling place a search or seizure is conducted, witnesses of investigative actions, and representatives must be informed of their right to be present at all the actions of the investigator and to make statements for entry in the record that pertain to such actions.

Article 170. Procedure for Conducting Seizure and Search. It shall not be permitted to conduct seizure or search at night, except in instances not permitting delay. In undertaking a seizure or search, an investigator shall be obliged to present a decree to such effect. When necessary, the investigator shall have the right to summon an appropriate specialist to participate in the conduct of a seizure or search.

When conducting a seizure after presentation of a decree, the investigator shall propose that the articles or documents subject to removal be given up, and in the event of a refusal to do so shall conduct a compulsory seizure.

When conducting a search after presentation of a decree, the investigator shall propose that the instruments of the crime, articles and valuables criminally acquired, or other articles or documents which might be of significance for the case, be given up. If they are given up voluntarily and there are no grounds to fear the concealment of the articles and documents being sought, the investigator shall have the right to limit himself to removing what has been given up without conducting further explorations.

When conducting search and seizure the investigator shall have the right to open locked premises and storehouses if the owner refuses to open them voluntarily, but the investigator must avoid unnecessary damage to locks, doors, and other articles.

The investigator shall be obliged to take measures to prevent the public disclosure of circumstances of the intimate life of the person occupying the premises, or of other persons, which are revealed during search or seizure.

The investigator shall have the right to prohibit persons in the premises or place where the search is being conducted, as well as persons arriving at the premises or place, from leaving it or from communicating with one another or with any other persons until the completion of the search.

[*Ved.* (1966), no. 36, item 1018, Edict August 31, 1966.]

Article 171. Removal of Articles and Documents During Seizure and Search. When conducting seizure and search an investigator must be strictly limited to removing articles and documents which may have a relation to the case. Articles and documents prohibited from circulation shall be subject to removal regardless of their relation to the case.

All the removed articles and documents shall be presented to the witnesses of investigative actions and to other persons present and when necessary shall be packed and sealed at the place of the seizure or search.

Article 172. Personal Search. Personal search shall be conducted in conformity with the rules of Articles 167–171 of the present Code.

Personal search may be conducted without the rendition of a separate decree to such effect and without the sanction of a procurator:

1. during detention or confinement under guard;

2. if there exist sufficient grounds to suppose that a person on the premises or in any other place where a seizure or search is being conducted is concealing on his person articles or documents which may be of significance for the case.

Personal search may be conducted only by a person of the same sex as the one being searched and in the presence of witnesses of investigative actions of the same sex as the one being searched.

Article 173. Conducting Search and Seizure on Premises of Diplomatic Missions. Seizure and search may be conducted on premises occupied by diplomatic missions, or on premises in which members of diplomatic missions and their families live, only upon the request or with the consent of the diplomatic representative. The consent of the diplomatic representative to seizure or search shall be obtained through the Ministry of Foreign Affairs.

The presence of a procurator and of a representative of the Ministry of Foreign Affairs shall be obligatory in the conduct of a seizure or search on the said premises.

Article 174. Seizure of Postal and Telegraphic Correspondence. The impounding of correspondence and its seizure at postal and telegraph offices may be carried out only with the sanction of a procurator or in accordance with a ruling or decree of a court.

When it is necessary to impound correspondence and to conduct a view and seizure of it, an investigator shall render a reasoned decree to such effect. After approval of the said decree by a procurator, the investigator shall refer the decree to the proper postal and telegraph office, shall propose that it hold the correspondence, and shall notify it of the time of his arrival to view and seize the correspondence. The view and seizure shall be conducted in the presence of witnesses of investigative actions from among the employees of the postal and telegraph office. When necessary the investigator shall have the right to summon a specialist to participate in the conduct of a seizure of postal and telegraphic correspondence.

An impounding of correspondence shall be canceled by decree of the investigator when there is no further necessity for the application of such measure.

[*Ved.* (1966), no. 36, item 1018, Edict August 31, 1966.]

Article 175. Impounding of Property. For the purpose of securing a civil suit or possible confiscation of property, an investigator shall be obliged to impound property of an accused, a suspect, or persons legally bearing material responsibility for their actions, or of other persons in possession of property criminally acquired.

The impounding of property may be carried out simultaneously with a seizure or search, or independently.

The investigator shall draw up a reasoned decree to impound property. The property to be impounded shall be described in conformity with the rules of Articles 169 and 170 of the present Code. All the property described must be presented to the witnesses of investigative actions and other persons present.

Articles necessary for the accused himself or for persons dependent on him may not be impounded. The list of such articles is established by legislation of the RSFSR.

Impounded property shall be transferred for safekeeping, at the discretion of the investigator, to a representative of the executive committee of the rural or settlement soviet of working people's deputies, or to a representative of the management of the apartment house, or to the owner of such property or a relative of his, or to any other person, and responsibility for the safekeeping of the property must be explained to such person and his signature to such effect must be obtained. When necessary the property which has been impounded may be removed.

When deposits of money are impounded the conduct of any operations in connection with them shall be terminated.

The impounding of property shall be canceled by decree of the investigator if there is no further necessity for the application of such measure.

Article 176. **Record of Seizure, Search, Impounding of Property.** A record of a seizure, search, or impounding of property shall be drawn up in conformity with the requirements of Articles 141 and 142 of the present Code. If in addition to the records a special inventory is drawn up of articles and documents removed or transferred for special safekeeping, the inventory shall be appended to the record. The record of the seizure, search, or impounding of property must contain an indication that the rights provided by Article 169 of the present Code were explained to the persons present, and the statements made by them.

With respect to articles and documents subject to removal, it must be indicated whether they have been given up voluntarily or removed compulsorily, and in exactly what place and under what circumstances they have been discovered. All the articles and documents removed as well as all the property described must be enumerated in the record or the inventory appended thereto, with a precise indication of quantity, size, weight, or individual indicia and as far as possible their value.

If in the seizure, search, or impounding of property there have been attempts to destroy or hide articles and documents, or instances of breach of order on the part of the persons being searched or other persons, the record must contain an indication thereof and of the measures taken by the investigator.

[*Ved.* (1970), no. 22, item 442, Edict May 21, 1970.]

Article 177. **Obligation to Hand Over Copy of Record.** A copy of the record shall be handed to, and a receipt obtained from, the person at whose dwelling place the seizure, search, or impounding of property has been conducted, or adult members of the family, or in their absence, a representative of the executive committee of the rural or settlement soviet of working people's deputies or the management of the apartment house.

If the seizure, search, or impounding of property has been conducted on premises belonging to an institution, enterprise, or organization, a copy of the record shall be handed to the appropriate official and a receipt obtained from him.

Chapter Fifteen: View and Examination

Article 178. **Grounds for Conduct of View.** An investigator shall conduct a view of the place of an incident, the locality, premises, articles, and documents, for the purpose of discovering traces of the crime and other real evidence, of elucidating the circumstances of the incident, or of discovering other circumstances of significance for the case.

In instances not permitting delay, a view of the place of an incident may be conducted before the initiation of a criminal case. In such instances, if there exist grounds therefor, a criminal case shall be initiated promptly after the conducting of the view of the place of the incident.

[*Ved.* (1963), no. 36, item 661, Edict September 10, 1963.]

Article 179. Procedure for Conduct of View. A view shall be conducted in the presence of witnesses of investigative actions.

An investigator shall have the right to enlist the accused, suspect, victim, or witness to participate in the conduct of a view.

When necessary, the investigator may engage an appropriate specialist to participate in the conduct of a view.

When necessary the investigator shall, during a view, make measurements, take photographs, make films, draw up plans and diagrams, and prepare molds and impressions of tracks.

A view of the articles and documents discovered during seizure, search, or view of the place of the incident, or of the locality, or premises shall be carried out by the investigator at the place of conducting the particular investigative action. In such event the results of the view shall be written down in the record of the said investigative action. If a view of the articles or documents will require a long time, or on other grounds, the investigator shall conduct the view at the place of conducting the investigation. When necessary the removed articles shall be packed and sealed.

A view of postal and telegraphic correspondence shall be conducted in conformity with the rules of Article 174 of the present Code.

[*Ved.* (1966), no. 36, item 1018, Edict August 31, 1966.]

Article 180. View of Corpse. An investigator shall view the exterior of a corpse at the place where it is discovered in the presence of witnesses of investigative actions and with the participation of a physician who is a specialist in the field of forensic medicine, or when it is impossible for him to participate, with the participation of any other physician. If it is necessary for viewing the corpse, another specialist may also be engaged.

If it is necessary to exhume a corpse from the place of burial, the investigator shall render a decree to such effect. Exhumation of a corpse shall take place in the presence of the investigator, the witnesses of investigative actions, and a physician who is a specialist in the field of forensic medicine.

[*Ved.* (1966), no. 36, item 1018, Edict August 31, 1966.]

Article 181. Examination. An investigator shall have the right to conduct an examination of an accused, suspect, witness, or victim to establish traces of a crime on his body or the presence thereon of particular marks, if a forensic medical expert examination is not required in this connection.

The investigator shall draw up a decree to conduct an examination. The decree to conduct an examination shall be binding upon the person with respect to whom it is rendered.

The examination shall be conducted in the presence of witnesses of investigative actions and when necessary with the participation of a physician.

The examination shall be conducted in the presence of witnesses of investigative actions of the same sex as the person being examined in those instances when such investigative action is accompanied by the disrobing of the person being examined.

The investigator shall not be present at the examination of a person of the opposite sex if the examination is accompanied by the disrobing of such person. In such event the examination shall be conducted by a physician in the presence of witnesses of investigative actions.

Actions lowering the dignity or dangerous to the health of a person being examined shall not be permitted during an examination.

Article 182. Record of View and Examination. A record shall be drawn up by an investigator concerning the conduct of a view or examination, in conformity with the requirements of Articles 141 and 142 of the present Code.

The record shall describe all the actions of the investigator and everything discovered during the view or examination in the sequence in which the view has been conducted and in the condition in which the discovered items have been observed at the time of the view or examination. The record shall also enumerate and describe everything removed in the view or examination.

Article 183. Investigative Experiment. For the purpose of verifying and precisely specifying data of significance for a case, an investigator shall have the right to conduct an investigative experiment by reproducing actions, a setting, or any other circumstances of a particular event and by performing necessary experimental actions. In this connection the investigator shall, when necessary, make measurements, take photographs, make films, and draw up plans and diagrams.

An investigative experiment shall be permitted provided that it does not lower the dignity and honor of the persons participating therein and their associates and does not create a danger to their health.

Witnesses of investigative actions must be present during an investigative experiment. When necessary a suspect, accused, victim, or witness may participate in an investigative experiment. The investigator shall also have the right to engage a specialist to participate in an investigative experiment.

A record shall be drawn up concerning the investigative experiment, in conformity with the requirements of Articles 141 and 142 of the present Code. The record shall set forth in detail the conditions, course, and results of the investigative experiment.

[*Ved.* (1966), no. 36, item 1018, Edict August 31, 1966.]

Chapter Sixteen: Conducting an Expert Examination

Article 184. Procedure for Assignment of Expert Examination. If an investigator deems an expert examination to be necessary, he shall draw up a decree to such effect, which shall indicate the grounds for assigning an expert examination, the surname of the expert or name of the institution at which the expert examination must be conducted, the questions placed before the expert, and the materials made available to the expert.

Before appointing an expert the investigator shall ascertain the necessary data about his specialty and competence.

The investigator shall be obliged to acquaint the accused with the decree assigning expert examination and to explain his rights as established by Article 185 of the present Code. A record thereof shall be drawn up, and signed by the investigator and the accused.

The decree to assign a forensic psychiatric expert examination and the opinion of the experts shall not be announced to the accused if his mental state makes this impossible.

Article 185. Rights of Accused During Assignment and Conduct of Expert Examination. During the assignment and conduct of an expert examination an accused shall have the right to:

(1) challenge the expert;

(2) request the assignment of an expert from among persons indicated by him;

(3) present additional questions in order to obtain the opinion of an expert concerning them;

(4) be present, with the permission of the investigator, at the expert examination and give explanations to the expert;

(5) become acquainted with the opinion of the expert.

In the event that he grants a petition of the accused, the investigator shall accordingly change or add to his decree to assign an expert examination.

In the event that he denies a petition, the investigator shall render a decree which shall be announced to the accused, and a receipt obtained from him.

Article 186. Obtaining Samples for Comparative Analysis. An investigator shall have the right to obtain from a suspect or accused samples of his handwriting or other samples necessary for comparative analysis, and he shall draw up a decree to such effect.

The investigator shall also have the right to obtain for comparative analysis samples of handwriting or any other samples from a witness or victim, but only when it is necessary to verify whether traces were left by the said persons at the place of the incident or on real evidence.

When necessary, the removal of samples for comparative analysis shall be carried out with the participation of a specialist.

A record shall be drawn up concerning the removal of samples for comparative analysis, in conformity with the requirements of Articles 141 and 142 of the present Code.

[*Ved.* (1966), no. 36, item 1018, Edict August 31, 1966.]

Article 187. Conduct of Expert Examination at Expert Institution. When entrusting an expert examination to an expert of an appropriate expert institution, an investigator shall send to such institution his decree and the materials necessary for conducting the expert examination.

Upon receiving the investigator's decree the director of the expert institution shall entrust the expert examination to one or several members of the given institution. Upon the commission of the investigator, the director of the expert institution shall explain to the members to whom the expert examination is entrusted the rights and duties of an expert as provided by Article 82 of the present Code and shall warn them of responsibility under Articles 181 and 182 of the RSFSR Criminal Code for refusing to give or evading giving an opinion or for giving an opinion known to be false, and a receipt shall be obtained from them which shall be sent to the investigator together with the expert's opinion.

Article 188. Commitment of Accused or Suspect to Medical Institution. If the necessity for constant observation arises during a forensic medical or forensic psychiatric expert examination, an investigator shall commit an accused or suspect to an appropriate medical institution, and the decree to assign the expert examination shall so indicate.

Commitment to a medico-psychiatric institution of an accused or suspect who is not being kept under guard shall be carried out with the sanction of the procurator.

Time spent in a psychiatric medical institution shall be counted in the period of confinement under guard.

If a suspect is referred to a forensic medical institution in connection with an expert examination, he shall be granted the rights established by Articles 184 and 185 of the present Code.

Article 189. Conduct of Expert Examination Outside Expert Institution. If an expert examination is conducted outside an expert institution, an investigator shall, after rendering the decree to assign an expert examination, summon the person to whom the expert examination has been entrusted, ascertain his identity, specialty, and competency, establish the relation of the expert to the accused, suspect, and victim, and shall also verify whether there are grounds for challenging the expert.

The investigator shall hand the expert the decree to assign an expert examination, shall explain to the expert the rights and duties provided by Article 82 of the present Code, and shall warn him of responsibility for refusing to give or evading giving an opinion or for giving an opinion known to be false. The investigator shall make a note that he has performed such actions in the decree to assign an expert examination, and such note shall be certified by the signature of the expert.

If the expert makes any declarations or submits petitions in the case, the investigator shall be obliged to draw up a record in conformity with the requirements of Articles 141 and 142 of the present Code.

Article 190. Presence of Investigator at Expert Examination. An investigator shall have the right to be present at an expert examination.

Article 191. Contents of Expert's Opinion. After conducting the necessary analyses an expert shall draw up an opinion, which must indicate when, where, by whom (surname, first name, and patronymic, education, specialty, academic degree and rank, office), on what basis the expert examination has been conducted, who has been present during the expert examination, what materials the expert has used, what analyses he has made, what questions have been presented to the expert, and his reasoned answers. If during an expert examination the expert establishes circumstances of significance for the case, concerning which questions have not been presented to him, he shall have the right to indicate them in his opinion.

The opinion shall be given in writing and shall be signed by the expert.

Article 192. Interrogation of Expert. An investigator shall have the right to interrogate an expert for the purpose of clarifying or adding to the opinion given by him. The expert shall have the right to set forth his answers in his own hand. The record of the interrogation of the expert shall be drawn up in conformity with the requirements of Articles 141 and 142 of the present Code.

Article 193. Presentation of Expert's Opinion to Accused. The opinion of an expert or his report of the impossibility of givng an opinion, as well as the record of the interrogation of the expert, shall be presented to the accused, who shall have the right to give his own explanations and submit objections as well as to request that additional questions be put to the expert and that supplementary or repeated expert examination be assigned. The performance of the said actions shall be noted in the record of the interrogation of the accused.

The rules of the present article shall also apply in instances when an expert examination has been conducted before prosecution of the person as the accused.

Article 194. Procedure for Assigning and Conducting Supplementary and Repeated Expert Examination. Supplementary and repeated expert examination shall be assigned in instances provided for by Article 81, and shall be conducted in conformity with the requirements of Articles 184–193 of the present Code.

Chapter Seventeen: Suspension and Completion of the Preliminary Investigation

Article 195. Grounds and Time Periods for Suspending Preliminary Investigation. A preliminary investigation shall be suspended:

(1) in the event that an accused has hidden from the investigation or from the court or when for other reasons his whereabouts are not established;

(2) in the event of a mental or other serious illness of the accused, certified by a doctor working in a medical institution;

(3) in the event that it is not established who is subject to prosecution as the accused.

If there exists one of these circumstances, the investigator shall render a reasoned decree to suspend the preliminary investigation. If two or several persons are being prosecuted in the case, but the grounds for suspension do not pertain to all the accused persons, the investigator shall have the right to disjoin and suspend the case with respect to individual accused persons or to suspend the whole proceeding.

In instances provided for by subsections 1 and 3 of the present article, the preliminary investigation shall be suspended only upon expiration of the period for conducting it; in instances provided for by subsection 2 of the present article, it may be suspended even before the end of the period for preliminary investigation.

Before suspending the preliminary investigation the investigator shall be obliged to perform all the investigative actions which can be conducted in the absence of the accused, and to take all measures to discover him or to establish the identity of the person who committed the crime.

A suspended proceeding shall be subject to termination upon expiration of the period of limitation established by criminal law.

Article 196. Search for Accused. If it is not known where an accused is, the investigator shall take the necessary measures to search for him. The investigator shall have thr right to commission agencies to conduct such search. Such commission of inquiry shall be indicated in the decree to suspend the preliminary investigation, or a special decree shall be rendered.

A search may be announced either at the time of the preliminary investigation or simultaneously with its suspension.

If there exist the grounds indicated in Article 89 of the present Code, the investigator may select a measure of restraint with respect to a person being sought. In instances provided for by Article 96 of the present Code, the investigator may, with the sanction of a procurator, select a measure of restraint in the form of confinement under guard.

Article 197. Measures for Ascertaining Person Subject to Prosecution as Accused. After suspending a preliminary investigation in an instance provided for by subsection 3 of Article 195 of the present Code, the investigator shall be obliged to take measures both directly and through agencies of inquiry to ascertain the person subject to prosecution as the accused.

Article 198. Reopening Preliminary Investigation. A suspended preliminary investigation shall be reopened by a reasoned decree of an investigator when the grounds for suspension have ceased to exist or when it becomes necessary to conduct additional investigative actions.

Article 199. Completion of Preliminary Investigation. A preliminary investigation shall be completed with the drawing up of a conclusion to indict or of a decree to refer the case to a court for consideration of the question whether to take compulsory measures of a medical character, or with the drawing up of a decree to terminate the case.

Article 200. Acquainting Victim, Civil Plaintiff, and Civil Defendant with Materials of Case. If an investigator deems a preliminary investigation to be completed and the evidence gathered to be sufficient for drawing up a conclusion to indict, he shall be obliged to notify the victim, civil plaintiff, and civil defendant or their representatives thereof and shall at the same time explain to them that they have the right to acquaint themselves with the materials of the case.

In the event of an oral or written petition on the part of any of the said persons, the investigator shall acquaint the victim and civil plaintiff or their representatives with the materials of the case, and shall acquaint the civil defendant or his representative with the materials of the case which pertain to the suit filed. If in the conduct of a preliminary investigation, films or sound-recordings are employed, they shall be replayed for the victim upon his petition.

Records shall be drawn up in conformity with the requirements of Articles 141 and 142 of the present Code concerning the acquainting of the victim, civil plaintiff, and civil defendant or their representatives with the materials of the case. The records shall note with what materials the victim, civil plaintiff, civil defendant or their representatives have been acquainted, as well as what petitions have been filed in this connection. Written petitions shall be attached to the file of the case.

If the investigator refuses to grant a petition in whole or in part, he shall render a reasoned decree to such effect. The decree shall be announced to the person who has filed the petition.

[*Ved.* (1966), no. 36, item 1018, Edict August 31, 1966.]

Article 201. Acquainting Accused With All Materials of Case. If an investigator deems the evidence gathered to be sufficient for drawing up a conclusion to indict and has fulfilled the requirements of Article 200 of the present Code, he shall announce to an accused that the investigation in his case has been terminated and that he has the right to become acquainted with all the materials of the case both personally and with the help of defense counsel, as well as to file petitions to supplement the preliminary investigation.

If the accused does not declare a desire to have defense counsel, all the materials of the case shall be presented to him for examination. In instances when the accused petitions to summon defense counsel to participate in becoming acquainted with the proceedings in the case, and in instances when defense counsel participates in the case from the moment of presentation of the accusation, the investigator shall present all the materials of the case to the accused and his defense counsel. In connection therewith the presentation of the materials of the case must be postponed until the appearance of defense counsel, but not for more than five days. If it is impossible for defense counsel selected by the accused to appear within the said period, the investigator shall take measures to summon other defense counsel. All the materials of the case shall be presented to the accused and his defense counsel in filed and numbered form. If in the conduct of a preliminary investigation, films or sound-recordings are employed, they shall be played back to the accused and his defense counsel. Upon request of the accused or his defense counsel the investigator shall have the right to allow them individually to acquaint themselves with the materials of the case.

If several persons are being prosecuted in the case, all the materials of the case shall be presented to each of them.

When the accused and his defense counsel have finished acquainting themselves with the materials of the case, the investigator shall be obliged to ask them whether they petition to supplement the investigation and in exactly what respect.

The accused shall have the right, in the process of acquainting himself with the materials of the case, to copy necessary information therefrom.

[*Ved.* (1966), no. 36, item 1018, Edict August 31, 1966.]

Article 202. Rights of Defense Counsel in Becoming Acquainted With All Materials of Case. An accused's defense counsel shall have the right:

(1) to meet with the accused alone;

(2) to acquaint himself with all the materials of the case and to copy necessary information therefrom;

(3) to discuss with the accused the question of filing petitions;

(4) to file petitions with respect to the conduct of investigative actions, the obtaining of evidence and having it attached to the file of the case, and all other questions of significance for the case;

(5) to file a challenge of an investigator, procurator, expert, specialist, or interpreter;

(6) to bring complaints to the procurator against actions of the investigator which violate or prejudice the rights of defense counsel or of the accused;

(7) to be present, with the permission of the investigator, during investigative actions performed in accordance with petitions filed by the accused and his defense counsel.

[*Ved.* (1966), no. 36, item 1018, Edict August 31, 1966.]

Article 203. Record of Announcing Termination of Preliminary Investigation and of Presenting Materials of Case to Accused and his Defense Counsel. An investigator shall draw up a record, in conformity with the requirements of Articles 141 and 142 of the present Code, of the presentation of all the materials of the case to the accused and his defense counsel for examination. The record shall note that the termination of the preliminary investigation has been announced to the accused, that his rights have been explained, exactly what materials (number of volumes and pages) have been presented for examination, where and for how long examination of the materials of the case has taken place, what petitions have been filed by the accused and his defense counsel, and what declarations they have made. If the accused refuses to acquaint himself with the materials of the case, this shall be indicated in the record, and the reasons for the refusal shall be set forth if the accused has communicated them.

Article 204. Petitions of Accused and His Defense Counsel to Supplement Preliminary Investigation. Petitions to supplement a preliminary investigation may be filed by an accused and his defense counsel orally or in writing. Petitions shall be entered in the record, and written petitions shall, in addition, be attached to the file of a case.

In the event that a petition is filed to elucidate circumstances of significance for the case, an investigator shall be obliged to supplement the preliminary investigation. If defense counsel is present during supplementary investigative actions, he shall have the right, with the permission of the investigator, to put questions to a witness, victim, expert, specialist, and accused, as well as to petition to have data of significance for the case entered in the record. The investigator may exclude questions proposed by the defense counsel, but an excluded question must be entered in the record.

If the investigator completely or partially refuses to grant a petition in whole or in part, he shall render a reasoned decree to such effect, which shall be announced to the petitioner.

After conducting supplementary investigative actions the investigator shall again be obliged to acquaint the accused and his defense counsel with the materials of the case, in conformity with the requirements of Articles 201–203 of the present Code.

[*Ved.* (1966), no. 36, item 1018, Edict August 31, 1966.]

Article 205. Conclusion to Indict. A conclusion to indict shall consist of a descriptive part and a resolutory part.

The descriptive part shall set forth the substance of the case: the place and time of commission of the crime, its methods, motive, consequences, and other material circumstances; information about the victim; evidence confirming the existence of a crime and guilt of the accused; circumstances tending to mitigate or aggravate the responsibility of the accused; arguments advanced by the accused in his defense and the results of verification of such arguments. The conclusion to indict must contain references to pages of the file of the case.

The resolutory part shall give information concerning the personality of the accused and shall set forth a formulation of the accusation with an indication of the article or articles of the criminal law which provide for the given crime.

The conclusion to indict shall be signed by the investigator with an indication of the place and time it is drawn up.

Article 206. Appendices to Conclusion to Indict. To a conclusion to indict there shall be appended a list of the persons who, in the opinion of the investigator, should be summoned to the judicial session, as well as information concerning the time periods of the investigation, measures of restraint selected with an indication of the time of confinement under guard, real evidence, the civil suit, measures taken to secure the civil suit and possible confiscation of property, and court costs.

The list of persons to be summoned to the judicial session shall indicate their domicile or whereabouts and the pages of the file of the case on which their testimony or opinions are set forth.

Article 207. Referral of Criminal Case to Procurator. After signing a conclusion to indict, an investigator shall immediately refer the case to a procurator.

Article 208. Grounds for Terminating Criminal Case. A criminal case shall be terminated:

(1) if there exists grounds indicated in Articles 5–9 of the present Code;

(2) if the participation of an accused in the commission of the crime has not been proved, and if all possibilities for collecting supplementary evidence have been exhausted.

If several accused persons have been prosecuted in the case, and the grounds for terminating the case do not pertain to all the accused persons, the investigator shall terminate the case with respect to individual accused persons.

Article 209. Decree to Terminate Criminal Case. With respect to termination of a case, an investigator shall draw up a reasoned decree, in which he shall set forth the substance of the case and the grounds for termination.

The decree must resolve the question of real evidence, of cancellation of the measure of restraint, and of the impounding of property. The decree shall be signed by the investigator with an indication of the place and time it is drawn up.

The investigator shall send to a procurator a copy of the decree to terminate the case. The investigator shall at the same time give written notification of the termination and grounds for termination of the criminal case to the person who has been prosecuted as the accused, the victim, and the person or institution upon whose declaration the case has been initiated, and shall explain the procedure for appeal.

If facts have been established by the investigation which require the application of measures of social, disciplinary, or administrative pressure to the person prosecuted as the accused or to other persons, the investigator shall, in terminating the criminal case, bring such facts to the attention of a social organization, comrades' court, collective of working people, or the administration of the appropriate enterprise or institution for the taking of social, disciplinary, or administrative measures of pressure.

The decree to terminate the case may be appealed to the procurator within five days from the moment of notification of termination of the case.

Article 210. Reopening of Terminated Case. A procurator shall have the right, if there exist grounds therefor, by his own decree to vacate a decree of the investigator terminating a criminal case and to reopen the case.

The reopening of a terminated case may take place only in the event that the periods of limitation have not expired.

If a case is terminated by the investigator under subsection 3 or 4 of Article 5 of the present Code, but the accused objects to termination, the investigator shall by his own decree reopen the case.

Chapter Eighteen: Supervision of the Procurator Over Execution of the Laws in the Conduct of the Inquiry and the Preliminary Investigation

Article 211. Powers of Procurator in Exercising Supervision Over Execution of Laws in Conduct of Inquiry and Preliminary Investigation. A procurator shall exercise supervision over the execution of the laws in the conduct of an inquiry or a preliminary investigation in accordance with the USSR Statute on Procuratorial Supervision.

(1) The procurator shall be obliged:

(a) to institute criminal proceedings against persons guilty of committing crimes, to take measures so that not a single crime remains undiscovered and not a single criminal escapes responsibility;

(b) strictly to see to it that not a single citizen is subjected to illegal or unfounded institution of criminal proceedings or any other illegal limitation of rights;

(c) to see to the undeviating observance of the procedure established by the present Code for conducting the inquiry and preliminary investigation;

(d) to exercise supervision so that no one is subjected to arrest otherwise than in accordance with a decree of a court or with the sanction of a procurator; in deciding the question of sanction for arrest the procurator shall carefully acquaint himself with all the materials upon which the arrest is founded and when necessary shall personally interrogate the accused or suspect.

(2) The procurator shall have the right:

(a) to give instructions concerning the conduct of the inquiry and preliminary investigation, concerning selection, change, or cancellation of measures of restraint with respect to the suspect or accused, concerning prosecution of one as the accused, classification of the crime and scope of the accusation, and concerning referral of the case, as well as concerning individual investigative actions and search for criminals in hiding;

(b) to demand for verification, from an agency of inquiry or an investigator, criminal files, documents, materials, and other information concerning crimes committed and concerning the course of the inquiry, the preliminary investigation, and the search for criminals;

(c) to participate in the inquiry and preliminary investigation and when necessary to conduct personally a preliminary investigation or individual investigative actions in any case;

(d) to return criminal cases to the agency of inquiry or the investigator with his written instructions concerning supplementary investigation;

(e) to vacate illegal and unfounded decrees of the agency of inquiry or investigator;

(f) to remove a person conducting an inquiry or an investigator from further conduct of the inquiry or investigation if he has permitted the law to be broken in the investigation of a case;

(g) to withdraw any case from an agency of inquiry and transfer it to an investigator, or to transfer a case from one investigator to another, for the purpose of securing more complete and more objective investigation of the case;

(h) to entrust to agencies of inquiry the performance of individual investigative actions and measures of search in cases being conducted by investigators of agencies of the Procuracy;

(i) to terminate criminal cases on grounds provided for by the present Code.

Article 212. **Binding Nature of Procurator's Instructions.** A procurator's instructions shall be given in writing and shall be binding upon an investigator and person conducting an inquiry. An appeal from instructions to a higher procurator shall not suspend their execution except in instances provided for by paragraph two of Article 127 of the present Code.

Article 213. Problems to Be Resolved by Procurator in Case Received With Conclusion to Indict. When he receives a case from an agency of inquiry or investigator, a procurator shall be obliged to verify:

(1) whether an act imputed to an accused has taken place, and whether the elements of a crime exist in such act;

(2) whether or not there exist circumstances in the case entailing termination of the case;

(3) whether the inquiry or preliminary investigation has been conducted thoroughly, completely, and objectively;

(4) whether the accusation is founded on evidence present in the case;

(5) whether an accusation is presented for all the criminal acts of the accused established by the inquiry or preliminary investigation;

(6) whether all persons discovered to have committed the crime are being prosecuted as the accused;

(7) whether the crime is properly classified;

(8) whether a measure of restraint is properly selected;

(9) whether measures are being taken to secure a civil suit and possible confiscation of property;

(10) whether circumstances that have facilitated commission of the crime are elucidated, and whether measures are being taken to eliminate them;

(11) whether the conclusion to indict is drawn up in conformity with the requirements of the present Code;

(12) whether all other requirements of the present Code are observed during the inquiry or preliminary investigation.

Article 214. Procurator's Decision Concerning Case Received With Conclusion to Indict. A procurator shall be obliged, within five days, to consider a case that has been received and to take one of the following decisions concerning it:

(1) if he deems that grounds exist for referring the case to court, to confirm the conclusion to indict with his own resolution;

(2) to return the case to the agency of inquiry or investigator, with his written instructions, for the conduct of a supplementary inquiry or investigation;

(3) to terminate the case, drawing up a decree to this effect in accordance with Article 209 of the present Code;

(4) in the event that the conclusion to indict is not in conformity with the requirements of Article 205 of the present Code, to return the case to the investigator or agency of inquiry, with his written instructions, for the drawing up of a new conclusion to indict;

(5) to draw up a new conclusion to indict, and to remove from the case the one previously drawn up, and return it to the agency of inquiry or the investigator with an indication of the mistakes discovered.

Article 215. Change of Accusation in Procurator's Confirmation of Conclusion to Indict. A procurator shall have the right, by his own decree, to exclude individual sections of an accusation from a conclusion to indict, as well as to apply a law concerning a less grave crime. In this connection, a new conclusion to indict shall be drawn up, when necessary.

If it is required to change the accusation to a graver one, or to one differing substantially in factual circumstances from the original accusation, the procurator shall return the case to the agency of inquiry or to the investigator for presentation of a new accusation.

Article 216. Change by Procurator of Measure of Restraint or of List of Persons Subject to Being Summoned to Judicial Session. A procurator shall have the right to cancel or change a measure of restraint previously selected or to select a measure of restraint if one has not been selected.

The procurator shall have the right also to change the list, appended to the conclusion to indict, of persons subject to being summoned to the judicial session.

Article 217. Referral of Case to Court by Procurator. If a procurator confirms a conclusion to indict or draws up a new conclusion to indict, he shall refer the case to the court in whose jurisdiction it lies, and shall inform the accused to what court the case is referred.

At the time he refers a case, the procurator shall simultaneously inform the court whether he considers it necessary to support the accusation in court.

After referral of the case to the court, all petitions and complaints in the case shall be referred directly to the court.

Chapter Nineteen: Appeal From Actions of the Agency of Inquiry, the Investigator, and the Procurator

Article 218. Procedure for Appeal. Appeals from actions of an agency of inquiry or an investigator shall be made to a procurator directly or else through the person conducting the inquiry or the investigator from whose actions an appeal is taken. Appeals may be both written and oral. Oral appeals shall be entered in the record, which shall be signed by the petitioner and by the person receiving the appeal.

The person conducting the inquiry or the investigator shall be obliged to refer an appeal that has been received to the procurator within twenty-four hours together with his explanation.

Until its resolution, the bringing of an appeal shall not suspend the execution of the action appealed from, if such is not found necessary by the person conducting the inquiry, the investigator, or the procurator, as appropriate.

Article 219. Consideration of Appeal by Procurator. A procurator shall be obliged to consider an appeal within three days of receiving it and to inform the petitioner of the results of his consideration. In the event of denial, the procurator shall be obliged to set forth the reasons for which the appeal is deemed unfounded.

Article 220. Appeal from Actions and Decisions of Procurator. Appeals from actions and decisions of a procurator shall be brought to a higher procurator.

Section Three: Proceedings in the Court of First Instance

Chapter Twenty: Bringing the Accused to Trial and Actions Preparatory to the Judicial Session

Article 221. * **Bringing to Trial.** If there exist sufficient grounds to consider a case in judicial session, a judge shall, without predetermining the question of guilt, render a decree to bring the accused to trial.

In instances when the judge disagrees with the findings of the conclusion to indict, as well as when it is necessary to change the measure of restraint selected with respect to the accused, the case shall be subject to consideration in an administrative session of the court. In this connection, regardless of the grounds for submitting the case for consideration by an administrative session, the court shall decide all questions pertaining to the administrative session.

The question of bringing to trial must be resolved by the judge or by the court in administrative session not more than fourteen days from the moment the case comes to court.

Article 222. Questions to Be Elucidated in Bringing to Trial. When a judge or a court in administrative session resolves the question of bringing an accused to trial, the following shall be elucidated with respect to each of the persons accused:

(1) whether the case is within the jurisdiction of the given court;

(2) whether the act imputed to the guilt of the accused contains the elements of a crime;

(3) whether or not there are circumstances entailing termination or suspension of the case;

(4) whether the evidence gathered for the case is sufficient for its consideration in judicial session;

(5) whether the requirements of the present Code have been observed in the initiation of the case and in the conduct of the inquiry or the preliminary investigation;

(6) whether the criminal law is correctly applied to the acts imputed to the accused;

(7) whether the conclusion to indict is drawn up in conformity with the requirements of the present Code;

(8) whether the measure of restraint is correctly selected with respect to the accused;

(9) whether measures are being taken to secure compensation for material loss caused by the crime and possible confiscation of property.

*The amendment of Article 36 of the Fundamental Principles of Criminal Procedure by the Edict of the Presidium of the Supreme Soviet of the USSR, of August 31, 1970, *Vedomosti SSSR*, September 9, 1970, no. 36, item 362, supplemented Article 221 by expanding the circumstances under which a case shall be subject to consideration in an administrative session of the court to include crimes of minors and crimes for which the death penalty may be imposed. As of March 1, 1972, the RSFSR Code of Criminal Procedure had not been amended to conform to the USSR edict.

Article 223. Consideration of Petitions and Declarations. When resolving the question of bringing an accused to trial, a judge or a court in administrative session shall be obliged to consider the petitions and declarations of persons and organizations concerning permission to participate in the case, further referral of the case, acquiring of supplementary evidence, change of measure of restraint, and the civil suit and measures to secure it. In this connection the judge or the court in administrative session shall have the right to summon the person or a representative of the organization that has filed a petition, in order to explain it.

A person or an organization that has filed a petition shall be informed of the result of the disposition of the petition. Denial of a petition shall not be subject to appeal; it may be renewed, however, at the judicial session.

Article 224. Composition of Court in Administrative Session. Criminal cases shall be considered in administrative sessions of all courts by a bench composed of a judge and two people's assessors.

Participation of a procurator in an administrative session shall be obligatory.

Article 225. Procedure of Administrative Session of Court. Consideration of a case in administrative session shall commence with the report of the judge, who shall give the grounds for his disagreement with the findings of the conclusion to indict or with the measure of restraint. Then the court shall hear the opinion of the procurator. Thereafter the persons summoned to the session of the court shall be invited to be heard in connection with the petitions filed by them. The court shall hear the conclusion of the procurator concerning the petitions filed. A ruling shall be rendered in the conference room.

The summoning of witnesses and experts to an administrative session shall not be permitted.

Article 226. Types of Rulings Rendered by Court in Administrative Session. A court in administrative session shall render one of the following rulings:

1. To bring an accused to trial;
2. To return the case for supplementary investigation;
3. To suspend proceedings in the case;
4. To refer the case to the proper jurisdiction;
5. To terminate the case.

Article 227. Bringing Accused to Trial in Administrative Session. If it reaches the conclusion that there exist sufficient grounds to consider a case in judicial session, a court in administrative session shall, without predetermining the question of guilt, render a ruling to bring the accused to trial. In connection therewith the court shall have the right to exclude individual sections of an accusation from the conclusion to indict or to apply a criminal law concerning a less grave crime, provided the new accusation does not differ substantially in its factual circumstances from the accusation contained in the conclusion to indict.

Reasons for a decision to exclude individual sections of an accusation or to apply another criminal law must be given in the ruling of the administrative session.

Article 228. Resolution of Questions Connected With Preparation for Consideration of Case in Judicial Session. Having found that there exist sufficient grounds for bringing an accused to trial, a judge or a court in administrative session shall be obliged also to resolve the following questions:

(1) whether a state accuser shall participate in the judicial examination;

(2) whether to permit a social accuser to participate in the judicial examination;

(3) whether to permit as defense counsel the person selected by the accused or whether to appoint defense counsel;

(4) whether to permit social defense counsel to participate in the judicial examination;

(5) which persons are subject to being summoned to judicial session as victim, civil plaintiff, civil defendant, their representatives, witnesses, experts, and specialists;

(6) whether to summon an interpreter;

(7) the place and time of the judicial examination;

(8) whether to consider the case in closed judicial session in instances provided for by Article 18 of the present Code.

A decree of a judge or ruling of the administrative session of a court that the participation of a procurator in the judicial examination is necessary shall be binding upon the latter.

If a procurator, in referring a case to court, states that he considers it necessary to support the accusation, the judge or the court in administrative session shall not have the right to deny this to him.

[*Ved.* (1966), no. 36, item 1018, Edict August 31, 1966.]

Article 229. Decree of Judge and Ruling of Administrative Session of Court. A decree of a judge or a ruling of an administrative session of a court must indicate:

(1) the time and place of rendering the decree or ruling;

(2) the office and surname of the judge rendering the decree or the composition of the court in administrative session, surname of the secretary, office and surname of the procurator taking part in the administrative session;

(3) the grounds and substance of the decisions taken.

A decree shall be signed by the judge. A ruling shall be signed by the person presiding and the people's assessors.

Article 230. Decree and Ruling to Bring to Trial. A decree of a judge or a ruling of an administrative session of a court to bring an accused to trial must contain: a finding that the evidence is sufficient to consider the case in judicial session, a decision to bring to trial, an indication of the person brought to trial and of the applicable criminal law, a decision concerning the measure of restraint with respect to the person brought to trial, as well as decisions concerning petitions filed and the questions enumerated in Article 228 of the present Code.

Article 231. Suspension of Case and Referral of It to the Proper Jurisdiction. If, in considering the question of bringing to trial, it is ascertained that an accused has hidden and his whereabouts are unknown, a judge or a court in administrative session shall render a decree or ruling to suspend proceedings in the case pending a search for the accused, and shall return the case to the procurator except in instances stated in subsection 1 of Article 246 and in Article 257 of the present Code.

In the event of grave illness of an accused, certified by a doctor working in a medical institution, which excludes the possibility of his participation in the judicial session, a judge or a court in administrative session shall render a decree or ruling to suspend proceedings in the case until the accused recovers.

If a judge or a court in administrative session establishes that a case is not within the jurisdiction of the given court it shall render a decree or ruling to refer the case to the proper jurisdiction.

Article 232. **Returning Case for Supplementary Investigation.** A court in administrative session shall refer a case for supplementary investigation in the event of:

(1) an insufficiency in the conduct of the inquiry or preliminary investigation;

(2) the substantial violation of criminal procedure law in the conduct of the inquiry or preliminary investigation;

(3) the existence of grounds for the presentation to the accused of another accusation connected with the one previously presented, or for changing the accusation to a graver one or one differing substantially in factual circumstances from the accusation contained in the conclusion to indict;

(4) the existence of grounds for instituting criminal proceedings against other persons in the given case when it is impossible to separate the materials of the case concerning them;

(5) incorrect joinder or disjoinder of a case.

A case shall be referred to the procurator for supplementary investigation. In this connection the court shall be obliged to indicate in its ruling upon what grounds the case is returned and what circumstances must be elucidated supplementarily.

When referring a case for supplementary investigation, a court shall be obliged to resolve the question of a measure of restraint with respect to the accused.

Article 233. **Measures of Securing Civil Suit and Confiscation of Property.** In the event that a person conducting an inquiry or an investigator has not taken measures of securing compensation of material loss caused by the crime, and possible confiscation of property, if such measures cannot be taken directly by a court, the judge or court in administrative session shall oblige the appropriate agencies to take the necessary measures of security.

Article 234. **Termination of Case.** If there exist circumstances stated in Articles 5–9 and subsection 2 of Article 208 of the present Code, a court in administrative session shall terminate the case. In this connection the court shall cancel the measures of restraint and the measures of securing the civil suit and confiscation of property and shall resolve the question of real evidence. A copy of the ruling to terminate the case shall be handed to the person against whom criminal proceedings have been instituted, and to the victim.

When facts are established requiring the application of measures of social pressure to the person against whom criminal proceedings have been instituted, the court shall, in terminating the case, bring such facts to the attention of an appropriate comrades' court, commission for cases of minors, or social organization or collective of working people.

When terminating a case on grounds stated in Article 9 of the present Code, a court shall notify the social organization or collective of working people of the granting of its petition and of the transfer to it on surety of the person against whom criminal proceedings have been instituted.

[*Ved.* (1970), no. 22, item 442, Edict May 21, 1970.]

Article 235. Record of Administrative Session. The record of an administrative session shall indicate the place and time of the session, the name and composition of the court, the secretary, the procurator, persons summoned by the court, the case under consideration, actions of the court in the order in which they have taken place, statements and petitions of the persons summoned to the administrative session, rulings rendered without retiring to the conference room, indication of the rulings rendered in the conference room.

The record shall be signed by the person presiding and the secretary.

Article 236. Securing Possibility of Becoming Acquainted With Materials of Case. After bringing an accused to trial, a judge shall be obliged to secure to the accuser, the person brought to trial, and defense counsel, as well as to the victim, civil plaintiff, civil defendant, or their representatives, an opportunity to become acquainted with all the materials of the case and to copy necessary information therefrom.

Article 237. Handing Copy of Conclusion to Indict. A copy of the conclusion to indict must be handed to the person brought to trial by the court.

If the accusation, the measure of restraint, or the list of persons subject to being summoned to court is changed when the question of bringing to trial is decided, a copy of the ruling of the court or decree of the judge must also be handed to the person brought to trial.

In cases of crimes provided for by Articles 112, 130 paragraph one and 131 of the RSFSR Criminal Code, if a preliminary investigation or inquiry has not been conducted concerning them, a copy of the declaration of the victim shall be handed to the person brought to trial.

The consideration of a case in judicial session may not be commenced earlier than three days from the moment such documents are handed to the person brought to trial.

Article 238. Summons to Judicial Session. A judge shall give directions concerning the summons to a judicial session of persons stated in his decree or in the ruling of the administrative session, shall secure the handing of the summons to them, and shall also take other measures to prepare for the judicial session.

Article 239. Time Limits for Considering Case in Judicial Session. The consideration of a case in judicial session must be commenced not later than fourteen days from the moment a judge renders a decree, or an administrative session a ruling, to bring an accused to trial.

Chapter Twenty-one: General Conditions of Judicial Examination

Article 240. Directness, Oral Nature, and Continuity of Judicial Examination. In considering a case, a court of first instance shall be obliged to analyze the evidence in the case directly: to interrogate persons brought to trial, victims, and witnesses, hear opinions of experts, view real evidence, and publicly disclose records and other documents.

The judicial session for each case shall proceed continuously except for time designated for rest. Consideration of other cases by the same judges before completion of the hearing of a case already commenced shall not be permitted.

Article 241. Inalterability of Composition of Court During Examination of Case. Each case must be considered by one and the same bench of judges. If any one of the judges is prevented from continuing to participate in the session, he shall be replaced by another judge, and examination of the case shall commence from the beginning except in instances provided for by Article 242 of the present Code.

Article 242. Reserve People's Assessor. In a case requiring a long time for its examination, a reserve people's assessor may be summoned. The reserve people's assessor shall be present in the courtroom from the commencement of the examination of a given case, and in the event of the departure of a people's assessor, he shall replace him.

If a reserve people's assessor who has taken the place of a departed one does not request the recommencement of judicial actions, the examination of the case shall continue.

Article 243. Person Presiding in Judicial Session. In a session of a district (city) people's court the president of such court or the people's judge shall preside, and in a session of any other court the president, deputy president, or member of the court shall preside.

The person presiding shall direct the judicial session, taking all measures provided by the present Code for a thorough, complete, and objective analysis of the circumstances of the case and for establishing the truth, eliminating from the judicial examination all that does not have a relation to the case, and securing the educational influence of the trial.

In the event that any person participating in the judicial examination objects to actions of the person presiding, such objections shall be entered in the record of the judicial session.

Article 244. Secretary of Judicial Session. A secretary of a judicial session shall keep a record of the judicial session. He shall be obliged to set forth in the record completely and correctly the actions and decisions of the court as well as the actions of participants in the trial which have taken place during the course of the session.

In the event that he disagrees with the person presiding concerning the contents of the record, the secretary shall have the right to append to the record his remarks, subject to consideration by the whole court.

Article 245. Equality of Rights of Participants in Judicial Examination. An accuser, person brought to trial, and defense counsel, as well as a victim, civil plaintiff, civil defendant, and their representatives at a judicial examination shall enjoy equal rights in presenting evidence, participating in the analysis of the evidence, and submitting petitions.

Article 246. Participation of Person Brought to Trial in Judicial Examination. The examination of a case in a session of a court of first instance shall proceed with the participation of the person brought to trial, whose appearance in court shall be obligatory.

The examination of a case in the absence of the person brought to trial may be permitted only in exceptional instances, if this does not obstruct the establishment of the truth in the case:

(1) when the person brought to trial is outside the USSR and evades appearance in court;

(2) when, in a case of a crime for which the punishment of deprivation of freedom may not be assigned, the person brought to trial petitions for examination of the case in his absence. A court shall have the right, however, to deem the appearance of the person brought to trial obligatory.

Article 247. Consequences of Nonappearance of Person Brought to Trial. If a person brought to trial does not appear, a case must be postponed, except in instances provided for by subsection 2 of Article 246 of the present Code. A court shall have the right to subject a person brought to trial who has not appeared to compulsory appearance, as well as to select or change a measure of restraint with respect to him.

Article 248. Participation of Procurator in Judicial Examination. A procurator shall support the state accusation before the court, shall participate in the analysis of the evidence, shall give opinions concerning questions arising during the judicial examination, and shall present to the court his views regarding the application of the criminal law and measures of punishment with respect to the accused.

In supporting the accusation, the procurator shall be guided by the requirements of the law and by his inner conviction founded on a consideration of all the circumstances of the case.

If, as a result of the judicial examination, the procurator becomes convinced that the data of the judicial investigation do not confirm the accusation presented to the person brought to trial, he shall be obliged to withdraw from the accusation and shall set forth to the court the reasons for so doing.

The procurator's withdrawal from the accusation shall not relieve the court from the duty to continue examination of the case and to resolve on the usual grounds the question of the guilt or innocence of the person brought to trial.

The procurator shall have the right to bring a civil suit or to support a civil suit brought by a victim if the protection of state or social interests or of the rights of citizens so requires.

Article 249. Participation of Defense Counsel in Judicial Examination. A defense counsel shall take part in the analysis of the evidence, shall express his opinion on questions arising during the judicial examination, shall set forth to the court the views of the defense on the substance of the accusation relating to circumstances tending to mitigate responsibility and concerning the measure of punishment and civil-law consequences of the crime.

Article 250. Participation of Social Accusers and Defense Counsel in Judicial Examination. Representatives of social organizations of working people may be permitted by ruling of a court to participate in the judicial examination of criminal cases as social accusers or social defense counsel.

A social accuser shall have the right to present evidence, take part in the analysis of the evidence, file petitions and challenges before the court, and participate in oral argument, setting forth to the court an opinion concerning whether the accusation has been proved, and concerning the social danger of the person brought to trial and of the act committed by him. The social accuser may express views regarding the application of the criminal law and the measure of punishment with respect to the person brought to trial and on other questions in the case. The social accuser shall have the right to withdraw from the accusation if the data of the judicial investigation give grounds therefor.

A social defense counsel shall have the right to present evidence, take part in the analysis of the evidence, file petitions and challenges before the court, and participate in oral argument, setting forth to the court an opinion concerning circumstances tending to mitigate the guilt of the person brought to trial or to acquit him, as well as concerning the possibility of mitigating the punishment of the person brought to trial, his conditional sentence or relief from punishment and transfer on surety to the social organization or collective of working people in whose name the social defense counsel speaks.

Article 251. Consequences of Nonappearance of Procurator, Social Accuser, Defense Counsel, or Social Defense Counsel. In the event that a procurator does not appear at a judicial session, the court shall resolve the question of the possibility of hearing the case in his absence or of postponing it. If the court deems the participation of the procurator to be necessary, the examination shall be postponed.

If a defense counsel does not appear and it is impossible to replace him in the session, examination of the case shall be postponed. The replacement of a defense counsel who has not appeared at a judicial session shall be permitted only with the consent of the person brought to trial.

If a social accuser or social defense counsel does not appear, the court, depending on the circumstances of the case, shall decide the question of postponing hearing of the case or of considering it in his absence.

A procurator or defense counsel who has newly entered a case must be granted the time necessary to prepare for participation in the judicial examination.

The court shall notify the appropriate higher procurator or presidium of the college of advocates of the nonappearance of a procurator or advocate without valid reason. The court shall notify the appropriate social organization if a social accuser or social defense counsel does not appear without valid reason.

Article 252. Consequences of Nonappearance of Civil Plaintiff or Civil Defendant. If a civil plaintiff or his representative does not appear, the court shall not consider the civil suit; in connection therewith the victim shall retain the right to bring the suit by way of civil proceedings.

The court shall have the right, upon the petition of the civil plaintiff, to consider the civil suit in his absence.

The court shall consider the civil suit regardless of the appearance of the civil plaintiff or his representative, if a procurator supports the suit or if the court deems this necessary.

The nonappearance of the civil defendant or his representative shall not stop consideration of the civil suit.

Article 253. Consequences of Nonappearance of Victim. If a victim does not appear, a court shall decide the question of examining the case or postponing it, depending on whether complete elucidation of all the circumstances of the case and protection of the victim's rights and legal interests are possible in his absence.

If the victim does not appear without valid reasons in cases of crimes provided for by Articles 112, 130 paragraph one, and 131 of the RSFSR Criminal Code and if a preliminary investigation or inquiry has not been conducted, the case shall be terminated; upon the petition of the person brought to trial, however, in such instances the case may be considered on the merits in the absence of the victim.

Article 253-1. Participation of Specialist in Judicial Examination. In instances provided for by the present Code, a specialist may be summoned to court who shall participate in the judicial examination in the procedure established by Article 133-1 of the present Code.

[*Ved.* (1966), no. 36, item 1018, Edict August 31, 1966.]

Article 254. Limits of Judicial Examination. The examination of a case in court shall be conducted only with respect to the accused and only in accordance with the accusation upon which he has been brought to trial.

The changing of an accusation in court shall be permitted if this does not worsen the position of the person brought to trial and does not violate his right to defense. If the changing of the accusation entails violation of the right to defense of the person brought to trial, the court shall refer the case for supplementary investigation or inquiry.

The changing of an accusation in court to a graver one or one differing substantially in factual circumstances from the accusation upon which the accused has been brought to trial shall not be permitted.

If the changing of an accusation consists of excluding part of it or excluding indicia of the crime that aggravate the responsibility of the person brought to trial, the court shall have the right to continue examination of the case.

Article 255. **Initiating of Criminal Case Upon New Accusation.** If a judicial examination establishes circumstances indicating that a person brought to trial has committed a crime for which no accusation has been previously presented to him, the court shall, without suspending examination, initiate a case upon a new accusation and shall refer the necessary materials for inquiry or preliminary investigation in the usual manner.

In the event that the new accusation is connected with the original one and their separate consideration is not possible, the whole case must be returned for supplementary investigation.

Article 256. **Initiating of Criminal Case With Respect to New Person.** If a judicial examination establishes circumstances indicating commission of a crime by a person against whom criminal proceedings have not been instituted, the court shall initiate a case with respect to such person and shall refer the necessary materials for inquiry or preliminary investigation.

In instances when a newly initiated case is connected with a case under consideration and their separate consideration is not possible, a court shall refer the whole case for supplementary investigation.

The initiation of a case with respect to a witness, victim, or expert who has given testimony or an opinion known to be false may take place only simultaneously with the decree of judgment.

A court shall have the right to apply a measure of restraint to a person with respect to whom a case is initiated, in accordance with the rules of Articles 89, 91, and 92 of the present Code.

Article 257. **Postponing of Examination and Suspending of Criminal Case.** When the examination of a case is impossible because of the nonappearance at a judicial session of any of the persons summoned or in connection with the necessity of acquiring new evidence, a court shall postpone examination and shall take measures to summon the persons who have not appeared or to acquire new evidence.

If a person brought to trial has hidden, or in the event of a mental or any other grave illness of the person brought to trial excluding the possibility of his appearance in court, the court shall suspend the proceeding with respect to such person brought to trial until a search for him is made, or until his recovery, and shall continue the examination with respect to the remaining persons brought to trial. If separate examination will impede the establishment of the truth, however, the entire proceeding in the case shall be suspended. A search for a person brought to trial who is in hiding shall be announced by a ruling of the court.

Article 258. Referring of Criminal Case for Supplementary Investigation. If circumstances indicated in Article 232 of the present Code are established during a judicial examination, the court shall refer the case for supplementary investigation.

When the case is received in court after completion of the supplementary investigation, the question of bringing the accused to trial shall be resolved in the usual manner.

Article 259. Terminating of Criminal Case in Judicial Session. A case shall be subject to termination in judicial session if during the judicial examination there are elucidated circumstances provided for by Article 5 of the present Code, except in instances stated in paragraph two of that article. A case shall also be subject to termination in judicial session in instances provided for by Articles 6, 7, 8, and 9 of the present Code.

Cases of crimes provided for by Articles 112, 130 paragraph one, and 131 of the RSFSR Criminal Code, in which a preliminary investigation or inquiry has not been conducted, shall also be subject to termination when the victim and the person brought to trial are reconciled, except in instances stated in paragraph four of Article 27 of the present Code.

[*Ved.* (1963), no. 36, item 661, Edict September 10, 1963.]

Article 260. Resolution of Question of Measure of Restraint. During the judicial examination the court shall have the right to select, change, or cancel a measure of restraint with respect to the person brought to trial.

Article 261. Procedure for Rendering Rulings in Judicial Session. A court shall render rulings on all questions which are resolved by the court during the judicial examination.

Rulings to refer a case for supplementary investigation, initiate a case upon a new accusation or with respect to a new person, terminate a case, select, change, or cancel a measure of restraint, concerning challenges, or to assign expert examination shall be rendered by the court in the conference room and shall be set forth as individual documents signed by the whole court.

All other rulings may, at the discretion of the court, be rendered either in the manner indicated above or after conference of the judges on the spot, with the ruling entered in the record of the judicial session.

Rulings rendered by the court during the judicial examination shall be subject to public disclosure.

Article 262. Routine of Judicial Session. When judges enter, all those present in a courtroom shall stand.

All participants in the trial shall stand when addressing the court, giving their testimony and making statements. Deviations from this rule may be permitted only with the permission of the person presiding.

All participants in the trial as well as all citizens present in the courtroom must unquestioningly obey the orders of the person presiding concerning observance of order in the judicial session.

If they are not accused persons or victims or witnesses in the case, persons younger than 16 shall not be permitted in the courtroom.

Article 263. Measures Taken With Respect to Violators of Order in Judicial Session. In the event that a person brought to trial violates order during a judicial session, and also if he does not obey orders of the person presiding, the person presiding shall warn the person brought to trial that if he repeats the aforesaid actions he will be removed from the courtroom. If the person brought to trial again violates order he may, upon a ruling of the court, be removed from the courtroom, and examination of the case shall continue in his absence. The judgment shall be proclaimed, however, in the presence of the person brought to trial or shall be announced to him immediately after proclamation.

In the event that an accuser or defense counsel does not obey the orders of the person presiding, the person presiding shall give him a warning. If the said person continues to disobey the orders of the person presiding, the hearing of the case may be postponed, upon a ruling of the court, if it does not appear possible without prejudice to the case to replace the given person with another. At the same time the court shall inform a higher procurator about this, or the presidium of the college of advocates or social organization, as appropriate.

A civil plaintiff, civil defendant, victim, and their representatives, an expert, a specialist, and an interpreter may be removed from the courtroom, upon a ruling of the court, in the event that they violate order in the judicial session or do not obey the orders of the person presiding.

The other persons present in the courtroom may be removed in similar instances upon the order of the person presiding. In addition a fine of up to 10 rubles may be imposed on them.

[*Ved.* (1966), no. 36, item 1018, Edict August 31, 1966.]

Article 264. Record of Judicial Session. The record of a judicial session shall indicate the place and date of the session with a designation of the time of commencement and completion, the name and composition of the court, the secretary, the interpreter, the accuser, the defense counsel, the person brought to trial, the victim, civil plaintiff, civil defendant, and their representatives, as well as the other persons summoned by the court, the case under consideration, data concerning the identity of the person brought to trial and the measure of restraint, actions of the court in the order in which they have taken place, statements and petitions of persons participating in the case, rulings rendered by the court without retiring to the conference room, indication of the rulings rendered in the conference room, the explanation to the persons participating in the case of their rights and duties, the detailed contents of the testimony, questions put to the expert and his answers, the results of views and other actions in collecting evidence conducted in the judicial session, indication of facts which persons participating in the case have asked to certify in the record, indication of facts of violations of order in the courtroom, if they have taken place, and identity of the violator, a summary of the oral argument and of the last word of the person brought to trial, and an indication that the judgment has been publicly disclosed and that the procedure and time limit for its appeal have been explained.

During the judicial examination the sound-recording of interrogations may be employed. In such event the phono-record shall be attached to the record of the judicial session, in which a note shall be made concerning the employment of a sound-recording.

The record of the judicial session must be prepared and signed not later than seventy-two hours after the completion of the judicial session.

The record shall be signed by the person presiding and by the secretary of the judicial session.

The person presiding shall be obliged to secure to participants in the trial an opportunity to become acquainted with the record.

[*Ved.* (1966), no. 36, item 1018, Edict August 31, 1966.]

Article 265. Remarks for Record of Judicial Session. Within three days after the signing of the record, the accuser, defense counsel, and person brought to trial, as well as the victim, civil plaintiff, civil defendant, and their representatives may file their remarks for the record.

Article 266. Consideration of Remarks for Record of Judicial Session. The remarks shall be considered by the person presiding, who shall, in the event that he is in agreement with the remarks, certify their correctness and attach them to the record of the judicial session.

If the person presiding is not in agreement with the remarks they shall be filed for consideration by an administrative session of the court, at which the person presiding and at least one of the people's assessors must be from among the judges who have participated in the examination of the case. When necessary the persons who have filed the remarks for the record shall be summoned.

As a result of considering the remarks the court shall render a reasoned ruling certifying their correctness or rejecting them. The remarks for the record and the ruling of the court shall be attached to the record of the judicial session.

Chapter Twenty-two: The Preparatory Part of the Judicial Session

Article 267. Opening of Judicial Session. The person presiding shall open the judicial session at the time assigned for consideration of the criminal case and shall announce which case is subject to examination.

Article 268. Verification of Appearance in Court. The secretary shall report concerning the appearance in court of the procurator, the social accuser, the person brought to trial, defense counsel, and social defense counsel as well as the victim, civil plaintiff, civil defendant, and their representatives, the interpreter, witnesses, experts, and specialists, and shall report the causes of the nonappearance of those who are absent.

[*Ved.* (1966), no. 36, item 1018, Edict August 31, 1966.]

Article 269. Explanation to Interpreter of His Duties. The person presiding shall explain to the interpreter his duty to translate to the court the testimony and statements of the persons participating in the case who do not have command of the language in which the proceedings are being conducted, and to translate to such persons the contents of the testimony, statements, and documents which are publicly disclosed in court as well as the orders of the person presiding and the decisions of the court.

The person presiding shall warn the interpreter of responsibility under Article 181 of the RSFSR Criminal Code for making a translation known to be incorrect.

Article 270. Removing of Witnesses From Courtroom. Witnesses who appear before the commencement of their interrogation shall be removed from the courtroom. The person presiding shall take measures so that witnesses who have been interrogated by the court do not communicate with witnesses who have not been interrogated.

Article 271. Establishing of Identity of Person Brought to Trial and Timely Handing to Him of Copy of Conclusion to Indict. The person presiding shall establish the identity of the person brought to trial, ascertaining his surname, first name, patronymic, the year, month, day, and place of birth, place of residence, occupation, education, family position. Then the person presiding shall ask the prisoner whether and exactly when copies of the documents enumerated in Article 237 of the present Code have been handed to him.

In the event that the said documents have not been handed to him within the period established by Article 237 of the present Code, examination of the case must be postponed.

Article 272. Announcing of Composition of Court and Explaining Right of Challenge. The person presiding shall announce the composition of the court, shall state who the accuser and defense counsel are, as well as the secretary, expert, specialist, and interpreter, and shall explain to the prisoner and other participants in the judicial examination their right to submit a challenge of the composition of the court or of any of the judges, the procurator, secretary, expert, specialist, or interpreter.

If a reserve people's assessor is present in the judicial session, the person presiding shall so announce. A reserve people's assessor may also be challenged.

Challenges shall be ruled on in accordance with the rules established by Articles 61–63 and 65–67 of the present Code.

[*Ved.* (1966), no. 36, item 1018, Edict August 31, 1966.]

Article 273. Explanation to Person Brought to Trial of his Rights. The person presiding shall explain to the prisoner his rights at the judicial examination as provided by Article 46 of the present Code.

Article 274. Explanation to Victim, Civil Plaintiff, and Civil Defendant of Their Rights. The person presiding shall explain to the victim, civil plaintiff, civil defendant, and their representatives their rights at the judicial examination as provided by

Articles 53–55 of the present Code, respectively. In addition, the victim must be informed of his right to reconciliation with the person brought to trial in cases of crimes provided for by Articles 112, 130 paragraph one, and 131 of the RSFSR Criminal Code, if a preliminary investigation or inquiry has not been conducted.

Article 275. Explanation to Expert of his Rights and Duties. The person presiding shall explain to the expert his rights and duties provided by Article 82 of the present Code, and shall warn him of responsibility for giving an opinion known to be false and for refusing to give an opinion, under Articles 181 and 182 of the RSFSR Criminal Code.

Article 275-1. Explanation to Specialist of His Rights and Duties. The person presiding shall explain to a specialist his rights and duties as provided by Article 133-1 of the present Code, and shall warn him of responsibility for refusing or evading the discharge of his duties.

[*Ved.* (1966), no. 36, item 1018, Edict August 31, 1966.]

Article 276. Filing and Disposition of Petitions. The person presiding shall ask the accuser, person brought to trial, and his defense counsel, as well as the victim, civil plaintiff, civil defendant, or their representatives, whether they have petitions to summon new witnesses, experts, and specialists or to acquire real evidence and documents. A person who has submitted a petition is obliged to indicate for the establishment of exactly what circumstances any supplementary evidence is necessary.

Having heard the opinion of the remaining participants in the judicial examination, the court must discuss each petition filed, must grant it if the circumstances subject to elucidation are of significance for the case, or render a reasoned ruling refusing to grant the petition.

The refusal of the court to grant a petition shall not limit the right of the person whose petition has been refused to file it in the future depending on the course of the judicial examination.

The court shall have the right, regardless of whether a petition has been filed, to render a ruling to summon new witnesses, assign an expert examination, or acquire documents and other evidence.

[*Ved.* (1966), no. 36, item 1018, Edict August 31, 1966.]

Article 277. Resolving of Question of Possibility of Considering Criminal Case in Absence of Any of Persons Participating in the Case. In the event of the nonappearance of any of the participants in a judicial examination or of a witness, expert, or specialist, the court shall hear the opinion of the person brought to trial, his defense counsel, the victim, civil plaintiff, civil defendant, or their representatives, and the opinion of the procurator, concerning the possibility of examining the case and shall render a ruling to continue the examination or to postpone it.

[*Ved.* 1966, no. 36, item 1018, Edict August 31, 1966.]

Chapter Twenty-three: The Judicial Investigation

Article 278. Commencement of Judicial Investigation. A judicial investigation shall begin with public disclosure of the conclusion to indict. In instances when an accusation has been changed in an administrative session of the court, the ruling of the administrative session shall also be publicly disclosed.

If a preliminary investigation or inquiry has not been conducted in the case, the judicial investigation shall begin with public disclosure of the victim's declaration.

The person presiding shall ask each person brought to trial whether he has understood the accusation, when necessary shall explain the substance of the accusation to the person brought to trial, and shall ask whether he acknowledges himself guilty. If the person brought to trial wishes, the person presiding shall grant him an opportunity to give reasons for his answer.

Article 279. Establishing of Order of Analyzing Evidence. After questioning of persons brought to trial on whether or not they acknowledge their guilt, a court shall hear the proposals of the accuser, person brought to trial, and defense counsel as well as of the victim, civil plaintiff, civil defendant, and their representatives concerning the sequence of interrogations of the persons brought to trial, victims, witnesses, and experts and shall render a ruling concerning the order of analyzing the evidence.

Article 280. Interrogation of Person Brought to Trial. The interrogation of a person brought to trial shall commence with the proposal of the person presiding that he give testimony regarding the accusation and the circumstances of the case known to him. Thereafter the judges, accuser, and victim, as well as the civil plaintiff, civil defendant, and their representatives, and defense counsel shall interrogate him. Then questions may be put to the person brought to trial by the other persons brought to trial and their defense counsel. The person presiding shall eliminate questions having no relation to the case.

The judges shall have the right to put questions to the person brought to trial at any moment of the judicial investigation.

The interrogation of a person brought to trial in the absence of another person brought to trial shall be permitted only upon a ruling of the court in exceptional instances when the interests of establishing the truth so require. In such event, after the return of the person brought to trial to the courtroom, the person presiding shall inform him of the contents of the testimony given in his absence and shall grant him an opportunity to put questions to the person brought to trial interrogated in his absence.

A person brought to trial may, with the permission of the person presiding, give testimony at any moment of the judicial investigation.

Article 281. Public Disclosure of Testimony of Person Brought to Trial. The public disclosure in court of testimony of a person brought to trial given during an inquiry or preliminary investigation may take place in the following instances:

(1) if there existed substantial contradictions between such testimony and testimony given in court by the person brought to trial;

(2) if the person brought to trial refuses to give testimony in court;

(3) when the case is being considered in the absence of the person brought to trial.

This rule shall extend as well to instances of public disclosure of testimony given in court by the person brought to trial.

The replaying of a sound-recording shall not be permitted without preliminary public disclosure of the testimony contained in the appropriate record of interrogation or record of judicial session. A note shall be made in the record of the judicial session concerning the replaying of the sound-recording.

[*Ved.* (1966), no. 36, item 1018, Edict August 31, 1966.]

Article 282. Warning of Witness of Responsibility for Refusing to Give Testimony and for Giving Testimony Known to be False. Before interrogation, the person presiding shall establish the identity of a witness, shall explain his civic duty and obligation to relate truthfully everything known to him in the case, and shall warn him of responsibility for refusing to give testimony and for giving testimony known to be false.

A signed statement shall be obtained from the witness concerning the fact that his obligations and responsibility have been explained to him. The signed statement shall be attached to the record of the judicial session.

The person presiding shall explain to witnesses who have not attained the age of 16 years the significance of complete and truthful testimony. Such witnesses shall not be warned of responsibility for refusing to give testimony or for giving testimony known to be false, and a signed statement shall not be obtained from them.

Article 283. Interrogation of Witnesses. Witnesses shall be interrogated separately and in the absence of witnesses not yet interrogated.

The person presiding shall ascertain the relationships among a witness and the person brought to trial and victim and shall propose to the witness that he communicate everything that is known to him in the case. Thereafter the judges and accusers, as well as the victim, the civil plaintiff, the civil defendant, and their representatives, defense counsel, and the persons brought to trial shall interrogate the witness. If a witness has been summoned to the judicial session upon a petition of one of the participants of the judicial examination, such participant shall put questions to such witness first. The person presiding shall eliminate questions having no relation to the case.

Judges shall have the right to put questions to a witness at any moment of the judicial investigation.

Witnesses who have been interrogated shall remain in the courtroom and may not withdraw before the completion of the judicial investigation without the permission of the court.

The person presiding may allow witnesses who have been interrogated to withdraw from the courtroom earlier than the completion of the judicial investigation only upon hearing the opinions of the accuser, person brought to trial, and defense counsel as well as of the victim, civil plaintiff, civil defendant, and their representatives.

Article 284. Use of Written Notes and Documents by Witness. When interrogated in court, a witness may use written notes in instances when his testimony relates to some kind of numerical or other data which are hard to remember. Such notes must be presented to the court upon its request.

A witness shall be allowed to read documents he has with him relating to the testimony given by him. Such documents shall be presented to the court and, upon a ruling of the court, may be attached to the file of the case.

Article 285. Interrogation of Minor Witness. In the interrogation of witnesses up to the age of 14 years and, at the discretion of the court, in the interrogation of witnesses aged 14 to 16, a teacher shall be summoned. When necessary, the parents or other legal representatives of the minor shall also be summoned. The said persons may, with the permission of the person presiding, put questions to such witness.

The interrogation of a minor witness may, upon a ruling of the court, be conducted in the absence of the person brought to trial, when the interests of establishing the truth so require. After the return to the courtroom of the person brought to trial he must be informed of the testimony of the witness and granted an opportunity to put questions to such witness.

A witness who has not attained the age of 16 years must be removed from the courtroom at the end of his interrogation, except in instances when the court deems necessary the further presence of such witness.

Article 286. Public Disclosure of Testimony of Witness. The public disclosure in court of testimony which has been given by a witness during an inquiry or preliminary investigation, as well as the replaying of a sound-recording of his testimony appended to the record, may take place in the following instances:

(1) if there exist substantial contradictions between such testimony and the testimony of the witness in court;

(2) in the absence of the witness at the judicial session for reasons which exclude the possibility of his appearance in court.

This rule shall extend as well to instances of public disclosure of the testimony of the witness which has been given in court.

The replaying of a sound-recording shall not be permitted without preliminary public disclosure of the testimony contained in the appropriate record of interrogation or record of judicial session. A note shall be made in the record of the judicial session concerning the replaying of the sound-recording.

[*Ved.* (1966), no. 36, item 1018, Edict August 31, 1966.]

Article 287. Interrogation of Victim. A victim shall be interrogated in accordance with the rules established for the interrogation of witnesses.

As a rule, a victim shall be interrogated before the interrogation of witnesses.

Article 288. Conduct of Expert Examination in Court. An expert shall participate in the analysis of circumstances of a case relating to the subject of the expert examination. He may put questions to the person brought to trial, victim, and witnesses concerning circumstances of significance for the giving of an opinion.

In the elucidation of all the circumstances of significance for the giving of an opinion, the person presiding shall propose to the accuser, defense counsel, and person brought to trial, as well as to the victim, civil plaintiff, civil defendant, and their representatives, that they present questions to the expert in writing. The questions must be publicly disclosed and the opinion of participants in the judicial examination and the opinion of the procurator must be heard concerning them. The court shall consider such questions, shall eliminate those which do not relate to the case or to the competence of the expert, and shall also formulate new questions, after which the expert shall proceed to draw up an opinion.

The opinion shall be given by the expert in writing, shall be publicly disclosed by him at the judicial session, and shall be attached to the file of the case together with the questions. An expert shall have the right to include in his opinion findings concerning circumstances of the case which relate to his competence but concerning which he has not been presented questions.

When it is necessary to present models to an expert for comparative analysis, the rules of Article 186 of the present Code shall be applied.

Article 289. Interrogation of Expert. After an expert has publicly disclosed his opinion, questions may be put to him to explain or supplement the opinion given by him.

Questions shall be put to an expert first by the judges and then by the accuser, victim, civil plaintiff, civil defendant, and their representatives, defense counsel, and the person brought to trial.

Article 290. Conduct of Supplementary or Repeated Expert Examination. In instances provided for by Article 81 of the present Code, a court may, by a reasoned ruling, assign supplementary or repeated expert examination.

Supplementary or repeated expert examination shall be conducted in accordance with the rules established by Articles 288 and 289 of the present Code.

Article 291. View of Real Evidence. Real evidence that is present in court or presented at a judicial session must be viewed by the court and presented to the accuser, person brought to trial, and defense counsel as well as to the victim, civil plaintiff, civil defendant, and their representatives. A view of real evidence may be conducted at any moment of a judicial investigation on the initiative of the court or in accordance with a petition of participants in the judicial examination. When necessary, real evidence may be presented to witnesses, an expert, and a specialist. Persons to whom real evidence is presented may direct the attention of the court to any circumstances connected with the view.

A view of real evidence which cannot be brought to the court shall be conducted, when necessary, by the whole court at the place where the real evidence is situated, with observance of the rules established by paragraph one of the present article.

[*Ved.* (1966), no. 36, item 1018, Edict August 31, 1966.]

Article 292. Public Disclosure of Documents. Documents attached to a file of a case or presented at a judicial session, if they set forth or verify circumstances of significance for the case, shall be subject to public disclosure. Documents may be publicly disclosed completely or partially at any moment of the judicial investigation both upon the initiative of the court and upon petition of the accuser, person brought to trial, or defense counsel or the victim, civil plaintiff, civil defendant, and their representatives. Documents presented at the judicial session may be attached to the file of the case upon a ruling of the court.

Article 293. View of Locality and Premises. If the court deems it necessary to view some premises or locality, a view shall be conducted by the whole court in the presence of the accuser, person brought to trial, and defense counsel as well as the victim, civil plaintiff, civil defendant and their representatives. When necessary, a view shall be conducted in the presence of witnesses, an expert, and a specialist.

Upon arrival at the place of the view, the person presiding shall announce the continuation of the judicial session, and the court shall commence the view; in this regard questions may be asked of the person brought to trial, victim, witnesses, expert, and specialist in connection with the view.

Persons present at the view may direct the attention of the court to everything which in their opinion can assist elucidation of the circumstances of the case.

[*Ved.* (1966), no. 36, item 1018, Edict August 31, 1966.]

Article 294. Completion of Judicial Investigation. After consideration of all the evidence, the person presiding shall ask the accuser, person brought to trial, and defense counsel, as well as the victim, civil plaintiff, civil defendant, and their representatives whether they wish to supplement the judicial investigation and exactly how. In the event that petitions are filed to supplement the judicial investigation, the court shall discuss such petitions and shall dispose of them.

Upon disposition of the petitions and performance of the necessary investigative actions, the person presiding shall announce that the judicial investigation is completed.

Chapter Twenty-four: Oral Argument and the Last Word Of the Person Brought to Trial

Article 295. Content and Procedure of Oral Argument. After completion of a judicial investigation, a court shall pass on to the hearing of oral argument. Oral argument shall consist of speeches of the accuser as well as of the civil plaintiff, civil defendant, or their representatives, of defense counsel, and of the person brought to trial if a defense counsel does not participate in the judicial session.

In cases of crimes provided for by Articles 112, 130 paragraph one, and 131 of the RSFSR Criminal Code, the victim or his representatives shall also participate in oral argument. In the event that in such cases counteraccusations are joined in one proceeding, the sequence of appearances in oral argument shall be determined by the court.

The order of appearance of the state and social accusers as well as the order of appearance of the defense counsel and the social defense counsel shall be established by the court on the basis of their proposals.

Participants in oral argument shall not have the right to refer to evidence which has not been the subject of consideration in the judicial investigation. In the event that it is necessary to present new evidence, they may petition to reopen the judicial investigation.

The court may not limit the duration of oral argument to a certain time, but the person presiding shall have the right to stop persons participating in the argument if they touch on circumstances having no relation to the case under consideration.

Article 296. **Rebuttals.** After all the participants in oral argument have given their speeches, they may each appear once more with a rebuttal of what was said in the speeches. The right of last rebuttal shall always belong to defense counsel and the person brought to trial.

Article 297. **Last Word of Person Brought to Trial.** After completion of oral argument the person presiding shall grant the person brought to trial the last word. Questions to the person brought to trial during his last word shall not be permitted.

The court may not limit to a certain time the duration of the last word of the person brought to trial, but the person presiding shall have the right to stop the person brought to trial in instances when he touches on circumstances clearly having no relation to the case.

If in the last word the person brought to trial reports new circumstances of substantial significance for the case, the court shall be obliged to reopen the judicial investigation.

Article 298. **Proposals of Participants in Judicial Examination Concerning Substance of Accusation.** Upon completion of oral argument, but before the court retires to the conference room, the accuser, defense counsel, and the person brought to trial, as well as the victim, civil plaintiff, and civil defendant, or their representatives, shall have the right to present to the court in writing their formulations of the decision of the questions stated in subsections 1–5 of Article 303 of the present Code. The proposed formulation shall not have binding force for the court.

Article 299. **Retirement of Court to Conference Room for Decreeing of Judgment.** Having heard the last word of the person brought to trial, a court shall immediately retire for conference to decree judgment, and the person presiding shall so announce to those present in the courtroom.

Chapter Twenty-five: The Decree of Judgment

Article 300. Rendering of Judgment in Name of RSFSR. A judgment of a court shall be rendered in the name of the Russian Soviet Federated Socialist Republic.

Military tribunals shall, in accordance with Article 43 of the Fundamental Principles of Criminal Procedure of the USSR and Union Republics, render judgment in the name of the Union of Soviet Socialist Republics.

Article 301. Legality and Well-founded Nature of Judgment. A judgment of a court must be legal and well-founded.

The court shall found the judgment only on evidence which has been considered at the judicial session.

The judgment of the court must be reasoned.

Article 302. Secrecy of Judges' Conference. A judgment shall be decreed by a court in the conference room. Only the judges comprising the membership of the court in a given case may be in the conference room during the judges' conference. The presence of any other persons shall not be permitted.

At nightfall, the judges shall have the right to interrupt the conference for rest. The judges may not divulge discussions which have taken place during the conference.

Article 303. Questions Resolved by Court When Decreeing Judgment. When decreeing judgment a court shall resolve the following questions in the conference room:

(1) whether the act which the person brought to trial is accused of committing has taken place;

(2) whether such act contains the elements of a crime and exactly which criminal law provides for it;

(3) whether the person brought to trial has committed such act;

(4) whether the person brought to trial is guilty of committing such crime;

(5) whether the person brought to trial is subject to punishment for the crime committed by him;

(6) exactly which punishment must be assigned to the person brought to trial and whether it is subject to being served by the person brought to trial;

(6-1) whether there are grounds for deeming the person brought to trial an especially dangerous recidivist; which type of correctional labor institution with the corresponding regimen must be determined for the person brought to trial in assigning him the punishment of deprivation of freedom;

(7) whether the civil suit is subject to satisfaction, in whose favor, and to what extent, and also, if a civil suit has not been brought, whether the material loss is subject to compensation;

(8) how to deal with the real evidence;

(9) on whom and in what amount court costs must be imposed;

(10) the measure of restraint with respect to the person brought to trial.

If the person brought to trial is accused of committing several crimes, the court shall resolve for each crime separately the questions indicated in subsections 1–6 of the present article.

If several persons brought to trial are accused of committing a crime, the court shall resolve these questions separately with respect to each person brought to trial.

[*Ved.* (1963), no. 36, item 661, Edict September 10, 1963;
Ved. (1970), no. 22, item 442, Edict May 21, 1970.]

Article 304. Discussion of Question of Observation of Conditionally Sentenced Person and of Carrying on of Educational Work With Him. In applying a conditional sentence, a court shall decide, in accordance with the procedure established by law, whom to charge with observation of the conditionally sentenced person and with the carrying on of educational work with him.

If there exists a petition concerning conditional sentence from a social organization or collective of workers, employees, or collective farm workers at the guilty person's place of work, the court may transfer the conditionally sentenced person to such organization or collective for reeducation and correction.

Article 305. Discussion of Question of Imputability of Person Brought to Trial. In instances when, during an inquiry, preliminary investigation, or judicial examination, the question has arisen of the imputability of a person brought to trial, the court shall be obliged to discuss this question again when decreeing judgment. If it deems that the person brought to trial was in a nonimputable state when committing the act or that after committing the crime he has contracted a mental illness which deprives him of the ability to realize the significance of his actions or to control them, the court shall render a ruling in accordance with the procedure of Chapter Thirty-three of the present Code.

Article 306. Procedure for Judges' Conference. The judges' conference shall precede the decreeing of judgment. The person presiding shall pose the questions to be resolved by the court in the order indicated in Article 303 of the present Code. Each question must be presented in such a form that either a positive or a negative answer might be given it.

All questions shall be decided by a simple majority vote. None of the judges shall have the right to abstain from voting. The person presiding shall give his vote last.

Article 307. Special Opinion of Judge. A person presiding or a people's assessor who maintains a special opinion shall have the right to set it forth in writing in the conference room. The special opinion shall not be announced when proclaiming the judgment, but shall be attached to the file of the case.

Article 308. Reopening of Judicial Investigation or Referral of Criminal Case for Supplementary Investigation. If, during discussion in the conference room of the questions indicated in Articles 303–305 of the present Code, a court deems necessary the ascertainment of any circumstances of significance for a case, it shall reopen the judicial investigation, and render a ruling to such effect. Upon completion of the judicial investigation the court shall again open the oral argument and shall hear the last word of the person brought to trial.

If the court in the conference room reaches the conclusion that it is necessary to refer the case for supplementary investigation, it shall render a reasoned ruling to such effect.

Article 309. Types of Judgments. A judgment of a court may be either of conviction or acquittal.

A judgment of conviction may not be founded on assumptions and shall be decreed only if during the course of the judicial examination the guilt of the person brought to trial in committing the crime is proved. The court shall decree a judgment of conviction without assigning punishment if, by the time the case is considered in court, the act has lost its social danger or the person who has committed it has ceased to be socially dangerous.

A judgment of acquittal shall be decreed in instances when:

(1) the event of a crime is not established;

(2) the act of the person brought to trial does not contain the elements of a crime;

(3) participation of the person brought to trial in the commission of the crime is not proved.

If, in decreeing a judgment of acquittal, because of lack of proof of the participation of the person brought to trial in the commission of the crime, the person who committed such crime remains undisclosed, the court shall, after the decree has taken legal effect, refer the case to the procurator to take measures to establish the person subject to prosecution as the accused.

[*Ved.* (1963), no. 36, item 661, Edict September 10, 1963.]

Article 310. Disposition of Civil Suit When Decreeing Judgment. When decreeing a judgment of conviction, a court shall completely or partially satisfy the civil suit or shall deny it, depending on whether the grounds and amount of the suit have been proved.

In exceptional instances, when it is impossible to carry out a detailed calculation in the civil suit without postponing examination of the case, the court may acknowledge the civil plaintiff's right to satisfaction of the suit and shall transfer the question of its amount for consideration by way of civil proceedings.

When a judgment of acquittal is decreed a court shall:

(1) deny satisfaction of the civil suit, if the event of the crime is not established or the participation of the person brought to trial in the commission of the crime is not proved;

(2) leave the suit unconsidered in the event of acquittal of the person brought to trial because of the absence of the elements of a crime.

Article 311. Securing of Civil Suit. In the event that a civil suit is satisfied, a court shall have the right, before the judgment takes legal effect, to decree that measures be taken to secure the suit, if such measures have not been taken earlier.

Article 312. Drawing up of Judgment. Upon deciding the questions stated in Articles 303–305 of the present Code, a court shall pass on to the drawing up of the judgment. It must be drawn up in clear, intelligible expressions, and shall be composed of an introductory part, a descriptive part, and a resolutory part.

The judgment shall be set forth in the language in which the judicial examination has proceeded.

The judgment must be written by one of the judges who participates in decreeing it, and shall be signed by all the judges. A judge who maintains a special opinion shall also sign the judgment.

Corrections in the judgment must be noted and the notations signed by all the judges in the conference room before proclamation of the judgment.

Article 313. Introductory Part of the Judgment. The introductory part of a judgment shall indicate:

(1) that the judgment is rendered in the name of the RSFSR or, in instances provided for by paragraph two of Article 300 of the present Code, in the name of the USSR;

(2) the time and place of decreeing judgment;

(3) the name of the court which has decreed judgment, the composition of the court, the secretary of the judicial session, the accuser, the defense counsel;

(4) the first name, patronymic, and surname of the person brought to trial, the year, month, day, and place of his birth, his place of residence, place of work, occupation, education, family position, and any other information about the personality of the person brought to trial which is of significance for the case;

(5) the criminal law which provides for the crime which the person brought to trial is accused of committing.

Article 314. Descriptive Part of Judgment. The descriptive part of a judgment of conviction must contain a description of the criminal act deemed proved, with an indication of the place, time, and method of its commission and the nature of the guilt, motives, and consequences of the crime; the evidence on which the court's conclusions are founded and the reasons for which the court has rejected other evidence; indications of circumstances tending to mitigate or aggravate responsibility; and in the event that part of the accusation is deemed unfounded, the grounds therefor; the court shall also be obliged to adduce the reasons for deeming the person brought to trial an especially dangerous recidivist, for changing the accusation, if such has been done in court, and, when necessary, the reasons relating to the measure of punishment selected. Reasons must be given, in addition, for the relief of the person brought to trial from punishment, the application of conditional conviction, as well as for the assignment of punishment lower than the lowest limit provided by the criminal law for the given crime, resort to another milder punishment, or the assignment of a type of correctional labor colony or educational labor colony with deviation from the general rules. If there is more than one person brought to trial in the case, the enumerated indications must be made with respect to each of the persons brought to trial individually.

The descriptive part of a judgment of acquittal shall set forth the substance of the accusation upon which the accused has been brought to trial; the circumstances of the case established by the court; it shall adduce the evidence serving as the basis for acquitting the person brought to trial, with an indication of the reasons explaining why the court rejects the evidence on which the accusation has been founded. Inclusion in a judgment of acquittal of formulations that cast doubt on the innocence of the acquitted person shall not be permitted.

The descriptive part of a judgment of conviction or acquittal must contain the reasons underlying the decision of the court with respect to the civil suit or compensation of the material loss caused by the crime.

[*Ved.* (1963), no. 36, item 661, Edict September 10, 1963; *Ved.* (1969), no. 4, item 89, Edict January 21, 1969; *Ved.* (1970), no. 22, item 442, Edict May 21, 1970.]

Article 315. Resolutory Part of Judgment of Conviction. The resolutory part of a judgment of conviction must indicate:

(1) the surname, first name, and patronymic of the person brought to trial;

(2) a decision to declare the person brought to trial guilty;

(3) the criminal law in accordance with which the person brought to trial is declared guilty;

(4) the type and extent of punishment assigned for the person brought to trial for each crime which is deemed proved; the final measure of punishment subject to being served in conformity with Articles 40 and 41 of the RSFSR Criminal Code; the type of correctional labor colony with the corresponding regimen in which a person sentenced to deprivation of freedom must serve punishment;

(5) the length of the probation period and who is charged with the duty of observation of the convicted person, in the event that a conditional sentence is applied;

(6) a decision to deduct preliminary confinement, if the person brought to trial has been kept under guard before the decree of judgment as a measure of restraint or of detention;

(7) a decision concerning a measure of restraint with respect to the person brought to trial until the judgment takes legal effect.

In the event that the person brought to trial is deemed an especially dangerous recidivist, the resolutory part of the judgment shall so indicate.

If an accusation is presented to the person brought to trial in accordance with several articles of the criminal law, the resolutory part of the judgment must indicate precisely under which of them the person brought to trial is acquitted and under which, convicted.

In the event that the person brought to trial is relieved from serving punishment, this shall be indicated in the resolutory part.

In all instances punishment must be designated in such manner that no doubts relating to the type or extent of punishment assigned by the court will arise during execution of the judgment.

In instances provided for by Article 36 of the RSFSR Criminal Code, the resolutory part of the judgment shall set forth the decision of the court, once the judgment has taken legal effect, to propose to the appropriate state agencies that the person brought to trial be deprived of an order, medal, or honorary, military or other title.

[*Ved.* (1963), no. 36, item 661, Edict September 10, 1963; *Ved.* (1969), no. 4, item 89, Edict January 21, 1969; *Ved.* (1970), no. 22, item 442, Edict May 21, 1970.]

Article 316. Resolutory Part of Judgment of Acquittal. The resolutory part of a judgment of acquittal must contain:

(1) the surname, first name, and patronymic of the person brought to trial;

(2) a decision to acquit the person brought to trial;

(3) an indication of cancellation of the measure of restraint, if one has been selected;

(4) an indication of cancellation of measures of securing confiscation of property, if such measures have been taken.

Article 317. Other Questions to Be Decided in Resolutory Part of Judgment. The resolutory part of both a judgment of conviction and a judgment of acquittal must contain, besides the questions enumerated in Articles 315 and 316, respectively, of the present Code:

(1) a decision concerning the civil suit presented or a decision concerning compensation for loss;

(2) a decision of the question of the real evidence;

(3) an indication of the distribution of court costs;

(4) an indication of the procedure and time limit for appealing from and protesting the judgment.

Article 318. Proclamation of Judgment. After signing a judgment, the court shall return to the courtroom and the person presiding or a people's assessor shall proclaim the judgment. All those present in the courtroom, including the members of the court, shall stand while hearing the judgment.

If the judgment is set forth in a language of which the person brought to trial does not have command, then after the proclamation of the judgment it must be read by an interpreter in translation in the native language of the person brought to trial or in another language of which he has command.

Article 319. Releasing From Guard of Person Brought to Trial. When acquitting a person brought to trial or relieving him from punishment or from serving punishment, or in the event that he is condemned to a punishment not connected with deprivation of freedom, the court shall release the person brought to trial immediately in the courtroom in the event that he is under guard.

Article 320. Handing Copy of Judgment to Convicted or Acquitted Person. Not later than three days after the proclamation of judgment, a copy thereof must be handed to the convicted or acquitted person.

Article 321. Special Ruling of Court. At the same time judgment is decreed, a court shall, when there exist grounds therefor, direct the attention of directors of institutions, enterprises, and organizations, and of other persons, by means of a special ruling, to the causes and conditions which have facilitated the commission of the crime and which require that appropriate measures be taken.

A copy of the special ruling shall be referred to the appropriate institution, enterprise, organization, or official, which shall be obliged within a month to inform the court of the measures taken by them.

The court shall have the right to direct the attention of appropriate officials, by a special ruling, to violations permitted in the conduct of the inquiry or preliminary investigation.

In accordance with materials of the judicial examination, the court shall have the right to direct the attention of social organizations or collectives of working people, by a special ruling, to the incorrect conduct of individual citizens at work or in daily life or to their violation of social duty. When necessary a copy of the special ruling may be referred to a comrades' court.

The special ruling shall be signed by all the judges and, at the discretion of the court, may be publicly disclosed at the judicial session.

Article 322. **Payment of Advocate Who Has Entered Case Upon Assignment.** In the event that an advocate has participated in a case upon assignment, a court shall, at the same time judgment is decreed, render a ruling concerning the extent of the remuneration payable for legal consultation by the person brought to trial.

Chapter Twenty-six: Procedure for Imposition of Monetary Exactions and Fines

Article 323. **Procedure for Decision by Court of Question of Imposing Monetary Exactions and Fines.** Monetary exactions in instances provided for by Articles 57, 94, 133-1, and 394 as well as fines in instances provided for by Article 263 of the present Code shall be imposed by the court which has jurisdiction of the corresponding criminal case. If the violation is committed in a judicial session, the decision to impose the exaction or fine shall be rendered by the court considering the case at the same session.

In remaining instances, the question of imposing a monetary exaction or fine shall be decided by the court in administrative session, with summons of the person upon whom the monetary exaction or fine may be imposed. Nonappearance of the person summoned, without valid reasons, shall not stop consideration of the case.

In the administrative session, the record drawn up by the person who has conducted the inquiry, the investigator, or the procurator, or an extract from the record of the judicial session, which sets forth the circumstances of the violation committed, shall be publicly disclosed. Thereafter the explanations of the violator and the conclusion of the procurator, if one is participating in the case, shall be heard, and a ruling shall be rendered.

If the court renders a ruling to impose a monetary exaction on an interpreter, a specialist, a surety, or a person who has violated order in the courtroom, it shall have the right to defer execution and arrange for payment in installments for a period of up to three months.

[*Ved.* (1966), no. 36, item 1018, Edict August 31, 1966.]

Article 324. Procedure for Converting Bail into State Revenue. When a court decides the question of converting bail into state revenue in connection with evasion of appearance by the accused at the investigation or in court, the rules of Article 323 of the present Code shall be applied.

Section Four: Proceedings in the Cassational Instance

Chapter Twenty-seven: Appealing From and Protesting Court Judgments, Rulings, and Decrees Which Have Not Taken Legal Effect

Article 325. Right of Cassational Appeal From and Protest of Judgment. A person brought to trial, his defense counsel and legal representative, as well as a victim and his representative, shall have the right to appeal by way of cassation from the judgment of a court.

A procurator shall be obliged to protest by way of cassation every illegal or unfounded judgment.

A civil plaintiff, civil defendant, and their representatives shall have the right to appeal from the judgment insofar as it relates to the civil suit.

A person acquitted by a court shall have the right to appeal by way of cassation from a judgment of acquittal insofar as the reasons and grounds of acquittal are concerned.

Judgments of the RSFSR Supreme Court shall not be subject to appeal or protest by way of cassation.

Article 326. Procedure for Appealing From and Protesting Judgments. Judgments which have not taken legal effect may be appealed from and protested by way of cassation as follows:

(1) judgments of district (city) people's courts to the supreme court of an autonomous republic, territorial, regional, or city court, court of an autonomous region, or court of a national area, as appropriate;

(2) judgments of supreme courts of autonomous republics, territorial, regional, or city courts, courts of autonomous regions, and courts of national areas – to the RSFSR Supreme Court;

(3) judgments of military tribunals, in accordance with the procedure established by Articles 20 and 21 of the Statute on Military Tribunals.

Cassational appeals and protests shall be brought through the court which has rendered judgment; however, filing of an appeal or protest directly to the cassational instance shall not be an obstacle to consideration of the appeal or protest.

A judgment rendered during a reconsideration of a case may be appealed from or protested in the usual manner.

Article 327. Notification of Protests and Appeals. A court of first instance shall notify the convicted person, acquitted person, and other participants in the trial whose interests the appeal or protest affects that a protest has been brought or an appeal filed.

The convicted person, acquitted person, and other participants in the trial shall have the right to acquaint themselves with protests and appeals which have been received in court and to submit their objections to them.

A copy of a victim's protest or appeal shall be handed to the convicted person or acquitted person upon his request.

Objections to an appeal or protest shall be attached to the file of the case or shall be referred within one day as a supplement to the file.

Article 328. Time Limits for Appealing From and Protesting Judgments. Appeals from and protests of a judgment of a court of first instance may be filed within seven days from the day judgment is proclaimed, but convicted persons kept under guard shall have the same period from the day a copy of the judgment is handed to them.

During the period established for appealing from a judgment, the file of the case may not be acquired from the court. The procurator, as well as the convicted person, acquitted person, their defense counsel and legal representatives, the victim, civil plaintiff, civil defendant, and their representatives shall have the right to acquaint themselves in court with the proceedings in the case and with the appeals and protests.

An appeal or protest filed after lapse of the time limit shall be returned to the person who has filed the appeal or protest.

Supplementary cassational appeals and protests and written objections thereto may be filed in the cassational instance before consideration of the case has commenced.

Article 329. Procedure for Extending Time Limit for Appealing or Protesting. In event that the time limit for appealing from or protesting a judgment has lapsed for valid reasons, persons who have the right to file a cassational appeal or protest may petition before the court which has decreed judgment to extend the lapsed time limit. The question of extending the time limit shall be decided in an administrative session of the court, which shall have the right to summon the person who has initiated the petition to give explanations.

A ruling of the court to refuse to extend a lapsed time limit may be appealed from or protested in the usual manner to a higher court, which shall have the right to extend the lapsed time limit and to consider the merits of the case on appeal or protest.

Article 330. Consequences of Submitting Appeal or Protest. The filing of a cassational appeal from or protest of a judgment shall suspend execution of the judgment.

Upon expiration of the time limit established for appealing and protesting, the court which has decreed judgment shall refer the case, with the appeals and protests, to the cassational instance.

Article 331. Appealing From and Protesting Ruling of Court of First Instance and Decree of Judge. A special appeal from or special protest of the ruling of a court of first instance or the decree of a judge in a criminal case may be brought by the persons specified in Article 325 of the present Code, with the following exceptions:

(1) rulings of a court to impose a monetary exaction or fine in instances provided for by the present Code and to initiate a criminal case in accordance with the procedure of Article 256 of the present Code may be appealed from by the persons with respect to whom they are rendered or may be protested by the procurator. A decree of a judge to refuse to initiate a case may be appealed from by the victim or protested by the procurator;

(2) rulings of a court and decrees of a judge rendered in instances provided for by Articles 227, 230, 232, 255, 258, 308 paragraph two, 321, 362, and 363 of the present Code shall not be appealable, but may be protested by the procurator;

(3) rulings of a court and decrees of a judge rendered in instances provided by Articles 43, 44, 223, 231, 247, 250, 257, 260, 263 (except rulings to impose a fine), 266, 276, 277, 279, 280, 285, 288, 308 paragraph one, 364, 365, 366, 367, 370, 401, and 402, of the present Code shall not be subject to appeal or protest.

In instances of an appeal from or protest of a ruling rendered during the judicial examination of a case that has ended with a decree of judgment, the case shall be subject to referral to the cassational instance only upon expiration of the time limit established for appealing from the judgment.

The rules established by Chapters Twenty-seven and Twenty-eight of the present Code relating to time limits and the procedure for filing and considering cassational appeals and protests shall extend to the time limits and procedure for filing and considering special appeals and special protests.

[*Ved.* (1963), no. 36, item 661, Edict September 10, 1963.]

Chapter Twenty-eight: Consideration of Cases on Cassational Appeal and Protest

Article 332. Verifying Legality and Well-founded Nature of Judgment. When considering a case by way of cassation, a court shall verify the legality and the well-founded nature of the judgment in accordance with the materials in the case and supplementary materials. The court shall not be bound by the arguments of the cassational appeal or protest and shall verify the case as a whole with respect to all the persons convicted including those who have not filed appeals and those with respect to whom no cassational protest has been brought. In the event that violations of the law are discovered entailing the vacating or changing of the judgment, the court shall be guided by the rules of Articles 339–342 of the present Code.

Article 333. Time Limits for Consideration of Criminal Case in Cassational Instance. A supreme court of an autonomous republic, territorial, regional, or city court, court of an autonomous region, or court of a national area, as well as a military tribunal, must consider a case on cassational appeal or protest not later than ten days, and the RSFSR Supreme Court not later than twenty days, from the receipt of the case.

Article 334. Open Consideration of Cases in Cassational Instance. The cassational instance shall consider cases in open judicial session, except in instances indicated in Article 18 of the present Code.

Article 335. Persons Participating in Consideration of Case by Way of Cassation. During consideration of a case by way of cassation, a procurator shall give an opinion concerning the legality and well-founded nature of the judgment. The defense counsel may participate in the session of the court considering the case by way of cassation.

The question of the participation of the convicted person in the session of the court considering the case by way of cassation shall be resolved by that court. A convicted or acquitted person who appears at the judicial session shall be permitted in all instances to give explanations.

The other persons specified in Article 325 of the present Code may also participate during consideration of the case by way of cassation.

Nonappearance of the said persons, if they have been given timely notice of the day of consideration of the case, shall not obstruct its consideration.

Article 336. Notification of Consideration of Case in Cassational Instance. Persons who have submitted cassational appeals must be notified of the day of consideration of the case by way of cassation in a supreme court of an autonomous republic, a territorial, regional, or city court, court of autonomous region, or court of national area.

The RSFSR Supreme Court shall give notice of the day of consideration of the case by way of cassation to those participants in the trial who so request in cassational appeals or in objections to a protest or appeal.

Nonappearance of the said persons, if they have been given notice of the day of consideration of the case, shall not obstruct its consideration.

An announcement must be posted in court concerning the time of consideration of a case not later than three days before its consideration by way of cassation.

Article 337. Presentation of New Materials in Cassational Instance. For confirmation or refutation of arguments set forth in an appeal or protest, the persons specified in Article 325 of the present Code shall have the right to present supplementary materials in the cassational instance both before and during consideration of a case, but before the procurator gives an opinion.

Article 338. Procedure for Consideration of Case in Cassational Instance. The person presiding shall open the judicial session and shall announce which case is subject to consideration. Then the person presiding shall certify who has appeared in the case, after which the court shall decide the question of the possibility of considering the case. Thereafter the person presiding shall announce the composition of the court and the surname of the procurator and interpreter and shall ask the persons who have appeared in the case whether they have any challenges to file.

The person presiding shall ask the persons who have appeared in the case concerning petitions they may have. The court shall render a ruling on the petitions filed.

Consideration of the case shall commence with the report of one of the members of the court, which shall set forth the substance of the case and the arguments of the appeal or protest. If the case is being heard on protest, the procurator shall substantiate the protest after the report of the member of the court. In the event that supplementary materials are presented, the presiding member of the court or a member of the court shall publicly disclose them and shall transfer them to the procurator and to the persons specified in Article 335 of the present Code, if they are participating in the session, to acquaint themselves with them.

Then the convicted or acquitted person, his defense counsel and legal representatives, the victim, civil plaintiff, and civil defendant, or their representatives, if they are participating in the session, shall give explanations. After the giving of explanations, the court shall hear the conclusion of the procurator and shall grant the convicted or acquitted person and his defense counsel a word for supplementary explanations and shall retire to the conference room to render a ruling.

The order of the judicial session and measures taken with respect to violators shall be determined by the rules of Articles 262 and 263 of the present Code.

Before the commencement of the judicial session, the person who has appealed from or protested the judgment shall have the right to withdraw his appeal or protest. A higher procurator shall have the right to withdraw a protest brought by a lower procurator.

Article 339. Rendering of Ruling. A court shall take one of the following decisions as a result of considering a case by way of cassation:

(1) to leave the judgment unchanged and the appeals or protests unsatisfied;

(2) to vacate the judgment and refer the case for new investigation or a new judicial consideration;

(3) to vacate the judgment and terminate the case;

(4) to change the judgment.

In rendering a ruling the court shall be guided by the requirements of Articles 306, 307, and 312 of the present Code. The ruling rendered shall be publicly disclosed directly in the courtroom by the person presiding or a member of the court.

Article 340. Impermissibility of Increasing Convicted Person's Punishment or of Applying to Him the Law for More Serious Crime in Cassational Instance. When considering a case by way of cassation a court may mitigate the punishment assigned by the court of first instance or apply the law for a less grave crime, but shall not have the right to increase the punishment or to apply the law for a graver crime.

A judgment may be vacated in connection with the necessity of applying the law for a graver crime or because of the mildness of the punishment only in instances when a procurator has brought a protest or a victim has filed an appeal on such grounds.

Article 341. **Vacating of Judgment of Acquittal.** A judgment of acquittal may not be vacated by way of cassation except on protest of a procurator or on appeal of a victim or on appeal of a person acquitted by a court.

Article 342. **Grounds for Vacating or Changing Judgment.** The grounds for vacating or changing a judgment in the consideration of a case by way of cassation are:

(1) one-sidedness or incompleteness of the inquiry or of the preliminary or judicial investigation;

(2) lack of correspondence of the court's findings, set forth in the judgment, with the factual circumstances of the case;

(3) substantial violation of the criminal procedure law;

(4) incorrect application of the criminal law;

(5) lack of correspondence of the punishment assigned by the court with the gravity of the crime or the personality of the convicted person.

Article 343. **One-sidedness or Incompleteness of Inquiry or of Preliminary or Judicial Investigation.** An inquiry or a preliminary or judicial investigation shall be deemed one-sided or incomplete if it has left circumstances unclarified whose establishment might have had substantial significance in decreeing judgment.

An inquiry or a preliminary or judicial investigation shall in every instance be deemed one-sided or incomplete if in the case:

(1) persons have not been interrogated whose testimony has substantial significance for the case, or expert examination has not been conducted when the conduct of it is legally obligatory, or documents or real evidence of substantial significance have not been acquired;

(2) circumstances indicated in the ruling of a court that has transferred the case for supplementary investigation or for new judicial consideration have not been analyzed;

(3) data concerning the personality of the accused are not established with sufficient completeness.

Article 344. **Lack of Correspondence of Court's Findings, Set Forth in Judgment, With Factual Circumstances of Case.** A judgment shall be deemed not to correspond with the factual circumstances of a case:

(1) if the court's findings are not corroborated by the evidence considered at the judicial session;

(2) if the court has not taken into account circumstances which might have substantially influenced the court's findings;

(3) when there exists contradictory evidence of substantial significance for the court's findings, if the judgment does not indicate on what grounds the court has accepted some evidence and rejected other evidence;

(4) if the court's findings, set forth in the judgment, contain substantial contradictions which influenced or might have influenced decision of the question of the guilt or innocence of the convicted or acquitted person, the correctness of the application of the criminal law, or the determination of the measure of restraint.

Article 345. Substantial Violation of Criminal Procedure Law. Those violations of the requirements of the articles of the present Code which, by depriving or restricting the rights guaranteed by law of participants in a case during consideration of the case or otherwise, have prevented a court from thoroughly examining the case and have influenced or might have influenced the decreeing of a legal and well-founded judgment shall be deemed substantial violations of the criminal procedure law.

A judgment shall be subject to being vacated in any event if:

(1) the criminal case has not been terminated by the court when there exist grounds provided for by Article 259 of the present Code;

(2) the judgment is rendered by an illegally constituted court;

(3) the case is considered in the absence of the person brought to trial in instances when his presence is legally obligatory;

(4) the case is considered without the participation of defense counsel in instances when his participation is legally obligatory;

(5) the secrecy of the judges' conference is violated when judgment is decreed;

(6) the judgment is not signed by one of the judges;

(7) the file of the case lacks a record of the judicial session.

Article 346. Incorrect Application of Criminal Law. The following constitute incorrect application of the criminal law:

(1) failure of a court to apply the applicable law;

(2) application of an inapplicable law;

(3) incorrect interpretation of a law, contradicting its precise meaning.

Article 347. Lack of Correspondence of Punishment Assigned by Court With Gravity of Crime and With Personality of Convicted Person. A punishment shall be deemed not to correspond with the gravity of a crime and with the personality of a convicted person when, although not exceeding the limits provided by the appropriate criminal law, it is nevertheless clearly unjust in its extent because of either mildness or severity.

Article 348. Consequences of Vacating Judgment With Referral of Case for New Consideration. In vacating a judgment and referring a case for new consideration, a court shall indicate in its ruling whether proceedings should commence with a supplementary inquiry or preliminary investigation, or with bringing to trial or judicial examination.

In the event that a judgment is vacated because of the necessity of presenting a graver accusation or an accusation which differs substantially in factual circumstances from that originally presented, the case shall be referred through the court which has decreed judgment to a procurator for supplementary investigation.

In the event that a judgment is vacated because of violations committed during consideration of the case in court, the case shall be referred for a new consideration to the court which has decreed judgment, but with other members, or to another court.

Article 349. Vacating of Judgment of Conviction With Termination of Case. In considering a case by way of cassation, a court shall vacate a judgment of conviction and terminate the case in the following instances:

(1) if there exist grounds indicated in Articles 5–9 or 402 of the present Code;

(2) if the evidence considered by the court of first instance does not corroborate the accusation presented to the person brought to trial and there are no grounds for conducting a supplementary investigation and a new judicial consideration.

[*Ved.* (1968), no. 20, item 859, Edict May 8, 1968.]

Article 350. Changing of Judgment. In the event that it is established during consideration of a case by way of cassation that the criminal law has been incorrectly applied by the court of first instance or punishment has been assigned which lacks correspondence with the gravity of the crime or with the personality of the convicted person, the cassational instance may, without transferring the case for a new consideration, introduce the necessary changes into the judgment, with observance of the requirements of Article 340 of the present Code; the punishment according to the changed judgment shall not, however, exceed the punishment originally assigned, and the law for a graver crime shall not be applied.

The cassational instance shall not have the right to introduce changes into the judgment based on circumstances not established by the court of first instance or on evidence rejected by it.

Article 351. Contents of Cassational Ruling. The cassational ruling must indicate:

(1) the time and place of rendering the ruling;

(2) the name and composition of the court which has rendered the ruling and of the procurator and other persons who have participated in consideration of the case in the cassational instance;

(3) the person who has brought the cassational appeal or protest;

(4) a summary of the judgment, the appeal or protest, the opinion of the procurator, and the explanations of persons participating in the case;

(5) the decision of the court of second instance concerning the appeal or protest.

When an appeal or protest is left unsatisfied, the ruling must indicate the grounds upon which the arguments of the appeal or protest are deemed incorrect or unsubstantial.

When a judgment is vacated or changed, the ruling must indicate those articles of the law whose requirements are violated and in what the violations consist or in what the groundlessness of the judgment consists.

When a case is transferred for supplementary investigation or new judicial consideration, the circumstances to be ascertained must be stated.

Article 352. Binding Nature of Instruction of Cassational Instance. The instructions of a court considering a case by way of cassation shall be binding during supplementary investigation and during a reconsideration of the case by a court.

The court considering the case by way of cassation shall not have the right to establish or consider as proved facts which have not been established in, or which have been rejected by, the judgment and also shall not have the right to predetermine the questions of whether or not the accusation has been proved, of the authenticity of any evidence, of the superiority of some evidence over other evidence, of the application by the court of first instance of one criminal law or another, or of the measure of restraint.

Article 353. Consideration of Case by Court of First Instance After Vacating of Original Judgment. After the vacating of an original judgment, a case shall be subject to consideration in the usual manner.

Increasing the punishment or applying the law for a graver crime in a new consideration of a case by a court of first instance shall be permitted only if the original judgment has been vacated because of the mildness of the punishment or in connection with the necessity of applying the law for a graver crime on cassational protest of a procurator or on appeal of a victim, or if circumstances are established in the new consideration of the case after the judgment is vacated which evidence the commission by the accused of a graver crime.

Article 354. Return of Ruling of Cassational Instance For Execution. A ruling of the cassational instance shall be final and may be protested only by way of judicial supervision.

Not later than five days after it is rendered, a ruling shall, together with the file of the case, be referred for execution to the court which has decreed judgment. The cassational appeal or protest and supplementary materials must be attached to the file.

If, on the basis of the ruling of the cassational instance, a convicted person is subject to release from guard, a copy of such ruling shall be referred for execution by the cassational instance within a day directly to the administration of the place of confinement.

Article 355. Special Ruling of Cassational Instance. A court considering a case by way of cassation shall have the right, by a special ruling, to direct the attention of appropriate officials to violations permitted during an inquiry or preliminary investigation or during consideration of a case by a court, as well as to render other special rulings provided for by Article 321 of the present Code.

Section Five: Execution of the Judgment

Chapter Twenty-nine: Execution of the Judgment

Article 356. Entry into Legal Effect of Judgment and Its Execution. A judgment shall take legal effect upon expiration of the period for bringing a cassational appeal or protest if it has not been appealed from or protested. In the event that a cassational appeal or protest is brought, the judgment shall take legal effect, if it is not vacated, upon consideration of the case by a higher court.

A judgment which is not subject to cassational appeal shall take legal effect from the moment it is proclaimed.

A judgment of conviction shall be executed when it takes legal effect.

A judgment of acquittal and a judgment relieving a person brought to trial from punishment shall be executed immediately upon proclamation of the judgment. In the event that the person brought to trial is under guard, the court shall release him from guard in the courtroom.

Supervision of the legality of the execution of judgments shall be exercised by a procurator.

Article 357. Entry into Legal Effect of Ruling of Court and of Decree of Judge and Their Execution. A ruling of a court and a decree of a judge shall take legal effect and be executed upon expiration of the period for bringing an appeal or protest or, in the event that a special appeal or protest is brought, upon consideration of the case by a higher court.

A ruling of a court and decree of a judge which are not subject to appeal or protest shall take effect and be executed immediately upon being rendered.

A procurator's protest of a ruling of a court concerning conditional early relief, concerning replacement of a punishment with a milder one and relief from serving punishment because of illness shall suspend execution of a ruling.

[*Ved.* (1970), no. 22, item 442, Edict May 21, 1970.]

Article 358. Binding Nature of Judgment, Ruling, and Decree of Court. In conformity with Article 54 of the Fundamental Principles of Criminal Procedure of the USSR and Union Republics, a judgment, ruling, or decree of a court which has taken legal effect shall be binding on all state and social institutions, enterprises, and organizations, officials and citizens and shall be subject to execution on the entire territory of the USSR.

Article 359. Procedure for Returning Judgment, Ruling, or Decree of Court for Execution. A court which has decreed judgment shall be charged with returning the judgment, ruling, or decree of the court for execution. An instruction to execute a judgment shall be sent by the judge or person presiding together with a copy of the judgment to the agency which is charged with the duty of executing the judgment. In the event that the judgment is changed in the consideration of the case by way of cassation or supervision, copies of the ruling or decree of the cassational or supervisory instance shall be appended to the copy of the judgment.

The agencies executing a judgment shall immediately notify the court which has decreed judgment that it has been executed. The administration of the correctional labor institution must notify the court which has rendered judgment of the place where the convicted person is serving the punishment.

A court which has rendered judgment shall be obliged to see that the judgment, ruling, or decree has been executed.

In the instances provided for by Article 304 of the present Code a court which has entrusted social organizations, collectives of working people, or individual persons with observation of a conditionally sentenced person and his reeducation and correction shall be obliged to send them a copy of the judgment and to inform itself periodically about the conduct of the conditionally sentenced person.

For the purpose of increasing the educational effect of a judgment, a court which has rendered a judgment shall, when necessary, send a copy of the judgment to the convicted person's place of work, study, or residence, upon its entry into legal effect.

After entry into legal effect of a judgment by which social censure is announced, it shall, when necessary, be brought to public attention through the press or in another manner.

[*Ved.* (1970), no. 22, item 442, Edict May 21, 1970.]

Article 360. Permitting Relatives to Meet With Convicted Person and Notifying Them of Execution of Judgment. Before a judgment is returned for execution, a people's judge or president of a court must grant near relatives of a convicted person kept under guard an opportunity to meet with him, upon their request.

After the entry into legal effect of a judgment under which a convicted person kept under guard is sentenced to deprivation of freedom or exile, the administration of the place of confinement shall be obliged to let the family of the convicted person know where he is sent for serving the punishment.

Article 361. Postponing Execution of Judgment. Execution of a judgment condemning a person to deprivation of freedom, exile, banishment, or correctional tasks without deprivation of freedom may be postponed if there exists one of the following grounds:

(1) serious illness of the convicted person, preventing him from serving the punishment – until he recovers;

(2) pregnancy of the convicted person – for a period of not more than one year after delivery;

(3) when immediate serving of the punishment may entail especially grave consequences for the convicted person or his family in view of a fire or other natural calamities, grave illness, the death of the only able-bodied member of the family, or other exceptional circumstances – for a period established by the court, but not of more than three months.

Payment of a fine may be deferred or arranged in installments for a period of up to six months if immediate payment of the fine is impossible for the convicted person.

Article 362. Relief From Serving Punishment Because of Illness. In the event that, while serving punishment, a sentenced person has contracted a chronic mental or other grave illness preventing serving the punishment, the court shall have the right, upon the proposal of the director of the agency conducting the execution of the punishment based on the opinion of a doctors' commission, to render a ruling to relieve him from further serving of the punishment.

When relieving from further serving of punishment a convicted person who has contracted a chronic mental illness, the court shall have the right to apply compulsory measures of a medical character or to transfer him to the care of agencies of public health.

When deciding the question of relieving from further serving of punishment persons who have contracted a grave illness other than persons who have contracted a mental illness, the court shall take into account the gravity of the crime committed, the personality of the convicted person, and other circumstances.

[*Ved.* (1971), no. 22, item 432, Edict May 28, 1971.]

Article 363. Conditional Early Relief From Punishment and Replacement of Punishment by Milder One. Conditional early relief from punishment and replacement of the unserved part of a punishment by a milder punishment in instances provided by Article 53 of the RSFSR Criminal Code shall be applied by a court upon the joint proposal of the agency charged with execution of the punishment and the supervisory commission of the executive committee of the local soviet of working people's deputies, and in instances of punishment served in a disciplinary battalion, upon the proposal of the command of the disciplinary battalion.

Conditional early relief from punishment and replacement of the unserved part of a punishment by a milder punishment, with respect to persons who have committed a crime while under the age of 18 years, and in accordance with Article 55 of the RSFSR Criminal Code, shall be applied by a court upon the joint proposal of the agency charged with execution of the punishment and the commission for cases of minors or the supervisory commission of the executive committee of the local soviet of working people's deputies.

Relief from punishment in the form of deprivation of the right to occupy specified offices or engage in specified activity shall be carried out by the court upon the petition of a social organization, collective of working people, or the convicted person.

In the event that a court refuses conditional early relief from punishment or replacement of the unserved part of a punishment with a milder punishment, a reconsideration of proposals on this question may not take place until six months from the day of rendering the ruling of refusal.

[*Ved.* (1970), no. 22, item 442, Edict May 21, 1970.]

Article 364. Change of Conditions of Confinement of Persons Sentenced to Deprivation of Freedom During Serving of Punishment. The transfer of a convicted person from a correctional labor colony of special regimen to a correctional labor colony of strict regimen, from a correctional labor colony of general, reinforced, or strict regimen to a colony-settlement, from a correctional labor colony of strict regimen to a correctional labor colony of special regimen, from a colony-settlement to a correctional labor colony of that type of regimen which was previously assigned to him by a court, from a prison to a correctional labor colony, or from a correctional labor colony to a prison, on grounds provided for by legislation of the USSR and RSFSR, shall be carried out by a court upon the joint proposal of the administration of a correctional labor colony and the supervisory commission of the executive committee of the local soviet of working people's deputies.

In the event of a refusal of a court to transfer from a correctional labor colony of special regimen to a correctional labor colony of strict regimen, from a correctional labor colony to a colony-settlement, or from a prison to a correctional labor colony, a reconsideration of the proposal on this question may take place not earlier than upon the expiration of six months from the day of rendering the ruling of refusal.

Transfer of a convicted person from an educational labor colony to a correctional labor colony and from an educational labor colony of general regimen to an educational labor colony of reinforced regimen on grounds provided for by legislation of the USSR and RSFSR shall be carried out by a court upon the joint proposal of the administration of the educational labor colony and the commission for cases of minors.

[*Ved.* (1963), no. 36, item 661, Edict September 10, 1963; *Ved.* (1969), no. 4, item 89, Edict January 21, 1969; *Ved.* (1970), no. 22, item 442, Edict May 21, 1970.]

Article 365. Replacing Correctional Tasks and Fine by Other Measures of Punishment. Replacement of correctional tasks by a fine, social censure, or imposition of the duty to make amends for harm caused, with respect to persons deemed incapable of working and in accordance with Article 27 of the RSFSR Criminal Code, as well as replacement of correctional tasks by deprivation of freedom in accordance with Article 28 of the RSFSR Criminal Code, shall be carried out by a court upon the proposal of the agency executing that type of punishment.

Replacement of a fine by correctional tasks shall be carried out by a court in accordance with Article 30 of the RSFSR Criminal Code.

[*Ved.* (1970), no. 22, item 442, Edict May 21, 1970.]

Article 366. Deduction of Time Spent in Medical Institution From Period of Serving Punishment. If a person serving punishment in the form of deprivation of freedom has been committed to a medical institution, the time spent there by the convicted person shall be deducted from the period of serving punishment.

Article 367. Execution of Judgment When There Exist Other Unexecuted Judgments. In the event that there exist several unexecuted judgments with respect to a convicted person of which the court which has decreed the latest judgment has not been notified, such court or a court of the same kind at the place of execution of the judgment shall be obliged to render a ruling to apply to the convicted person punishment in accordance with all the indicated judgments, being governed by Articles 40 and 41 of the RSFSR Criminal Code.

Article 368. Courts Resolving Questions Connected With Execution of Judgment. A court which has decreed judgment shall resolve the questions of postponement of execution of judgment and nonexecution of judgment in accordance with Article 49 of the RSFSR Criminal Code, replacement of a fine and correctional tasks without deprivation of freedom by other measures of punishment in instances provided for by Article 365 of the present Code, inclusion of time for serving correctional tasks without deprivation of freedom in general job seniority in accordance with Article 27 of the RSFSR Criminal Code, replacement of the duty to make amends for the harm caused by correctional tasks, a fine, dismissal from office, or social censure in accordance with Article 32 of the RSFSR Criminal Code, reduction of the probation period in a conditional conviction in accordance with Article 44 of the RSFSR Criminal Code, institution of criminal proceedings against the guilty person in the event that the social organization or collective of working people renounces surety in accordance with Article 52 of the RSFSR Criminal Code, change or termination of the application of compulsory measures of a medical character to mentally ill persons in accordance with Article 60 of the RSFSR Criminal Code, extension or termination of compulsory treatment with respect to alcoholics and drug addicts in accordance with Article 62 of the RSFSR Criminal Code, as well as every sort of doubt and vagueness which arise in execution of the judgment.

If a judgment is executed outside the district in which the court which has decreed judgment operates, these questions shall be resolved by a court of the same kind, or, in the absence of a court of the same kind in the district in which the judgment is to be executed, by a higher court. In such event a copy of the ruling shall be delivered to the court which has decreed judgment.

Questions of relief from serving punishment because of illness, conditional early relief from punishment, replacement of the unserved part of the punishment by a milder punishment, transfer from one correctional labor or educational labor colony to another colony of a different type of regimen, from an educational labor colony to a correctional labor colony, from a correctional labor colony to a prison, and from a prison to a correctional labor colony, shall be resolved by a ruling of a district (or city) people's court at the place the convicted person is serving punishment regardless of which court has rendered the judgment.

[*Ved.* (1963), no. 36, item 661, Edict September 10, 1963; *Ved.* (1969), no. 4, item 89, Edict January 21, 1969); *Ved.* (1970), no. 22, item 442, Edict May 21, 1970.]

Article 369. Procedure for Resolving Questions Connected With Execution of Judgment. Questions connected with the execution of a judgment shall be resolved by a court in judicial session with participation of a procurator.

As a rule, the convicted person shall be summoned to the session. If the question concerns the execution of the part of a judgment relating to a civil suit the civil plaintiff shall also be summoned. Nonappearance of the specified persons shall not stop consideration of the case.

When a court decides the question of release of a convicted person because of illness or of committing him to a hospital, the presence of a representative of the doctors' commission which has given the opinion shall be obligatory.

When a court considers the question of conditional early relief from punishment, replacement of the unserved part of the punishment by a milder one, transfer from one correctional labor or educational labor colony to another colony of a different type of regimen, from an educational labor colony to a correctional labor colony, from a correctional labor colony to a prison, and from a prison to a correctional labor colony, a representative of the agency which is charged with execution of the punishment shall be summoned.

In instances when a case is considered by a court upon the joint proposal of the agency which is charged with execution of the punishment and the supervisory commission of the executive committee of the local soviet of working people's deputies or commission for cases of minors, or upon the proposal of the agency which is charged with execution of the punishment, with the consent of these commissions, the court shall notify the commissions of the time and place of consideration of the petition.

Consideration of a case shall commence with the report of the person presiding, after which the court shall hear the persons who have appeared at the session and the opinion of the procurator. Then the court shall retire for conference to render a ruling.

[*Ved.* (1963), no. 36, item 661, Edict September 10, 1963; *Ved.* (1969), no. 4, item 89, Edict January 21, 1969; *Ved.* (1970), no. 22, item 442, Edict May 21, 1970.]

Article 370. Consideration by Courts of Petitions to Expunge Record of Conviction. A question concerning expunging of a record of conviction in accordance with Article 57 of the RSFSR Criminal Code shall be decided by a district (city) people's court at the place of residence of the person serving the punishment, upon petition of such person or of social organizations.

A procurator shall be notified of a petition which has been received. Nonappearance of the procurator at the judicial session shall not stop consideration of the petition.

The presence in court of the person with respect to whom a petition is being considered to expunge the record of conviction shall be obligatory. In the event that a petition to expunge the record of conviction is initiated by a social organization, the presence of a representative of such organization shall also be obligatory.

Consideration of a petition to expunge the record of conviction shall commence with the report of the person presiding, after which the court shall hear the persons summoned and the conclusion of the procurator.

In the event that the court refuses to expunge the record of conviction, a new petition to that effect may not be initiated until one year from the day of rendering the ruling of refusal.

Section Six: Review of Judgments, Rulings, and Decrees Which Have Taken Legal Effect

Chapter Thirty: Proceedings in the Supervisory Instance

Article 371. Review by Way of Judicial Supervision of Judgment, Ruling, or Decree of Court Which Has Taken Legal Effect. The review by way of judicial supervision of a judgment, ruling, or decree of a court which has taken legal effect shall be permitted only on protest of a procurator or a chairman of a court or their deputies, as designated in the present article.

The following shall have the right to bring protests:

(1) the USSR Procurator General – of judgments, rulings, and decrees of any court of the RSFSR;

(2) the President of the USSR Supreme Court – of decrees of the Presidium as well as of judgments and rulings of the Judicial Division for Criminal Cases of the RSFSR Supreme Court, acting as a court of first instance;

(3) USSR Deputy Procurators General – of judgments, rulings, and decrees of any court of the RSFSR with the exception of decrees of the Presidium of the RSFSR Supreme Court;

(4) Deputy Presidents of the USSR Supreme Court – of judgments and rulings of the Judicial Division for Criminal Cases of the RSFSR Supreme Court, acting as a court of first instance;

(5) the RSFSR Procurator and President of the RSFSR Supreme Court and their deputies – of judgments, rulings, and decrees of any court in the RSFSR with the exception of decrees of the Presidium of the RSFSR Supreme Court.

(6) the president of the supreme court of an autonomous republic, territorial, regional, or city court, court of an autonomous region, or court of a national area, procurator of an autonomous republic, territory, region, autonomous region, or national area – of a judgment or ruling of a district (city) people's court or a ruling of a judicial division for criminal cases of the supreme court of the autonomous republic, territorial, regional, or city court, court of an autonomous region, or court of a national area, respectively, which has considered the case by way of cassation.

Protests of judgments of military tribunals shall be brought in accordance with the procedure established by Articles 20 and 21 of the Statute on Military Tribunals.

A person who has brought a protest shall have the right to withdraw it. A protest brought by a procurator may be withdrawn by a higher procurator. Withdrawal of a protest shall be permitted only before the commencement of the judicial session during which the protest is subject to consideration.

Article 372. Suspending Execution of Judgment, Ruling, or Decree of Court. In accordance with Article 48 of the Fundamental Principles of Criminal Procedure of the USSR and Union Republics, the USSR Procurator General and the President of the USSR Supreme Court and their deputies, the Chief Military Procurator and the President of the Military Division of the USSR Supreme Court shall have the right, within the limits of their competence, to suspend the execution of a protested judgment, ruling, or decree of a court until resolution of the case by way of judicial supervision.

The RSFSR Procurator and the President of the RSFSR Supreme Court and their deputies shall have the right to suspend the execution of a protested judgment, ruling, or decree of any court of the RSFSR except a decree of the Presidium of the RSFSR Supreme Court until resolution of the case by way of judicial supervision.

Article 373. **Protest by Way of Judicial Supervision of Mildness of Punishment, Termination of Case, or Judgment of Acquittal.** The review by way of judicial supervision of a judgment of conviction or ruling or decree of a court because of the mildness of the punishment or the necessity of applying to the convicted person the law for a graver crime, as well as review of a judgment of acquittal or ruling or decree of a court to terminate a case, shall be allowed only during a year from their entry into legal effect.

Article 374. **Courts Considering Cases on Protests by Way of Supervision.** The presidium of the supreme court of an autonomous republic, territorial, regional, or city court, court of an autonomous region, or court of a national area shall consider cases on protests of cassational rulings of such courts, of judgments and rulings of district (city) people's courts which have taken legal effect, and of rulings of people's judges to bring to trial.

The Judicial Division for Criminal Cases of the RSFSR Supreme Court shall consider cases on protests of judgments and rulings rendered by all courts of the republic which have taken legal effect, of decrees of judges of supreme courts of autonomous republics, territorial, regional, and city courts, courts of autonomous regions, and courts of national areas to bring to trial, if the judgments, rulings, and decrees have not been the subject of consideration in the RSFSR Supreme Court, and also cases on protests of decrees of presidia of supreme courts of autonomous republics, territorial, regional, and city courts, courts of autonomous regions, and courts of national areas.

The Presidium of the RSFSR Supreme Court shall consider cases on protests of judgments and rulings of the Judicial Division for Criminal Cases of the RSFSR Supreme Court, and also of decrees of judges of the RSFSR Supreme Court to bring to trial.

A member of a presidium of a court who has taken part in consideration of a case in first or second instance or by way of judicial supervision as a member of the Judicial Division for Criminal Cases of the RSFSR Supreme Court may not participate in the consideration of the case as a member of the presidium of the court.

If a majority of the members of the presidium of the supreme court of an autonomous republic, territorial, regional, or city court, court of an autonomous region, or court of a national area have taken part in the consideration of a given case in a court of first instance or in cassational instance, and a protest has been brought by the president of such court or by the procurator of the autonomous republic, territory, region, city, autonomous region, or national area, the person who has brought the protest shall refer the case to the President of the RSFSR Supreme Court or the RSFSR Procurator, as appropriate, for discussion of the question of bringing the protest to the RSFSR Supreme Court by way of judicial supervision. In instances when a protest of such a case has been brought by the USSR Procurator General, President of the RSFSR Supreme Court, or the RSFSR Procurator or their deputies, the case shall be transferred for consideration by way of judicial supervision to the Judicial Division for Criminal Cases of the RSFSR Supreme Court.

[*Ved.* (1963), no. 36, item 661, Edict September 10, 1963.]

Article 375. **Acquiring File of Criminal Case.** The persons specified in Article 371 of the present Code shall have the right to acquire, within the limits of their competence, the file of any criminal case for resolution of the question of bringing a protest of a judgment, ruling, or decree of a court which has taken legal effect.

The right to acquire the file of a case from district (city) people's courts shall also belong to the procurators of the districts (cities), who shall, when necessary, submit to a higher procurator a proposal concerning the bringing of a protest by way of judicial supervision.

Article 376. **Taking Decision Concerning Acquired Case.** Upon perceiving that the judgment, ruling, or decree of a court in a case of which the file has been acquired is illegal or unfounded, a person specified in Article 371 of the present Code shall bring a protest and shall refer the case with the protest to the appropriate supervisory instance.

In the event that a person who has acquired the file of a case has not detected therein grounds for bringing a protest, he shall so inform the person, institution, or organization upon whose petition the file of the case has been acquired for verification, with an indication of the reasons for refusal. The file of the case shall be returned to the court from which it has been acquired.

Article 377. **Procedure for Consideration of Case on Protest.** A case on protest of a judgment, ruling, or decree which has taken legal effect shall be considered by a supervisory instance in judicial session not later than fifteen days or, in the RSFSR Supreme Court, not later than a month, from the moment of receiving the case with the protest.

The following shall take part in consideration of a case by way of judicial supervision:

(1) in the presidium of the supreme court of an autonomous republic, territorial, regional, or city court, court of an autonomous region, or court of a national area – the procurator of the respective autonomous republic, territory, region, city, autonomous region, or national area;

(2) in the Judicial Division for Criminal Cases of the RSFSR Supreme Court – a procurator empowered by the RSFSR Procurator;

(3) in the Presidium of the RSFSR Supreme Court – the RSFSR Procurator or his deputy.

A court considering a case by way of judicial supervision shall, when necessary, have the right to summon to the judicial session the convicted or acquitted person or his defense counsel.

The case shall be reported by the president of the court or, upon his assignment, by a member of the presidium or a member of the court who has not previously participated in consideration of the case. The reporter shall set forth the circumstances of the case, the content of the judgment, ruling, or decree, and the content of the protest. Questions may be put to the reporter. If the convicted or acquitted person or his defense counsel is participating in the judicial session, he shall have the right, after the report of the judge, to give his oral explanations.

Then the procurator shall be granted the opportunity to support the protest brought by him or to give an opinion on the protest of the president of the court or his deputy, after which the judges shall render a decree, or the Judicial Division for Criminal Cases of the RSFSR Supreme Court a ruling, which shall be taken by a majority vote. If there is a tie vote, the protest shall be considered voted down for not having mustered a majority.

Article 378. Rulings and Decrees of Court Considering Protest. As a result of considering a case by way of supervision, a court may:

(1) leave the protest unsatisfied;

(2) vacate the judgment and all subsequent judicial rulings and decrees and terminate proceedings in the case or transfer it for new investigation or new judicial consideration;

(3) vacate the cassational ruling as well as subsequent judicial rulings and decrees if any have been rendered and transfer the case for new cassational consideration;

(4) vacate the rulings and decrees rendered by way of judicial supervision and leave unchanged or change the judgment of the court and cassational ruling;

(5) change the judgment, ruling, or decree of the court.

Article 379. Grounds for Vacating or Changing Judgment, Ruling or Decree of Court Which Has Taken Legal Effect. The circumstances stated in Article 342 of the present Code shall constitute the grounds for vacating or changing a judgment in the consideration of a case by way of judicial supervision.

Rulings of a court of first instance, decrees of a judge, rulings of the cassational instance, and rulings and decrees of the supervisory instance shall be subject to being vacated or changed if the court considering the protest deems that by such ruling or decree the court of first instance has rendered an illegal or unfounded decision, or that a higher court has without basis left unchanged, vacated, or changed previous rulings, decrees, or the judgment in the case, or that in the consideration of the case in the higher court violations of the law have been permitted which have affected or might have affected the correctness of the ruling or decree rendered by it.

Article 380. Limits of Rights of Supervisory Instance. In the consideration of a protest by way of judicial supervision, a court shall not be bound by the arguments of the protest and shall be obliged to verify all the proceedings in the case in their entirety. If several persons have been convicted in the case but the protest is brought with respect to only one or some of the convicted persons, the court shall be obliged to verify the case with respect to all the convicted persons.

In the consideration of a case by way of judicial supervision, a court may mitigate the punishment assigned to the convicted person or apply the law for a less grave crime but shall not have the right to increase the punishment or to apply the law for a graver crime.

If it deems incorrect the acquittal of the person brought to trial or termination of the case in a court of first or cassational instance or the assignment of punishment to the person brought to trial which by its mildness does not correspond to the act committed, a court of supervisory instance shall have the right, under the conditions established in Article 373 of the present Code, to vacate the judgment or ruling and refer the case for a new consideration by the court of first or cassational instance, as appropriate. In this connection, in returning a case to the court of first instance, the court of supervisory instance must indicate the stage from which the new consideration of the returned case must commence.

If unfounded termination of a case or illegal mitigation of the punishment for the convicted person has been permitted in the consideration of a case by way of supervision, a higher supervisory instance shall have the right to vacate the ruling or decree of a lower supervisory instance and leave unchanged the judgment of the court of first instance or ruling of the cassational instance.

In the event that several persons brought to trial have been convicted or acquitted in the case, the court shall not have the right to vacate the judgment, ruling, or decree concerning those acquitted or convicted persons with respect to whom a protest is not submitted if vacating of the judgment, ruling, or decree worsens their position.

The instructions of a court considering a case by way of judicial supervision shall be binding during supplementary investigation and during a reconsideration of the case by a court.

The court considering the case by way of judicial supervision shall not have the right to establish or consider as proved facts which have not been established in, or which have been rejected by, the judgment and also shall not have the right to predetermine the questions of whether or not the accusation has been proved, of the authenticity or lack of authenticity of any evidence, of the superiority of some evidence over other evidence, of the application by the court of first instance of one criminal law or another, or of the measure of restraint.

Similarly, in the consideration of a case by way of judicial supervision a court, in vacating the cassational ruling, shall not have the right to predetermine the findings which may be made by the cassational instance during a reconsideration of the case.

Article 381. Content of Ruling or Decree. A decree rendered in the consideration of a case by the presidium of a court or a ruling of the Judicial Division for Criminal Cases of the RSFSR Supreme Court by way of judicial supervision must correspond to the requirements of Article 351 of the present Code.

A ruling shall be signed by the whole court and a decree shall be signed by the person presiding in the session of the presidium.

The ruling or decree of the court shall be attached to the file of the case together with the protest.

Article 382. Consideration of Case After Vacating of Original Judgment or of Ruling of Cassational Instance. After the vacating of an original judgment or of a cassational ruling, a case shall be subject to consideration in the usual manner.

An increase of punishment or application of a law for a graver crime in the consideration of the case by a court of first or second instance, respectively, shall be permitted only if the original judgment or ruling has been vacated by way of supervision because of the mildness of the punishment or in connection with the necessity of applying a law for a graver crime, or if in the reconsideration of the case after the vacating of the judgment circumstances are established which testify to commission by the accused of a graver crime. A judgment decreed by a court of first instance during a reconsideration of a case may be appealed from and protested in the usual manner.

Article 383. Submitting New Protests. A protest of a new judgment, ruling, or decree rendered in connection with the vacating of previous ones by way of cassation or by way of judicial supervision may be submitted on the usual grounds regardless of the reasons for which the first judgment, ruling, or decree of the court has been vacated.

Chapter Thirty-one: Reopening Cases on the Basis of Newly Discovered Circumstances

Article 384. Grounds for Reopening Cases on Basis of Newly Discovered Circumstances. A judgment, ruling, or decree of a court which has taken legal effect may be vacated on the basis of newly discovered circumstances.

The following shall constitute grounds for reopening a criminal case on the basis of newly discovered circumstances:

(1) the establishment by a judgment of a court which has taken legal effect of the known falsity of the testimony of a witness or opinion of an expert as well as the fraudulent character of real evidence, records of investigative and judicial actions or other documents, or known falsity in a translation, resulting in the decreeing of an unfounded or illegal judgment;

(2) the establishment by a judgment of a court which has taken legal effect of criminal abuses by judges permitted by them in the consideration of a given case;

(3) the establishment by a judgment of a court which has taken legal effect of criminal abuses by persons who have conducted the investigation in the case, resulting in the decreeing of an unfounded or illegal judgment or of a ruling of the court to terminate the case;

(4) any other circumstances unknown to the court when decreeing the judgment or ruling which in themselves, or together with circumstances established earlier, prove that the convicted person is not guilty or that he has committed

a less grave or graver crime than that of which he has been convicted, or prove that an acquitted person or a person with respect to whom a case has been terminated is guilty.

If it is impossible to render a judgment because of the expiration of periods of limitation, the promulgation of an act of amnesty, the pardoning of individual persons, or the death of the accused, the newly discovered circumstances indicated in subsections 1–3 of the present article shall be established by an investigation conducted in accordance with the procedure provided by Article 387 of the present Code.

Article 385. Periods for Reopening Cases on Basis of Newly Discovered Circumstances. The review of a judgment of acquittal or ruling or decree of a court to terminate a case, as well as the review of a judgment of conviction, ruling, or decree of a court for reasons of the mildness of the punishment or the necessity of applying to the convicted person the law for a graver crime, shall be permitted only within the periods of limitation for instituting criminal proceedings established by Article 48 of the RSFSR Criminal Code and not later than one year after the discovery of the new circumstances.

The review of a judgment of conviction on the basis of newly discovered circumstances in favor of the convicted person shall not be limited by time periods.

The death of a convicted person shall not obstruct the reopening of a case concerning him on the basis of newly discovered circumstances for the purpose of rehabilitating such convicted person.

Article 386. Initiating Proceedings on Basis of Newly Discovered Circumstances. The statements of citizens and communications of institutions, enterprises, organizations, and officials concerning newly discovered circumstances shall be referred to a procurator.

If there exists one of the grounds provided for by Article 384 of the present Code, the procurator shall, within the limits of his competence, render a decree to initiate proceedings on the basis of newly discovered circumstances and shall conduct an investigation of such circumstances or shall commission an investigator to do so. When investigating the newly discovered circumstances, interrogations, views, expert examinations, seizures, and any other necessary investigative actions may be conducted, in accordance with the rules of the present Code.

If the procurator does not perceive grounds to initiate proceedings on the basis of newly discovered circumstances, he shall refuse to do so by a reasoned decree. The procurator's decree must be communicated to interested persons, institutions, enterprises, or organizations, who may appeal from it to a higher procurator.

Article 387. Actions of Procurator Upon Completion of Investigation of Newly Discovered Circumstances. Upon completion of the investigation of newly discovered circumstances, if there exist grounds for reopening a case, a procurator shall refer the case to a court with the materials of the investigation and his opinion, being governed in this connection by the rules of Article 388 of the present Code.

In the absence of grounds for reopening the case, the procurator shall terminate the proceedings by a reasoned decree. Such decree must be communicated to interested persons, institutions, enterprises, or organizations, who may appeal from it to a higher procurator.

Article 388. Resolution by Court of Question of Reopening Case on Basis of Newly Discovered Circumstances. Cases shall be reopened on the basis of newly discovered circumstances:

(1) with respect to judgments and rulings of district (city) people's courts, by the presidium of the appropriate higher court;

(2) with respect to judgments, rulings, and decrees of supreme courts of autonomous republics, territorial, regional, or city courts, courts of autonomous regions, and courts of national areas, by the Judicial Division for Criminal Cases of the RSFSR Supreme Court;

(3) with respect to judgments and rulings rendered in the first instance and decrees of the RSFSR Supreme Court, by the Presidium of the RSFSR Supreme Court.

The previous consideration of a case by way of cassation or by way of judicial supervision shall not obstruct its consideration in the same judicial instance by way of reopening on the basis of newly discovered circumstances.

The reopening of a case on the basis of newly discovered circumstances shall be carried out in judicial session in accordance with the rules established in Article 377 of the present Code.

Article 389. Rulings and Decrees of Court Considering Conclusion of Procurator. The presidium of a court which has considered a case on the basis of newly discovered circumstances shall render a decree, and the Judicial Division for Criminal Cases of the RSFSR Supreme Court a ruling:

(1) to vacate the judgment, ruling, or decree of the court and to transfer the case for new investigation or new judicial examination;

(2) to vacate the judgment, ruling, or decree of the court and to terminate the case;

(3) to decline to adopt the opinion of the procurator.

Article 390. Procedure After Reopening Case on Basis of Newly Discovered Circumstances. The preliminary investigation and judicial examination after the reopening of a case in connection with the vacating of a judgment on the basis of newly discovered circumstances, as well as an appeal from a newly rendered judgment, shall be conducted on the usual grounds.

In the judicial examination of a case in which the judgment has been vacated in connection with newly discovered circumstances, the court of first instance shall not be bound by the punishment assigned in the vacated judgment.

Section Seven: Proceedings in Cases of Minors

Chapter Thirty-two: Proceedings in Cases of Minors

Article 391. Method of Conducting Proceedings in Cases of Minors. Judicial proceedings in cases of minors shall be determined by the general rules of the present Code and, in addition, by the following articles.

The regulations in the present chapter shall be applied in cases of persons who have not attained the age of 18 years at the moment of committing a crime.

Article 392. Circumstances to be Established in Cases of Minors. In the conduct of the preliminary investigation and the judicial examination in cases of minors, it is necessary to direct special attention to ascertainment of the following circumstances:

(1) the age of the minor (day, month, and year of birth);

(2) conditions of life and upbringing;

(3) the causes and conditions facilitating commission of the crime by the minor;

(4) the existence of adult instigators and other accomplices.

If there exist data concerning mental retardation of the minor not connected with mental illness, it must also be ascertained whether he could completely realize the significance of his actions. To establish these circumstances, the parents of the minor, his teachers and educators, and other persons capable of giving the necessary information must be interrogated, the necessary documents must be acquired, and other investigative and judicial actions must be conducted.

Article 393. Detention and Confinement Under Guard of Minors. Detention and confinement under guard as a measure of restraint may be applied to a minor only in exceptional instances when such is called for by the gravity of the crime committed and if there exist grounds stated in Articles 91, 96, and 122 of the present Code.

[*Ved.* (1970), no. 22, item 442, Edict May 21, 1970.]

Article 394. Release of Minor Under Care. Besides the measures of restraint provided by Article 89 of the present Code, minors may be released under the care of parents, guardians, or curators, and minors who are being educated in boarding institutions for children may be released under the supervision of the administration of these institutions.

A release under the care of parents, guardians, curators, or the administration of boarding institutions for children shall consist in an undertaking by any of the specified persons of a written obligation to ensure the appearance of the minor before the investigator and in court as well as his proper behavior.

In the obtaining of a signed statement to accept under care, the parents, guardians, curators, or directors of boarding institutions for children shall be warned of the character of the crime of which the minor is suspected or accused and of their responsibility in the event of violation of the obligation undertaken by them.

In the event that they violate the obligation undertaken by them, the measures provided by paragraph two of Article 94 of the present Code shall be applied to parents, guardians, and curators under whose care a minor has been released.

[*Ved.* (1970), no. 22, item 442, Edict May 21, 1970.]

Article 395. Procedure for Summoning Accused. The summoning of a minor before an investigator and to court shall be carried out, as a rule, through his parents or other legal representatives. Any other procedure shall be permitted only in the event that such is called for by the circumstances of the case.

A minor who is under guard shall be summoned through the administration of the place of confinement.

Article 396. Disjoinder of Case Concerning Minor into Separate Proceeding. If a minor has participated in the commission of a crime together with adults, the case concerning him must, when possible, be disjoined into a separate proceeding at the stage of the preliminary investigation.

In the event that disjoinder into a separate proceeding concerning the minor may create substantial obstacles to the thorough, complete, and objective analysis of the circumstances of the case, the rules of the present chapter shall be applicable to a minor prosecuted as an accused in the same case with adults.

Article 397. Participation of Teacher in Interrogation of Accused Minor. At the discretion of an investigator or procurator or upon a petition of defense counsel, a teacher may participate in the interrogation of an accused minor who has not attained the age of 16 years. The participation of a teacher is also possible in the interrogation of a minor over the age of 16 if he is deemed mentally retarded.

A teacher participating in an interrogation shall have the right, with the permission of the investigator, to put questions to the accused. Upon completion of the interrogation, a teacher who has participated therein shall have the right to acquaint himself with the record of the interrogation and to make written remarks concerning the correctness and completeness of the entries in it. Before commencement of the interrogation of a minor the investigator shall be obliged to inform the teacher of his rights and a note to such effect shall be made in the record of the interrogation.

Article 398. Acquainting Legal Representative of Accused Minor With Materials of Case. When the termination of a preliminary investigation is announced to a minor and the materials of the case are presented to him in order that he may acquaint himself with them, the legal representative of the accused must be admitted if he so petitions.

The investigator may refuse to permit the legal representative of the minor to participate in the acquainting of the accused with the materials of the case if he deems that this may be harmful to the interests of the minor.

Article 399. Participation in Judicial Session by Legal Representatives of Minor Prisoner. The parents or other legal representatives of a minor prisoner may be summoned to the judicial session. They shall have the right to participate in the analysis of evidence at the judicial investigation, to present evidence, and to submit petitions and challenges. The said rights must be explained to them at the opening of the judicial session.

When it is necessary to interrogate the parents or other legal representatives of the person brought to trial as witnesses, a court shall hear their testimony. The legal representatives of the person brought to trial shall be present in the courtroom during the entire judicial examination.

In exceptional instances, when participation in the judicial session by a legal representative may be harmful to the interests of an accused minor, the court shall have the right by a reasoned ruling either to bar completely the legal representative from participation in the judicial session or to limit his participation to a particular part of the judicial session.

Nonappearance of the legal representatives of the person brought to trial shall not suspend consideration of the case if the court does not find their participation necessary.

Article 400. Participation in Judicial Session by Representatives of Educational Institutions and Social Organizations. For the purpose of strengthening the educational effect of the judicial examination of a case concerning a minor, the court shall notify the school or other educational institution in which the minor has been studying as well as social organizations at his place of study or work of the time and place of consideration of the case. When necessary, the court shall have the right to summon to the judicial session representatives of such organizations as well as representatives of social organizations at the place of work of the parents, guardian, or curator of the person brought to trial.

Article 401. Removal from Courtroom of Minor Brought to Trial. When it has heard the opinion of the defense counsel and the legal representative of the person brought to trial and the conclusion of the procurator, the court shall have the right by its ruling to remove the minor from the courtroom during the time that circumstances are analyzed which might have a negative influence on the minor.

Article 402. Court's Application to Minor of Compulsory Measures of Educational Character. If as a result of consideration of a case the court reaches the conclusion that without application of criminal punishment it is possible to correct a person who, while under the age of 18 years, has committed a crime not representing a great social danger, it shall render a ruling to terminate the criminal case and to apply to the minor one of the compulsory measures of an educational character provided by Article 10 of the RSFSR Criminal Code.

In the rendering of the ruling, the requirements of Articles 261, 339, and 377 of the present Code shall be observed.

Termination of a criminal case with respect to a minor may be carried out by the court in addition, in an administrative session in accordance with Article 8 of the present Code.

[*Ved.* (1968), no. 20, item 859, Edict May 8, 1968.]

Section Eight: Proceedings for the Application of Compulsory Measures of a Medical Character

Chapter Thirty-three: Proceedings for the Application of Compulsory Measures of a Medical Character

Article 403. Grounds for Applying Compulsory Measures of Medical Character. Compulsory measures of a medical character provided by Article 58 of the RSFSR Criminal Code shall be applied by a court to persons who have committed socially dangerous acts provided for by the criminal law while in a state of nonimputability, or who, after committing a crime, have contracted a mental illness which deprives them of the ability to realize the significance of their actions or to control them, if such persons represent a danger to society because of the character of the act committed by them and their state of illness.

Legal proceedings for application of compulsory measures of a medical nature shall be determined by the general rules of the present Code and, in addition, by the following articles.

Article 404. Procedure for Preliminary Investigation. In cases of socially dangerous acts of nonimputable persons as well as of crimes of persons who have contracted a mental illness after committing a crime, it shall be obligatory to conduct a preliminary investigation.

The following circumstances must be ascertained in the preliminary investigation:

(1) the time, place, method, and other circumstances of committing the socially dangerous act;

(2) the commission of the socially dangerous act by the given person;

(3) whether the person who has committed the socially dangerous act has been mentally ill in the past, the degree and character of the mental illness at the moment of committing the socially dangerous act and at the time of the investigation of the case;

(4) the behavior of the person who has committed the socially dangerous act both before and after its commission;

(5) the character and extent of the damage caused by the socially dangerous act.

Referral of the person for examination by a forensic psychiatric expert shall be permitted only if there exist sufficient data to indicate that this very person has committed the socially dangerous act regarding which the criminal case has been initiated and the investigation is being conducted.

If, by virtue of his mental state, the conduct of investigative actions with the participation of the person who has committed the socially dangerous act is impossible, the investigator shall draw up a record to this effect.

Article 405. Participation of Defense Counsel. In cases of persons who have committed socially dangerous acts while in a state of nonimputability as well as of persons who have contracted a mental illness after committing a crime, the participation of defense counsel shall be obligatory.

Defense counsel shall be permitted to participate in a case from the moment the fact of the mental illness of the person who has committed the socially dangerous act is established.

Article 406. Completion of Preliminary Investigation. Upon completion of a preliminary investigation an investigator shall render a decree:

(1) to terminate proceedings in the case, in instances provided for by Article 208 of the present Code or in instances when, because of the character of the socially dangerous act and his mental state, the person who has committed such act does not represent a danger to society;

(2) to refer the case to court, if grounds have been established for applying compulsory measures of a medical character to the person who has committed the socially dangerous act.

The decree to refer the case to court must set forth all the circumstances of the case established by the preliminary investigation and the grounds for application by the court of compulsory measures of a medical character.

The decree shall be referred, together with the file of the case, to a procurator, who, if he is in agreement with the decree, shall transfer the case to court, or if he is not in agreement, shall return the case for supplementary investigation. In the absence of grounds for the application of measures of a medical character the procurator shall terminate the case.

In terminating the case, when the person who has committed the socially dangerous act does not represent a danger to society because of the nature of the act committed and his mental state, but is mentally ill, the investigator or the procurator shall inform the local agency of public health concerning him.

Article 407. Actions Preparatory to Judicial Session. If a people's judge or president of a court receives a case from a procurator, he shall assign it for consideration in a judicial session, shall notify the procurator, defense counsel, and legal representatives of the person who has committed the socially dangerous act, and shall summon the victims, witnesses, and also, when necessary, experts.

The people's judge or the chairman of the court shall have the right to order the person concerning whom the case is being considered to be summoned to the judicial session if the character of his illness does not prevent this.

In instances when the people's judge or the chairman of the court perceives grounds for terminating proceedings for application of compulsory measures of a medical character or grounds for returning the case for supplementary investigation, he shall bring the case to the consideration of an administrative session of the court.

Article 408. Judicial Examination in Criminal Case. The judicial examination in a case received in court under the procedure of Article 406 of the present Code shall proceed in judicial session in accordance with the rules of Chapters Twenty-one through Twenty-three of the present Code with obligatory participation of a procurator and defense counsel.

In the judicial session evidence tending to establish or disprove the commission by the given person of a socially dangerous act provided for by the criminal law must be verified, the opinion of experts concerning the mental state of the accused must be heard, and other circumstances which are of substantial significance for deciding the question of the application of compulsory measures of a medical character must be verified.

Upon completion of the judicial investigation the court shall hear the procurator and the defense counsel.

Article 409. Resolution of Case by Court. A court shall resolve a case by its ruling, which shall be rendered in the conference room.

When rendering a ruling the court must resolve the following questions:

(1) whether there has taken place a socially dangerous act provided for by the criminal law;

(2) whether the person concerning whom the case is being considered has committed that act;

(3) whether the given person has committed the socially dangerous act while in a state of nonimputability;

(4) whether after committing the crime the given person has contracted a mental illness which deprives him of the ability to realize the significance of his actions or to control them, and whether or not such illness is a temporary derangement of mental activity requiring only the suspension of proceedings in the case;

(5) whether a compulsory measure of a medical character is applicable and exactly which one.

Article 410. Ruling of Court. If it deems proved that a given person has, while in a state of nonimputability, committed a socially dangerous act provided for by the criminal law, or that, after committing the crime, such person has contracted a chronic mental illness which deprives him of the ability to realize the significance of his actions or to control them, a court shall render a ruling in accordance with Article 11 of the RSFSR Criminal Code to release such person from criminal responsibility or punishment, as appropriate, and to apply to him a compulsory measure of a medical character with an indication of exactly which one, or to terminate the case and not apply such measures in instances when the person, because of the nature of the act he has committed and his mental state, does not represent a danger to society and does not need compulsory treatment. In such instances the court shall notify the agencies of public health concerning the sick person.

If it deems that nonimputability of the person concerning whom the case is being considered is not established or that the illness of the person who has committed the crime does not eliminate the application to him of measures of punishment, the court shall, by its ruling, return the case for supplementary investigation and further referral of the case in the usual manner.

In the event that the court deems that participation of the given person in the commission of a socially dangerous act has not been proved or if the circumstances provided for by Article 5 of the present Code have been established, the court shall render a ruling to terminate the case on the ground established by it regardless of the existence or the character of the person's illness and shall notify the agencies of public health.

In the ruling the court shall resolve the questions indicated in Article 317 of the present Code.

Article 411. **Appealing From and Protesting Ruling of Court.** Within seven days a ruling of a court may be appealed from by defense counsel, the victim and his representative, or a near relative of the person concerning whom the case has been considered, or protested by the procurator to a higher court.

Article 412. **Cancellation or Change of Compulsory Measure of Medical Character.** If because of the recovery of a person deemed nonimputable or because of a change in the state of his health the necessity ceases for further application of a compulsory measure of a medical character previously taken, a court shall consider, in accordance with the procedure established by paragraphs one and six of Article 369 of the present Code, the question of canceling or changing the compulsory measure of a medical character, upon proposal of the administration of the medical institution in which the given person is kept, based on the conclusion of a commission of doctors.

The same rules shall be applied with respect to a person who has contracted a chronic mental illness after committing a crime if, because of a change which has occurred in the state of his health, such person does not need further application of compulsory measures of a medical character, although he remains mentally ill.

Near relatives of the person deemed nonimputable and other interested persons may initiate a petition to cancel or change the compulsory measures of a medical character. In such instances the court shall inquire of the appropriate agencies of public health concerning the state of health of the person concerning whom the petition is initiated.

The questions stated in this article shall be resolved by the court which has rendered the ruling to apply a compulsory measure of a medical character or by a court at the place of application of such a measure, with the obligatory participation of a procurator.

Article 413. **Reopening Case With Respect to Person to Whom Compulsory Measure of Medical Character Has Been Applied.** If a person to whom a compulsory measure of a medical character has been applied because of a mental illness contracted by him after commission of the crime is deemed by a doctors' commission to have recovered, a court shall render a ruling, on the basis of the opinion of the medical institution and in accordance with the rules of Article 369 of the present Code, to cancel the compulsory measure of a medical character and shall decide the question of referring the case for inquiry or preliminary investigation, prosecution of the given person as the accused, or transfer of the case to a court in the usual manner.

The time spent in the medical institution shall be included in the time of being kept under guard.

Section Nine: Proceedings in Cases of Hooliganism

Chapter Thirty-four: Proceedings in Cases of Hooliganism

Article 414. Method of Conducting Proceedings in Cases of Hooliganism. The method of conducting proceedings in cases of hooliganism shall be determined by the general rules of the present Code with the exceptions established by the articles of the present chapter.

[*Ved.* (1966), no. 35, item 946, Edict August 24, 1966.]

Article 415. Procedure for Referring Materials to Court. In cases of crimes provided for by paragraph one of Article 206 of the Criminal Code of the RSFSR, agencies of the police and other agencies of inquiry shall within fifteen days establish the circumstances of the crime which has been committed and the identity of the lawbreaker; receive the explanations of the lawbreaker, the victim, and the eyewitnesses; demand and obtain information concerning the existence or nonexistence of the lawbreaker's convictions, character references from his place of work or study, and other materials having significance for the consideration of the case in court.

A record shall be drawn up concerning the detention of the lawbreaker, the establishment of his identity, and the circumstances of the crime which has been committed, to which shall be attached all the materials as well as a list of persons subject to court summons. The record shall be confirmed by the chief of the agency of inquiry, after which all the materials shall be presented to the lawbreaker so that he may acquaint himself with them, and a corresponding notation to this effect shall be made in the record. The record together with the materials shall be referred to a court with the sanction of the procurator.

[*Ved.* (1966), no. 35, item 946, Edict August 24, 1966.]

Article 416. Conduct of Inquiry. In cases of crimes provided for by paragraph two of Article 206 of the Criminal Code of the RSFSR, an inquiry shall be conducted by investigators of agencies of internal affairs, who shall use the powers therefor provided by Article 127 of the present Code.

An inquiry in cases of crimes provided for by paragraph one of Article 206 of the Criminal Code of the RSFSR shall be conducted by agencies of inquiry in the following instances:

a) when the criminal case is initiated by the chief of an agency of inquiry, if within fifteen days it is impossible to ascertain the essential circumstances of the commission of the crime;

b) when the file of the case or the materials are returned by a court for ascertaining essential supplementary circumstances, if they cannot be established in the judicial session.

In instances provided for by the present article, the inquiry must be concluded not later than twenty days from the day of the initiation or return of the criminal case.

[*Ved.* (1966), no. 35, item 946, Edict August 24, 1966; *Ved.* (1970), no. 22, item 442, Edict May 21, 1970.]

Article 417. Conduct of Preliminary Investigation. Preliminary investigation shall be conducted in cases of crimes provided for by paragraph three of Article 206 of the Criminal Code of the RSFSR, as well as in instances provided for by paragraph two of Article 126 of the present Code.

The preliminary investigation must be concluded not later than one month from the day the criminal case was initiated.

[*Ved.* (1966), no. 35, item 946, Edict August 24, 1966; *Ved.* (1970), no. 22, item 442, Edict May 21, 1970.]

Article 418. Detention and Application of Measure of Restraint. Persons who have committed crimes provided for by Article 206 of the Criminal Code of the RSFSR shall be detained by agencies of the police or other agencies of inquiry and shall be confined under guard. The grounds and method of detention shall be determined by Article 122 of the present Code.

Prior to the consideration of the case in court, confinement under guard shall, as a rule, be selected as the measure of restraint for persons detained for hooliganistic acts.

Prior to the initiation of the case and its consideration in court, the measure of restraint for persons detained for the commission of a crime provided for by paragraph one of Article 206 of the Criminal Code of the RSFSR shall be selected in conformity with paragraph two of the present article.

[*Ved.* (1966), no. 35, item 946, Edict August 24, 1966.]

Article 419. Initiation of Case in Court. Having deemed the materials on a crime provided for by paragraph one of Article 206 of the Criminal Code of the RSFSR to be sufficient for consideration in a judicial session, the court shall render a ruling to initiate a criminal case and to bring the lawbreaker to trial and shall consider the case in a judicial session or shall return the materials so that an inquiry or preliminary investigation may be conducted, but in the absence of grounds for initiating a criminal case it shall refuse to initiate a criminal case.

A single judge may personally render a decree to initiate a criminal case, to bring the lawbreaker to trial, and to assign the case for consideration in a judicial session.

[*Ved.* (1966), no. 35, item 946, Edict August 24, 1966.]

Article 420. Consideration of Case in Court. Cases of crimes provided for by paragraph one of Article 206 of the Criminal Code of the RSFSR shall be subject to consideration in court not later than fifteen days from the moment they are entered in court. In considering such cases the court shall have the right to return them so that an inquiry or preliminary investigation may be conducted if it becomes necessary to ascertain essential supplementary circumstances which cannot be established in a judicial session.

Cases of hooliganism in which an inquiry or preliminary investigation has been conducted shall be considered by a court not later than ten days from the moment they are entered in court.

[*Ved.* (1966), no. 35, item 946, Edict August 24, 1966.]

The Law on Court Organization of the RSFSR

October 27, 1960, as Amended to March 1, 1972

Chapter One: General Provisions

Article 1. Judicial System. In accordance with Article 107 of the Constitution of the RSFSR, justice in the RSFSR shall be administered by the Supreme Court of the RSFSR, by supreme courts of autonomous republics, by territorial, regional, and city courts, by courts of autonomous regions, by courts of national areas, and by district (or city) people's courts.

Article 2. Goals of Justice. Justice in the RSFSR is called upon to protect from any infringements:

(a) the social and state system secured by the USSR Constitution, by the RSFSR Constitution, and by constitutions of autonomous republics, the socialist system of economy, and socialist ownership;

(b) political, labor, housing, and other personal and property rights and interests of citizens guaranteed by the USSR Constitution, by the RSFSR Constitution, and by constitutions of autonomous republics;

(c) rights and legally protected interests of state enterprises, institutions, collective farms, cooperative and other social organizations.

Justice in the RSFSR has as its task the securing of the strict and undeviating execution of the laws by all institutions, organizations, officials, and citizens.

Article 3. Tasks of Court. By all its activity a court shall educate citizens in the spirit of loyalty to the Motherland and to the cause of communism, and in the spirit of strict and undeviating execution of Soviet laws, care for socialist ownership, observance of labor discipline, an honorable attitude toward state and social duty, and respect for the rights, honor, and dignity of citizens and for rules of socialist community life.

In applying measures of criminal punishment a court not only chastises criminals but also has as its purpose their correction and reeducation.

Article 4. Administration of Justice Through Judicial Consideration of Civil and Criminal Cases. Justice in the RSFSR shall be administered through:

(a) consideration and resolution in judicial sessions of civil cases concerning disputes affecting the rights and legal interests of citizens, state enterprises, institutions, collective farms, and cooperative and other social organizations;

(b) consideration in judicial sessions of criminal cases and either the application of measures of punishment established by law to persons guilty of committing a crime or the acquittal of the innocent.

Article 5. Equality of Citizens Before Law and Courts. Justice in the RSFSR shall be administered on the basis of equality of citizens before the law and the courts, without regard to their social, property, or occupational status, nationality, race, or religious confession.

Article 6. Administration of Justice in Strict Accordance With Law. Justice in the RSFSR shall be administered in strict accordance with legislation of the USSR, the RSFSR, and autonomous republics.

Article 7. Independence of Judges and Their Subordination Only to Law. In accordance with Article 116 of the Constitution of the RSFSR, judges and people's assessors in administering justice shall be independent and subordinate only to law.

Article 8. Formation of All Courts on Basis of Election. In accordance with Articles 110–113 of the Constitution of the RSFSR, all courts in the RSFSR shall be formed on the basis of election.

Article 9. Conditions Required for Candidates for Judges and People's Assessors. Every citizen of the USSR who possesses the right to vote and has attained the age of 25 years by election day may be elected a judge or a people's assessor.

Article 10. Collegial Consideration of Cases in All Courts. Cases in courts shall be considered collegially.

Consideration of cases in all courts of first instance shall be by a judge and two people's assessors.

Cases on appeal or on protest shall be considered in judicial divisions of higher courts in benches of three members of the particular court.

Cases on protests of decisions, judgments, rulings, and decrees of courts which have taken legal effect shall be considered in judicial divisions of the Supreme Court of the RSFSR, in benches of three members of the court.

Presidia of courts shall consider cases with a majority of the members of the presidium being present.

Article 11. Equal Rights of People's Assessors and Judges in Administration of Justice. During discharge of their duties in court the people's assessors shall exercise all the rights of a judge.

Article 12. Open Examination of Cases in All Courts. In accordance with Article 115 of the Constitution of the RSFSR, examination of cases in all courts of the RSFSR shall be open, insofar as an exception is not provided by law.

Article 13. Securing to an Accused the Right to Defense. In accordance with Article 115 of the Constitution of the RSFSR, an accused shall be secured the right to defense.

Article 14. Language in Which Judicial Proceedings Shall Be Conducted. In accordance with Article 114 of the Constitution of the RSFSR, judicial proceedings in the RSFSR shall be conducted in the Russian language or in the language of the autonomous republic or autonomous region or national area, but in instances provided by constitutions of autonomous republics [they shall be conducted] in the language of the majority of the population of the district, persons not having command of that language being secured a full acquaintance with materials of the case through an interpreter and also the right to speak in court in their native language.

Article 15. Period for Which People's Assessors Shall Be Called Upon for Discharge of Duties in Court. People's assessors shall be called upon for discharge of their duties in courts in turn, according to a list, for not more than two weeks a year, except in instances when extension of this period is necessitated to complete the consideration of a case commenced with their participation.

Article 16. Retention of Wages for People's Assessors During Discharge of Their Duties in Court. People's assessors who are workers, employees, or collective farmers shall receive their average wages at their place of work for the time during which they discharge their duties in court.

People's assessors who are not workers, employees, or collective farmers, shall be compensated for expenses connected with discharge of their duties in court.

The manner and the amount of reimbursement shall be established by the Presidium of the Supreme Soviet of the RSFSR.

[*Ved.* (1968), no. 37, item 1349, Edict September 9, 1968.]

Article 17. Reports of People's Judges to Voters. People's judges shall systematically report to voters on their work and the work of the people's court.

Article 18. Accountability of Courts to Agencies Which Elect Them. Territorial, regional, and city courts, courts of autonomous regions, and courts of national areas shall be accountable to the respective soviets of working people's deputies.

Supreme courts of autonomous republics shall be accountable to supreme soviets of the autonomous republics or, in the interval between sessions, to presidia of supreme soviets of the autonomous republics.

The Supreme Court of the RSFSR shall be accountable to the Supreme Soviet of the RSFSR or, in the interval between sessions, to the Presidium of the Supreme Soviet of the RSFSR.

Article 19. Early Recall of Judges and People's Assessors. Judges and people's assessors may be prematurely deprived of their powers only by recall of the voters or the agency which elected them or by reason of a judgment of a court passed on them.

The procedure for recall of judges and people's assessors is established by the Statute on Early Recall of Judges and People's Assessors, confirmed by the Presidium of the Supreme Soviet of the RSFSR.

Article 20. Relief of Judges From Office. Judges may be relieved from office before expiration of the term of office in connection with lengthy illness or transfer to other work, and also upon their request if there exist valid reasons.

The early relief of people's judges shall be carried out by a decision of the executive committee of the soviet of working people's deputies of the national area, autonomous region, city, region, or territory, by preliminary agreement with the Supreme Court of the RSFSR and, in an autonomous republic, by decree of the presidium of the supreme soviet of the autonomous republic or by preliminary agreement with the Supreme Court of the RSFSR.

The early relief of presidents, vice presidents, and members of territorial, regional, and city courts, courts of autonomous regions, and courts of national areas shall be carried out by decision of the soviets of working people's deputies of the territory, region, city, autonomous region, or national area, respectively.

The early relief from office of a president, vice president, or member of a supreme court of an autonomous republic or of the Supreme Court of the RSFSR shall be carried out in accordance with a decree of the presidium of the supreme soviet of the autonomous republic or the Presidium of the Supreme Soviet of the RSFSR, respectively, with subsequent submission for confirmation by the supreme soviet of the autonomous republic or the Supreme Soviet of the RSFSR.

[*Ved.* (1964), no. 8, item 81, Edict February 20, 1964.]

Article 21. Procedure for Elections of People's Judges to Replace Those Who Have Departed Before Expiration of Term of Office. In the event of departure of a people's judge before the expiration of his term of office, the election of a people's judge to replace him for the remainder of his term of office shall be organized by the presidium of the supreme soviet of the autonomous republic or by the executive committee of the territorial, regional, or city soviet of working people's deputies, of the soviet of working people's deputies of the autonomous region, or of the soviet of working people's deputies of the national area, in accordance with the Statute on Elections of District (or City) People's Courts of the RSFSR.

Article 22. Procedure for Elections of President, Vice Presidents, and Members of Courts to Replace Those Who Have Departed Before Expiration of Term of Office. In the event of departure before expiration of the term of office of a president, vice presidents, or members of courts of national areas, courts of autonomous regions, city, regional, or territorial courts, supreme courts of autonomous republics, or the Supreme Court of the RSFSR, the elections of a new president, vice presidents, and members of courts for the remainder of the term of office shall be conducted at a regular session of the soviets of working people's deputies of the national area, autonomous region, city, region, territory, supreme soviets of autonomous republics or the Supreme Soviet of the RSFSR, respectively.

Article 23. College of Advocates. Colleges of advocates shall operate for the purpose of providing defense at preliminary investigations and in court, and also for rendering other legal aid to citizens, enterprises, institutions, and organizations.

Colleges of advocates are voluntary societies of persons engaged in advocacy, and they shall operate on the basis of a Statute confirmed by the Supreme Soviet of the RSFSR.

Article 24. Participation of Procurator in Court. The Procurator General of the USSR, the Procurator of the RSFSR, and procurators subordinate to them, on the basis of and in accordance with the procedure established by law, shall participate in administrative sessions and in judicial sessions during consideration of criminal and civil cases, shall support the state accusation in court, shall present and support suits in court, and shall exercise supervision over the legality and validity of judgments, decisions, rulings, and decrees rendered by courts, as well as over the execution of judgments.

Article 25. Social Accusers and Social Defense Counsel. Social accusation and defense in court may be carried out by representatives of social organizations in accordance with the procedure established by law.

In instances provided for by legislation, victims of a crime may also support an accusation.

Article 26. Direction and Control of Activity of RSFSR Courts. The Supreme Court of the RSFSR shall exercise direction and control of the activity of all courts of the RSFSR.

Supreme Courts of autonomous republics, territorial, regional, and city courts, courts of autonomous regions, and courts of national areas shall exercise direction and control of the activity of the district (or city) people's courts of autonomous republics, territories, regions, cities, autonomous regions, and national areas, respectively.

[*Ved.* (1964), no. 8, item 81, Edict February 20, 1964.]

Chapter Two: District (or City) People's Courts

Article 27. Formation of District (or City) People's Courts. District (or city) people's court shall operate in each district or in a city not divided into districts.

The Council of Ministers of the RSFSR, upon the recommendation of the Supreme Court of the RSFSR, may form one people's court for a district and city, or for a district and cities and settlements situated on the territory of such district, or for a city and part of a rural district.

[*Ved.* (1964), no. 8, item 81, Edict February 20, 1964.]

Article 28. Procedure for Election of District (or City) People's Courts. People's judges of district (or city) people's courts shall be elected by citizens of the district (or city) on the basis of universal, equal, and direct suffrage by secret ballot for a term of five years.

People's assessors of district (or city) people's courts shall be elected by open ballot for a term of two years at general meetings of workers, employees, and peasants at their place of work or residence, and at general meetings of military personnel in their military units.

The procedure for elections of district (or city) people's courts is established by the Statute on Elections of District (or City) People's Courts of the RSFSR confirmed by the Presidium of the Supreme Soviet of the RSFSR.

Article 29. Number of People's Judges and People's Assessors. The number of people's judges and people's assessors for each district (or city) people's court shall be established by the executive committee of the territorial, regional, or city soviet of working people's deputies, soviet of working people's deputies of the autonomous region, or soviet of working people's deputies of the national area, upon the recommendation of the president of the territorial, regional, or city court, court of the autonomous region, or court of the national area, respectively.

The number of people's judges and people's assessors for each district (or city) people's court in an autonomous republic shall be established by the presidium of the supreme soviet of the autonomous republic upon the recommendation of the president of the supreme court of the autonomous republic.

[*Ved.* (1964), no. 8, item 81, Edict February 20, 1964.]

Article 30. Competence of District (or City) People's Courts. District (or city) people's courts shall consider all criminal and civil cases with the exception of cases referred by law to the jurisdiction of other courts.

Article 31. Presidents of District (or City) People's Courts. In a district where several people's judges are elected, the district soviet of working people's deputies, and in a city not divided into districts, the city soviet of working people's deputies, upon the recommendation of the president of the supreme court of the autonomous republic, territorial, regional, or city court, court of the autonomous region, or court of the national area, respectively, shall appoint a president of the district (or city) people's court from among the elected people's judges.

The president of a district (or city) court shall:

(a) preside at judicial sessions or assign people's judges to do so;

(b) direct the study of the judicial practice of the court;

(c) direct the work of the court's secretarial office;

(d) appoint sheriffs and direct their work;

(e) exercise general organizational direction of the work of the court.

Article 32. Replacement of Temporarily Absent Presidents of District (or City) People's Courts. In the event of the temporary absence (illness, vacation, etc.) of the president of a district (or city) people's court, discharge of his duties shall be entrusted to one of the people's judges by the executive committee of the district (or city) soviet of working people's deputies.

In the event of the temporary absence of a people's judge, discharge of his duties shall be entrusted to a people's judge of the same district or to a people's judge of another district by the president of the supreme court of the autonomous republic, territorial, regional, or city court, court of the autonomous region, or court of the national area, respectively, or to one of the people's assessors by the executive committee of the district (or city) soviet of working people's deputies.

Chapter Three: Territorial, Regional, and City Courts, Courts of Autonomous Regions, and Courts of National Areas.

Article 33. **Procedure for Election of Territorial, Regional, and City Courts, Courts of Autonomous Regions, and Courts of National Areas.** In accordance with Article 112 of the Constitution of the RSFSR, territorial, regional, and city courts, courts of autonomous regions, and courts of national areas shall be elected for terms of five years by territorial, regional, and city soviets of working people's deputies, soviets of working people's deputies of autonomous regions and soviets of working people's deputies of national areas, respectively.

The numerical composition of territorial, regional, and city courts, courts of autonomous regions, and courts of national areas shall be established by the territorial, regional, and city soviets of working people's deputies, soviets of working people's deputies of the autonomous regions, and soviets of working people's deputies of national areas, respectively, at the time of election of the court.

Article 34. **Competence of Territorial, Regional, and City Courts, Courts of Autonomous Regions, and Courts of National Areas.** Territorial, regional, and city courts, courts of autonomous regions, and courts of national areas shall consider:

(a) civil and criminal cases of first instance, referred by law to their jurisdiction;

(b) cases on appeals and on protests of decisions, judgments, and rulings of district (or city) people's courts which have not taken legal effect;

(c) cases on protests of decisions, judgments, and rulings of district (or city) people's courts which have taken legal effect and on protests of decrees of people's judges to bring to trial.

Territorial, regional, and city courts, courts of autonomous regions, and courts of national areas shall check the work of district (or city) people's courts, shall render practical help in their work, shall exercise direction and control over their activity, and shall organize the study and summarizing of judicial practice.

[*Ved.* (1964), no. 8, item 81, Edict February 20, 1964.]

Article 35. **Composition of Territorial, Regional, and City Courts, Courts of Autonomous Regions, and Courts of National Areas.** A territorial, regional, or city court, court of autonomous region, or court of national area shall consist of a president, deputy president, members of the court, and people's assessors, and shall include:

a. A judicial division for civil cases;
b. A judicial division for criminal cases;
c. A presidium of the court.

Article 36. **Judicial Divisions of Territorial, Regional, and City Courts, Courts of Autonomous Regions, and Courts of National Areas.** The judicial division for civil cases and the judicial division for criminal cases of a territorial, regional, or city court, court of an autonomous region, or court of a national area shall consider, respectively, cases of first instance referred by law to the jurisdiction of such courts, as well as cases on appeals and on protests of decisions, judgments and rulings of district (or city) people's courts, which have not taken legal effect.

The organizational direction of the work of judicial divisions shall be carried out by the presidents of the judicial divisions.

The presidents of judicial divisions shall be appointed by the executive committee of the respective soviet of working people's deputies upon the recommendation of the president of the territorial, regional, and city court, court of autonomous region, and court of national area, from among the deputy presidents or members of the court.

Article 37. **Presidia of Territorial, Regional, and City Courts, Courts of Autonomous Regions, and Courts of National Areas.** The presidium of a territorial, regional, or city court, court of an autonomous region, or court of a national area shall consist of the president, deputy presidents, and members of the court in a number determined by the executive committee of the soviet of working people's deputies of the territory, region, city, autonomous region, or national area, respectively.

The members of the presidium shall be appointed by the executive committee of the respective soviet of working people's deputies upon the recommendation of the president of the territorial, regional, or city court, court of autonomous region, or court of the national area.

The participation of the procurator of the territory, region, city, autonomous region, or national area in a session of the presidium shall be obligatory during the consideration of judicial cases.

[*Ved.* (1964), no. 8, item 81, Edict February 20, 1964.]

Article 38. **Competence of Presidia of Territorial, Regional, and City Courts, Courts of Autonomous Regions, and Courts of National Areas.** The presidium of a territorial, regional, or city court, court of an autonomous region, or court of a national area shall consider cases on protests of decisions, judgments, and rulings of district (or city) people's courts which have taken legal effect, on protests of decrees of people's judges to bring to trial, as well as on protests of rulings of judicial divisions of the territorial, regional, and city court, court of autonomous region, or court of national area rendered with respect to appeals and protests.

The presidium of a territorial, regional, or city court, court of an autonomous region, or court of a national area shall consider questions concerning the work of judicial divisions, materials of judicial statistics and of summarizing judicial practice, and questions of work with cadres.

Article 39. **Presidents of Territorial, Regional, and City Courts, Courts of Autonomous Regions, and Courts of National Areas.** The president of a territorial, regional, or city court, court of an autonomous region, or court of a national area shall:

(a) preside at judicial sessions of divisions or assign his deputy, the president of a judicial division, or a member of the court to do so;

(b) protest, in accordance with the procedure established by law, decisions, judgments, and rulings of district (or city) courts which have taken legal effect, decrees of people's judges to bring to trial, as well as rulings of judicial divisions rendered with respect to appeals and protests;

(c) convoke the presidium of the court and preside at its sessions; submit for consideration by the presidium questions requiring its decisions;

(d) assign members of the court to judicial divisions;

(e) organize the work of summarizing judicial practice and keeping judicial statistics;

(f) entrust discharge of the duties of a people's judge, in the event of his temporary absence, to a people's judge of the same district or to a people's judge of another district;

(g) appoint sheriffs for district (or city) people's courts;

(h) exercise general organizational direction of the work of the court.

In the absence of the president of the court, the deputy president of the court shall exercise his rights and duties.

[*Ved.* (1964), no. 8, item 81, Edict February 20, 1964.]

Chapter Four: Supreme Courts of Autonomous Republics

Article 40. Supreme Courts of Autonomous Republics as Highest Judicial Agencies of Autonomous Republics. The supreme court of an autonomous republic shall be the highest judicial agency of the autonomous republic.

The supreme court of an autonomous republic shall be entrusted with the supervision of judicial activity of all courts of the autonomous republic.

The supreme court of an autonomous republic shall possess the right of legislative initiative.

Article 41. Procedure for Election of Supreme Courts of Autonomous Republics. In accordance with Article 111 of the Constitution of the RSFSR, the supreme court of an autonomous republic shall be elected by the supreme soviet of the autonomous republic for a term of five years.

The numerical composition of the supreme court of an autonomous republic shall be established by the supreme soviet of the autonomous republic at the time of election of the court.

Article 42. Competence of Supreme Courts of Autonomous Republics. The supreme court of an autonomous republic shall consider:

(a) civil and criminal cases of first instance referred by law to its jurisdiction;

(b) cases on appeals and on protests of decisions, judgments, and rulings of district (or city) people's courts which have not taken legal effect;

(c) cases on protests of decisions, judgments, and rulings of district (or city) people's courts which have taken legal effect and on protests of decrees of people's judges to bring to trial.

The supreme court of an autonomous republic shall perform checks of the work of district (or city) people's courts, render practical help in their work, exercise direction and control over their activity, and organize the study and summarizing of judicial practice.

[*Ved.* (1964), no. 8, item 81, Edict February 20, 1964.]

Article 43. Composition of Supreme Courts of Autonomous Republics. The supreme court of an autonomous republic shall consist of a president, vice president, members of the court, and assessors, and shall include:

a. A judicial division for civil cases;
b. A judicial division for criminal cases;
c. A presidium of the court.

Article 44. Judicial Divisions of Supreme Courts of Autonomous Republics. The judicial division for civil cases and the judicial division for criminal cases of the supreme court of an autonomous republic shall consider, respectively, civil and criminal cases of the first instance referred by law to the jurisdiction of such court, as well as cases on appeals and on protests of decisions, judgments, and rulings of district (or city) people's courts which have not taken legal effect.

The organizational direction of the work of judicial divisions shall be carried out by the presidents of the judicial divisions.

The presidents of judicial divisions shall be appointed by the presidium of the supreme soviet of the autonomous republic upon the recommendation of the president of the supreme court of the autonomous republic.

Article 45. Presidia of Supreme Courts of Autonomous Republics. The presidium of the supreme court of an autonomous republic shall consist of the president, vice presidents, and members of the supreme court in a number determined by the presidium of the supreme court of the autonomous republic.

The members of the presidium of the supreme court shall be appointed by the presidium of the supreme soviet of the autonomous republic upon the recommendation of the president of the supreme court of the autonomous republic.

The participation of the procurator of the autonomous republic in a session of the presidium of the court during the consideration of judicial cases shall be obligatory.

[*Ved.* (1964), no. 8, item 81, Edict February 20, 1964.]

Article 46. Competence of Presidia of Supreme Courts of Autonomous Republics. The presidium of the supreme court of an autonomous republic shall consider cases on protests of decisions, judgments, and rulings of district (or city) people's courts which have taken legal effect, on protests of decrees of people's judges to bring to trial, as well as on protests of rulings of judicial divisions of the supreme court rendered with respect to appeals and protests.

The presidium of the supreme court of an autonomous republic shall consider questions concerning the work of judicial divisions, materials of checks on the work of district (or city) people's courts, materials of judicial statistics and of summarizing of judicial practice, and questions of work with cadres.

[*Ved.* (1964), no. 8, item 81, Edict February 20, 1964.]

Article 47. Presidents of Supreme Courts of Autonomous Republics. The president of the supreme court of an autonomous republic shall:

(a) preside at judicial sessions of divisions or assign his deputy, the president of the judicial division, or a member of the court to do so;

(b) protest, in accordance with the procedure prescribed by law, decisions, judgments, and rulings of district (or city) people's courts which have taken legal effect, decrees of people's judges to bring to trial, as well as rulings of judicial divisions rendered with respect to appeals or protests;

(c) convoke the presidium of the court and preside at its sessions; submit for consideration by the presidium questions requiring its decisions;

(d) assign members of the court to judicial divisions;

(e) organize the work of summarizing judicial practice and keeping judicial statistics;

(f) entrust discharge of the duties of a people's judge, in the event of his temporary absence, to a people's judge of the same district or to a people's judge of another district;

(g) appoint sheriffs for district (or city) people's courts;

(h) exercise general organizational direction of the work of the court.

In the absence of the president of the supreme court of an autonomous republic, the vice president of the court shall exercise his rights and duties.

[*Ved.* (1964), no. 8, item 81, Edict February 20, 1964.]

Chapter Five: Supreme Court of the RSFSR

Article 48. Supreme Court of RSFSR – the Highest Judicial Agency of RSFSR. In accordance with Article 109 of the Constitution of the RSFSR, the Supreme Court of the RSFSR shall be the highest judicial agency of the RSFSR.

The Supreme Court of the RSFSR shall be entrusted with the supervision of judicial activity of all judicial agencies of the RSFSR.

The Supreme Court of the RSFSR shall possess the right of legislative initiative.

Article 49. Procedure for Election of Supreme Court of RSFSR. In accordance with Article 110 of the Constitution of the RSFSR, the Supreme Court of the RSFSR shall be elected by the Supreme Soviet of the RSFSR for a term of five years.

The numerical composition of the Supreme Court of the RSFSR shall be established by the Supreme Soviet of the RSFSR at the time of election of the court.

Article 50. Competence of Supreme Court of RSFSR. The Supreme Court of the RSFSR shall consider:

(a) civil and criminal cases of first instance referred by law to its jurisdiction;

(b) cases on appeals and on protests of decisions, judgments, and rulings of supreme courts of autonomous republics, of territorial, regional, and city courts, courts of autonomous regions, and courts of national areas, which have not taken legal effect;

(c) cases on protests of decisions, judgments, rulings, and decrees of all courts of the RSFSR which have taken legal effect.

The Supreme Court of the RSFSR shall give explanatory directives to courts for the application of RSFSR legislation.

The Supreme Court of the RSFSR shall perform checks of the work of supreme courts of autonomous republics, territorial, regional, and city courts, courts of autonomous regions, courts of national areas, and district (or city) people's courts, render practical help in their work, exercise direction and supervision over their activity, study and summarize judicial practice, and keep judicial statistics for the republic.

[*Ved.* (1964), no. 8, item 81, Edict February 20, 1964.]

Article 51. Composition of Supreme Court of RSFSR. The Supreme Court of the RSFSR shall consist of a President, Vice Presidents, members of the Supreme Court of the RSFSR, and people's assessors, and shall include:

a. A judicial division for civil cases;
b. A judicial division for criminal cases;
c. A Presidium of the Supreme Court of the RSFSR;
d. A Plenum of the Supreme Court of the RSFSR.

Article 52. Judicial Divisions of Supreme Court of RSFSR. The judicial division for civil cases and the judicial division for criminal cases of the Supreme Court of the RSFSR shall consider:

(a) civil and criminal cases of first instance referred by law to the jurisdiction of the Supreme Court of the RSFSR, as well as cases on appeals and on protests of decisions, judgments, and rulings rendered by territorial, regional, and city courts, by courts of autonomous regions, and by courts of national areas, which have not taken legal effect;

(b) cases on protests of decisions, judgments, and rulings rendered by all courts of the republic which have taken legal effect and of decrees to bring to trial of judges of supreme courts of autonomous republics, territorial, regional, and city courts, courts of autonomous regions, and courts of national areas, if the decisions, judgments, rulings, and decrees have not been the subject of consideration on appeal in the Supreme Court of the RSFSR, as well as cases on protests of decrees of presidia of supreme courts of autonomous republics, territorial, regional, and city courts, courts of autonomous regions, and courts of national areas.

[*Ved.* (1964), no. 8, item 81, Edict February 20, 1964.]

Article 53. Presidents of Judicial Divisions of Supreme Court of RSFSR. The presidents of judicial divisions of the Supreme Court of the RSFSR shall be appointed by the Presidium of the Supreme Soviet of the RSFSR upon the recommendation of the President of the Supreme Court of the RSFSR from among the Vice Presidents or members of the court.

The presidents of judicial divisions shall:

(a) exercise organizational direction of the work of the respective divisions;

(b) present reports on the activity of the division to the Plenum of the Supreme Court of the RSFSR.

Article 54. **Presidium of Supreme Court of RSFSR.** The Presidium of the Supreme Court of the RSFSR shall consist of the President of the Court, his Deputies, and members of the court in a number established by the Presidium of the Supreme Soviet of the RSFSR.

The members of the Presidium of the Supreme Court of the RSFSR shall be appointed by the Presidium of the Supreme Soviet of the RSFSR upon the recommendation of the President of the Supreme Court of the RSFSR.

The participation of the Procurator of the RSFSR or his deputy in a session of the Presidium of the Supreme Court of the RSFSR during the consideration of judicial cases shall be obligatory.

[*Ved.* (1964), no. 8, item 81, Edict February 20, 1964.]

Article 55. **Competence of Presidium of Supreme Court of RSFSR.** The Presidium of the Supreme Court of the RSFSR shall consider:

(a) cases on protests of decisions, judgments, and rulings of judicial divisions of the Supreme Court of the RSFSR, as well as decrees of judges of the Supreme Court of the RSFSR to bring to trial;

(b) checks on the work of courts, judicial statistics and of the summarizing of judicial practice;

(c) questions of work with cadres;

(d) questions of the work of judicial divisions and departments of the Supreme Court of the RSFSR.

The Presidium of the Supreme Court of the RSFSR shall issue instructions and methodological directives concerning questions of the work of courts.

Decrees of the Supreme Court of the RSFSR shall be adopted by a simple majority vote.

[*Ved.* (1964), no. 8, item 81, Edict February 20, 1964.]

Article 56. **Plenum of Supreme Court of RSFSR.** The Plenum of the Supreme Court of the RSFSR shall consist of the President, Vice Presidents, and all members of the Supreme Court of the RSFSR.

The participation of the Procurator of the RSFSR in sessions of the Plenum shall be obligatory.

The Plenum of the Supreme Court of the RSFSR shall be convoked not less than once every three months.

A session of the Plenum shall be considered authorized to act if not less than two thirds of its membership is present.

Decrees of the Plenum shall be adopted by a simple majority of members of the Plenum of the Supreme Court of the RSFSR participating in the session.

[*Ved.* (1964), no. 8, item 81, Edict February 20, 1964.]

Article 57. Competence of Plenum of Supreme Court of RSFSR. The Plenum of the Supreme Court of the RSFSR shall:

(a) during consideration of civil and criminal cases as well as the recommendation of the Procurator of the RSFSR, give courts explanatory directives on questions of application of RSFSR legislation, on the basis of the summarizing of judicial practice, judicial statistics, and decisions rendered in cases considered by the Supreme Court of the RSFSR;

(b) make recommendations to the Presidium of the Supreme Soviet of the RSFSR on questions which are subject to resolution by legislative procedure and on questions of interpretation of RSFSR laws;

(c) hear reports of the presidents of judicial divisions of the Supreme Court of the RSFSR on the activity of the divisions;

(d) assign the members of judicial divisions of the Supreme Court of the RSFSR from among the members of the Supreme Court of the RSFSR;

(e) hear questions concerning the work of the Presidium of the Supreme Court of the RSFSR.

[*Ved.* (1964), no. 8, item 81, Edict February 20, 1964.]

Article 58. President of Supreme Court of RSFSR. The President of the Supreme Court of the RSFSR shall:

(a) preside at judicial sessions of divisions or assign his deputy, the president of the judicial division, or members of the court to do so;

(b) protest, in accordance with the procedure prescribed by law, decisions, judgments, rulings, and decrees of all courts of the RSFSR, and also decrees of judges to bring to trial;

(c) suspend the execution of a protested decision, judgment, ruling, or decree of any court of the RSFSR;

(d) convoke the Presidium and Plenum of the Supreme Court of the RSFSR and preside at their sessions;

(e) submit for consideration by the Presidium and Supreme Court of the RSFSR questions requiring their decision;

(f) exercise general organizational direction of the work of the Supreme Court of the RSFSR;

(g) organize the work of checking the activity of the courts, of rendering practical help to them, of studying and summarizing judicial practice, and of keeping judicial statistics;

(h) organize the work of selecting and training cadres of judicial agencies.

In the absence of the President of the Supreme Court of the RSFSR, the Deputy President of the Supreme Court of the RSFSR shall exercise his rights and duties.

[*Ved.* (1964), no. 8, item 81, Edict February 20, 1964.]

Article 59. Procedure for Approving Table of Organization of Supreme Court of RSFSR. The table of organization of the Supreme Court of the RSFSR shall be issued by the Presidium of the Supreme Soviet of the RSFSR.

Article 60. Bulletin of Supreme Court of RSFSR. The Supreme Court of the RSFSR shall publish the Bulletin of the Supreme Court of the RSFSR.

Chapter Six: Sheriffs

Article 61. Procedure for Naming Sheriffs. There shall be sheriffs for district (or city) people's courts.

Sheriffs shall be appointed by the president of a district (or city) people's court or by a people's judge and shall be confirmed in office by the president of the supreme court of an autonomous republic, of a territorial, regional, or city court, of a court of an autonomous region, or of a court of a national area.

Article 62. Competence of Sheriffs. Sheriffs shall be charged with the execution of decisions, rulings, and decrees in civil cases, as well as with the execution of court judgments, rulings, and decrees in criminal cases to the extent that they involve property exactions.

Requirements imposed by sheriffs for execution of court decisions, judgments, rulings, and decrees shall be binding upon all officials and citizens.

Chapter Seven: Responsibility of Judges

Article 63. Procedure for Instituting Criminal Proceedings Against Judges and People's Assessors. Criminal proceedings may not be instituted against judges nor may they be removed from their posts in such connection or subjected to arrest:

(a) with respect to people's judges, presidents, deputy presidents, and members of territorial, regional, and city courts, courts of autonomous regions, courts of national areas, and supreme courts of autonomous republics, without the consent of the Presidium of the Supreme Soviet of the RSFSR;

(b) with respect to the President, Vice Presidents, and members of the Supreme Court of the RSFSR, as well as people's assessors of that court, without the consent of the Supreme Soviet of the RSFSR, and in the interval between sessions, of the Presidium of the Supreme Soviet of the RSFSR.

Article 64. Disciplinary Responsibility of Judges. For dereliction of duty and unworthy acts undermining the authority of justice, judges shall bear disciplinary responsibility.

The procedure for disciplinary responsibility of judges is established by the Statute on Disciplinary Responsibility of Judges of Courts of the RSFSR, confirmed by the Presidium of the Supreme Soviet of the RSFSR.

[*Ved.* (1964), no. 8, item 81, Edict February 20, 1964.]

Appendices

Appendix I

Table of Corresponding Provisions of the Fundamental Principles of Criminal Legislation of the USSR and the Criminal Code of the RSFSR

USSR Fundamental Principles	*RSFSR Code*
1	1
2	2
3	3
4	4
5	5
6	6
7	7
8	8
9	9
10	10
11	11
12	12
13	13
14	14
15	15
16	16
17	17
18	18
19	19
20	20
21	21, 22
22	23
23	24
24	25, 26
25	27, 28
26	29
27	30, 31, 32
28	33
29	34
30	35
31	36
32	37
33	38
34	39
35	40
36	41, 42
37	43
38	44, 45

USSR Fundamental Principles	*RSFSR Code*
39	46
40	47
41	48
42	49
43	50, 51, 52
44	53, 54
45	55
46	56
47	57, 58, 59, 60, 61, 62, 63

Appendix II

Table of Corresponding Provisions of the Fundamental Principles of Criminal Procedure of the USSR and the Code of Criminal Procedure of the RSFSR

USSR Fundamental Principles	*RSFSR Code*
1	1
2	2
3	3
4	4
5	5
6	11, 12
7	13
8	14
9	15
10	16
11	17
12	18
13	19
14	20
15	68
16	69
17	71
18	23
19	24
20	25
21	46
22	47
23	51
24	53
25	54
26	55
27	58
28	125, 126
29	117, 118, 119, 120
30	127
31	211
32	122
33	89, 90
34	96, 97
35	167, 168, 169, 170
36	221
37	240
38	245

USSR Fundamental Principles	*RSFSR Law*
39	246
40	248
41	250
42	254
43	301, 309
44	325
45	332
46	340
47	341
48	371
49	342, 379
50	384, 385
51	352
52	353
53	356
54	358

Appendix III

Table of Corresponding Provisions of the Fundamental Principles of Legislation on Court Organization of the USSR and the Union and Autonomous Republics and the Law on Court Organization of the RSFSR

USSR Fundamental Principles	*RSFSR Law*
1	1
2	2
3	3
4	4
5	5
6	6
7	8
8	10
9	7
10	14
11	12
12	13
13	23
14	24
15	25
16, 17	–
18	1
19	28
20	33
21	35
22	40, 41, 42
23	43
24	48, 49, 50
25	51
26, 27, 28	–
29	9
30	11
31	15
32	16
33	17
34	18
35	19
36	63
37	64
38	62

Glossary of Legal Terms

Abduction (see also Stealing)	Pokhishchenie
Ability	Sposobnost'
Abortion	Abort
Abuse	Zloupotreblenie
Accessory	Posobnik
Accomplice	Souchastnik
Accusation	Obvinenie
Accused	Obviniaemyi
Accuser	Obvinitel'
Acknowledgment of guilt	Priznanie viny
Acquisition	Priobretenie
Acquittal	Opravdanie
Act	Deianie
Action	Deistvie
Activity	Deiatel'nost'
Additions (to plans, documents, etc.)	Pripiski
Administration	Upravlenie
Administrative offense	Administrativnoe narushenie
Administrative pressure	Administrativnoe vozdeistvie
Administrative session (of court)	Rasporiaditel'noe zasedanie
Advocate	Advokat
Agency	Organ
Aggravating circumstances	Obstoiatel'stva, otiagchaiushchie otvetstvennost'
Aggregation (of punishments, of crimes)	Sovokupnost'
Agitation	Agitatsiia
Appeal	Zhaloba
Application, Declaration	Zaiavlenie
Application (of laws)	Primenenie
Appropriation	Prisvoenie
Argument, oral	Preniia
Arrest (noun) (see also Detain, Detention)	Arest

Arrogation	Samoupravstvo
Article (of code)	Stat'ia
Article (object)	Predmet
Assault with intent to rob	Razboi
Assign (punishment, etc.)	Naznachit'
Assumption	Predpolozhenie
Attempt	Pokushenie
Attitude	Otnoshenie
Autonomous	Avtonomnyi
Bail	Zalog
Banditry	Banditizm
Banishment	Vysylka
Basis (see also Grounds)	Osnovanie
Begging	Poproshainichestvo
Bigamy	Dvoezhenstvo
Blood feud	Krovnaia mest'
Blow (noun)	Poboi
Bodily injuries	Telesnye povrezhdeniia
Bribery	Vziatochnichestvo
Bride price	Vykup za nevestu
Business, trade	Promysel
Buying up	Skupka
Capacity (see Ability)	
Case, File of case	Delo
Cassation, by way of	V kassatsionnom poriadke
Challenge	Otvod
Chastisement	Kara
Check, Verify	Proverit'
Circumstance	Obstoiatel'stvo
Civil defendant	Grazhdanskii otvetchik
Civil plaintiff	Grazhdanskii istets
Civil procedure	Grazhdanskii protsess
Civil proceedings	Grazhdanskoe sudoproizvodstvo
Civil status, acts of	Akty grazhdanskogo sostoianiia
Civil suit	Grazhdanskii isk
Clarification	Vyiasnenie
Client, Entruster	Doveritel'
Code	Kodeks, Ustav
Collective farm	Kolkhoz
College of advocates	Kollegiia advokatov
Collegiality	Kollegial'nost'
Commercial middleman, activity as	Kommercheskoe posrednichestvo
Commission (assignment)	Poruchenie

Communal life	Obshchezhitie
Compensation	Vozmeshchenie
Competence (of court, etc.)	Kompetentsiia
Complicity	Souchastie
Compulsion	Prinuzhdenie
Compulsory appearance	Privod
Comrades' court	Tovarishcheskii sud
Conclusion	Vyvod
Conclusion to indict	Obvinitel'noe zakliuchenie
Conditional	Uslovnoe
Conference	Soveshchanie
Confession (see Acknowledgment of guilt)	
Confinement	Zakliuchenie
Confiscation	Konfiskatsiia
Confrontation	Ochnaia stavka
Consideration (judicial)	Rassmotrenie
Conspiracy	Zagovor
Convicted person	Osuzhdennyi
Conviction (see also Judgment of conviction)	Osuzhdenie
Conviction, record of	Sudimost'
Correction	Ispravlenie
Correctional labor colony	Ispravitel'no-trudovaia koloniia
Correctional tasks	Ispravitel'nye raboty
Costs (court)	Izderzhki
Court	Sud
Courtroom	Zal sudebnogo zasedaniia
Crime	Prestuplenie
Crime, elements of	Sostav prestupleniia
Criminal Code	Ugolovnyi kodeks
Criminal group	Prestupnaia gruppirovka
Criminal legislation	Ugolovnoe zakonodatel'stvo
Criminal procedure, Criminal proceedings	Ugolovnoe sudoproizvodstvo
Curator	Popechitel'
Currency transactions	Valiutnye operatsiia
Customs, local	Mestnye obychai
Damage (in transport)	Avariia
Data	Dannye
Death penalty	Smertnaia kazn'
Deception	Obman
Decision	Reshenie
Declare	Zaiavliat'
Decree	Postanovlenie

Deem	Priznat'
Defamation	Kleveta
Defense counsel	Zashchitnik
Defense, necessary	Neobkhodimaia oborona
Defense, right to	Pravo na zashchitu
Den of debauchery	Priton razvrata
Denunciation	Ogovor
Depraved actions	Razvratnye deistviia
Deprivation of freedom	Lishenie svobody
Deputy	Zamestitel'
Detain (arrest)	Zaderzhat'
Detention	Zaderzhanie
Dignity	Dostoinstvo
Disciplinary Code	Ditsiplinarnyi Ustav
Disjoinder (of cases)	Vydelenie
Dismissal of suit	Otkaz v iske
Dismissal from office	Uvol'nenie ot dolzhnosti
Dissipation	Promotanie
Distraint of property	Opis' imushchestvo
District	Raion
Division (criminal, civil, etc., of court)	Kollegiia
Divulgence	Razglashenie
Document	Dokument
Duty (see also Obligation)	Dolg, Obiazannost'
Dwelling space	Zhilishche
Economic crime	Khoziaistvennoe prestuplenie
Educational	Vospitatel'nyi
Election	Vybor
Embezzlement	Rastrata
Enterprise	Predpriiatie
Equal rights	Ravnopraviia
Escape	Pobeg
Espionage	Shpionazh
Eviction (see also Resettlement)	Vyselenie
Evidence (see also Proof)	Dokazatel'stvo
Examination (judicial)	Razbiratel'stvo
Examination (of real evidence)	Osvidetel'stvovanie
Execution (of judgment, laws, etc.)	Ispolnenie
Exile	Ssylka
Expert	Ekspert
Expert examination	Ekspertiza
Explanatory directives	Rukovodiashchie raz''iasneniia
Expunging	Pogashenie

Extortion	Vymogatel'stvo
Eye-witness	Ochevidets
Fabrications	Izmyshleniia
Failure to render aid	Neokazanie pomoshchi
Failure to report	Nedonesenie
False report	Lozhnyi donos
File (verb)	Zaiavliat'
Findings of court	Vyvody suda
Fine	Shtraf
Force	Nasilie
Forensic, Judicial	Sudebnyi
Forgery	Podlog
Full power	Polnomochie
Fundamental principles	Osnovy, Osnovnye nachala
Gambling	Azartnye igry
Giving oneself up	Iavka s povinnoi
Grave	Tiazhkii
Groundless, Unfounded, Unjustified	Neobosnovannyi
Grounds (see also Basis)	Osnovaniia
Group (see also Criminal group)	Gruppa
Guard (see also People's Guard)	Strazha
Guardian	Opekun'
Guilt	Vina
Harm	Vred
Helpless condition, in a	Bespomoshchnyi
Homicide	Ubiistvo
Hooliganism	Khuliganstvo
Impounding of property	Nalozhenie aresta na imushchestvo
Imprisonment	Zakliuchenie v tiurme
Imputability	Vmeniaemost'
Indicia	Priznaki
Indict, conclusion to	Obvinitel'noe zakliuchenie
Information	Svedeniia
Infringement	Posiagatel'stvo
Initiation (of criminal case)	Vozbuzhdenie
Injury	Povrezhdenie
Inquiry	Doznanie
Inspection	Reviziia
Instance (judicial)	Instantsiia
Instigation	Podstrekatel'stvo
Institution	Uchrezhdenie

Institution of criminal proceedings	Privlechenie k ugolovnoi otvetstvennosti
Insubordination	Nepovinovenie
Insult	Oskorblenie
Intent	Umysel
Intentional	Umyshlennyi
Interpretation	Tolkovanie
Interrogation	Dopros
Intoxication	Op'ianenie
Investigation	Sledstvie
Investigative jurisdiction	Podsledstvennost'
Investigator	Sledovatel'
Inviolability	Neprikosvennost'
Issuing (noun)	Vypusk, Vydacha, Sbyt
Job seniority	Trudovoi stazh
Joinder (of cases)	Soedinenie
Judge	Sud'ia
Judgment	Prigovor
Judgment of acquittal	Opravdatel'nyi prigovor
Judgment of conviction	Obvinitel'nyi prigovor
Judicial division	Sudebnaia kollegiia
Jurisdiction (of court)	Podsudnost'
Justice, administration of	Pravosudie
Knowingly, known to be	Zavedomo
Last word	Poslednoe slovo
Law (in general; see also Rights)	Pravo
Law (individual)	Zakon
Leaving in danger	Ostavlenie v opasnosti
Legality	Zakonnost'
Legislation	Zakonodatel'stvo
Limitation, period of	Srok davnosti
Loss	Ushcherb
Maiming	Chlenovreditel'stvo
Maintenance, Support	Alimenty
Making amends for harm	Zagladit' vred
Malicious	Zlostnyi
Malingering	Simuliatsiia bolezni
Mass disorders	Massovye besporiadki
Material loss	Material'nyi ushcherb
Materials (of a case)	Materialy
Measures of social pressure	Mery obshchestvennogo vozdeistviia
Mental agitation	Dushevnoe volnenie
Mental illness	Dushevnaia bolezn'

Mercenary motives	Korystnye pobuzhdeniia
Military service for a regular term, persons in	Voennosluzhashchii srochnoi sluzhby
Military tribunals	Voennye tribunaly
Mistreatment of prisoners of war	Durnoe obrashchenie s voennoplennymi
Mitigating circumstances	Obstoiatel'stva, smiagchaiushchie otvetstvennost'
Motherland	Rodina
National area	Natsional'nyi okrug
Nationality	Natsional'nost
Nationalization	Natsionalizatsiia
Necessity, extreme	Krainaia neobkhodimost'
Neglect (of official duty)	Khalatnost'
Negligence	Neostorozhnost'
Nonimputability	Nevmeniaemost'
Notify, Notice	Soobshchit', Soobshchenie
Obligation	Obiazatel'stvo
Observation	Nabliudenie
Occupational activities	Zaniatiia
Occupational duties	Sluzhebnye obiazannosti
Occupational status (see also Official position)	Sluzhebnoe polozhenie
Office	Dolzhnost'
Official (adj.)	Dolzhnostnoi, sluzhebnyi
Official (noun)	Dolzhnostnoe litso
Official crime	Dolzhnostnoe prestuplenie
Official position	Sluzhebnoe polozhenie
Omission	Bezdeistvie
Opinion (of expert, procurator, medical institution)	Zakliuchenie
Organization	Organizatsiia
Organizer	Organizator
Owner	Vladelets
Ownership (see also Property)	Sobstvennost'
Page (of file of case)	List
Pandering	Svodnichestvo
Paragraph	Chast'
Parasitic way of life	Paraziticheskii obraz zhizni
Pardon	Pomilovanie
Passing (counterfeit money)	Sbyt
Passport	Pasport
Pederasty	Muzhelozhstvo
People's assessor	Narodnyi zasedatel'

People's court	Narodnyi sud
People's guard (collective)	Narodnaia druzhina
People's guard (individual)	Druzhinnik
People's judge	Narodnyi sud'ia
Period (time, term)	Srok
Perpetrator (of crime)	Ispolnitel'
Person	Litso
Person brought to trial	Podsudimyi
Person without citizenship	Litso bez grazhdanstva
Personality	Lichnost', Litso
Personal ownership	Lichnaia sobstvennost'
Petition	Khodataistvo
Petty (stealing, speculation, etc.)	Melkii
Phono-record	Fonogramm
Pillage	Maroderstvo
Plenum	Plenum
Pogrom	Pogrom
Police	Militsiia
Policeman	Rabotnik militsii
Polygamy	Mnogozhenstvo
Preliminary investigation	Predvaritel'noe sledstvie
Preparation	Prigotovlenie
Present evidence, Prove	Dokazyvat'
President	Predsedatel'
Presidium	Prezidium
Pressure	Vozdeistvie
Prison	Tiurma
Prisoner (in labor colony, etc.)	Zakliuchennyi
Private entrepreneurial activity	Chastnopredprinimatel'skaia deiatel'nost'
Probation period	Ispytatel'nyi srok
Procuracy	Prokuratura
Procurator	Prokuror
Procurator General	General'nyi Prokuror
Procuratorial supervision	Prokurorskii nadzor
Products	Produktsiia
Profit, for the purpose of making a	S tsel'iu nazhivy
Promise, signed	Podpiska
Proof (see also Evidence)	Dokazyvanie, Dokazannost', Dokazatel'stvo'
Propaganda	Propaganda
Propagandizing of war	Propaganda voiny
Property (see also Ownership)	Imushchestvo
Property status	Imushchestvennoe polozhenie
Prosecute as the accused, as civil defendant	Privlekat' v kachestve obviniaemogo, grazhdanskogo otvetchika
Prosecutor	Obvinitel'

Protest	Protest
Prove, Present evidence	Dokazyvat'
Provocation	Provokatsiia
Public (noun; see also Social)	Obshchestvennost'
Public disclosure, Announcement	Oglashenie
Public order	Obshchestvennyi poriadok
Publicity (of judicial examination)	Glasnost'
Psychiatric	Psikhiatricheskii
Punishment	Nakazanie
Race (see also Nationality)	Rasa
Rape	Iznasilovanie
Real evidence	Veshchestvennoe dokazatel'stvo
Reasoned	Motivirovannyi
Recidivist	Retsidivist
Reconciliation	Primirenie
Record (of proceedings)	Protokol
Record of conviction	Sudimost'
Reeducation	Perevospitanie
Refer	Napravliat'
Referral of file of case	Napravlenie dela
Refusal (to commit crime)	Otkaz
Regime	Vlast'
Region	Oblast'
Regional (court, soviet, etc.)	Oblastnoi
Rehabilitation	Reabilitatsiia
Relief (from punishment, etc.)	Osvobozhdenie
Relief, conditional early	Uslovno-dosrochnoe osvobozhdenie
Religious rites	Religioznye obriady
Resistance (of policeman, etc.)	Soprotivlenie
Repentance	Raskaianie
Representative	Predstavitel'
Reprimand	Vygovor
Responsibility	Otvetstvennost'
Republic	Respublika
Resettlement (see also Eviction)	Vyselenie
Restraint, measure of	Mer presecheniia
Retroactive force	Obratnaia sila
Rights	Prava
Rules for safe movement	Pravila bezopasnosti dvizheniia
Ruling	Opredelenie
Rural district	Sel'skii raion
Sabotage	Diversiia
Sale	Sbyt
Search	Obysk

Secrecy of correspondence	Taina perepiska
Secret, state	Gosudarstvennaia taina
Secretary	Sekretar'
Securities	Tsennye bumagi
Seizure	Zakhvat
Sentence	Osuzhdenie
Session	Zasedanie
Settlement (village)	Poselka
Sheriff	Sudebnyi ispolnitel'
Shooting	Rasstrel
Slander (see Defamation)	
Smuggling	Kontrabanda
Social accusation	Obshchestvennoe obvinenie
Social accuser	Obshchestvennyi obvinitel'
Social censure	Obshchestvennoe poritsanie
Social danger	Obshchestvennaia opasnost'
Social defense	Obshchestvennaia zashchita
Social defense counsel	Obshchestvennyi zashchitnik
Social organization	Obshchestvennaia organizatsiia
Social pressure	Obshchestvennoe vozdeistvie
Social property	Obshchestvennoe imushchestvo
Social status	Obshchestvennoe polozhenie
Social worker	Obshchestvennyi rabotnik
Socialist legal consciousness	Sotsialisticheskoe pravosoznanie
Socialist ownership	Sotsialisticheskaia sobstvennost'
Sound-recording	Zvukopis'
Speculation	Spekuliatsiia
State (noun)	Gosudarstvo
State accuser	Gosudarstvennyi obvinitel'
State, crime against	Gosudarstvennoe prestuplenie
State farm	Sovkhoz
State ownership	Gosudarstvennaia sobstvennost'
State property	Gosudarstvennoe imushchestvo
State security agency	Organ gosudarstvennoi bezopasnosti
Statute	Polozhenie
Stealing (of property generally) (see also Abduction)	Pokhishchenie
Stealing (of state or social property)	Khishchenie
Stealing, open (see also Theft, Assault with intent to rob)	Grabiozh, Otkrytoe pokhishchenie
Subsection	Punkt
Subversion	Podryv
Suffering	Stradanie
Suicide	Samoubiistvo
Summons	Vyzov
Supervision	Nadzor

Supervision, by way of	V poriadke nadzora
Supervisory instance	Nadzornaia instantsiia
Supplementary	Dopolnitel'nyi
Surety	Poruka
Surety, release on	Peredat' na poruki
Surrender	Sdacha
Surveillance	Nabliudenie
Survivals of local customs	Perezhitki mestnykh obychaev
Suspect	Podozrevaemyi
Swindling	Moshennichestvo
Task	Zadacha
Tasks, correctional	Ispravitel'nye raboty
Taxes	Nalogi
Teacher	Pedagog
Term, Time period	Srok
Termination (of case)	Prekrashchenie
Territory	Krai
Terrorist act	Terroristicheskii akt
Testimony	Pokazaniia
Theft (secret stealing)	Krazha
Threat	Ugroza
Time period, Term	Srok
Title, honorary	Pochetnoe zvanie
Torment	Muchenie
Torture	Istiazanie
Traces	Sledy
Trade, prohibited	Zapreshchennyi promysel'
Trade (commerce)	Torgovlia
Trademark	Tovarnyi znak
Trade union	Profsoiuz
Transfer, sale (see also Issuing)	Sbyt
Transport	Transport
Treason	Izmena rodine
Treasury note	Kaznacheiskii bilet
Treatment (medical)	Lechenie
Trial	Protsess
Trial, bring to	Peredat' sudu
Trust	Doverie
Unconscientious	Nedobrosovestnyi
Union republic	Soiuznaia respublika
Unwarranted (seizure, construction, absence, etc.)	Samovol'nyi
Use, criminally wrongful	Prestupno-nebrezhnoe ispol'zovanie

Vacate	Otmenit'
Vagrancy	Brodiazhnichestvo
Verify, Check	Proverit'
Verification	Proverka
Victim	Poterpevshii
View	Osmotr
Violation	Narushenie
Voluntary	Dobrovol'nyi
Vote, right to	Izbiratel'noe pravo
Wages	Zarabotok
Warning	Predosterezhenie
Without foundation	Neobosnovannyi
Witness	Svidetel'
Witness of investigative actions	Poniatoi
Wrecking	Vreditel'stvo
Wrongful	Nebrezhnyi

Index

Note: The page numbers in italics refer to pages of the Introduction; the other numbers refer to articles of the relevant codes – C.C. (Criminal Code); C.C.P. (Code of Criminal Procedure); L.C.O. (Law on Court Organization).

Russian Research Center Studies

1. *Public Opinion in Soviet Russia: A Study in Mass Persuasion*, by Alex Inkeles
2. *Soviet Politics—The Dilemma of Power: The Role of Ideas in Social Change*, by Barrington Moore, Jr.*
3. *Justice in the U.S.S.R.: An Interpretation of Soviet Law*, by Harold J. Berman. Revised edition, enlarged*
4. *Chinese Communism and the Rise of Mao*, by Benjamin I. Schwartz
5. *Titoism and the Cominform*, by Adam B. Ulam*
6. *A Documentary History of Chinese Communism*, by Conrad Brandt, Benjamin Schwartz, and John K. Fairbank*
7. *The New Man in Soviet Psychology*, by Raymond A. Bauer
8. *Soviet Opposition to Stalin: A Case Study in World War II*, by George Fischer*
9. *Minerals: A Key to Soviet Power*, by Demitri B. Shimkin*
10. *Soviet Law in Action: The Recollected Cases of a Soviet Lawyer*, by Boris A. Konstantinovsky; edited by Harold J. Berman*
11. *How Russia Is Ruled*, by Merle Fainsod. Revised edition
12. *Terror and Progress USSR: Some Sources of Change and Stability in the Soviet Dictatorship*, by Barrington Moore, Jr.
13. *The Formation of the Soviet Union: Communism and Nationalism, 1917–1923*, by Richard Pipes. Revised edition
14. *Marxism: The Unity of Theory and Practice—A Critical Essay*, by Alfred G. Meyer. Reissued with a new introduction
15. *Soviet Industrial Production, 1928–1951*, by Donald R. Hodgman
16. *Soviet Taxation: The Fiscal and Monetary Problems of a Planned Economy*, by Franklyn D. Holzman*
17. *Soviet Military Law and Administration*, by Harold J. Berman and Miroslav Kerner*
18. *Documents on Soviet Military Law and Administration*, edited and translated by Harold J. Berman and Miroslav Kerner*
19. *The Russian Marxists and the Origins of Bolshevism*, by Leopold H. Haimson
20. *The Permanent Purge: Politics in Soviet Totalitarianism*, by Zbigniew K. Brzezinski*

21. *Belorussia: The Making of a Nation—A Case Study*, by Nicholas P. Vakar
22. *A Bibliographical Guide to Belorussia*, by Nicholas P. Vakar*
23. *The Balkans in Our Time*, by Robert Lee Wolff (also American Foreign Policy Library)
24. *How the Soviet System Works: Cultural, Psychological, and Social Themes*, by Raymond A. Bauer, Alex Inkeles, and Clyde Kluckhohn†
25. *The Economics of Soviet Steel*, by M. Gardner Clark*
26. *Leninism*, by Alfred G. Meyer*
27. *Factory and Manager in the USSR*, by Joseph S. Berliner†
28. *Soviet Transportation Policy*, by Holland Hunter
29. *Doctor and Patient in Soviet Russia*, by Mark G. Field†
30. *Russian Liberalism: From Gentry to Intelligentsia*, by George Fischer
31. *Stalin's Failure in China, 1924–1927*, by Conrad Brandt
32. *The Communist Party of Poland: An Outline of History*, by M. K. Dziewanowski
33. *Karamzin's Memoir on Ancient and Modern Russia: A Translation and Analysis*, by Richard Pipes*
34. *A Memoir on Ancient and Modern Russia*, by N. M. Karamzin, the Russian text edited by Richard Pipes*
35. *The Soviet Citizen: Daily Life in a Totalitarian Society*, by Alex Inkeles and Raymond A. Bauer†
36. *Pan-Turkism and Islam in Russia*, by Serge A. Zenkovsky
37. *The Soviet Bloc: Unity and Conflict*, by Zbigniew K. Brzezinski. Revised and enlarged edition‡
38. *National Consciousness in Eighteenth-Century Russia*, by Hans Rogger
39. *Alexander Herzen and the Birth of Russian Socialism, 1812–1855*, by Martin Malia
40. *The Conscience of the Revolution: Communist Opposition in Soviet Russia*, by Robert Vincent Daniels*
41. *The Soviet Industrialization Debate, 1924–1928*, by Alexander Erlich
42. *The Third Section: Police and Society in Russia under Nicholas I*, by Sidney Monas
43. *Dilemmas of Progress in Tsarist Russia: Legal Marxism and Legal Populism*, by Arthur P. Mendel
44. *Political Control of Literature in the USSR, 1946–1959*, by Harold Swayze
45. *Accounting in Soviet Planning and Management*, by Robert W. Campbell
46. *Social Democracy and the St. Petersburg Labor Movement, 1885–1897*, by Richard Pipes
47. *The New Face of Soviet Totalitarianism*, by Adam B. Ulam
48. *Stalin's Foreign Policy Reappraised*, by Marshall D. Shulman
49. *The Soviet Youth Program: Regimentation and Rebellion*, by Allen Kassof*
50. *Soviet Criminal Law and Procedure: The RSFSR Codes*, translated by Harold J. Berman and James W. Spindler: introduction and analysis by Harold J. Berman
51. *Poland's Politics: Idealism vs. Realism*, by Adam Bromke

52. *Managerial Power and Soviet Politics*, by Jeremy R. Azrael
53. *Danilevsky: A Russian Totalitarian Philosopher*, by Robert E. MacMaster
54. *Russia's Protectorates in Central Asia: Bukhara and Khiva, 1865–1924*, by Seymour Becker
55. *Revolutionary Russia*, edited by Richard Pipes
56. *The Family in Soviet Russia*, by H. Kent Geiger
57. *Social Change in Soviet Russia*, by Alex Inkeles
58. *The Soviet Prefects: The Local Party Organs in Industrial Decision-making*, by Jerry F. Hough
59. *Soviet-Polish Relations, 1917–1921*, by Piotr S. Wandycz
60. *One Hundred Thousand Tractors: The MTS and the Development of Controls in Soviet Agriculture*, by Robert F. Miller
61. *The Lysenko Affair*, by David Joravsky
62. *Icon and Swastika: The Russian Orthodox Church under Nazi and Soviet Control*, by Harvey Fireside
63. *A Century of Russian Agriculture: From Alexander II to Khrushchev*, by Lazar Volin
64. *Struve: Liberal on the Left, 1870–1905*, by Richard Pipes
65. *Nikolai Strakhov*, by Linda Gerstein
66. *The Kurbskii-Groznyi Apocrypha: The Seventeenth-Century Genesis of the "Correspondence" Attributed to Prince A. M. Kurbskii and Tsar Ivan IV*, by Edward L. Keenan
67. *Chernyshevskii: The Man and the Journalist*, by William F. Woehrlin
68. *European and Muscovite: Ivan Kireevsky and the Origins of Slavophilism*, by Abbott Gleason
69. *Newton and Russia: The Early Influence, 1698–1796*, by Valentin Boss
70. *Pavel Axelrod and the Development of Menshevism*, by Abraham Ascher

* Out of print.

† Publications of the Harvard Project on the Soviet Social System.

‡ Published jointly with the Center for International Affairs, Harvard University.

www.ingramcontent.com/pod-product-compliance
Lightning Source LLC
Chambersburg PA
CBHW031145200626
46927CB00012B/482
* 9 7 8 0 6 7 4 8 2 6 3 6 6 *